**49th EDITION**

*Warman's*

# Antiques &
# Collectibles

## 2016

**NOAH FLEISHER**

Published by

Krause Publications, a division of F+W, A Content + eCommerce Company
700 East State Street • Iola, WI 54990-0001
715-445-2214 • 888-457-2873
www.krausebooks.com

To order books or other products call toll-free 1-800-258-0929
or visit us online at www.krausebooks.com

ISBN-13: 9781440243844
ISBN-10: 1440243840
ISSN: 1076-1985

Cover Design by Nicole MacMartin
Designed by Nicole MacMartin & Sandi Carpenter
Edited by Mary Sieber

Printed in China

**On the cover, clockwise from upper left:** Orange patent leather Chanel East-West flap bag with silver and orange leather chain and silver hardware. $775 (Courtesy of Heritage Auctions); "Breakfast at Tiffany's" rare large format poster, Paramount, 1961, 30" x 40". $5,378 (Courtesy of Heritage Auctions); Tiffany flowerform glass vase signed on underside "L.C.T. O1965." $4,740 (Courtesy of James D. Julia Auctioneers, Fairfield, Maine, www.jamesdjulia.com); rare Patek Philippe platinum wristwatch. $242,500 (Courtesy of Heritage Auctions); Nesbitt's advertisement by Charles Showalter, "A Soft Drink Made of Real Oranges," offset lithograph on paper. $275 (Courtesy of Heritage Auctions); and Hans Wegner contemporary ox chair, leather and metal, originally designed in 1960. $8,000-$10,000

**On the back cover:** 1940s Coca-Cola cooler sign with Sprite Boy, 31" long. $1,200 (Courtesy of Morphy Auctions); Beatles vintage record player (NEMS, 1964), one of approximately 5,000 producted. $4,000 (Courtesy of Heritage Auctions)

# Contents

# Introduction

By Noah Fleisher

**NOAH FLEISHER** received his Bachelor of Fine Arts degree from New York University and brings more than a decade of newspaper, magazine, book, antiques and art experience to his position as Public Relations Director of Heritage Auctions, one of the country's foremost auction houses. He is the former editor of *Antique Trader, New England Antiques Journal* and *Northeast Antiques Journal*, is the author of *Warman's Modern Furniture*, and has been a longtime contributor to *Warman's Antiques & Collectibles.*

Welcome to the 2016 edition of *Warman's Antiques & Collectibles!* Those of you steeped in the tradition of preserving our important material culture, I salute you!

As I write this I'm reflecting back on an interesting and record-setting year in the world of antiques and collectibles – a $3.2 million copy of *Action Comics #1*, anybody? Sold on eBay, no less? Fascinating stuff, to say the least – and a tough one personally, as far as the business goes. While I know this introduction is not a diary, I feel it necessary to mention the passing of my mentor in the antiques business, Harold Hanson of Catskill, New York, formerly of his Hudson, New York shop *Verso* and publisher of the now-defunct *Northeast Antiques Journal,* the first antiques paper I wrote for. I loved him and I thank him for his guidance, and because what he taught me is 100% germane to this year's introduction.

When I first started writing about antiques back in 2000, it was something I did for a little extra money. I was good at it, but not too interested. Harold was. He spent his life steeped in it. He saw something in me that fit the business and took it upon himself to educate me. He was such pleasant company, I went along solely for the rides. Harold was all about the "getting there." Our destinations? One of myriad antique shows throughout the Northeast and New England. We drove for hours on back roads, discussing life and antiques, and he introduced me to show promoters and dealers, many of whom I got to know fairly well, at county fairgrounds and elementary school gyms all over the place.

The first, and best, aphorism that he taught me regarding the collecting of antiques for business and pleasure: Quality always sells. This is all you need to know, I believe.

I was quickly hooked on the stuff, and I was quickly hooked on the feel and excitement (most of the time) of a show. It's only appropriate, then, as I reflect on the influence Harold Hanson was in my life, that we open the 49th edition of *Warman's* with a look at the State of the Antique Show.

The three promoters interviewed here come from culturally

and geographically different areas of the country. They represent venerable venues, top-shelf dealers and all manner of antiques and collectibles. They are a representative trio of the dozens of show promoters in America, and they offer a straightforward assessment of the antiques show, viewed from perches overseeing the show floor. Has the Internet had an effect on the business? What about TV? What are people buying? Is it worth getting in the car and driving a couple hours to a show?

Frank Gaglio is the show promoter behind the seven-show stable at Barnstar Promotions (Barnstar.com) of Rhinebeck, New York. He is a 20-year veteran as a promoter, with more under his belt as a noted American antiques dealer. His shows include the Mid-Week Twilight Tuesday and Thursday Pickers Market Antiques Shows during Antiques Week in New Hampshire, the revered Wilton Fall Antiques Market in Wilton, Connecticut, and the Armonk Antiques Show in Armonk, New York.

Christine Palmer is the owner of Christine Palmer & Associates (ChristinePalmer.net), formerly the antiques and collectibles venue famously known as Palmer-Wirfs in Portland, Oregon. The company operates the Portland Expo Center Show in March, July and October, along with the Puyallup Fairgrounds Show in February and November, and the Clark County Fairgrounds Show in January. The company has operated shows all over Oregon and California in the 40 years since Don Wirfs first set up his Sunday antiques flea market in Portland. Christine's past is one that is rich in collectibles and antiques and long on business sense.

David Lamberto, the owner and operator of Hertan's Antiques Shows (HertansBrimfield.com), knows what it means to be at the heart of the action in Brimfield, Massachusetts, one of America's most famous and well-trafficked antiques venues. Three times a year – in May, July, and September – for more than 30 years, when the antiques world focuses on Brimfield, Lamberto's field is right in the middle of town

and always packed. Brimfield is famous for its sheer variety and the stunning finds that come out of the fields. Hertan's has provided more than its share of great pieces, and the atmosphere is among the most festive and friendly in the place.

▶ **Warman's 2016: What is the current state of the antique show right now as compared to the broader business (online, auctions, and shops)?**

Frank Gaglio (FG): The antiques show is in a state of correction. For the past three decades or more, antiques shows served several purposes in our economy. An important one was as a platform for fund-raising (witness the Winter Antiques Show benefiting the East Side Settlement House Show in New York City or the Philadelphia Antiques Show benefiting the Penn Medicine Health Care System). Collectors and supporters would pony up thousands of dollars in preview party tickets for their organization and support the antiques dealers exhibiting with sales. Today, collectors are no longer adding to their collections or are divesting as they age. Their children seldom share the same passions, so it's donated or goes to auction.

In comparing antiques shows to online sales, there is no question the computer age has had an effect on the antiques show. However, you cannot sit on a chair, feel the fabric, or experience the glaze on fine porcelain from a computer. The true collector wants to experience the object in hand, and that's where the antiques show will never be replaced. Auctions are a "buyer beware" environment, where both bad as well as good hits the market.

The introduction decades ago of the "buyer's premium," or "buyer's penalty" as I call it, changed the auction business forever, shutting out dealers by consuming whatever profit a dealer might make after a hard day's work. Some auction houses see the BP as necessary to remain competitive. I feel they were doing just fine for decades when

◄ *Orson Byron Lowell (American, 1871-1956), "Home for Christmas," oil on canvas, 40" x 32", signed lower center "Orson Lowell," signed and titled verso "Home for Christmas By Orson Lowell / Orson / Lowell / 501 5th Ave / N.Y."* **$15,000**

customer service and creative marketing gave them the edge over competition – not penalizing buyers. As for antiques shops, they've been replaced by group shops or consignment shops, leaving the landscape vacant of the wonderful mom-and-pop shops that used to dot country roads and make for a wonderful Sunday outing. They are very much missed.

**David Lamberto (DL):** The state of the antiques show right now is changing, but it's always changing, as all things do. We've seen continued strength for our spring show in May and our fall show in September, and a slowdown for our summer show in July. Many of the dealers have difficulty finding enough inventory in the short time between our spring and our summer shows. Also, for many people, the weather will be too hot or humid, although many years it is beautiful.

**Christine Palmer (CP):** After a serious impact (negative), people are coming back to shows. Buying vintage from the web is a dry experience. Shopping a show is interactive, entertaining, and you can see it and touch it before you buy. Plus, thanks to "Antiques Roadshow" and all the other programming on television, there's a spotlight on discovering that buy-in-the-sky. It becomes not so much the item, but what it's worth. Many think they can duplicate what they see on TV. We've also become much more entertainment-oriented. For our shows, we always have a feature display, live music and – for the last 15 years – we've offered an "Evaluation and Identification" booth (making it clear that they get a verbal market evaluation, that we don't evaluate anything purchased at the show, that we staff the booth with ISA appraisers, and that the money goes to a charity partner). Shopping in the broader market, beyond vintage items, has to have an entertainment component today. We provide that.

► **Warman's 2016: What is selling right now (and in the last few years) and who is buying? Are shows attracting crowds and are they attracting quality material?**

**CP:** Our customers are looking for decorative pieces more as a lifestyle thing (period lighting, kitchenware, prints and art, garden items, etc.). They're buying pieces that set them apart, such as vintage clothing and costume jewelry. Decorative items and vintage clothing are examples of different and unique things, instead of a cookie cutter look. Nostalgia is also driving sales of toys from the 1970s and 1980s – this is what draws the 35-40-year-olds to our shows. We've always been America's largest antiques and collectibles shows and, thanks to the "and collectibles," we've survived the last decade. Fine antiques still sell. Estate jewelry is another hot seller today. You can get a lot of dollar value in one booth and people love it. They like the fact that it was worn by someone else who loved it.

As far as exhibitors go, we're facing the aging of many dealers. The business is hard work, merchandise can be hard to find, and a person in his 70s isn't about to change to a better-selling category at this stage in his career. We've held seminars letting people know that there is room in this industry for them and attracted recent retirees looking for something to do, who over-collected and need to divest. Our speakers make it clear that it's hard work, there's a learning curve, and capital is needed to get started. However, our seminars alone aren't keeping pace with the loss. We also produce a Christmas Bazaar, and it's been our recent experience that we're selling out our booth space (900 booths).

**DL:** My customers tell me that fine art, Chinese and Japanese art and objects, mid-century modern, industrial, vintage clothing, and folk art are some of the categories that are selling well. We get a good crowd for our show openings and buyers are made up of collectors, designers, and pickers of every sort. We've noticed that more people from Asia are coming to buy.

**FG:** The antiques business and collecting in general is subject to trends and styles as the fashion industry is. In the past, if Martha Stewart was buying green glass dinnerware, that became the craze; if Barbra Streisand was collecting Mission, that became hot. That's changed as younger people appear to be less inclined to collect traditional antiques or even have an interest in them, as that was "their parents' thing." Though true period antiques are still in demand, certain fields are leading the way with a younger generation, including art, watches, vintage photography, posters, designer jewelry, mid-century and modern furniture and design, industrial furniture plus

objects that fit into a modern lifestyle and – most important – are practical.

Young people today don't want to be burdened by collections of anything, as they're more mobile and like the freedom of sparsely decorated environments. The shows that seem to be attracting crowds these days are those without a specific focus, more of a general show, in major cities where the population can easily get to the show, often by walking. Whether the shows are presenting quality material is another story, as these shows are sometimes less "vetted" by the show managers and more about filling booth space and collecting booth rents.

▶ **Warman's 2016: What is the future of the antiques show? Is the demise of the traditional show exaggerated?**

**FG:** The reality, as we see it here in the Northeast, is that dealers who made a living exhibiting at better quality shows are getting older, and exhibiting at shows is very hard work: the preparation, loading a van, setting up, standing on your feet attending to customers for hours, staying at motels, eating out, reloading the van after the show, driving home, unloading what didn't sell, adding the cost of gasoline and booth rental…the business takes much more commitment and stamina than it did 20-30 years ago.

There's a future for shows that keep their exhibitors' and customers' best interests in mind. That includes making the show experience as seamless and problem-free as possible, introducing special events such as appraisal clinics, guest speakers, and special exhibits, giving the consumer more bang for their admission dollars. On the bright side, too, [there's] the "Antiques Week" show concept, or cluster shows, where several events under different show managers take place in the span of a week or longer, such as Antiques Week in New Hampshire, Round Top in Texas, Americana Week in New York City, and Madison-Bouckville, New York. By virtue of collective advertising, these types of events thrive where other shows do not. Dealers like the opportunity to shop all the other events and share in the camaraderie with one another.

**CP:** I'll acknowledge that we're concerned. Are we dinosaurs-to-be? To stave off demise, I've patterned our business after the mainstream consumer shows, such as home and garden, RV, boat and sportsman shows. We used to be supported by the die-hard collector. Those collectors are now in divesting (selling) mode, if they haven't liquidated their collections already. Unfortunately, their collections can be obsolete (Hopalong Cassidy lunch boxes, as an example). I've had a mentor, a home and garden show producer who, for 20 years, has shared how he draws attendees. For the last decade we've used radio, television, transit advertising, social media, digital, sponsorship and other tools of the mainline consumer shows. It's helpful that here, in the Pacific Northwest, we're one of two antique show producers. The other one is more than 200 miles from us. To some degree, we have this particular market to ourselves.

**DL:** I haven't heard talk of the demise of the traditional show, thankfully. I'm optimistic about the future; we've always had ups and downs as trends come and go. The experience of buying antiques and collectibles at shows is nothing like doing so online or at shops. There's a place for all of these types of outlets for selling.

▶ **Warman's 2016: What has the effect of the Internet been on your business and on the role of the antiques show in general? Has eBay or Amazon had an effect? Has the accessibility of online pricing information and online auctioneers and dealers had an effect? If so, what?**

**DL:** The Internet has provided an easy way for individuals to get information. Especially when combined with smart phone technology, the savvy shopper can do some preliminary research on the spot. This can help a buyer make a final decision to purchase an item, or give a good idea of a fair price range. People have to remember that asking prices do not represent fair market values.

When eBay first came on the scene there seemed to be a rush to use it and, perhaps, a rise in prices for some items as they became visible to a global marketplace. Then prices evened out and the novelty wore off. I've seen some dealers discontinue eBay selling because it can be so impersonal and asocial.

**CP:** The Internet has made nothing very rare. It used to be that there might be one of an item at a particular show. Now that item can be found easily, which lowers prices for it. Online pricing through websites like Worthpoint.com is valuable as they show realized prices. Customers at our shows walk around with their cell phones tuned into these sites as they shop. The dealers don't like it, but that's the way it is today. If they're confronted with someone comparing their price to the same thing on the web, they're pretty comfortable telling that customer to buy it from the web. Most collectors want it hot and now, and will take it home that day from the show rather than wait.

Antiques shows are about passion and relying on impulse buying to some extent. That's why it is so important that the dealer at a show puts together a good-looking booth, merchandises well, and is friendly and accommodating. Our heyday in the late 1990s is never coming back. Our 400-booth shows are, however, maintaining themselves well from an exhibitor and attendee perspective. Our flagship shows are 1,000 booths. We're not selling out of any of them, but it's been exactly the same in numbers for the last eight years and I think we've finally plateaued. Like any retail business, I am ever vigilant and hopeful.

**FG:** The Internet has opened up a whole new world to both dealer and collector, including me and my business. Some show managers have actually tried to put their shows online, though in my observation, unsuccessfully, as there is no substitute for attending a show live. As a manager you can take photos of your show floor and upload them to your website for people to see, but that's where the system loses ground. As far as eBay or Amazon having a significant effect on antiques sales, I think not, as only certain mass-produced commodities can be sold successfully, having been manufactured by the hundreds or within a certain price category.

With regard to the accessibility of online pricing information and online auctioneers, I find online pricing only relevant to the origin of a piece, condition, size and age. I can imagine the hundreds of people who watch "Antiques Roadshow" and see the same piece they have in their living room being appraised by the Keno brothers for half a million dollars, only to take their item to a local auctioneer and find it was sold from a Sears catalog in 1950! Online pricing can be very helpful if you know where to look and how to decipher the information.

▶ **Warman's 2016: Is there a way for nuts-and-bolts antiques shows to incorporate new technology and make it relevant to shows, or vice versa, for new technology to incorporate a live element and make it relevant to consumers?**

**CP:** I think so. We've toyed with writing an app guiding a person through the show from a distance. We use the usual: social media, digital advertising, etc., but I don't think we want to emulate buying online. We're a brick and mortar business and have pluses that the web doesn't, such as the entertainment factor.

**DL:** I think the traditional antiques show can certainly incorporate new technology to enhance the buying and selling experience. We've recently seen the development of a smart phone app, which is proving to be very helpful to dealers and buyers at our Brimfield shows.

We also offer free wi-fi hotspots so that dealers and buyers can do immediate research when they see an item of interest. Buyers have abandoned the walkie-talkies they used to use to tell colleagues what they're seeing when they're physically apart. Now they snap a photo, send it with a text, and get a reply in seconds with their cell phones.

**FG:** Nuts-and-bolts antiques shows don't have the budget to invest in experimental new technology to make their shows relevant, aside from using social media such as Constant Contact to get the word out about their events. Even then, the process is limited to email addresses the show manager has at his disposal. The first step is to gather email addresses of new attendees at shows or share email addresses with other show managers when event dates are not in conflict. I find Facebook, Twitter, and online discount event sites of little help. You just don't get the response at the gate you would if you were hosting a vodka party.

Aside from getting bodies to attend the shows, we need interested buyers to support exhibiting dealers. For new technology to incorporate a "live" element to an antiques show, the show would have to run one full week or longer, giving online consumers time to visit the show site during their work week. Unfortunately, expenses for participating dealers would go up prohibitively. I think shows will be a one- or two-day event and serious collectors will attend. The challenge will fall to show managers to make it work.

Courtesy of Mark Mussio, Humler & Nolan

▶ *Weller Sicard vase with cuttings of daisy flower heads and foliage strewn about circumference, metallic textured border surrounds base, Weller Sicard signature, excellent condition, 7 1/4" high.* **$600**

▶ **Warman's 2016: What's the best advice you can give someone heading to his/her first show, or who has just started buying at shows?**

**FG:** Research a show's history and attend the show. Consider the location of the show, number of exhibitors, admission fee, amenities, and special events, and focus on what you're looking to collect. I always suggest walking around a show in one direction, then reversing and walking the other way. You would be amazed at what you've missed. Ask if there's a show program with the exhibitors' contact information should you want to consider a purchase after the show.

If you decide to make a purchase, rule number one is ask for a receipt with the dealer's name and full contact information, date of sale, description of the object's origin, period, condition, any restorations or repairs, and price all listed for you, as this is your insurance policy that what you are purchasing is authentic. Most importantly, have fun and don't be afraid to ask questions, even if you are not ready to buy. Knowledge is king in this business, and every good dealer should be willing and happy to share it with you, as you never know when object and buyer make that special connection.

**DL:** Seek knowledge about the items you want to collect from dealers, books, and Internet searches. When you find an item of interest, buy it right away so that you aren't disappointed when you return to find it's been sold. Bargain politely with dealers; they can be insulted if your offer is low. Dress comfortably, keep hydrated, and be prepared for an adventure. Take your time to have a good look in the various booths and keep a good attitude.

**CP:** Have some idea of what type of things you're looking for in general terms [and] whether it's for decorating your home, buying a unique gift, or a hobby.

We offer something we call "Keyword Kiosk" where a customer can ask where the booths are in certain categories. We print a list in location order for them. If a show offers something similar, take advantage of it so you don't run out of steam before you feel that you've seen what's there. We have a lot of dealers who are likely to have a teddy bear next to a slot machine, so sometimes better advice is to arrive rested, with comfortable shoes and a bottle of water, ready to treasure hunt.

Know the correct verbiage for asking a dealer to come down in price: Can you do any better? What's the best you can do? Would you consider "X," a price reflecting a 10-20% discount at the most, so you don't insult a hard-working dealer? Take advantage of early admission, a feature of many shows. Not all shows offer it, but it's a good investment; the early bird gets the worm, you know.

## In the Beginning

Edwin G. Warman was an entrepreneur in Uniontown, Pennsylvania. He dabbled in several ventures, including ownership of a radio station. He was also an avid antiques collector who published his price listings in response to requests from friends and fellow collectors. The first modest price guide was published in 1948 as *Warman's Antiques and Their Current Prices*. It was a bold move. Until then, antiques were sold primarily through dealers, antiques shops, and at auctions. The sellers and buyers negotiated prices and were forced to do their own research to determine fair prices. Under Warman's care, the price guide changed all that forever. Warman also published some specialized price guides for pattern glass and milk glass, as well as his "Oddities and Curiosities" editions, under the banner of the E.G. Warman Publishing Co.

Although the name varied slightly over the years, *Warman's Antiques and Their Current Prices* covered such collectible areas as mechanical banks, furniture, and silver, just like the Warman's of today. His pages consisted of a brief statement about the topic, either relating to the history or perhaps the "collectibility" of the category. A listing of current prices was included, often containing a black and white photograph.

E.G. Warman died in 1979. His widow, Pat Warman, continued the tradition and completed work on the 15th edition after his death. The estate sold the E.G. Warman Publishing Co. to Stanley and Katherine Greene of Elkins Park, Pennsylvania, in 1981. Chilton Books bought the Warman Publishing Co. in the fall of 1989. With the 24th edition, Warman's was published under the Wallace-Homestead imprint. Krause Publications purchased both the Warman's and Wallace-Homestead imprints in 1997.

We are proud to continue the rich tradition started 65 years ago by Mr. Warman, a man driven by his love of antiques and collectibles and by a thirst for sharing his knowledge.

## The Warman's Advantage

The Warman's Advantage manifests itself in several important ways in the 2016 edition. As we reviewed past volumes, we wanted to make this book as easy to use as possible. To that end, we've consolidated and reorganized how we present several key categories. Our new mantra is, "What is it first?"

For instance, an antique clock may also have an advertising component, an ethnic element (like black memorabilia), reflect a specific design theme (like Art Deco), and be made of cast iron. But first and foremost, it's a clock, and that's where you'll find it listed, even though there are other collecting areas involved.

There are some categories that remain iconic in the collecting world. Coca-Cola collectibles cross many interests, as do folk art, Asian antiques, and Tiffany designs, to name a few. These still have their own broad sections.

*New categories in this edition:* Beatles pop culture, celebrity collectibles, children's literature, contemporary art, and animation art.

## Prices

The prices in this book have been established using the results of auction sales across the country, and by tapping the resources of knowledgeable dealers and collectors. These values reflect not only current collector trends, but also the wider economy. The adage that "an antique (or collectible) is worth what someone will pay for it" still holds. A price guide measures value, but it also captures a moment in time, and sometimes that moment can pass very quickly.

Beginners should follow the same advice that all seasoned collectors will share: Make mistakes and learn from them; talk with other collectors and dealers; find reputable resources (including books and websites); and learn to invest wisely, buying the best examples you can afford.

## Words of Thanks

This 49th edition of the *Warman's* guide would not be possible without the help of countless others. Dozens of auction houses have generously shared their resources, but a few deserve special recognition: Heritage Auctions, Dallas; Backstage Auctions, Houston; Woody Auction, Douglass, Kansas; Greg Belhorn, Belhorn Auction Services LLC, Columbus, Ohio; Andrew Truman, James D. Julia Auctioneers, Fairfield, Maine; Anthony Barnes at Rago Arts and Auction Center, Lambertville, New Jersey; Karen Skinner at Skinner, Inc., Boston; Morphy Auctions, Denver, Pennsylvania; Susan Pinnell at Jeffrey S. Evans & Associates, Mount Crawford, Virginia; Rebecca Weiss at Swann Auction Galleries, New York; and Leslie Hindman Auctioneers, Chicago. And, as always, special thanks to Catherine Saunders-Watson for her many contributions and continued support.

## Read All About It

There are many fine publications that collectors and dealers may consult about antiques and collectibles in general. Space does not permit listing all of the national and regional publications in the antiques and collectibles field; this is a sampling:

- *Antique Trader,* published by Krause Publications, 700 E. State St., Iola, WI, 54990 – *www.antiquetrader.com*

- *Antique & The Arts Weekly,* 5 Church Hill Rd., Newton, CT 06470 – *www.antiquesandthearts.com*

- *AntiqueWeek,* P.O. Box 90, Knightstown, IN 46148 – *www.antiqueweek.com*

- *Maine Antique Digest,* P.O. Box 358, Waldoboro, ME 04572 – *www.maineantiquedigest.com*

- *New England Antiques Journal,* 24 Water St., Palmer, MA 01069 – *www.antiquesjournal.com*

- *The Journal of Antiques and Collectibles,* P.O. Box 950, Sturbridge, MA 01566 – *www.journalofantiques.com*

- *Southeastern Antiquing & Collecting Magazine,* P.O. Box 510, Acworth, GA 30101 – *www.go-star.com/antiquing*

## Visit an Antiques Show

One of the best ways to enjoy the world of antiques and collectibles is to take the time to really explore an antiques show. Some areas, like Brimfield, Massachusetts, and Manchester, New Hampshire, turn into antiques meccas for a few days each summer when dealers and collectors come for both specialized and general antiques shows, plus auctions.

Here are a few of our favorites:

- **Brimfield, Massachusetts, shows,** held three times a year in May, July, and September, www.brimfield.com

- **Round Top, Texas, antique shows,** held spring and fall, www.roundtop.com/antique1.htm

- **Antiques Week** in and around Manchester, New Hampshire, held every August, www.antiquesweeknh.com

- **Christine Palmer & Associates,** including the Portland, Oregon, Expos, christinepalmer.net

- **The Original Miami Beach Antique Show,** www.dmgantiqueshows.com

- **Merchandise Mart International Antiques Fair,** Chicago, www.merchandisemartantiques.com

- **High Noon Western Americana Show and Auction,** Phoenix, www.highnoon.com

 # LET US KNOW
# WHAT YOU THINK

We're always eager to hear what you think about this book and how we can improve it.

Contact:
Paul Kennedy
Editorial Director
Antiques & Collectibles Books
Krause Publications
700 E. State St.
Iola, WI 54990-0001
715-445-2214, Ext. 13470
Paul.Kennedy@fwcommunity.com

## CONTRIBUTORS

*John Adams-Graf*
*Tom Bartsch*
*Eric Bradley*
*Brent Frankenhoff*
*Kyle Husfloen*
*Paul Kennedy*
*Karen Knapstein*
*Mark B. Ledenbach*
*Kristine Manty*
*Michael Polak*
*Antoinette Rahn*
*Ellen T. Schroy*
*Mary Sieber*
*Susan Sliwicki*
*David Wagner*
*Martin Willis*

# Auction Houses

**Sanford Alderfer Auction & Appraisal**
501 Fairgrounds Rd.
Hatfield, PA 19440
215-393-3000
www.alderferauction.com
*Full service*

**American Bottle Auctions**
915 28th St.
Sacramento, CA 95816
800-806-7722
www.americanbottle.com
*Antique bottles, jars*

**American Pottery Auction**
Waasdorp Inc.
P.O. Box 434
Clarence, NY 14031
716-983-2361
www.antiques-stoneware.com
*Stoneware, redware*

**American Sampler**
P.O. 371
Barnesville, MD 20838
301-972-6250
www.castirononline.com
*Cast-iron bookends, doorstops*

**Antiques and Estate Auctioneers**
861 W. Bagley Rd.
Berea, OH 44017
440-647-4007
Fax: 440-647-4006
www.estateauctioneers.com
*Full service*

**Auctions Neapolitan**
1100 First Ave. S.
Naples, FL 34102
239-262-7333
www.auctionsneapolitan.com
*Full service*

**Belhorn Auction Services, LLC**
P.O. Box 20211
Columbus, Ohio 43220
614-921-9441
www.belhorn.com
*Full service, American art pottery*

**Backstage Auctions**
448 West 19th St., Suite 163
Houston, TX 77008
713-862-1200
www.backstageauctions.com
*Rock 'n' roll collectibles and memorabilia*

**Bertoia Auctions**
2141 DeMarco Dr.
Vineland, NJ 08360
856-692-1881
www.bertoiaauctions.com
*Toys, banks, holiday, doorstops*

**Bonhams**
101 New Bond St.
London, England W1S 1SR
44-20-7447-7447
www.bonhams.com
*Fine art and antiques*

**Brian Lebel's Old West Auction**
3201 Zafarano Dr., Suite C585
Santa Fe, NM 87507
480-779-9378
www.codyoldwest.com
*Western collectibles and memorabilia*

**Brunk Auctions**
P.O. Box 2135
Asheville, NC 28802
828-254-6846
www.brunkauctions.com
*Full service*

**Caroline Ashleigh Associates, LLC**
1000 S. Old Woodward, Suite 201
Birmingham, MI 48009-6734
248-792-2929
www.auctionyourart.com
*Full service, vintage clothing, couture and accessories, textiles, western wear*

**Cedarburg Auction Co., Inc.**
227 N. Main St.
Thiensville, WI 53092
262-238-5555
www.cedarburgauction.com
*Full service*

**Christie's New York**
20 Rockefeller Plaza
New York, NY 10020
www.christies.com
*Full service*

**Clars Auction Gallery**
5644 Telegraph Ave.
Oakland, CA 94609
510-428-0100
www.clars.com
*Full service*

**Coeur d'Alene Art Auction**
8836 Hess St., Suite B
Hayden Lake, ID 83835
208-772-9009
www.cdaartauction.com
*19th and 20th century Western and American art*

**Cowan's**
6270 Este Ave.
Cincinnati, OH 45232
513-871-1670
www.cowanauctions.com
*Full service, historic Americana, Native American objects*

**Doyle New York**
175 E. 87th St.
New York, NY 10128
212-427-2730
www.doylenewyork.com
*Fine art, jewelry, furniture*

**DuMouchelles Art Gallery**
409 E. Jefferson Ave.
Detroit, MI 48226
313-963-6255
www.dumouchelle.com
*Fine art and antiques, art glass*

**Early Auction Co., LLC.**
123 Main St.
Milford, OH 45150
513-831-4833
www.earlyauctionco.com
*Art glass*

**Elder's Antiques**
901 Tamiami Trail (US 41) S.
Nokomis, FL 34275
941-488-1005
www.eldersantiques.com
*Full service*

**Elite Decorative Arts**
1034 Gateway Blvd. #106
Boynton Beach, FL 33426
561-200-0893
www.eliteauction.com

**Greg Martin Auctions**
660 Third St., Suite 100
San Francisco, CA 94107
415-777-4867
*Firearms, edged weapons, armor, Native American objects*

**Great Gatsby's Antiques and Auctions**
P.O. Box 660488
Atlanta, GA 30366
770-457-1903
www.greatgatsbys.com
*Fine art, fine furnishings, lighting, musical instruments*

**Grey Flannel**
13 Buttercup Ln.
Westhampton Beach, NY 11977
631-288-7800
www.greyflannel.com
*Sports jerseys, memorabilia*

**Guernsey's**
65 E 93rd St.
New York, NY 10128
212-794-2280
www.guernseys.com
*Art, historical items, pop culture*

**Guyette Schmidt & Deeter**
24718 Beverly Road
P.O. Box 1170
St. Michaels, MD 21663
410-745-0487
www.guyetteandschmidt.com
*Antique decoys*

**Hake's Americana & Collectibles Auctions**
P.O. Box 12001
York, PA 17402
717-434-1600
www.hakes.com
*Character collectibles, pop culture*

**Heritage Auctions**
3500 Maple Ave., 17th Floor
Dallas, TX 75219-3941
800-872-6467
www.ha.com
*Full service, coins, pop culture*

**Humler & Nolan**
225 E. Sixth St., 4th Floor
Cincinnati, OH 45202
513-381-2041 or 513-381-2015
www.humlernolan.com
*Antique American and European art pottery and art glass*

**iGavel, Inc.**
229 E. 120th St.
New York, NY 10035
866-iGavel6 or 212-289-5588
igavelauctions.com
*Online auction, arts, antiques and collectibles*

**Jackson's International Auctioneers and Appraisers**
2229 Lincoln St.
Cedar Falls, IA 50613
319-277-2256
www.jacksonsauction.com
*Full service, religious and Russian objects, postcards*

**James D. Julia, Inc.**
203 Skowhegan Rd.
Fairfield, ME 04937
207-453-7125
www.juliaauctions.net
*Full service, toys, glass, lighting, firearms*

**Jeffrey S. Evans & Associates**
2177 Green Valley Ln.
Mount Crawford, VA 22841
540-434-3939
www.jeffreysevans.com
*Full service, glass, lighting, Americana*

**John Moran Auctioneers, Inc.**
735 W. Woodbury Rd.
Altadena, CA 91001
626-793-1833
www.johnmoran.com
*Full service, California art*

**Keno Auctions**
127 E. 69th St.
New York, NY 10021
212-734-2381
www.kenoauctions.com
*Fine antiques, decorative arts*

**Lang's Sporting Collectibles**
663 Pleasant Valley Rd.
Waterville, NY 13480
315-841-4623
www.langsauction.com
*Antique fishing tackle and memorabilia*

**Leland Little Auctions & Estate Sales, Ltd.**
620 Cornerstone Ct.
Hillsborough, NC 27278
919-644-1243
www.llauctions.com
*Full service*

**Leslie Hindman Auctioneers**
1338 W. Lake St.
Chicago, Il 60607
312-280-1212
www.lesliehindman.com
*Full service*

**Litchfield County Auctions, Inc.**
425 Bantam Road (Route 202)
Litchfield, CT 06759
860-567-4661
212-724-0156
www.litchfieldcountyauctions.com
*Full service*

**McMasters Harris Auction Co.**
1625 W. Church St.
Newark, OH 43055
800-842-3526
www.mcmastersharris.com
*Dolls and accessories*

**Michaan's Auctions**
2751 Todd St.
Alameda, CA 94501
800-380-9822
www.michaans.com
*Antiques, fine art*

**Michael Ivankovich Auction Co.**
P.O. Box 1536
Doylestown, PA 18901
215-345-6094
www.wnutting.com
*Wallace Nutting objects*

**Morphy Auctions**
2000 N. Reading Rd.
Denver, PA 17517
717-335-3435
www.morphyauctions.com
*Toys, banks, advertising, pop culture*

**Mosby & Co. Auctions**
5714-A Industry Ln.
Frederick, MD 21704
240-629-8139
www.mosbyauctions.com
*Mail, phone, Internet sales*

**Neal Auction Co.**
4038 Magazine St.
New Orleans, LA 70115
504-899-5329
800-467-5329
www.nealauction.com
*Art, furniture, pottery, silver, decorative arts*

**New Orleans Auction Gallery**
801 Magazine St.
New Orleans, LA 70130
800-501-0277
www.neworleansauction.com
*Full service, Victorian*

**Noel Barrett Vintage Toys @ Auction**
P.O. Box 300
Carversville, PA 18913
215-297-5109
www.noelbarrett.com
*Toys, banks, holiday, advertising*

**Old Town Auctions**
11 St. Paul St.
Boonsboro, MD 21713
240-291-0114
301-416-2854
*Toys, advertising, Americana;
no Internet sales*

**Old Toy Soldier Auctions USA**
P.O. Box 13324
Pittsburgh, PA 15243
Ray Haradin
412-343-8733
800-349-8009
www.oldtoysoldierauctions.com
*Toy soldiers*

**Old World Auctions**
4325 Cox Rd.
Glen Allen, VA 23060
804-290-8090
www.oldworldauctions.com
*Maps, documents*

**Past Tyme Pleasures**
5424 Sunol Blv., #10-242
Pleasanton, CA 94566
925-484-6442
www.pasttyme1.com
*Internet catalog auctions*

**Philip Weiss Auctions**
74 Morrick Rd.
Lynbrook, NY 11563
516-594-0731
www.prwauctions.com
*Full service, comic art*

**Pook & Pook, Inc.**
463 E. Lancaster Ave.
Downingtown, PA 19335
610-629-4040
www.pookandpook.com
*Full service, Americana*

**ATM Antiques & Auctions LLC**
811 SE US Hwy 19.
Crystal River, FL 34429
800-542-3877
www.charliefudge.com
*Full service*

**Quinn's Auction Galleries
& Waverly Auctions**
360 S. Washington St.
Falls Church, VA 22046
703-532-5632
www.quinnsauction.com
www.waverlyauctions.com
*Full service, rare books and prints*

**Rago Arts and Auction Center**
333 N. Main St.
Lambertville, NJ 08530
609-397-9374
www.ragoarts.com
*Arts & Crafts, modernism, fine art*

**Red Baron's Antiques, Inc.**
8655 Roswell Rd.
Atlanta, GA 30350
770-640-4604
www.rbantiques.com
*Full service, Victorian,
architectural objects*

**Rich Penn Auctions**
P.O. Box 1355
Waterloo, IA 50704
319-291-6688
www.richpennauctions.com
*Advertising and country-store objects*

**Richard D. Hatch & Associates**
913 Upward Rd.
Flat Rock, NC 28731
828-696-3440
www.richardhatchauctions.com
*Full service*

**Robert Edward Auctions, LLC**
P.O. Box 7256
Watchung, NJ 07069
908-226-9900
www.robertedwardauctions.com
*Baseball, sports memorabilia*

**Rock Island Auction Co.**
7819 42nd St. West
Rock Island, IL 61201
800-238-8022
www.rockislandauction.com
*Firearms, edged weapons
and accessories*

**St. Charles Gallery, Inc.**
1330 St. Charles Ave.
New Orleans, LA 70130
504-586-8733
*Full service, Victorian*

**Samuel T. Freeman & Co.**
1808 Chestnut St.
Philadelphia, PA 19103
215-563-9275
www.freemansauction.com
*Full service, Americana*

**Seeck Auctions**
P.O. Box 377
Mason City, IA 50402
641-424-1116
www.seeckauction.com
*Full service, carnival glass*

**Skinner, Inc.**
63 Park Plaza
Boston, MA 02116
617-350-5400
www.skinnerinc.com
*Full service, Americana*

**Sloans & Kenyon**
7034 Wisconsin Ave.
Chevy Chase, MD 20815
301-634-2330
www.sloansandkenyon.com
*Full service*

**Slotin Folk Art**
Folk Fest Inc.
5619 Ridgetop Dr.
Gainesville, GA 30504
770-532-1115
www.slotinfolkart.com
*Naïve and outsider art*

**Sotheby's New York**
1334 York Ave.
New York, NY 10021
212-606-7000
www.sothebys.com
*Fine art, jewelry, historical items*

**Strawser Auctioneers & Appraisers**
P.O. Box 332, 200 N. Main
Wolcottville, IN 46795
260-854-2859
www.strawserauctions.com
*Full service, majolica, Fiestaware*

**Susanin's Auctions**
900 S. Clinton St.
Chicago, IL 60607
312-832-9800
www.susanins.com
*Fine art, Asian, fine furnishings,
silver, jewelry*

**Swann Galleries, Inc.**
104 E. 25th St., #6
New York, NY 10010-2999
212-254-4710
www.swanngalleries.com
*Rare books, prints,
photographs, posters*

**Ted Owen and Co. Auctions/
The Fame Bureau**
Suite 71
2 Old Brompton Rd.
SW7 3DQ London, United Kingdom
http://famebureau.com

**Theriault's**
P.O. Box 151
Annapolis, MD 21404
800-638-0422
www.theriaults.com
*Dolls and accessories*

**Tom Harris Auction Center**
203 S. 18th Ave.
Marshalltown, IA 50158
641-754-4890
www.tomharrisauctions.com
*Full service, clocks, watches*

*Auction Houses (cont.)*

**John Toomey Gallery**
818 North Blvd.
Oak Park, IL 60301
708-383-5234
www.treadwaygallery.com
*Arts & Crafts, modernism, fine art*

**Tradewinds Antiques**
**& Auctions**
P.O. Box 249
24 Magnolia Ave.
Manchester-By-The-Sea, MA
01944-0249
978-526-4085
www.tradewindsantiques.com
*Canes*

**Treadway Gallery**
2029 Madison Rd.
Cincinnati, OH 45208
513-321-6742
www.treadwaygallery.com

**Turkey Creek Auctions, Inc.**
13939 N. Highway 441
Citra, FL 32113
352-622-4611
800-648-7523
antiqueauctionsfl.com

**Victorian Casino**
**Antiques Auction**
4520 Arville St. # 1
Las Vegas, NV 89103
702-382-2466
www.vcaauction.com

**Waverly Auctions**
360 S. Washington St.
Falls Church, VA 22046
703-532-5632
www.quinnsauction.com
www.waverlyauctions.com
*Full service, rare books
and prints*

**Woody Auction**
P.O. Box 618
317 S. Forrest
Douglass, KS 67039
316-747-2694
www.woodyauction.com
*Glass*

# Ask an Expert

Many contributors have proved invaluable in sharing their expertise during the compilation of the 48th edition of the *Warman's* guide. For more information on their specialties, call or visit their websites.

**Caroline Ashleigh**
Caroline Ashleigh Associates, LLC
1000 S. Old Woodward,
Suite 201
Birmingham, MI 48009-6734
248-792-2929
www.auctionyourart.com
*Vintage clothing, couture and
accessories, textiles,
western wear*

**Tim Chambers**
Missouri Plain Folk
501 Hunter Ave.
Sikeston, MO 63801-2115
573-620-5500
moplainfolk@gmail.com
*Folk art*

**Noah Fleisher**
noah.fleisher@yahoo.com
*Modernism*

**Reyne Haines**
Reyne Gallery
2311 Westheimer Rd.
Houston, TX 77098
513-504-8159
www.reyne.com
reyne@reyne.com
*20th century decorative
arts, lighting, fine jewelry,
wristwatches*

**Ted Hake**
Hake's Americana &
Collectibles Auctions
P.O. Box 12001
York, PA 17402
717-434-1600
hakes@hakes.com
*Pop culture, Disneyana, political*

**Mary P. Manion**
Landmarks Gallery &
Restoration Studio
231 N. 76th St.
Milwaukee, WI 53213
800-352-8892
www.landmarksgallery.com
*Fine art and restoration*

**Suzanne Perrault**
Perrault Rago Gallery
333 N. Main St.
Lambertville, NJ 08530
609-397-9374
www.ragoarts.com
 suzanne@ragoarts.com

**David Rago**
Rago Arts and Auction Center
333 N. Main St.
Lambertville, NJ 08530
609-397-9374
www.ragoarts.com
*Art pottery, Arts & Crafts*

**Dennis Raleigh Antiques**
**& Folk Art**
P.O. Box 745
Wiscasset, ME 04578
734-604-0898
www.dennisraleighantiques.com
dgraleigh@myfairpoint.net
*Decoys, silhouettes,
portrait miniatures*

**Henry A. Taron**
Tradewinds Antiques
P.O. Box 249
Manchester-By-The-Sea,
MA 01944-0249
978-526-4085
www.tradewindsantiques.com
*Canes*

**Andrew Truman**
James D. Julia, Inc.
203 Skowhegan Rd.
Fairfield, ME 04937
207-453-7125
www.juliaauctions.net
*Toys, dolls, advertising*

# Advertising

By Noah Fleisher

The enduring appeal of antique advertising is not hard to understand. The graphics are great, they hearken back to a simpler time and a distinct American identity, and – perhaps best of all – are available across all price levels. That means buyers from all tax brackets and walks of life.

"It's like anything in collectibles and antiques," according to Dan Matthews, petroliana/automobilia advertising expert with Morphy Auctions, former president and owner of Matthew's Auction in Moline, Illinois, and author of *The Fine Art of Collecting and Displaying Petroliana.* "The best stuff, the very top, sells no matter what. Right now the medium market is doing OK and the lower continues to drag a bit behind."

The most reliable value in Matthews' market continues to be top-of-the-line petroliana – names like Harbo Petrolium, Keller Springs, Quiver, or Must-go can command tens of thousands of dollars – but there is a definite hierarchy at play and, if you are thinking of expanding your collecting horizons to include antique signage, you would do well to know the market.

Seasoned collectors will warn, with good reason, that money should not be the motivating factor in the hobby, so it may be somewhat deceptive to start this discussion with the idea of monetary value. The true value of antique advertising signs, from gas stations to country stores to soda pop, lies in the context of their production and the nostalgia they evoke of that time.

The best antique advertising evokes the meat of the first half of the 20th century, when signs were the most effective ways to catch the eyes of car culture consumers. The signs and symbols evolved to reflect the values and styles of the regions where they were posted and the products they reflected. A sign with bold color, great graphics, and a catchy slogan can transport a collector back decades in an instant. Collectors feel a rapport with a piece; they don't see dollar signs.

"Buy it because you like it," said Matthews, "because you can live it with it and it means something to you. Never get into something because you think you'll make money."

**NOAH FLEISHER** received his Bachelor of Fine Arts degree from New York University and brings more than a decade of newspaper, magazine, book, antiques and art experience to his position as Public Relations Director of Heritage Auctions, one of the country's foremost auction houses. He is the former editor of *Antique Trader, New England Antiques Journal* and *Northeast Antiques Journal,* is the author of *Warman's Modern Furniture,* and has been a longtime contributor to *Warman's Antiques & Collectibles.*

Courtesy of Heritage Auctions

*American hand-carved cigar store Indian, colorful headdress, bear-claw necklace with central medallion, fringed skirt, holding small bundle of cigars, base 5 1/2" high x 16" wide x 20 1/2" deep, headdress to toes 75 1/2".*
**$203,150**

Look at the market for one of the most collectible and popular markets: Coca-Cola. Fifteen years ago the best Coke pieces in the middle market could reliably command several thousand dollars. Coca-Cola manufactured hundreds of thousands of signs and related ephemera, millions even, and they began to come out of the woodwork. There is little more evocative of classic Americana than the red and white of Coke, but as everybody sold their pieces and everybody acquired their bit of nostalgia, the market cooled and prices went down significantly. Pieces that had routinely brought $500-$1,000 could suddenly be had for significantly less, and people stopped selling.

Now, however, with several years of very quiet action in the books, the cycle seems to be turning around. New collectors have entered the market and older collectors are leaving. Those collections are finding new owners at a decent price.

"Coca-Cola does seem to be coming back," said Matthews. "It's been stagnant for the past five years, but good clean signs are finding good homes at good prices."

As with any category, the very best antique advertising will bring top dollar no matter what, as a look through the recent advertising sales database of prices realized at an auction house like Morphy's will attest to. In those sales it can be seen that the rarest of Coca-Cola paper and tin routinely bring tens of thousands of dollars.

That said, then, let's talk money. Antique advertising provides a tangible place for collectors to put real money. Looking through recent prices realized at the top auction venues – like Morphy Auctions, Heritage Auctions and William Morford – it's obvious that top dollar can be had for the true rarities in the business and that the middle market provides a solid outlet for design-minded collectors as opposed to those who collect to amass a sizable grouping.

There are opportunities everywhere for the educated collector – from the country auction to the flea market. Going head to head, out of the blocks, with the top collectors in the business at the top auctions can result in frustration. Rather, if you're just getting your feet wet, research online, email experts and ask for resources, do your due diligence in seeing what the market is bringing and, then, take those skills to unlikely places and see what turns up.

"All the fields we deal in seem to be doing quite well right now," said Matthews. "Gas and oil, which there's more of than anything else, keeps going up more and more. The best thing to do is buy from reputable auction houses and dealers, from people who guarantee your product."

Barring the finds you can make at small antiques shows, shops and markets, expect to go into an auction ready to spend an average of $500 for a quality piece of petroliana, for pieces like rare

oil and gas cans. A sharp and patient buyer can grab a steal for $10 or a masterpiece for $1,000. As with anything else, a seasoned and practical eye comes with practice. The prices broaden greatly when the market is expanded to include country store advertising and specific brand advertising, like Campbell's Soup.

"Like most kinds of collectibles, everybody starts out buying middle grade stuff and graduates to the higher stuff," said Matthews. "Collectors in this hobby are very dedicated; prices on the best stuff haven't peaked yet, that's for sure."

A lot of the steadiness in the market is coming from the exposure antique advertising is getting in places like cable television, via shows like "American Pickers" and "Pawn Stars," where a premium is placed on supreme objects.

"These kinds of shows are only helping the hobby get bigger," Matthews added. "Take Ford Oil cans, for instance. Before these shows, the market was dominated by a handful of players. The prices ran way up. Those guys all got out, cans went down to $500 or so from $1,000 or more. Then these shows premiered, oil cans got some attention, and now a lot more collectors are back in at $1,000."

Factor in the pop culture value, as blue collar treasures are increasingly regarded as art , and the horizon is bright for this working-man's collectible.

"I see younger generations continuing to get into this hobby more and more," said Matthews. "As long as we have to put gas in our cars and food in our mouths, people will collect this stuff."

Courtesy of Heritage Auctions

*"They All Want Budweiser... Nothing Else," oil on canvas, 13 1/2" x 33".* **$2,250**

**RECOMMENDED READING**

**Picker's Pocket Guide Signs.** Pick antiques like a pro with the Picker's Pocket Guide, a handy how-to guide that explains the ins and outs of buying and selling advertising signs.
www.krausebooks.com

Courtesy of Heritage Auctions

*Goudey Gum sign, circa 1933, tin litho with sprite whispering in young boy's ear, "The Goudey Gum Co. Boston – Chicago," near mint condition with light minor scratches, yellow metal frame, 7 1/2" x 15 1/2".* **$286**

Courtesy of Skinner, Inc., www.skinnerinc.com

*Polychrome painted wooden "T. DOUGLAS LADIES & GENTS QUICK LUNCH" trade sign, American, late 19th century, tall wooden panel depicting portly gentleman with "I Lunch Here" inscribed above, 84" high x 26 1/4" wide.* **$21,330**

▲ *Freestone R.H. Cate & Co. Distillers, Knoxville, Tennessee, self-framed tin sign, circa 1905, all original in excellent condition, 28" x 22".*
**$3,500**

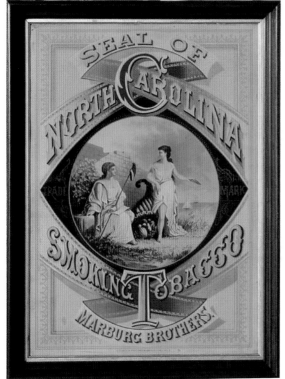

*Seal of North Carolina Smoking Tobacco sign, signed Wells & Hope Co., litho on tin, Philadelphia, rare color in deep walnut frame, circa 1880, near mint condition, 32" high x 23 1/2" wide.*
**$25,750**

*Rare Swift's Fertilizer flange sign.*
**$1,250**

Courtesy of Lang's Auction

▼ *Heddon Tackle tri-fold advertising die-cut display sign, leaping bass with red head shiner scale Zig Wag lure in mouth, 1930, 26" x 52" high, opens to reveal shelf for product, "copyright 1930, James Heddon's Sons and printed by James T. Igoe Co. of Chicago, IL."* **$3,000**

Courtesy of Morphy Auctions

*Soapine reverse on glass sign, circa 1890s, some restoration, excellent condition, 35" x 29".* **$6,000**

Courtesy of Rich Penn Auctions

▶ *Apothecary trade sign, circa 1880-1910, druggist mortar, curved etched ruby glass advertising panels on top and bottom in formed metal frame, jeweled center band, excellent condition with professional restoration on lower advertising panels, rare, 42" high x 25" diameter.* **$12,500**

Courtesy of Rock Island Auction Co.

◄ *Rare stoneware tin sign by The American Art Works Co. of Coshocton, Ohio, "STONEWARE / THE BEST FOOD / CONTAINER" at top and "WE SELL ALL SIZES" on bottom, cardboard with folding stand, back stamped with The American Art Works cleaning instructions, 19" x 13".* **$600**

Courtesy of Brian Maloney

▲ *Creek Chub Bait Co. embossed tin sign with rare turquoise background.* **$1,250**

Courtesy of Brian Maloney

◄ *Milkmaid Milk porcelain sign, wooden frame, 51".* **$1,300**

▶ *No. 1 Chocolate Brownies sign, circa 1880s, single-sided lithograph on tin cardboard, possible Palmer Cox-style Brownies carrying stack of chocolate candies, very good condition, 6" square.* **$300-$400**

▲ *Tobacco figure of Punch, Lord of Misrule, circa 1885, much original paint, "Wm. Demuth & Co. Manufacturers New York" cast into base, back fitted with metal tube for making puffs of smoke flow through cigar clenched between teeth, rare, 18 1/2" high.* **$80,662**

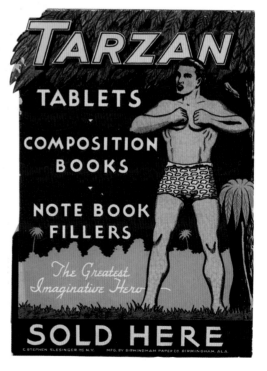

*Tarzan school paper supplies cardboard store sign, circa 1930s, Birmingham Paper Co., very good condition.* **$167**

*Drink Vernor's Ginger Ale double-sided die-cut flange tin sign, 18" x 21".* **$300**

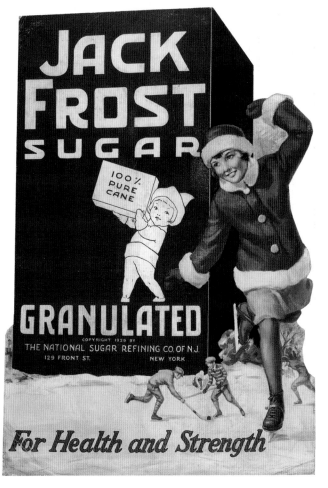

*National Sugar Refining Co., known as Jack Frost, advertising sign on heavy stock material, excellent condition, 21" x 30".* **$358**

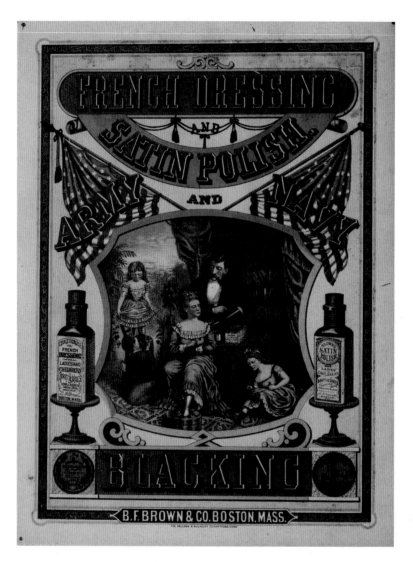

Courtesy of R.W. Oliver Auctions

*Tin sign advertising French dressing shoe polish, circa 1870s, B.F. Brown & Co., Boston, Kellog and Bulkely Litho, considered one of the finest advertising signs to exist, 17" x 23".* **$3,000-$5,000**

# ART

# Animation Art

By Noah Fleisher

**NOAH FLEISHER** received his Bachelor of Fine Arts degree from New York University and brings more than a decade of newspaper, magazine, book, antiques and art experience to his position as Public Relations Director of Heritage Auctions, one of the country's foremost auction houses. He is the former editor of *Antique Trader, New England Antiques Journal* and *Northeast Antiques Journal*, is the author of *Warman's Modern Furniture*, and has been a longtime contributor to *Warman's Antiques & Collectibles*.

Cartoons were a tremendous part of my childhood, as they were for so many people. I was raised in the prime years of Saturday morning cartoons, the mid-1970s. Those endless weekend mornings, perched in front of the tube with a box of Cheerios and a gallon of milk, I was set for the cavalcade of Bugs Bunny and Hanna-Barbera that was a well-deserved reward for a week of school, homework, and dodging the various perils of kid-dom.

The nostalgia I feel for those mornings, where names like Grape Ape, The Super Friends, Schoolhouse Rock, and Hong Kong Phooey reside, is palpable. Great characters live with us, they become embedded in our collective consciousness and are guides along the way. So many of the lessons I learned in life came to me directly from cartoons: the laws of physics were mutable, how to deal with bullies, good usually triumphs over bad, and you should never, ever cross Bugs Bunny.

This nostalgia, and these lessons, are nothing new to me and my Generation X cohorts. The love and influence of animation goes all the way back to the early 20th century and the inception of the art form. It took firm hold of American hearts and souls in the 1920s with the advent of Walt Disney's revolutionary mouse and his groundbreaking Silly Symphonies. It continued in the 1940s with Warner Brothers cartoons and Merry Melodies. It soared through the 1950s and 1960s with cartoons from Jay Ward and Hanna-Barbera, who dominated the 1970s as well.

The 1980s saw the beginning of the end of traditional hand-animated cartoons as digital animation began its march toward dominance, but it was in the 1980s and 1990s that animation art itself would experience its first great boom as well as its first great crash.

When the kids who had grown up on The Wonderful World of Disney in the 1950s and 1960s realized they could actually buy and own the individual animation cels from the movies and cartoons they watched and loved so well as children, well, a market was born. Prices on the best Disney pieces soared.

In the mid-1990s the market, over-saturated, soured. Prices fell. Key master cels and master backgrounds used in the making of the great animated films of Disney, for instance, stopped bringing six-figure and high five-figure prices.

Twenty years later, animation is on the move again. Auction houses are posting sales with results that routinely surpass $1 million. Classic pieces of Disney art, with key names attached, are again bringing five-figure prices, sometimes flirting with $100,000 and above. Two generations have aged into collecting, nostalgia is strong, and wallets are open. What's more, as hunger for classic Disney and Warner Brothers cartoons heats back up, so too has the desire among Gen-X collectors for the cartoons of their childhoods. Super Friends and Schoolhouse Rock animation cels and related pieces routinely bring several thousand dollars when they show up. They are actively tracked and bid on by a whole new generation of collectors looking to capture exactly what the previous generations were: their childhoods.

For insight into today's market, *Warman's* turned to one of the leading dealers of animation today: Deborah Weiss, the owner of Wonderful World of Animation in Orange County, California.

Weiss needs no introduction to serious collectors; she has been in the business for decades, has dealt with some of

Courtesy of Heritage Auctions

*"Pinocchio" Geppetto and Pinocchio production cel and background (Walt Disney, 1940), original hand-inked and hand-painted production cels of Geppetto, Pinocchio, and Figaro from early scene in which Pinocchio's finger catches fire, key master set-up with cels placed over hand-painted production background; Geppetto 10", Pinocchio 6", and Figaro approximately 2" x 2 1/4".* **$17,925**

Courtesy of Heritage Auctions

*Woody Woodpecker production cel and pan background (Walter Lantz, circa 1960s), 12-field cel with 4" hand-painted Woody mounted to piece; hand-painted background 46" high x 9" wide.* **$2,271**

the greatest pieces of animation art in existence, and has an impeccable eye for good pieces. Collectors turn to her for pieces of all vintages, and for objective advice and fair deals on these pieces. A routine look around her website, www. WonderfulWorldofAnimation.com, confirms all of this. There is plenty to choose from across price points and generations.

**Warman's:** Please give me a brief overview of the market for Animation Art right now. What's hot? What's not?

**Deborah Weiss (DW):** The animation market is very much on an upward swing right now and appears to be getting stronger all the time. A stronger economy, strong results in auction, and the recently built museums are all adding to the momentum. We had our best month in our 20+ years at the gallery recently and have sold a number of pieces in the $30,000-$100,000 range.

Strong classic Disney art is hot. Master set-ups and concept art from the classics – Gustav Tenggren, David Hall, Mary Blair, etc. – have been selling very well.

What's not? The limited edition market got over-supplied and many of those pieces now sell for a quarter of their original price.

**Warman's:** Where are the best buys right now? What genre, characters, etc.?

**DW:** I've always advised collectors to buy what they love. If it goes up in value, that's an added bonus. The safest thing to do is to buy the best pieces you can afford. Cels of "classic" recognizable characters in their quintessential poses should always have the most general appeal: Cinderella in a ball gown, Lady and Tramp spaghetti scene, etc. Best buys, as far as contemporary cartoons go? The Simpsons. It's a record-breaking show and each year more of its fans are growing up and able to afford the cels. For vintage Disney drawings, collectors can pick up lovely drawings from the 1930s-1950s in the $300-$1,000 range, very affordable.

**Warman's:** What's the appeal of animation art? Why should it be taken seriously as an art form?

**DW:** You own a one-of-a-kind piece used to make a film. My favorite thing is to pause the DVD, then look at my wall and think, "I own that! I actually own a piece of Snow White." How fantastic is that? Hang a Simpsons cel in your house and probably every single person who sees it will know what it is. There's serious skill needed to create characters that live in our collective consciousness and are loved the world over. The skill level, attention to detail and quality is on the level of many artists that are deemed more "serious." Keep in mind, though, that pieces reside in the permanent collections of some of the world's most famous museums now, including MoMA.

**Warman's:** How has the market changed since the heyday of the 1980s and early 1990s?

*"Challenge of the Super Friends" title cel and background (Hanna-Barbera, 1978). After the success of "Super Friends" (1973) and "The All New Super Friends Hour" (1977), Hanna-Barbera brought to ABC this third installment of the franchise that pits the Justice League of America against the Legion of Doom.* **$5,676**

**DW:** That era had a lot of things going on. It was the first time that animation art had reached a big audience and the Internet did not exist. Since then, what the market saw was prices on OK-ish art falling, like Pink Panther cels, while the very rare items, like Snow White master set-ups, are once again approaching, and in some cases exceeding, the levels of the early '90s.

Nowadays, it's much easier for collectors to find galleries, and the perception of availability and how rare something is can get skewed. There aren't more Pinocchio pieces in existence than there were 25 years ago, but when one sees a few on a number of sites, the idea of how "rare" something is can change.

On the other hand, so many new collectors have come along – people who otherwise would've never known this type of art exists to collect – that we have collectors from all over the world finding us and purchasing, keeping prices competitive.

**Warman's:** What should a collector look for when starting an animation art collection? What's the best advice you could give them?

**DW:** This is an easy one. It's the same [advice] I followed

*"Mickey's Service Station" Mickey and Goofy production cel and master background (Walt Disney, 1935), from one of Mickey Mouse's last black and white cartoons featuring work by the best of the early Disney stable; original hand-inked and painted production nitrate cel of Mickey and Goofy, with Pete's car, placed over master hand-painted background from film, completely original, no restoration.* **$98,588**

when I started collecting: Do some research, familiarize yourself with definitions and prices, and collect what appeals to you – it's your collection and you should buy what you like. Call a few galleries and ask them questions. Find galleries that you feel comfortable dealing with and you feel are trying to show you the pieces that best match your collecting goals.

**Warman's:** Real, hand-drawn animation is a diminishing art in modern TV and film. Is there a future for animation collecting 50 or 100 years from now?

**DW:** Absolutely. It's unfortunate that there is not art to collect from newer TV and films, but every generation has a place in its heart for the classics; they'll continue to be sought-after. The collector base grows each year as more and more people realize this type of art exists to collect.

**Warman's:** What drew you to animation art? How did you end up in the business?

**DW:** When I was little, I collected comic books. Not only did I collect comic books, I dreamed of comic books and counted the days until the new Overstreet arrived. My first cel was a gift – an Archie cel – and after that I was completely head-over-heels hooked. I used to trade Latin American equities on Wall Street, and I really enjoyed my job, but I lived and breathed animation. How lucky was I that I could have a career doing what I love!

Courtesy of Heritage Auctions

▲ *"Snow White and the Seven Dwarfs" original Courvoisier hand-inked and hand-painted production cel set-up of Snow White's encounter with the Old Hag (Walt Disney, 1937); Snow White 4", Old Hag 4 1/4" in 9 1/2" x 7 3/4" image area.* **$26,290**

Courtesy of Heritage Auctions

*"Snow White and the Seven Dwarfs" Evil Queen original Courvoisier production cel (Walt Disney, 1937), hand-inked, hand-painted; Queen 10" in 9 1/4" x 12" image area.* **$14,340**

Courtesy of Heritage Auctions

*Peanuts "It Was a Short Summer, Charlie Brown" pan production cel set-up (Bill Melendez, 1969), hand-painted, with 11 Peanuts characters including Charlie Brown, Lucy, Linus, Violet, Schroeder, Pigpen, and Peppermint Patty, hand-painted key master production overlays and hand-painted key master production background; 35 1/2" x 8 1/2" image area.* **$12,548**

Courtesy of Heritage Auctions

▲ *Charlie Brown/Peanuts Ford Falcon commercial, Charlie Brown, Linus, and Snoopy production cel and pan background (Bill Melendez/ Playhouse Pictures, 1961); Charlie Brown and Linus 1 3/4", Snoopy 2 1/4".* **$12,548**

Courtesy of Heritage Auctions

◄ *Charlie Brown/Peanuts Ford Falcon commercial, Charlie Brown, Snoopy, and Linus production cel set-up with background (Bill Melendez/Playhouse Pictures, 1962), cels on key master hand-painted background, Charlie Brown watching television, Linus adjusting Snoopy's dog ears like antenna; characters 3" average.* **$6,573**

Courtesy of Heritage Auctions

*Mary Blair "It's a Small World" original art (Walt Disney, 1964), tempera and watercolor on board, 15" x 20". Blair's artwork was the inspiration and major force in the design and implementation of the global attraction seen by millions of people every year.* **$17,925**

Courtesy of Heritage Auctions

*Beatles "Yellow Submarine" Paul McCartney, George Harrison, Ringo Starr, and John Lennon rare, original hand-painted color model cel animation art (United Artists/King Features, 1968), Beatles in "everyday" outfits for film, with color instructions written in ink and china marker on acetate; approximately 13 3/4" x 10".* **$14,340**

Courtesy of Heritage Auctions

*Chuck Jones Pepe Le Pew original signed watercolor painting original art (Warner Brothers, undated), rare, on acid-free art rag paper, Jones' signature at bottom right; 13" x 8".* **$13,743**

Courtesy of Heritage Auctions

*"The Charlie Brown and Snoopy Show" World War I Flying Ace production cels and animation drawing group (Bill Melendez, 1982), series of three sequenced hand-painted production cels of Snoopy as World War I Flying Ace; 6" x 5" each.* **$11,950**

Courtesy of Heritage Auctions

▲ *Winsor McCay "Gertie the Dinosaur" production drawing (Winsor McCay, 1914), #252, Gertie rolling around by shore, 6" from tail to nose. This pioneering animated short was the first cartoon to catch the public's attention and give birth to an industry. Gertie was animation's true first star, and McCay drew each scene complete on paper before the use of acetate, nitrate, or any type of cels or background art.* **$7,768**

Courtesy of Heritage Auctions

◄ *"Red Hot Riding Hood" production cel (MGM, 1943), animated by Preston Blair, from sequence of Red performing song, "Daddy," which inspires Wolf's reaction that is now cartoon history; Red 7 1/2".* **$4,332**

*"The Jungle Book" "I Wanna Be Like You" Baloo and King Louie hand-painted production cel setup and master background (Walt Disney, 1967), with Baloo, King Louie, and Louie's monkeys, hand-painted master production background of King Louie's castle.* **$5,079**

*"The New Batman/Superman Adventures" "Mad Love" Arkham Asylum production background set-up (Warner Brothers, 1997), view of Gotham City's Arkham Asylum as seen from outside gate.* **$5,079**

*"Duck Amuck" Daffy Duck production cel set-up (Warner Brothers, 1953, cartoon with Bugs Bunny's classic "Ain't I a stinker?" line), hand-inked and hand-painted; Daffy Duck 6 1/2", 12" x 9" image area.* **$5,079**

Courtesy of Heritage Auctions

*"Dr. Seuss' How the Grinch Stole Christmas" Grinch production cel signed by Chuck Jones (Warner Brothers, 1966), original 12-field, hand-painted production cel of Grinch looking down at Max the dog.* **$4,780**

Courtesy of Heritage Auctions

*"Dr. Seuss' How the Grinch Stole Christmas" Max and Grinch production cel set-up signed by Chuck Jones (MGM, 1966), two cel set-up of Grinch doing sewing repair work on Santa Claus outfit sleeve as worn by Max; Grinch 6", Max 3".* **$3,466**

Courtesy of Heritage Auctions

▲ *"The Little Mermaid" Ariel and King Triton production cel (Walt Disney, 1989), hand-painted, from last Disney feature animation film to use hand-painted production cels; Ariel 6", Triton 7".* **$3,884**

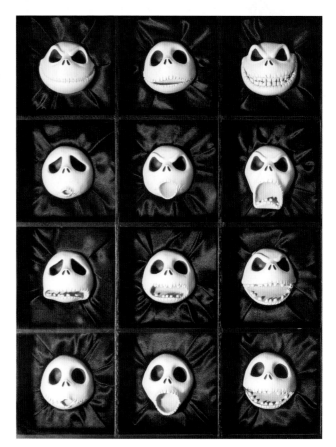

Courtesy of Heritage Auctions

▶ *Tim Burton's "The Nightmare Before Christmas" "Twelve Faces of Jack" limited edition set, 32/275 (Disney Art Editions, 1993), 12 hand-painted cast heads of Jack Skellington, back of box signed by Tim Burton.* **$3,585**

Courtesy of Heritage Auctions

*"Space Ghost" opening title
production cel set-up signed
by Bill Hanna and Joe Barbera
(Hanna-Barbera, 1966), with
hand-lettered title on separate cel,
placed over custom hand-painted
non-production background;
11 1/2" x 9 1/2" image area.*
**$1,494**

Courtesy of Heritage Auctions

▲ *"The Smurfs" model-size
comparison color model cel
(Hanna-Barbera, 1981), with 23
hand-painted Smurfs characters,
rare, used for reference; 47" long.*
**$2,629**

Courtesy of Heritage Auctions

*"Steamboat Willie" Mickey Mouse
production drawing (Walt Disney,
1928), 12-field animation drawing
of Mickey Mouse from his first
theatrical short, drawn by Ube
Iwerks and directed by Walt Disney,
"70" circled next to drawing; Mickey
5" from arm to arm.* **$3,107**

Courtesy of Heritage Auctions

▲ *"The Simpsons" opening
title production cel set-up and
master background (Fox, 1992),
family does kick-step dance in
rare opening title "Couch Gag
Sequence" that continues with
walls falling away, revealing the
Rockettes in dance production
scene; from "Lisa's First Word,"
10th episode from fourth season;
2 1/2" x 7".* **$3,585**

Courtesy of Heritage Auctions

◄ *"The Simpsons" Bart and
Homer production cel with key
master painted background from
first episode of first season (Fox,
1990), hand-painted 12-field cel
from episode "Bart the Genius,"
which aired on Jan. 21, 1990.*
**$2,032**

Courtesy of Heritage Auctions

*"The Flintstones" "Fred Flintstone in Car" title sequence production cel (Hanna-Barbera, 1960), original hand-inked and hand-painted cel from opening title sequence; 6 1/2" x 4".* **$2,868**

Courtesy of Heritage Auctions

*"Duck Dodgers in the 24 1/2th Century" Daffy Duck production cel set-up (Warner Brothers, 1953), hand-inked and hand-painted, from short with third appearance of Marvin the Martian; Daffy 4 1/2", 11 1/2" x 8 1/2" image area.* **$2,988**

Courtesy of Heritage Auctions

*"Heavenly Puss" Tom and Jerry publicity cel set-up and background (MGM, 1949), with original hand-painted production background, possibly color model or publicity cel set-up because scene doesn't appear in cartoon; Tom 3 1/2", Jerry 2".* **$2,629**

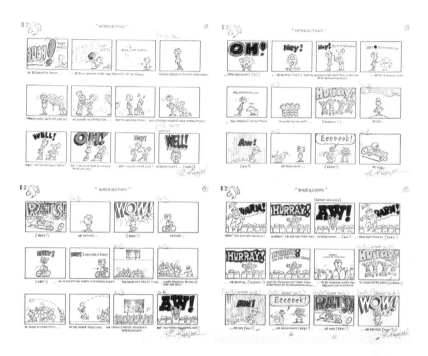

Courtesy of Heritage Auctions

*"Schoolhouse Rock" "Interjections!" storyboards (Walt Disney, 1974), six pages with graphite notations, many panels partially hand-colored. One of the most loved and remembered of the classic first season of "Schoolhouse Rock."* **$3,884**

Courtesy of Heritage Auctions

*"The Jetsons" publicity cel (Hanna-Barbera, 1985), hand-painted, one of five cels signed by voice cast at final taping of show.* **$2,151**

*"Star Trek" production title cel setup and master background (Filmation, 1973), original 12-field hand-painted title cel; ship 6" long.* **$2,629**

*"Batman: The Animated Series" "Two-Face, Part Two" production cel set-up and background (Warner Brothers, 1992), unpainted line art cel placed over fully painted cel and brick wall backdrop, placed over key master background hand-painted artwork.* **$1,434**

*"The Jackson 5ive" production cel (Rankin-Bass, 1972), rare 12-field hand-painted cel with all five Jacksons – Marlon, Jackie, Tito, Jermaine, and Michael – from Season 2, Episode 1, "Who's Hoozis?" (airdate: Sept. 9. 1972), in which group sang "Rockin' Robin" and "Wings of My Love"; 5" to 8" each.* **$896**

*"Fat Albert and the Cosby Kids"
Fat Albert and Dumb Donald
production cel (Filmation Studios,
1972-1984), original hand-
painted 12-field cel; 7" x 6" and
4" x 7 1/2," respectively.* **$203**

*"The Godzilla Power Hour"
Godzilla and Godzooky
publicity cel (Hanna-Barbera,
1978); approximately 12 1/2"
x 10 1/2", Godzilla 8" and
Godzooky 3".* **$125**

*"The Wise Hen" Donald Duck
and Peter Pig production cel
(Walt Disney, 1934), from
Donald Duck's big screen debut,
Donald 3". Very few production
cels of Donald Duck are known to
exist from this landmark cartoon.*
**$8,365**

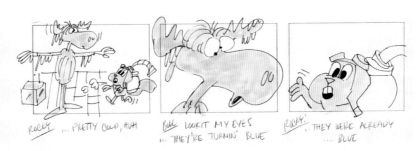

Courtesy of Heritage Auctions

*"The Bullwinkle Show" storyboard group (Jay Ward Studios, 1961), three rare trimmed storyboards by Roy Morita for episode titled "Buried Treasure," on Ward, Inc. storyboard paper.* **$33,460**

▲ *"Lady and the Tramp" three-cel set-up with Disney oil-painted art props background (Walt Disney, 1955), "Bella Notte" production cel set-up with Lady on one cel, Tramp with mouth full of spaghetti on second cel, and third with table and tablecloth, spaghetti and meatballs on plate, breadsticks and candle; Tramp 5", Lady 4".* **$33,460**

▶ *Chuck Jones early Wile E. Coyote concept sketch (Warner Brothers, 1950s), on 12-field animation paper, one of the first ever made of iconic character.* **$9,560**

*"The Mighty Hercules" production cel and drawing (Adventure Cartoon Productions, 1963), original hand-inked cel of Hercules and secondary character from 1963 cartoon series; both approximately 5".* **$311**

◄ *"Dumbo" Dumbo with Timothy and crows production cel Courvoisier set-up (Walt Disney, 1941), hand-inked and painted, Dumbo with feather, Timothy Mouse riding in Dumbo's hat, with all five crows (Fat Crow, Jim Crow, Glasses Crow, Preacher Crow, and Straw Hat Crow); Dumbo 6" long.* **$5,378**

▼ *"The Lion King" presentation cel and production background (Walt Disney, 1994), background with production overlay of Simba with Zazu and villain Scar; Scar 8", Simba and Zazu 4" long x 2 1/2" at upper point.* **$3,107**

# Contemporary Art

By Noah Fleisher

**NOAH FLEISHER** received his Bachelor of Fine Arts degree from New York University and brings more than a decade of newspaper, magazine, book, antiques and art experience to his position as Public Relations Director of Heritage Auctions, one of the country's foremost auction houses. He is the former editor of *Antique Trader, New England Antiques Journal* and *Northeast Antiques Journal,* is the author of *Warman's Modern Furniture,* and has been a longtime contributor to *Warman's Antiques & Collectibles.*

The proliferation of eight- and nine-figure artworks in the last five years has been hard to miss, unless you live in a cave, and no sector has seen a bigger uptick than contemporary art.

If you have a spare $10 million to $100 million, then the seasonal sales at high-end art auctions, where sums of money that equal or exceed some nations' GDP regularly change hands, are for you. One hundred million dollars for a couple of Warhols, anyone (Christie's, May 2014)? How about a Francis Bacon triptych for $142+ million (Christie's again, November 2013)? How about $1+ million for a Damien Hirst (Sotheby's, June 2104)? Look out your window now, toward the gilded art halls of New York, London and Paris, and tell me if you can see the bubble growing.

It sounds to me, sometimes, like the idle rich have too much Monopoly money on their hands and are blowing it all in a battle royale aimed simply at keeping up with the Joneses, or buying art by the yard to decorate expansive chateaus and tony beach houses.

Forgive the cynicism, if you will, but it seems to me that the market is simply being ruined for the rest of us, meaning those of us who can't afford to spend eight figures on a canvas, who can often only spend a few thousand, if that.

Really, though, where does the middle market – which has taken it in the shorts, by most accounts, across most categories, in the last decade – stand amidst all this conspicuous consumption? Is there a bubble forming? How can we even tell?

The truth is somewhere in-between, according to Brandon Kennedy, a Contemporary and Modern Art Specialist at Heritage Auctions, a specialty auction house that, while it hasn't seen $10 million or $100 million paintings, has seen an increase in prices and buyers for its modern auctions in the last few years.

"Now that we're six years beyond the economic downturn, things are definitely on the upswing," said Kennedy. "There's always a little bit of the 'good, bad, and the ugly' in the market and it largely depends on where you're standing. As of late, the talk is of a bubble and whether or not it exists. Only time will tell."

The best place to stand would be on your own two feet, I have to guess, on a firm foundation. That foundation, first and foremost, has

to be built on a solid understanding of exactly what you are looking at. Just what is the definition of contemporary art, and how is it separated from modern art?

According to Kennedy, the term "modern art" is used to define a period starting in the late 19th century and extending to sometime in the 1960s-1970s, depending on who you ask, largely defined by styles and movements within a certain historical moment. "Contemporary art" is generally thought of taking shape post-1965 or so, when the lines between strict divisions and traditional mediums begin to dissolve and even wander outside the gallery or institutional framework.

Kennedy is quick to point out that, with the rapid evolution of mediums (including digital artwork, 3-D printers and new mediums for sculpture), even those definitions are becoming hazy. There is a definite post-modern movement, but is such a thing as post-contemporary even possible?

What can we make of recent sales at big auction houses and galleries of work by young artists done in those non-traditional mediums, specifically computer prints (or is it computer art?) that sell for seven and eight figures? How philosophically and financially sound or unsound is this?

"Artwork created by digital or other technological means is now always present and will continue to evolve with the available technology at hand," said Kennedy. "Whether sound or unsound, it

Courtesy of Heritage Auctions

*Sam Francis (American, 1923-1994), "Untitled," 1988, acrylic on canvas, estate stamp verso, 79 1/2" x 120".*
**$515,000**

*Frank Stella (American, b. 1936), "Eskimo Curlew (3X)," 1977, enamel, oilstick and crushed glass on corrugated aluminum, 54" x 69" x 13 1/2".*
**$317,000**

largely boils down to the market and personal taste and where the two overlap."

Let's go a little further, then: Doesn't the very artificiality of such a medium change value for the lower in the long run?

"There are plenty of high rollers and lower-level speculators treating contemporary art like a futures market," Kennedy said, "and many others simply follow along and get burnt on the back-side of a transaction when they try to resell the work. A lot of the time, the contemporary art market can sound like it's somewhere in-between a horse race and interior decorating, and, unfortunately, it is sometimes as simple as that."

Can't an artist just print out another print, if it's a digital piece? Absolutely, and sometimes they do. In the topsy-turvy modern world, that can even enhance the value of a piece, at least in the short-term, even when an artist "creates" more digital work in a sort of protest against what could become a quickly bloated market.

Take the case of artist Wade Guyton, for example, a well-known, mid-career artist.

"Upon hearing that one of his Epson UltraChrome inkjet works on canvas would soon be offered at a major house with an estimate of $3.5 million to $4.5 million," Kennedy said, "he made dozens of

*David Hammons
(American, b. 1943),
"Feed Folks," 1974,
mixed media, 39 3/4" x
29 1/2", signed in pencil
lower right: Hammons.*
**$1,205,000**

duplicates and then posted photos to his Instagram account of them lingering about in his studio."

The original print that Kennedy is referring to, "If I Live I'll See You Tuesday," offered in Christie's late spring 2014 sale, still brought north of $3.5 million.

Most of us, again, don't play in those sandboxes. If you're serious about getting in, where do you even begin? What area of contemporary art is the hottest right now and who are the hottest artists who might not necessarily be household names?

"Names like Warhol, Bacon and Gerhard Richter are still fetching premium prices, at all levels of work, and that's no surprise," Kennedy said. "Bruce Nauman and Ed Ruscha are still producing great work and fetching premium prices, as is the work of artists like David Hammons, John Baldessari, Jasper Johns and Richard Serra. There are also a slew of hot, young artists who graduate from the gallery scene to the auction block in the blink of an eye and, by the time you realize that you could've capitalized

Courtesy of Heritage Auctions

*Gerhard Richter (German, b. 1932), "Untitled, 3.3," 1986, oil on paper, signed and dated upper left: 3.3.86/ Richter, 23 3/4" x 33 1/4".* **$286,800**

on their ascendancy, they're already on the decline. I won't name names specifically because of the aforementioned problem."

Is contemporary art, then, a market that's even open to first-time buyers and those without massive bank accounts?

"Absolutely," said Kennedy. "Start small and look at editions and prints of an established artist that you have heard of before. Pop and abstract expressionism are good movements to consider when pondering this question. Otherwise, visit local art galleries and the artists who show there. Spend a season or two surveying what's available and educating yourself, and eventually your heart and taste will lead you down the right road."

Kennedy is 100% right in this approach, which will work no matter what the category. Ask experts for their opinion. Get to know the people behind the industry, go to auctions and gallery openings and museum exhibitions. Continue to educate yourself in every aspect of art culture and the market.

"Educate yourself and continue to do so over the course of your life," he said, "but only buy what you love and can't stop thinking about."

Courtesy of
Heritage Auctions

*Dale Chihuly
(American, b.
1941), "Cobalt
Chandelier," 2003,
handblown glass,
steel armature,
94" x 72" x 72".*
**$158,500**

Courtesy of Heritage Auctions

*Christo and Jeanne-Claude, "The Umbrellas (Project for Japan and USA)," 1987, graphite, charcoal, pastel, wax crayon, map and acrylic on paper collage laid down on panel, in two parts, signed, titled and dated, inscribed with installation instructions and numbered on reverse, together 65" x 57".* **$149,000**

Courtesy of Heritage Auctions

*Francois-Xavier Lalanne (French, 1927-2008), "Bélier (Ram)" (from "Les Nouveaux Moutons"), 1994, epoxystone and patinated bronze, ed. 169/250, stamped with signature, initialed, numbered and with foundry stamp: Landowski Fondeur, 36 5/8" x 40 1/4" x 15".* **$137,000**

Courtesy of Heritage Auctions

*Enrique Toledo (Cuban, b. 1966), "Homage to Dalí (Untitled 12)," 2009, oil on canvas, signed and dated lower right, 39 1/2" x 51".*
**$1,688**

Courtesy of Heritage Auctions

*Andy Warhol (American, 1928-1987), "Souper Dress," circa 1968, color screenprint on cellulose and cotton, labeled "The Souper Dress" at neck, 37 1/2" x 21 1/2".*
**$10,625**

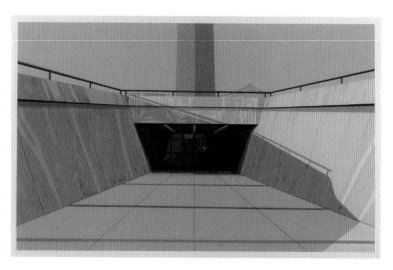

*Richard Estes
(American, b.
1932), "Arch,
St. Louis" (from
"Urban Landscapes
I" series), 1972,
silkscreen in colors,
ed. 17/75, signed
and numbered in
pencil lower right,
14 1/2" x 23 3/4".*
**$1,500**

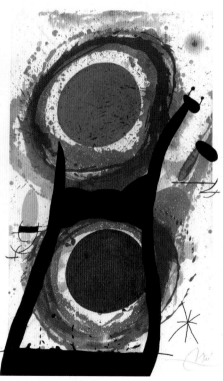

*Yinka Shonibare MBE, "China Love," 2011, paper,
pen, gold leaf, collage and fabric, 47 1/2" x 31 1/2".*
**$11,000**

*Joan Miró (Spanish, 1893-1983), "L'Adorateur du
Soleil," 1969, etching and aquatint in colors with
carborundum, signed and annotated in pencil on
bottom edge, 41 1/2" x 26 3/4".* **$10,938**

Courtesy of Heritage Auctions

*Gustavo Montoya (Mexican, 1905-2003), "Niña del Caballito," 1969, oil on canvas, signed lower right: Gustavo Montoya, 24" x 18".* **$10,625**

Courtesy of Heritage Auctions

*Kikuo Saito (Japanese, b. 1939), "Silver Snail," 1995, acrylic on canvas, signed, titled and dated verso, 77 1/2" x 82".* **$10,625**

Courtesy of Heritage Auctions

*Richard Diebenkorn (American, 1922-1993), "Green," 1986, etching with aquatint and drypoint printed in colors, ed. 37/60, initialed and dated lower right: RD86, 44" x 35 1/2".*
**$262,900**

Courtesy of Heritage Auctions

*Richard Serra (American, b. 1939), "Patience," 1984, screenprint in colors with paint stick, ed. 19/20, signed, dated and numbered in paint stick, 62" x 52 1/2".* **$10,625**

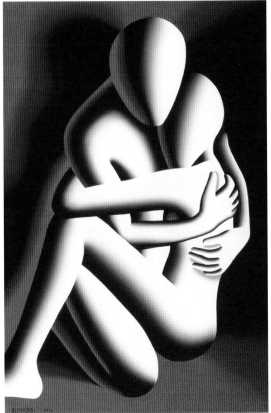

Courtesy of Heritage Auctions

*Mark Kostabi (American, b. 1960), "The Embrace," 1990, oil on canvas, signed and dated lower left: Kostabi 1990, 54" x 36".* **$10,625**

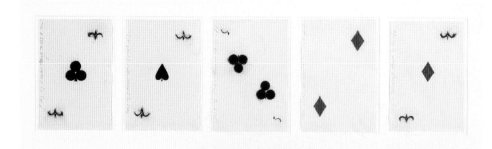

Courtesy of Heritage Auctions

▲ *Donald Sultan (American, b. 1951), "King of Clubs, March 17; King of Spades, April 8; Jack of Clubs, March 17; Two Diamonds, March 20; King of Diamonds, March 30 (5)," 1989, conte crayon and charcoal on paper, signed with initials, titled and dated, each 11 1/2" x 8".* **$10,158**

Courtesy of Heritage Auctions

▶ *Valerie Jaudon (American, b. 1945), "Carlisle," 1983, oil on canvas, titled, signed and dated on reverse: Carlisle / Valerie Jaudon '83, 22" x 22".* **$4,183**

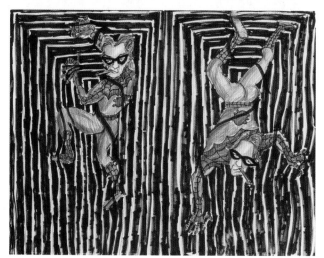

Courtesy of Heritage Auctions

*Red Grooms (American, b. 1937), "Spiderman on Stripe Paintings (Frank Stella)," 1986, marker and colored pencil on graph paper, signed and dated upper right: Red Grooms 1986, 17" x 22".* **$4,063**

Courtesy of Heritage Auctions

*David H. Ligare (American, b. 1945), "Still Life With Lemons and Figs," 1983, oil on canvas, signed lower right, 18" x 29".* **$9,375**

Courtesy of Heritage Auctions

*Liu Hong (Chinese, b. 1956), "Lip Language #4," 2010, oil on canvas, signed and dated lower right, 39 1/4" x 33 1/2".* **$9,100**

Courtesy of Heritage Auctions

*Alex Katz (American, b. 1927), "Joan," 1986, aquatint in colors, ed. 28/65, signed and numbered lower left: Alex Katz, 31 1/2" x 38 1/2".* **$8,963**

Courtesy of Heritage Auctions

*Hong Hao (Chinese, b. 1965),*
*"Guide-Yuanmingynan and Long*
*March (2)," 2001, chromogenic*
*prints, ed. 12/12, 9/9, each signed,*
*numbered and titled on reverse,*
*47 1/4" x 86 1/2".* **$3,884**

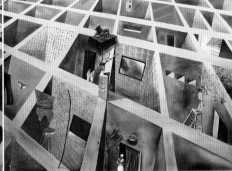

Courtesy of Heritage Auctions

*Pratul Dash (Indian, b. 1974), "Living Space," 2011 (diptych), watercolor and mixed media on Fabriano paper, signed, dated and inscribed on reverse, 28" x 78".* **$4,063**

Courtesy of Heritage Auctions

*Brice Marden (American, b. 1938), "Obama Letter" (from portfolio "Artists for Obama"), 2012, photogravure and etching, ed. 31/150, signed, dated and numbered in pencil on bottom edge, 14" x 14".* **$3,906**

Courtesy of Heritage Auctions

*Joan Mitchell (American, 1926-1992), "Trees IV" (on two sheets), 1992, color lithograph on paper, ed. 4/34, signed and dated in graphite lower right: Joan Mitchell 1992, 56 3/4" x 82 1/2".* **$4,183**

Courtesy of Heritage Auctions

*Marc Quinn (British, b. 1964),*
*"Image 1 (Garden 2)," 2000,*
*pigment print, ed. 45/45, signed*
*and dated verso: Marc Quinn*
*2000, 31 1/2" x 48 1/2".* **$1,793**

Courtesy of Heritage Auctions

*Jeff Koons (American, b. 1954),*
*"A Suite of Three Monkey Train*
*Skate Decks," 2006, thermoformed*
*and silkscreened plywood, printed*
*signature and inscription: MONKEY*
*TRAIN/JK on base of each deck,*
*each 31 3/4" x 7 3/4" x 1/2".* **$3,750**

Courtesy of Heritage Auctions

▲ *James Hyde (American, b. 1958), "Climate," 2002, mixed media with sewn nylon webbing, 88" x 88" x 8".* **$3,585**

Courtesy of Heritage Auctions

*Thomas Hirschhorn (Swiss, b. 1957), from series "Utopia Utopia = One World One War One Army One Dress: Deny Flight," 2003, paper, prints, adhesive tape, marker, ballpoint, signed, titled and dated on reverse, 19 1/2" x 23 1/4".* **$3,585**

Courtesy of Heritage Auctions

*Jules De Balincourt (French, b. 1972), "Custom," 2003, spray paint on Masonite, signed, titled and dated on reverse, 12" x 13".* **$9,063**

Courtesy of Heritage Auctions

*Jasper Johns (American, b. 1930), "Savarin," 1977, lithograph in colors, ed. 42/50, signed, dated and numbered in pencil on bottom edge, 38 1/4" x 28 1/4".* **$100,000**

Courtesy of Heritage Auctions

*Rodolfo Opazo (Chilean, b. 1935),*
*"El Amanecer; Angel (two works),"*
*1973, 1975, oil on canvas, each*
*signed, dated and titled verso,*
*24" x 18" and 20 x 15".* **$3,750**

Courtesy of Heritage Auctions

*Fang Runsheng, James*
*Fong AKA Ultraman*
*(Chinese, b. 1968), "Ultra*
*Iron Qee Robot," 2007,*
*high-gloss effect spray*
*on fiberglass, signed and*
*dated on bottom of torso,*
*36 1/2" x 19" x 15".*
**$3,750**

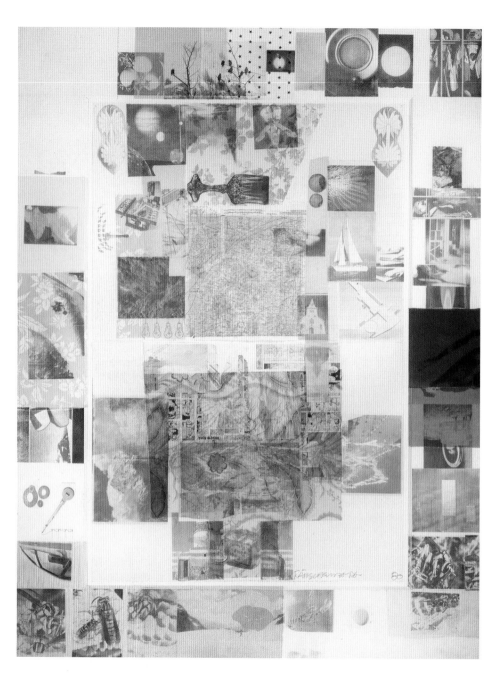

Courtesy of Heritage Auctions

*Robert Rauschenberg (American, 1925-2008), "Rush 1" (from "Cloister" series), 1980, solvent transfer on paper and collage laid on panel, signed and dated lower right, 98 1/4" x 74".* **$168,000**

Courtesy of
Heritage Auctions

*Jack Golsdstein
(American, 1945-
2003), "Untitled,"
1983, acrylic on
canvas, 96" x 132".*
**$203,150**

Courtesy of
Heritage Auctions

*Jo Baer (American,
b. 1929), "Untitled
(Double Bar
Orange)," 1972, oil
on canvas, signed
and dated on reverse,
72" x 72".* **$83,650**

# Fine Art

Fine art, created for aesthetic purposes and judged by its beauty rather than its utility, includes original painting and sculpture, drawing, watercolor, and graphics. It is appreciated primarily for its imaginative, aesthetic, or intellectual content.

Today's fine art market is a global one, grossing $47.4 billion in 2013, second only to 2007 as the most prosperous year on record. After being dominated by Chinese and Asian buyers in 2010 and 2011, the 2012 fine art market recorded the entrance of major buyers from Russia and the Middle East. Currently, the United States tops the list with China in second place. Post-war and contemporary art dominate the market.

Courtesy of Heritage Auctions

*Bernard Finegan Gribble (British, 1873-1962), "Out For Adventure," oil on canvas, signed lower left "B.F. Gribble," 28" x 36".* **$2,000**

Courtesy of Coeur d'Alene Art Auction

◀ *Bob Kuhn (1920-2007), "Foraging Fox – Sniffing for Mice," acrylic on board, 8" x 10", 1991.* **$55,575**

Courtesy of Heritage Auctions

▼ *Alexander John Drysdale (American 1870-1934), "Louisiana Bayou," watercolor on paper, signed lower left in pencil "A J Drysdale," 10" x 29".* **$3,884**

Courtesy of Pook & Pook, Inc.

*Itzchak Tarkay (Serbian/Israeli 1935-2012), oil on canvas of woman seated at table, signed lower left, 24" x 16".* **$3,936**

Courtesy of Heritage Auctions

*Marcel Dyf (French, 1899-1985), "Roses et gueules de loup," 1970, oil on canvas, signed lower right "Dyf," 30" x 24".* **$7,500**

Courtesy of Heritage Auctions

*Louis Comfort Tiffany (American 1848-1933), "Architecture Study, Hagia Sofia, Istanbul," watercolor on paper, signed lower left "L.C. Tiffany," 8" x 11 3/4".* **$8,365**

Courtesy of Skinner, Inc.; www.skinnerinc.com

*Pablo Picasso (Spanish, 1881-1973), "Femme retenant son peignoir," graphite on wove paper, circa 1923, signed "Picasso" in pencil lower right, framed, deckled edges, foxing, mat burn, paper tape hinged to backing mat, sheet size 12 5/8" x 9 11/16".* **$159,000**

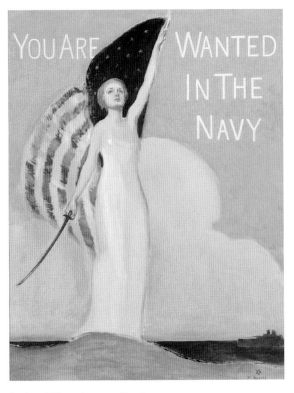

Courtesy of Skinner, Inc.; www.skinnerinc.com

*Frederick Andrew Bosley (American, 1881-1942), "You are Wanted in the Navy," oil on canvas, framed, signed "F. Bosley" lower right, scattered retouch, 31" x 24".* **$1,968**

Courtesy of Coeur d'Alene Art Auction

*Charles M. Russell (1864-1926), "Bear with a Jug," bronze, 5 1/2" high.* **$18,720**

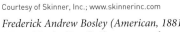

Courtesy of Pook & Pook, Inc.

*Portrait of young girl, oil on canvas, circa 1840, Genevieve White of Baltimore, in red dress holding flower basket, 34" x 24".* **$7,200**

Courtesy of Skinner, Inc.; www.skinnerinc.com

*David Davidovich Burliuk (Ukrainian, 1882-1967), "House of Van Gogh," oil on canvas, dated, signed, and inscribed "1950 BURLiUK Arles" lower right, titled and identified on label from ACA Galleries, New York, with stamp from Burliuk Gallery, New York, on stretcher, minor surface grime, 18" x 24".* **$31,980**

Courtesy of Coeur d'Alene
Art Auction

*James Earle Fraser
(1876-1953), "The End
of the Trail," bronze,
36" high (49" high at
top of spear).* **$921,000**

Courtesy of Skinner, Inc.;
www.skinnerinc.com

*Saliba Douaihy (Lebanese, 1915-
1994), "Milking the Cow," oil on
canvas, framed, signed "S Douaïhy"
lower right, surface grime, 17" x 21".*
**$49,200**

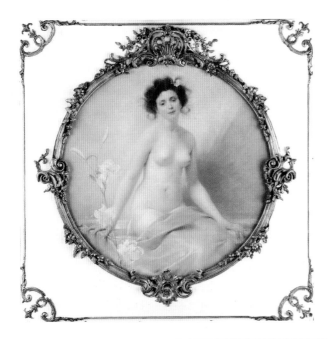

Courtesy of Heritage Auctions

*Edouard-Marie-Guillaume
Dubufe (1853-1909), "A Seated
Nude with Yellow Hibiscus,"
French, 1898, pastel on paper
laid on canvas, signed and dated
"1898/ G. Dubufe," 28 1/2" x
28 1/2" unframed.* **$5,676**

Courtesy of Heritage Auctions

▲ *Victor Tchetchet (American
1891-1974), "Night Club Girl,"
pastel on paper, signed center left,
overall very good condition, 26" x
19 1/2".* **$1,554**

Courtesy of Heritage Auctions

◄ *Edward Frederick Ertz
(American, 1862-1954), "Trees
along a Creek," 1895, oil on
canvas, signed and dated lower
left "E. Ertz 95," 32" x 24".* **$4,063**

Courtesy of Coeur d'Alene Art Auction

*Dylan Lewis (b. 1964), "Leopard Pair Maquette," bronze, 17" high.* **$11,700**

Courtesy of Pook & Pook, Inc.

*Andrew Wyeth (American 1917-2009), color lithograph, "End of Olsons," published by The Metropolitan Museum of Art, signed in pencil lower left and numbered 288/300, 18 1/4" x 19 1/4".* **$461**

Courtesy of Skinner, Inc.; www.skinnerinc.com

*Frank Weston Benson (American, 1862-1951), three works: "House in a Field" (shown), "Skyline with Spruces," and "Woodlands," each unsigned, watercolor and graphite on paper, unframed, tears, toning, losses, abrasions, tack holes, folds/creases, sheet sizes to 15 3/4" x 14". Provenance: Descended within family of artist.* **$3,690**

Courtesy of Coeur d'Alene Art Auction

*Birger Sandzén (1871-1954), "Willows and Cottonwoods," oil on board, 16" x 20", 1933.* **$26,325**

Courtesy of Skinner, Inc.;
www.skinnerinc.com

*James King Bonnar (American, 1883-1961), "Vermont Covered Bridge," oil on canvas, framed, signed "James K Bonnar" lower right, titled and inscribed ".../by James K. Bonnar Newtonville Mass" on stretcher, surface grime, 22" x 26 1/4".* **$2,460**

Courtesy of Coeur d'Alene Art Auction

*Frederic Remington (1861-1909),*
*"A Rearer," pen and ink and*
*gouache on paper, 1890, 12" x 9".*
**$35,100**

Courtesy of Coeur d'Alene Art Auction

*Thomas Moran (1837-1926),*
*"Icebergs," watercolor on paper,*
*1891, 10" x 14".* **$70,200**

Courtesy of Coeur d'Alene Art Auction

*Keith Shackleton (b. 1923), "Elephants," oil on board, 1965, 43" x 71 1/2".* **$10,530**

Courtesy of Coeur d'Alene Art Auction

▲ *Morgan Weistling (b. 1964), "Tea and Sympathy," oil on canvas, 2003, 26" x 30".* **$29,250**

Courtesy of Heritage Auctions

◄ *Ralph Albert Blakelock (American, 1847-1919), "Adirondack Landscape," oil on canvas, circa 1868, initialed lower left "R.A.B.," 7 1/2 x 4 1/2".* **$5,938**

Courtesy of Heritage Auctions

*Christian Riese Lassen (American, b. 1949), "Sunlit Waves and a Waterfall," acrylic on board, signed lower right Christian R. Lassen, 24" x 36".* **$4,688**

Courtesy of Heritage Auctions

*Edmund Adler (German, 1871-1957), "The Little Soldier," oil on canvas, signed lower right Edmund Adler, 22" x 27".* **$10,000**

Courtesy of Coeur d'Alene Art Auction

▲ *Richard Schmid (b. 1934), "Still Life with Flowers and Oranges," oil on canvas, 36" x 48".* **$43,875**

Courtesy of Coeur d'Alene Art Auction

◄ *Sydney Laurence (1865-1940), "Northern Lights," oil on canvas, 10" x 8".* **$9,360**

# Illustration Art

By Brent Frankenhoff and Maggie Thompson

Collectors, whether looking for a distinctive decoration for a living room or seeking a rewarding long-term investment, will find something to fit their fancy – and their budget – when they turn to illustration art.

Pieces of representational art – often, art that tells some sort of story – are produced in a variety of forms, each appealing in a different way. They are created as the source material for political cartoons, magazine covers, posters, story illustrations, comic books and strips, animated cartoons, calendars, and book jackets. They may be in color or in black and white. Collectible forms include:

- Mass-market printed reproductions. These can range from art prints and movie posters to engravings, clipped advertising art, and bookplates. While this may be the least-expensive art to hang on your wall, a few rare items can bring record prices.

- Limited-run reproductions. These range from signed, numbered lithographs to numbered prints.

- Tangential items. These are hard-to-define, oddball pieces. One example is printing plates (some in actual lead, some in plastic fused to lightweight metal) used by newspapers and comic-book printers to reproduce the art.

- Unique original art. These pieces have the widest range of all, from amateur sketches to finished paintings. The term "original art" includes color roughs produced by a painter as a preliminary test for a work to be produced, finished oil paintings, animation cels for commercials as well as feature films, and black-and-white inked pages of comic books and strips. They may be signed and identifiable or unsigned and generic.

"Illustration art" is often differentiated from "fine art," but its pop culture nature may increase the pool of would-be purchasers. Alberto Vargas (1896-1982) and Gil Elvgren (1914-1980) bring high prices for pin-up art; Norman Rockwell (1894-1978), James Montgomery Flagg (1877-1960), and J.C. Leyendecker (1874-1951) were masters of mainstream illustration; and Margaret Brundage (1900-1976) and Virgil Finlay (1914-1971) are highly regarded pulp artists.

**MAGGIE THOMPSON** was among the pioneering amateurs who formed the foundation in the 1960s of today's international anarchy of comic-book collecting. With her late husband, Don, she edited *Comics Buyer's Guide* and remains active as a collector and essayist. **BRENT FRANKENHOFF** is a lifelong collector and former editor of *Comics Buyer's Guide*.

Courtesy of Heritage Auctions

▲ *Walter Biggs (American, 1886-1968), "Seated Lady in the Park," 1941, oil on canvas, signed and dated lower left "W Biggs 41," 33" x 36".* **$12,500**

Courtesy of Swann Galleries

◄ *W.W. Denslow, Scarecrow and two Munchkins illustration from* The Wonderful Wizard of Oz, *original pen and ink and pencil on paper, signed in ink with seahorse monogram, published as first in-text illustration of Chapter 4 (page 43), with headpiece, in* The Wonderful Wizard of Oz, *Chicago: George M. Hill, 1900, light age-toning, 13 1/4" x 12 1/4".* **$30,720**

Courtesy of Heritage Auctions

*Jessie Willcox Smith (American, 1863-1935), "Children Playing in the Snow," mixed media on board, signed lower right "JESSIE WILLCOX SMITH," inscribed verso "For Tille Anne who would be a perfect model for her / Mothers friend / Jessie Willcox Smith," 20" x 16".* **$56,250**

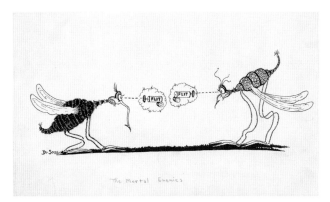

Courtesy of Swann Galleries

*Dr. Seuss (Theodor Geisel), "The Mortal Enemies," pen and ink drawing on card, circa 1930s, advertisement for Flit insecticide, signed in ink lower left, and captioned in Seuss's hand in pencil, lower margin, light marginal smudges, faint impression from paperclip at upper left margin with light rust stain visible on verso only, on exhibition mount, 8 1/4" x 14".* **$12,800**

Courtesy of Swann Galleries

*Marc Tauss, "Vanished New York," photography, dyes, color pencil, airbrush, and glaze on chromogenic print paper, 6 1/2" x 6 3/4" (image), mounted to Bainbridge board with archival tape along wide margins, matted, cover art for Jay McInerney's* Bright Lights, Big City, *New York: Vintage Books, 1984.* **$11,250**

Courtesy of Swann Galleries

*Arthur Saron Sarnoff, "Learning to Live," gouache and tempera on board, signed lower right, light soiling, corners with creasing, 29 3/4" x 40".* **$2,000**

Courtesy of Swann Galleries

*Al Hirschfeld, "I Love Lucy," pen and ink on illustration board, signed lower right, matted and framed to overall size of 37" x 30 1/2", published in* Collier's Magazine, *April 30, 1954, 21 1/2" x 17 1/2".* **$8,125**

Courtesy of Swann Galleries

*Eleanor B. Campbell, "Gerber Baby," oil on canvas, signed lower right, abrasion along signature, 25 3/4" x 20 3/4".* **$1,280**

Courtesy of Swann Galleries

*George Herriman, "Krazy Kat and Ignatz," watercolor on paper, with signed presentation inscription at bottom, "To Fred Myer / who had the nerve to / ask for it - / from Geo. Harriman / who had the nerve to / give it to him / 1933," contemporary matte and frame, 22 1/2" x 20".* **$21,250**

Courtesy of Swann Galleries

*Charles Archibald MacLellan, woman with autumn foliage bouquet, oil on canvas, mounted on linen, cover design for* Modern Priscilla *magazine, October 1926, signed and dated in oil lower left within bouquet, 28" x 22 1/4".* **$4,000**

Courtesy of Heritage Auctions

▲ *Norman Rockwell (American, 1894-1978), "For Double Reason You'll Prefer Double Rich," Schenley Cream of Kentucky whiskey advertisement, 1940, pastel and charcoal on board, signed lower right "Norman Rockwell," 16 1/2" x 19".* **$59,375**

Courtesy of Swann Galleries

*George Timothy Tobin, "Madonna and Child," watercolor, ink and pencil on paper, cover design for* Harper's Bazar *(magazine began publishing in 1867, but years passed before misspelled title was corrected), December 1906, matted and framed, 10 1/4" x 7 3/4".* **$1,500**

Courtesy of Heritage Auctions

*James Montgomery Flagg (American, 1877-1960), "The World: Good Versus Evil,"* Life *magazine cover, July 23, 1908, ink and watercolor on board, signed lower right "JAMES MONTGOMERY FLAGG," 23" x 17 1/2" (sight).* **$35,000**

Courtesy of Skinner, Inc.;
www.skinnerinc.com

*Amos Sewell (American, 1901-1983), illustration from* Huckleberry Finn, *mixed media on illustration board, unframed, signed "AMOS/SEWELL" lower left, foxing to margins, mild surface grime, 13" x 23 3/4".* **$3,198**

Courtesy of Swann Galleries

*Johnny Gruelle, "Raggedy Ann," colored pencil and ink on paper, circa 1930s, signed lower right, 9 1/4" x 6 1/4".* **$1,152**

Courtesy of Swann Galleries

*Max Ginsburg, "A Separate Peace," oil on canvas, signed lower left, original cover art for 1982 Bantam Books edition of John Knowles' A Separate Peace, New York, 1981-1982, 40" x 24".* **$10,000**

Courtesy of Swann Galleries

*Constantin Alajálov, "Standing Room Only," tempera on illustration board, signed lower right with presentation inscription, "To Elinor and Martin Bush," printer's marks in margins on recto, penciled date and exhibition label in artist's hand on verso, published as* The New Yorker *cover, Oct. 21, 1944, 13 1/2" x 9 1/2" (image).* **$4,000**

Courtesy of Heritage Auctions

*McClelland Barclay (American, 1891-1943), "The Confrontation," oil on canvas, signed upper right "McClelland Barclay," 29" x 30".* **$4,531**

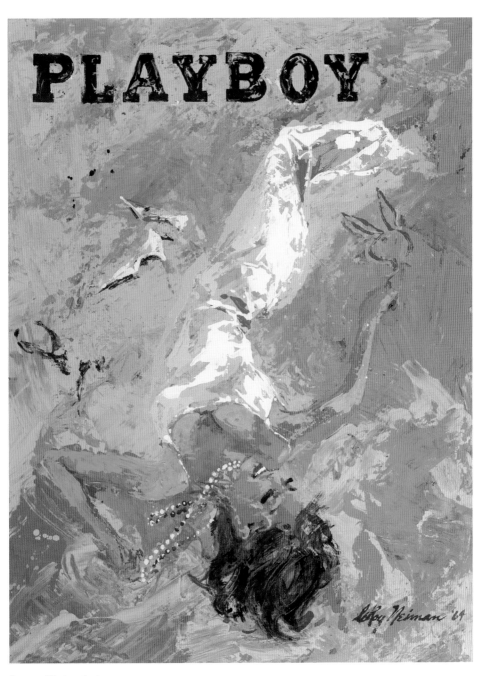

Courtesy of Heritage Auctions

*LeRoy Neiman (American, 1921-2012), "Lying Down in Her Party Dress,"* Playboy, *1964, oil on Masonite, signed and dated lower right "Leroy Neiman '64," 30" x 22 1/2".* **$115,625**

Courtesy of Heritage Auctions

*Frank Xavier Leyendecker (American, 1877-1924), "Pierrot and Columbine,"* Vanity Fair *magazine cover, June 1915, oil on board, signed lower right "Frank X. Leyendecker," 23 1/2" x 16 1/2".* **$118,750**

◄ *Howard Chandler Christy, "…She was made for love and capture, was Polly," ink, watercolor, gouache full-length portrait on board, published in story, "Being Engaged to Polly" by Ellis Parker Butler in* Good Housekeeping Magazine, *November 1913, page 620, signed, inscribed, and dated lower right,* Good Housekeeping *stamp on verso and archival tape along edges attaching image to window matte, framed, 39 1/4" x 28 1/2".* **$16,250**

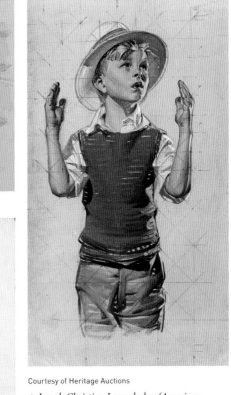

▲ *Joseph Christian Leyendecker (American, 1874-1951), "Young Boy in a Hat," oil on canvas mounted on board, 16" x 9".* **$6,875**

◄ *Ernest H. Shepard, "Their Search for Small," pen and ink on board, illustration for page 39 of A. A. Milne's* House at Pooh Corner, *London, 1928, full sheet, signed in ink in image lower left, titled in pencil lower margin, and signed in full on verso in brown ink "Ernest H. Shepard / Shamley Green / Guildford," 14 1/2" x 10 1/2".* **$47,500**

# Asian

Art and antiques from Asia have fascinated collectors for centuries because they are linked with the rich culture and fascinating history of the Far East. Their beauty, artistry and fine craftsmanship have lured collectors through the ages.

The category is vast and includes objects ranging from jade carvings to cloisonné to porcelain, the best known of these being porcelain.

Large quantities of porcelain have been made in China for export to America from the 1780s. A major source of this porcelain was Ching-te-Chen in the Kiangsi province, but the wares were also made elsewhere. The largest quantities were blue and white.

Prices for Asian antiques and art fluctuate considerably depending on age, condition, decoration, etc.

Courtesy of
Elite Decorative Arts

*Antique Chinese blue and white brush washer, porcelain, in shape of butterfly, nine-character mark to inside, 6 3/8" wide x 1 1/2" high, total weight 672.8 grams.*
**$2,000**

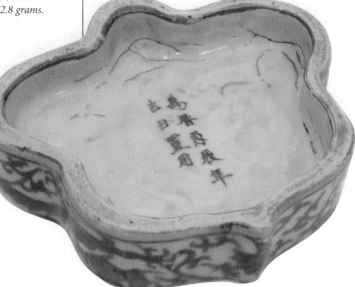

Courtesy of Heritage Auctions

*Two Chinese snuff bottles, one coral, one green, lid of green bottle missing a section, general wear commensurate with age and indicative of use, taller bottle 2 3/4" high.* **$500**

Courtesy of Heritage Auctions

*Japanese patinaed metal floor vase, Meiji Period, small nicks to metal around cartouche edges, 24 1/2" high x 12" wide.* **$1,125**

Courtesy of Heritage Auctions

*Carved coral figural group depicting woman and child with three monkeys, 20th century, good condition, 9" high.* **$15,000**

▲ *Chinese Rose Medallion porcelain punch bowl, very good condition, 9" high x 23 1/4" diameter.* **$7,500**

▶ *Pair of Japanese patinated bronze elephants, Meiji Period, surface scratches commensurate with age, 22 1/2" x 24 1/2" x 14".* **$7,500**

▶ *Burmese repoussé silver bowl, maker unknown, late 19th century, stand late 20th century, unmarked, bulbous bowl with central band of Eastern figures engaged in battle in high relief repoussé with chased detail on textured ground, polished rim above band of stylized foliate, band of repeating foliate forming scrolls enclosing diaper-work ground, chased peacock figure with feathers spread to underside, with later pierced rosewood stand, monogrammed MO to underside, 6" high x 8 1/2" diameter, 49.58 troy ounces.* **$1,375**

*Japanese Meiji
Period patinated
bronze oval planter
on stand, 19th
century, some loss
to patination, 9"
x 14 1/4" x 9".*
**$1,500**

*Buddha's Hand, patinated bronze on wooden base,
moderate surface wear, scratches, and oxidation
commensurate with age, generally good condition,
11" x 7" x 3 1/2".* **$1,250**

*Chinese green jade censer, 20th century, good
condition, one tusk broken to elephant finial, small
scratch to underside, 5 1/2" high.* **$625**

Courtesy of Heritage Auctions

▶ *Chinese cloisonné double covered dish, 20th century, chipping of enamel to interior and interior of handle, otherwise with wear commensurate with age, 11 7/8" long.* **$250**

Courtesy of Heritage Auctions

▲ *Monumental Japanese patinated bronze palace urn, 64" high.* **$2,750**

Courtesy of Heritage Auctions

▶ *Chinese painted porcelain vase, glaze chipping in some areas, in painting to interior of rim, overall in good condition with general wear commensurate with age, 17 5/8" high.* **$2,250**

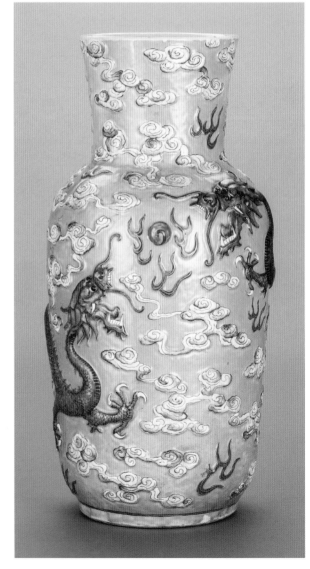

▲ *Chinese red fluted Peking glass bowl on carved wood stand, 20th century, fleabite to one corner, 4 3/4" x 12" 1/2".* **$1,375**

◄ *Carved wood ruyi scepter, China, Qing Dynasty, hardwood, carved with Daoist Immortals and auspicious motifs representing longevity, wealth, and power, four characters, Yi Pin Dang Chao indicating highest rank of Imperial court, 22" long.* **$135,000**

Courtesy of Heritage Auctions

*Tibetan silver and hardstone-covered ewer, circa 1900, unmarked, baluster-form with fluted waisted neck, repoussé and chased geometric and stylized foliate decoration throughout, body centered with single cartouche decorated with seated figure to one side, other side with animals, removable lid secured with chain from finial to serpentine-form handle, spout with pear-shaped blue hardstone and issuing from mouth of zoomorphic head mounted to body, bezel set blue hardstones to shoulder, 10" high, 39.7 ounces.* **$1,625**

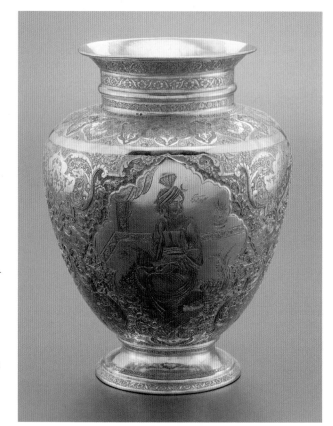

Courtesy of Heritage Auctions

*Persian silver gilt vase attributed to Vartan, early 20th century, marks: 84, (script), ovoid baluster-form vase with ground of chased repoussé floral and foliate design within tight scrolling framework with diapered fields on textured ground, framing three cartouches with chased repoussé scenes of men in various pursuits dressed in robe and turban, two cartouches are signed, good condition with minor loss to gilt surface, 10 3/4" high, 52.1 ounces.* **$3,250**

Courtesy of Skinner, Inc.; www.skinnerinc.com

*Longquan celadon dish, China, Song Dynasty style, decorated with fish design and fluted exterior border, good condition with minor chips to foot rim, 8 1/4" diameter.* **$9,225**

Courtesy of Skinner, Inc.; www.skinnerinc.com

*Tall Wucai Gu vase, China, Qing Dynasty, upper section depicting horsemen bringing tributes to official and bordered at top by "cracked ice" motif, middle band depicting scholar's rock among peonies, bottom section depicting groups of pomegranates, peaches and finger citron, 17" high.* **$8,610**

Courtesy of Skinner, Inc.; www.skinnerinc.com

*Ten-panel folding screen (Songhakdo), Korea, 1907, Yang Gihun (1843-after 1919), depicting five cranes with pine and bamboo trees, inscribed with couplet by Shi Yannian (994-1041), poet from Northern Song Dynasty, signed "Seok-yeon No-eo" with three seals, each panel 78 3/8" x 12 7/8", painting 50 1/8" x 12 7/8".* **$8,610**

*Painting of a mouse, China, Qing Dynasty, perched on lychee branch and eating ripe fruit, ink and color on silk, framed and glazed, small area of wear at center of painting, 19 1/2" x 18 1/2".* **$7,995**

*Pair of Mandarin duck-shaped makie incense holders, Japan, 19th/20th century, with details in shakudo hiramakie on kinji ground, inlaid black beads for eyes, interiors in nashiji, in wood box, good condition with minor surface wear to base, to 2 7/8" high x 4 3/8" long.* **$1,722**

*Cloisonné ruyi scepter, China, 19th century or later, decorated with three shaped insets depicting Immortal with deer, bats, and lingzhi mushrooms, and peach branch, four-character Qianlong mark to back, in good condition with minor surface dirt, minor loss of enamel, 17" high.* **$7,380**

Courtesy of Skinner, Inc.; www.skinnerinc.com

◄ *Gold lacquered inro with ivory ojime, Japan, 19th century, oval column-shape with five cases, each side depicting eagle in gold and silver hiramakie, takamakie, and kirikane on kinji ground, interior and risers in gold and red hirame ground, fitted with ivory ojime depicting boy and lotus in relief, 3 3/4" high.* **$3,567**

Courtesy of Elite Decorative Arts

▲ *Antique Japanese large bronze dragon relief vase, 19th century, unsigned, 12" high.* **$150**

Courtesy of Elite Decorative Arts

◄ *Large vintage Thai double bronze dancers, early to mid-20th century, antique wooden base, 18 1/2" high, total weight 7,200 grams.* **$150**

Courtesy of Heritage Auctions

*Chinese painted porcelain fruit cooler with gilt bronze mounts in Louis XV taste, 18th century with later gilt bronze, small chip to lid, 18" x 16 1/2" x 9".* **$4,375**

Courtesy of Skinner, Inc.;
www.skinnerinc.com

*Sencha tea tray, Japan, 19th/ early 20th century, burlwood, leaf-form tray for Chinese-style tea ceremony, handles carved to depict two different types of chrysanthemums, scattered abrasion to edge with one crack, 17 1/2" long x 16" wide x 1/8" deep.* **$3,998**

Courtesy of Skinner, Inc.;
www.skinnerinc.com

*Carved box and cover, Japan, 18th/19th century, with rugged and lacquered surface, decorated with carved worms and insects picked out in takamakie and various metal inlays, cover carved to conform undulating mouth rim, topped with acorn sprig and worm, underside lacquered in red and gold, 4 1/8" high x 5 7/8" diameter.* **$1,968**

# Autographs

By Zac Bissonnette

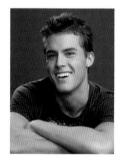

**ZAC BISSONNETTE** is a *New York Times* bestselling finance author and has been featured on The Today Show, The Suze Orman Show, CNN, and National Public Radio. In addition to his work in the antiques field, he has served as a financial journalist for *Glamour, The Daily Beast, The New York Times, The Huffington Post,* and *AOL Money & Finance.* He has a degree in art history from the University of Massachusetts and is a former editor of *Warman's Antiques & Collectibles.*

In *The Meaning and Beauty of Autographs,* first published in 1935 and translated from the German by David H. Lowenherz of Lion Heart Autographs, Inc. in 1995, Stefan Zweig explained that to love a manuscript, we must first love the human being "whose characteristics are immortalized in them." When we do, then "a single page with a few lines can contain the highest expression of human happiness, and ... the expression of deepest human sadness. To those who have eyes to look at such pages correctly, eyes not only in the head, but also in the soul, they will not receive less of an impression from these plain signs than from the obvious beauty of pictures and books."

John M. Reznikoff, founder and president of University Archives, has been a leading dealer and authority on historical letters and artifacts for 32 years. He described the current market for autographs as "very, very strong on many fronts. Possibly because of people being afraid to invest in the market and in real estate, we are seeing investment in autographs that seems to parallel gold and silver."

Reznikoff suspects that Civil War items peaked after Ken Burns' series but that Revolutionary War documents, included those by signers of the Declaration of Independence and the Constitution, are still undervalued and can be purchased for under $500.

Currrently, space is in high demand, especially Apollo 11. Pop culture, previously looked at as secondary by people who dealt in Washingtons and Lincolns, has come into its own. Reznikoff anticipates continued growth in memorabilia that includes music, television, movies, and sports. Babe Ruth, Lou Gehrig, Ty Cobb, and Tiger Woods are still good investments, but Reznikoff warns that authentication is much more of a concern in sports than in any other field.

The Internet allows for a lot of disinformation and this is a significant issue with autographs. There are two widely accepted authentication services: Professional Sports Authenticator

CLOSE-UP!

Courtesy of Nate D. Sanders

*Scarce first edition of* Fantasia *signed by animation pioneer Walt Disney, first edition published by Simon and Schuster, New York, 1940.*
**$3,125**

(PSA/DNA) and James Spence Authentication (JSA). A dealer's reliability can be evaluated by seeing whether he is a member of one or more of the major organizations in the field: the Antique Booksellers Association of America, UACC Registered Dealers Program, and the National Professional Autograph Dealers Association (NPADA), which Reznikoff founded.

There is an additional caveat to remember and it is true for all collectibles: rarity. The value of an autograph is often determined less by the prominence of the signer than by the number of autographs he signed.

Courtesy of Iconic Auctions

*Clint Eastwood signed color photograph with Academy Awards, PSA/DNA, 11" x 14".* **$181**

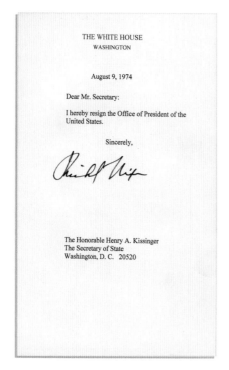

Courtesy of Nate D. Sanders

*Richard Nixon typed presidential resignation souvenir letter, dated Aug. 9, 1974, signed "Richard Nixon" at conclusion in black felt tip.* **$1,511**

Courtesy of Nate D. Sanders

*Eva Perón, aka Evita, First Lady of Argentina from 1946-1952, signed photo display, dedication in Spanish written in script above signature.* **$938**

Courtesy of Collect Auctions

*Everlast boxing gloves with high-grade Muhammad Ali signature on right glove, probably signed in early 1980s, signature pre-certified by PSA/DNA.* **$1,026**

Courtesy of Legendary Auctions

*Color magazine photo of Roger Maris in his Cardinals uniform, circa 1967-1968, his last two Major League seasons.* **$508**

Courtesy of Iconic Auctions

*Wayne Gretzky signed pro-model Hespeler hockey stick.* **$360**

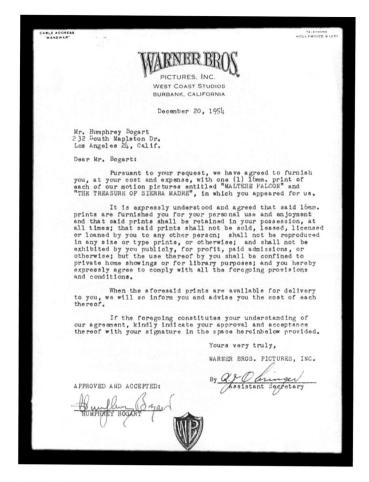

Courtesy of Legendary Auctions

*1954 Humphrey Bogart signed Warner Brothers agreement regarding "Maltese Falcon" and "Treasure of Sierra Madre" on official Warner Bros. stationery.* **$1,434**

Courtesy of SCP Auctions

*Goose Gossage signed empty bottle of 1920 Mouton Rothschild wine purchased at a 1977 dinner to celebrate his new contract with New York Yankees.* **$180**

Courtesy of
Legendary Auctions

*White, unused OML (Selig) ball signed on sweet spot by 39th U.S. President Jimmy Carter.* **$269**

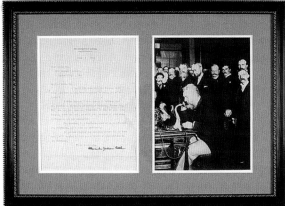

Courtesy of Robert Edward Auctions

▲ *Photo signed by famed German World War 1 pilot, Manfred Von Richthofen (1892-1918), the infamous "Red Baron," affixed to blank front page of a German book titled* Der Rote Kampfflieger, *JSA, 3 1/4" x 5 1/2".* **$5,036**

Courtesy of Iconic Auctions

◄ *Alexander Graham Bell signed one-page typed letter dated June 6, 1912, in custom framed display.* **$1,595**

Courtesy of Legendary Auctions

*Irving Berlin signed album page in framed display, with "White Christmas" song sheet, JSA.* **$448**

**CLOSE-UP!**

Courtesy of Legendary Auctions

*ZZ Top 1979 album "Deguello" signed by all three members of the band, Barry Gibbons, Dusty Hill and Frank Beard.* **$149**

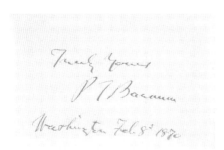

Courtesy of Legendary Auctions

*P.T. Barnum cut signature, dated Feb. 8, 1870,*
*3" x 4 3/4".* **$508**

Courtesy of Legendary Auctions

*Barack Obama 1968 "150th Anniversary Illinois" signed*
*First Day Cover, 6 1/2" x 3 5/8" envelope.* **$478**

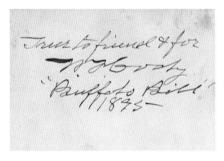

Courtesy of Iconic Auctions

*William F. "Buffalo Bill" Cody cut signature,*
*"True to friend & foe, W.F. Cody, 'Buffalo Bill',*
*1895."* **$1,056**

Courtesy of Collect Auctions

*NASA-issued Gemini IV photo (labeled NASA S-65-*
*29635) signed by Edward H. White II in black felt*
*tip pen, PSA/DNA, 8" x 10". White was the first*
*American to "walk" in space on June 3, 1965 and*
*died on Feb. 21, 1967 during a pre-launch test of the*
*first manned Apollo mission at Cape Kennedy.* **$846**

Courtesy of Collect Auctions

*Index card with Oprah Winfrey signature in*
*blue Sharpie, PSA/DNA, 3" x 5".* **$89**

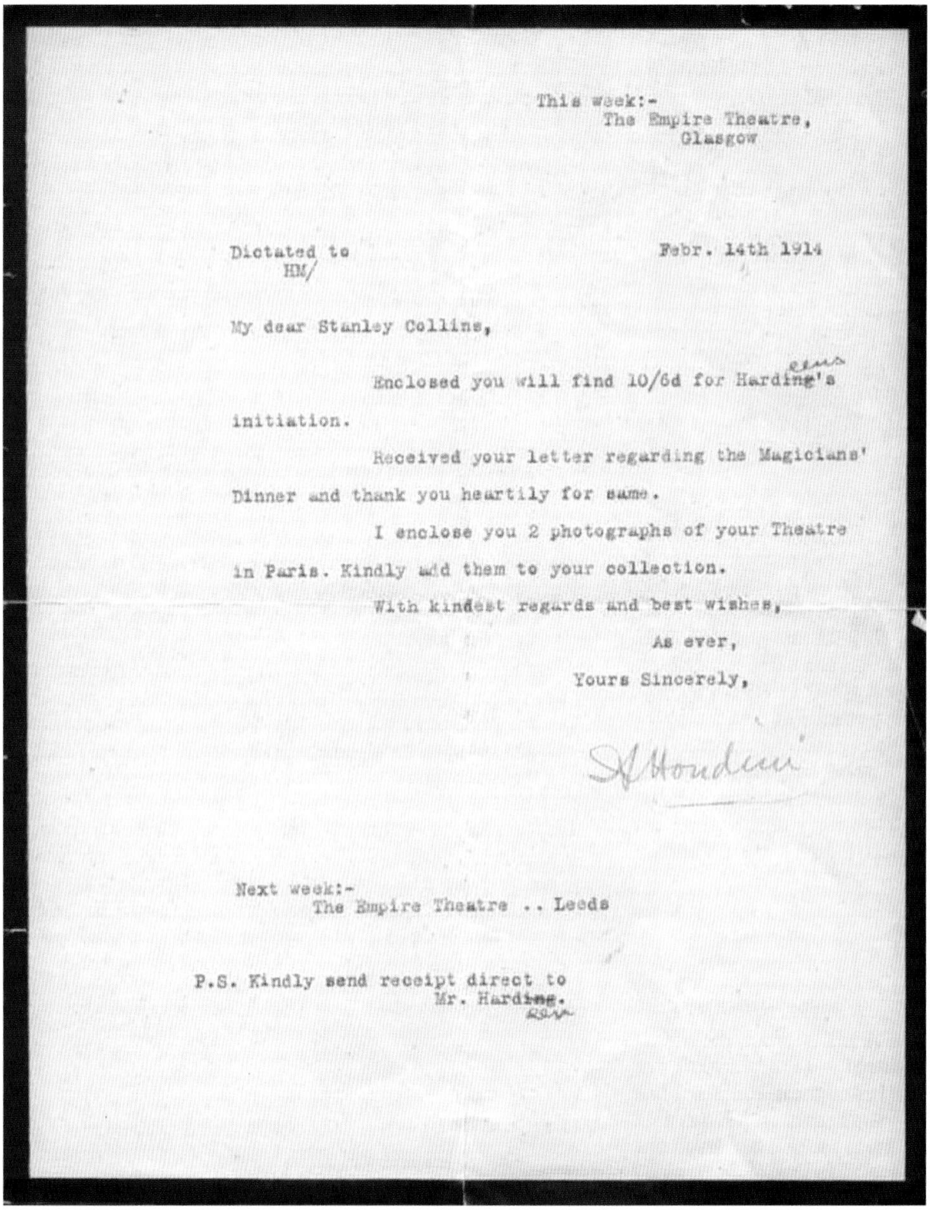

This week:-
The Empire Theatre,
Glasgow

Dictated to
HM/

Febr. 14th 1914

My dear Stanley Collins,

Enclosed you will find 10/6d for Harding's
initiation.

Received your letter regarding the Magicians'
Dinner and thank you heartily for same.

I enclose you 2 photographs of your Theatre
in Paris. Kindly add them to your collection.

With kindest regards and best wishes,

As ever,

Yours Sincerely,

Next week:-
The Empire Theatre .. Leeds

P.S. Kindly send receipt direct to
Mr. Harding.

Courtesy of Iconic Auctions

*Harry Houdini signed and typewritten letter dated 1914, PSA/DNA.* **$1,755**

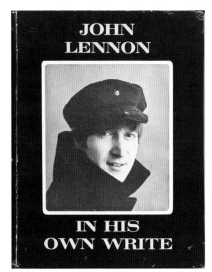

INSIDE LOOK!

**THE BEATLES**

Courtesy of Iconic Auctions

*The Beatles group-signed* John Lennon In His Own Write *hardcover book, graded Minr 9, PSA/DNA, "Paul McCartney," "John Lennon," "George Harrison" and "Ringo Starr."* **$17,558**

Courtesy of Collect Auctions

*Framed display of vintage 8" x 10" photograph of Mae West on right with oversized signature on left above nameplate, "Come up and see me sometime, Mae West" and dated "1938," PSA/DNA, 22" x 17".* **$60**

**MISTER ROGERS' NEIGHBORHOOD**

Family Communications, Inc.   4802 Fifth Avenue   Pittsburgh, PA 15213   (412) 687-2990   FAX (412) 687-1226

March, 1994

Dear Sam Oliver, Rex Morgan, and Oscar Peters,

It was a pleasure to get to know you from Fred Boyd's
letter. He told me you enjoy collecting baseball cards and
autographed pictures, and it meant a lot to me that you
would like to include my autograph in your collection. How
fortunate you are to have a friend like Fred who cares so
much about you and about the things that are important to
you. From what he wrote in his letter, your friendship
means a lot to him, too.

A few years ago, I was honored to be named the Celebrity
Captain of the Pittsburgh Penguin hockey team. There were
hockey cards made with my picture, and I thought you might
enjoy having those for your collection.

Best wishes from all of us here in the Neighborhood.

Sincerely,

*Fred Rogers*

MISTER ROGERS' NEIGHBORHOOD is underwritten by Public Television Stations
and the Corporation for Public Broadcasting.

**CLOSE-UP!**

*Fred Rogers*

Courtesy of Nate D. Sanders

*Typed letter signed
by beloved children's
television personality
Fred Rogers on "Mister
Rogers' Neighborhood"
letterhead, dated
March 1994.* **$313**

Courtesy of Nate D. Sanders

*Postcard signed by Ted Healy,
creator of the Three Stooges,
with Healy advertising his
new Stooges lineup, dated
October 30, 1937.* **$313**

October 30, 1937

Dear Friend:

On November 4th I will be on the air with my new
stooges for the first time. A Metro-Goldwyn-Mayer broadcast sponsored by the Maxwell House Coffee thru the
courtesy of National Broadcasting Company at 6 P. M.,
California time. Please listen to this program and send me a
card or letter stating your reaction as soon after the broadcast as possible care National Broadcasting Company,
Hollywood, California. A card or letter from your friends
would also be appreciated.

Sincerely,

TED HEALY

Courtesy of Robert Edward Auctions

*1785 Paul Revere signed partial document in framed display, PSA/DNA, JSA.* **$7,110**

# Banks

By Eric Bradley & Karen Knapstein

**ERIC BRADLEY** is one of the young guns of the antiques and collectibles field. Bradley, who works for Heritage Auctions, is a former editor of *Antique Trader* magazine and an award-winning investigative journalist with a degree in economics. His work has received press from *The New York Times* and *The Wall Street Journal.* He also served as a featured guest speaker on investing with antiques. He has written several books, including the critically acclaimed *Mantiques: A Manly Guide to Cool Stuff.*

**KAREN KNAPSTEIN** is the print editor of *Antique Trader* magazine. A lifelong collector and student of antiques, she has written dozens of articles on antiques and collectibles. She lives in Wisconsin with her husband and daughter.

Banks that display some form of action while accepting a coin are considered mechanical banks. Mechanical banks date back to ancient Greece and Rome, but the majority of collectors are interested in those made between 1867 and 1928 in Germany, England, and the United States. More than 80 percent of all cast iron mechanical banks produced between 1869 and 1928 were made by J. & E. Stevens Co. of Cromwell, Connecticut. Tin banks are usually of German origin.

The mechanical bank hobby continues to catch headlines as some of the best examples of rare banks head to the auction block. Morphy Auctions is a world leader in selling mechanical and still banks most desired by collectors; the firm has offered more than 6,000 mechanical banks in the last 12 years, and nearly 2,700 still banks.

According to Dan Morphy, owner and founder of Morphy Auctions, condition – like all other categories of collecting – is king. "Banks in top condition seem to be the trend these days," he said.

It's not uncommon for desirable banks to earn four- and five-figure results. But you don't need to be able to fill a bank to start collecting them. Auctions abound with more affordable character banks and premium banks from the mid-20th century. Designs are as varied as your imagination and cover a number of historical events, political figures, and landmarks. Unlike other collecting areas, many rare forms of mechanical and still banks (banks with no mechanical action) are highly valued, even if they are not in perfect condition. However, one should always buy the best condition afforded; when investing in a collection, quality should always outweigh quantity.

Those interested in mechanical banks are encouraged to learn more about the Mechanical Bank Collectors of America (www.mechanicalbanks.org), a non-profit organization consisting of around 400 members from the United States and several foreign countries. Organized in 1958, it is dedicated to expanding the knowledge and availability of antique mechanical banks. The MBCA can be reached at info@mechanicalbanks.org or by writing

*Dreadnaught still bank, Sydenham & McOustra, England, circa 1915, 7" high.* **$155**

*Arcade Flat Top Taxi bank, cast iron, nickel lights and disc wheels with painted centers, spare tire on rear, seated driver, coin slot in hood, 8" long.* **$740**

to Mechanical Bank Collectors of America, P.O. Box 13323, Pittsburgh, PA 15242.

Another valuable resource is the Still Bank Collectors Club of America (www.stillbankclub.com), a non-profit organization founded in 1966 that now consists of nearly 500 collectors from the United States, Canada, Germany, Denmark, Australia and England. Learn more about the SBCCA by writing to SBCCA Membership Chairman, 440 Homestead Ave., Metairie, LA 70005.

Courtesy of Bertoia Auctions

*Palace still bank, Ives, circa 1885, historical building with extraordinary casting details, 7 1/2" x 8".* **$1,975**

Courtesy of Bertoia Auctions

*Cabin mechanical bank, J. & E. Stevens Co., designed by Edward L. Morris, Boston, patented June 2, 1885; place coin on roof above man's head, move handle of whitewash brush, man stands on his head and kicks coin into bank.* **$525**

Courtesy of Bertoia Auctions

*State still bank, Kenton, circa 1900, japanned overall with gold and bronze highlights, 5 3/4" high.* **$555**

Courtesy of Bertoia Auctions

*1939 New York World's Fair still bank, lithographed tin sphere ball bank with original thermometer, 5" to 12 1/4" high.* **$525**

Courtesy of Bertoia Auctions

*Cat and Mouse mechanical bank, J. & E. Stevens Co., designed by James H. Bowen, patented April 21, 1891; place coin in front of mouse, press lever, and as coin disappears into bank, kitten in fancy dress appears, turning somersault, holding mouse and ball.* **$1,112**

Courtesy of Bertoia Auctions

▶ *McKinley-Teddy Roosevelt elephant still bank, circa 1900, scarce example with busts of both men embossed on one side with their platform of "Prosperity" on other side, 3 1/2" high.* **$985**

Courtesy of Bertoia Auctions

*Indian Shooting Bear mechanical bank with box, J. & E. Stevens Co., designed by Charles A. Bailey, circa 1883; place coin in proper position on barrel of rifle, press lever, and Indian takes aim and shoots coin into bear (paper cap may be inserted).* **$33,138**

Courtesy of Bertoia Auctions

▲ *Trick Dog mechanical bank, six-part base, Hubley Manufacturing Co.; coin is placed in dog's mouth, and by touching lever dog jumps through hoop and deposits coin in barrel.* **$432**

Courtesy of Noel Barrett

▶ *Lion and Monkey mechanical bank, Kyser & Rex, painted cast iron, exceptional example, original locking trap, no key, monkey recast, 9" long.* **$1,452**

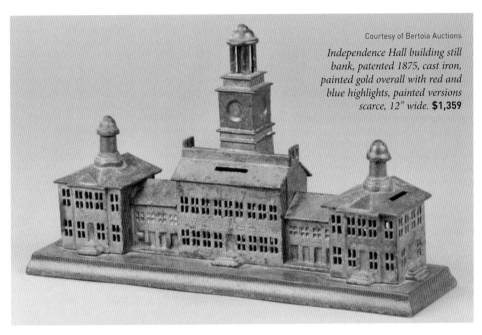

Courtesy of Bertoia Auctions

*Independence Hall building still bank, patented 1875, cast iron, painted gold overall with red and blue highlights, painted versions scarce, 12" wide.* **$1,359**

Courtesy of Bertoia Auctions

*Mammy and Child mechanical bank, Kyser & Rex Co., yellow, designed by Alfred C. Rex, patented Oct. 21, 1884; place coin in slot on mammy's apron and press lever, mammy lowers spoon as if feeding baby, her head lowers, baby's legs rise.* **$54,225**

Courtesy of Noel Barrett

*Clown on Globe mechanical bank, painted cast iron, J. & E. Stevens Co., 9" high when seated; bank's violent action caused few to survive in very fine condition and even fewer in near mint condition.* **$19,360**

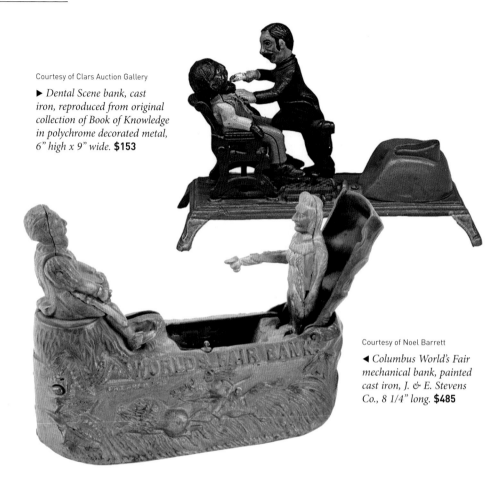

Courtesy of Clars Auction Gallery

▶ *Dental Scene bank, cast iron, reproduced from original collection of Book of Knowledge in polychrome decorated metal, 6" high x 9" wide.* **$153**

Courtesy of Noel Barrett

◀ *Columbus World's Fair mechanical bank, painted cast iron, J. & E. Stevens Co., 8 1/4" long.* **$485**

Courtesy of Bertoia Auctions

*Baby in Cradle still bank of young baby sleeping under blanket, circa 1890s, very rare, nickeled cast iron and steel bed, 3 1/4" x 4".* **$988**

Courtesy of Bertoia Auctions

*Squirrel and Tree Stump mechanical bank, Mechanical Novelty Works, designed by Robert E. Turnbull, patented June 28, 1881; place coin in squirrel's forepaws, touch spring, and squirrel bounds forward and throws coin into bank.* **$6,793**

Courtesy of Skinner, Inc.; www.skinnerinc.com

*Bill E. Grin mechanical bank, cast iron, painted, J. & E. Stevens Co., Cromwell, Connecticut, circa 1890, 4 1/4" high.* **$613**

Courtesy of Morphy Auctions

*Mikado mechanical bank, cast iron, Kyser & Rex, blue variation, one cone reattached, works fine, near mint condition, 6 3/4" high.* **$192,000**

Courtesy of Morphy Auctions

*Harlequin mechanical bank, cast iron, J. & E. Stevens Co., original first casting, working condition, minor touch up to paint, 7" high.* **$49,200**

Courtesy of Skinner, Inc.; www.skinnerinc.com

*Leapfrog mechanical bank, cast iron, Shepard Hardware Co., Buffalo, New York, patented 1891, 4 7/8" high x 7 1/2" wide.* **$577**

Courtesy of Clars Auction Gallery

*Paddy and Pig mechanical bank, cast iron, J. & E. Stevens Co., circa 1882, designed by James H. Bowen, black coat and red stockings, marked on base "ENG PAT JULY 28 1882 and US PAT AUG 8 1882"; place coin on nose of pig, press lever, pig strikes coin with foot, man opens his mouth, catches coin on tongue, swallows coin, at same time eyes roll, giving face pleased expression, 8 1/2" x 7".* **$1,452**

Courtesy of Lloyd Ralston Gallery

*Statue of Liberty still bank,
Kenton, painted cast iron, missing
trap, 6 3/8" high.* **$290**

Courtesy of Bertoia Auctions

*Charlie McCarthy still bank figure,
die-cast, with suitcase by side, slot in
back, stenciled "Charlie McCarthy"
on suitcase, 8" high.* **$432**

# Beatles
## Pop Culture

By Noah Fleisher

**NOAH FLEISHER** received his Bachelor of Fine Arts degree from New York University and brings more than a decade of newspaper, magazine, book, antiques and art experience to his position as Public Relations Director of Heritage Auctions, one of the country's foremost auction houses. He is the former editor of *Antique Trader, New England Antiques Journal* and *Northeast Antiques Journal,* is the author of *Warman's Modern Furniture,* and has been a longtime contributor to *Warman's Antiques & Collectibles.*

Transcendent. Brilliant. Singular. Throw out a handful of superlatives and every last one could be applied to The Beatles. The boys from Liverpool are unmatched in the annals of music history, and for good reason. Everybody knows the group and everybody knows at least a few of their tunes.

My earliest memories of music are of playing Beatles 8-tracks in my living room as a seven-year-old, digging through compilations that started with "I Wanna Hold Your Hand" and went through "Let it Be." I remember the stunned reaction of the world when John Lennon was shot and killed in 1980. I remember falling hard for "Abbey Road" and "Sgt. Pepper's" in high school and, now, as a 44-year-old father of an eight-year-old girl, it pleases me to no end to hear her say that she could never marry a boy who didn't love The Beatles – as good a litmus test as I can think of.

The Beatles also rule the world of music and entertainment memorabilia like few others. I might even venture to say, having watched the market in the best Beatles material explode in the last five years, that they may well be the only sure-fire bet in music memorabilia that a collector could have right now.

Collectors will always look for the pieces of their past that can help them recapture their youth, or a key moment, but often the music and musicians that represent those moments are not evergreen like the Fab Four. Even Elvis is no guarantee, at least not on par with The Beatles.

The Beatles have made new fans in every single generation that has followed their American debut in 1964. For 50 years parents have turned their kids on to Beatles music, and those kids have carried that torch forward to the next generation. You name it – autographs, clothing, instruments, images, toys – all of them are commanding top dollar from flea markets to conventions, auctions, shows, shops, and everything in between.

*Beatles signed "Sgt. Pepper's Lonely Hearts Club Band" mono UK gatefold cover (Parlophone PMC 7027, 1967).* **$290,500**

When it comes to selling Beatles memorabilia, there are few, if any, who can match Darren Julien, the CEO and president of Julien's Auctions in Los Angeles. Julien has a knack for finding the best Beatles material (among the amazing troves of other music and entertainment memorabilia he manages to dig up), bringing it to auction amidst tremendous international attention, and then getting incredibly strong prices for it.

"The Beatles are so popular because their music is still relevant and their fan base is not only global but it transcends all age groups," Julien told *Warman's*. "Their fan base only continues to increase and, for many, buying an item from their life or career is like buying a memory from their past. The Beatles are on the high end of the collector scale as they were really the first on many levels and no other group has had so many hits. Their talent as artists coming together was unprecedented, and in my opinion won't ever be repeated."

It becomes easy to see why the band occupies a perch all its own in terms of collectors.

"Beatles memorabilia is the blue chip of the collectibles market," Julien told *Warman's*. "Items from their career tend to go up gradually and consistently, unlike some celebrities who spike high and sometimes end low."

That assessment, certainly true as evidenced by continued collector mania, can carry with it the same type of issues that collectors have to be on the lookout for with any other hot collectible: fakes.

"The problem with this market, as it is with all markets, is that companies are selling fake items, such as signatures or property, that do not have proper provenance," said Julien. "Fortunately, there are several very good and reputable auction houses that consistently sell authentic property, which helps stabilize the market. Also, collectors are becoming more educated on items, knowing what to look for when buying something Beatles-related."

The Internet, a plethora of written material, and images have indeed now put the power in the hands of the increasingly better-educated consumer. As any top level auctioneer or dealer will tell you, Julien echoes the cry of educating oneself before jumping in, no matter what level a collector is looking at. A few hundred or a few hundred thousand dollars, patience, study, and a trusted ally will go far.

"Do your research," said Julien. "There's so much information online that can give you an idea of what an item is worth and if it's authentic. It's also very important to buy from a reputable auction house or dealer who knows how to vet the authenticity of an item."

This is sage advice indeed, and it rings true the deeper you go into your research and the closer you get to buying. Listen to the expert:

"The provenance is the most important thing to look for on an item, and make sure that it can be matched up to photographs or videos to ensure the items are authentic," Julien said. "When it comes to Beatles instruments, the best resource is Andy Babuik's *Beatles Gear* book. Andy has had access to the archives of The Beatles members and has done an impressive job of detailing the history of the items used by the band."

Okay, but not all of us are in the market for a George Harrison guitar. Still, collectors need to familiarize themselves with the high and the low ends of the market to make the best choice. How does this break down where John, Paul, George, and Ringo are concerned?

"The items that bring the most and are the most sought-after are items that were used/worn on stage," Julien said. "The market for these items has dramatically increased. For instance, guitars that Christie's sold for around $100,000 in recent years, we now sell for more than $500,000. Beatles garments have also dramatically increased in recent years as museums and investors now look for iconic items that can be on display or that will increase in value."

You can do the math from there. Don't have six figures to drop on a pristine signed album, or a suit John wore in 1965? Know your limit and look for the autographs you can afford, or a Beatles bobblehead, lunchbox, or record player, etc.

Let's look ahead. The pursuit of Beatles material has grown so much over the last decade, has it topped out? Julien doesn't think so, and he's well-positioned to posit an overview.

"The Beatles are not going anywhere," he said. "I think their legendary status and collectibility will only continue to increase. Items

Courtesy of Julien's Auctions

*"The Beatles" TV cartoon 16 mm film.* **$384**

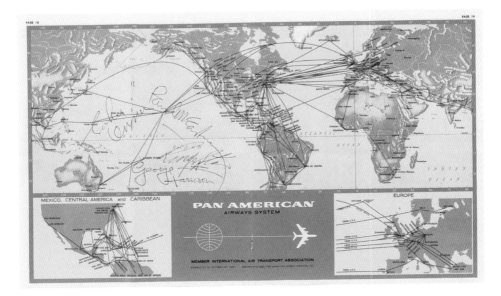

*Beatles signed Pan Am Airways route map obtained on their flight to America on Feb. 7, 1964.*
**$23,750**

that we see selling for $500,000 now, I believe, will be worth $2 million to $3 million in 50 years."

Where does this put the rest of rock n' roll memorabilia, then? Is it remotely possible for a modern band (1980 onward) to have the same impact on music (and subsequently memorabilia) as The Beatles? Julien thinks so, but the path that a band carves, while building on the music and the market that the Beatles created, will have to be unique to itself or there is no chance of a lasting impact.

"There'll be other bands that will have a similar impact on music," he said. "I think that rock n' roll memorabilia, as a whole, is on the rise. Most of this is due to the Internet and accessibility to collectors, fans, museums, and investors globally. Now, rather than someone taking the time to fly to a destination to bid in an auction and spending the money, they can bid from the comfort of their own home or office. Asia and Russia have become huge markets for Beatles memorabilia, and they are buying up everything."

Understand, then, that the Beatles are king and may always be, but keep a keen eye on the market, on popular music, and on collector tastes. You may not score the Holy Grail of Fab Four memorabilia, but by respecting their position in the market and understanding their genius as artists, you may just be able to parlay your understanding into a great Beatles acquisition down the road or into a solid investment in a different band or artist on the rise that may be able to capture in a bottle just a hint of the lightning that made The Beatles the pinnacle of the music memorabilia market.

*The Beatles "Let It Be" U.K. film poster.* **$768**

*The Beatles signed merchandising poster.* **$12,160**

*The Beatles 1964 press conference and performance.* **$1,280**

Courtesy of Julien's Auctions

*The Beatles First State "butcher cover" sleeve.* **$32,000**

Courtesy of Julien's Auctions

*The Beatles signed "With the Beatles" album.* **$32,000**

Courtesy of Julien's Auctions

*"Beatles '65" original album cover artwork mock-up.* **$896**

*John Lennon and Yoko Ono original signed "Bed-In" drawing.* **$185,000**

*The Beatles Rickenbacker guitar.* **$605,000**

*Photograph of The Beatles performing in 1963.* **$75**

*The Beatles signed 1965 tour program.* **$19,200**

*John Lennon/George Harrison's Vox guitar.*
**$408,000**

*George Harrison's handwritten lyrics for "Isn't It a Pity."* **$8,320**

*The Beatles platinum record award.* **$2,560**

Courtesy of Julien's Auctions

▲ *The Beatles gold record award.* **$2,880**

Courtesy of Julien's Auctions

▲ *Paul McCartney presentation bass.* **$201,800**

Courtesy of Julien's Auctions

▶ *The Beatles "Sgt. Pepper's Lonely Hearts Club Band" outtake photograph.* **$320**

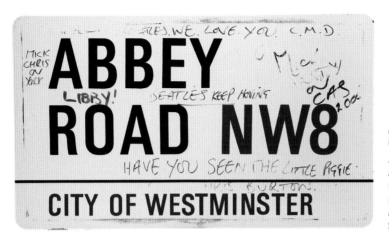

*Abbey Road street
sign; this heavier
version adorned
road in late 1960s
and early 1970s.*
**$16,730**

ELVIS

8/27/65

*Beatles autographs on Elvis Presley's personal
stationery, Aug. 27, 1965.* **$59,750**

*The Beatles, Ed Sullivan, and Brian Epstein signatures
from historic first American appearance on the "Ed
Sullivan Show," Feb. 9, 1964."* **$125,000**

CLOSE-UP!

*The Beatles Dodger Stadium tickets and program.* **$512**

*Beatles hand-painted Mold (Wales) assembly hall concert poster, 1963.* **$3,750**

*The Beatles Shampoo box (1964), one of few known to survive.* **$1,554**

Courtesy of Heritage Auctions

Beatles "Hey Jude" acetate, unreleased extended version (Allied New York imprint, 1968). $1,673

Courtesy of Heritage Auctions

G Vintage 1960s Kodak M26 Instamatic movie camera, owned and used by John Lennon in mid-1960s at his Kenwood home in Weybridge, England. $3,525

Courtesy of Heritage Auctions

Peach-colored end mezzanine ticket to The Beatles' Sept. 3, 1964, Thursday afternoon (5:00) show at Indiana State Fair. $1,625

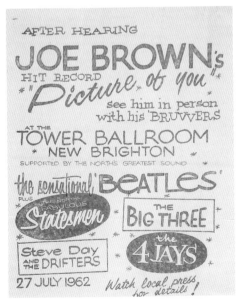

Courtesy of Heritage Auctions

The Beatles Tower Ballroom concert handbill, 1962, one of only eight known to still exist. $1,494

Courtesy of Heritage Auctions

Beatles vintage record player (NEMS, 1964), one of approximately 5,000 produced, complete and in working order. $4,000

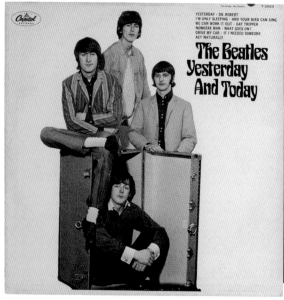

Courtesy of Heritage Auctions

▲ Beatles "Yesterday and Today"
second state "butcher cover"
mono LP (Capitol T 2553, 1966),
pasted over original infamous
"butcher cover." **$1,375**

Courtesy of Heritage Auctions

▲ Beatles perpetual tabletop
calendar (UK, circa 1963). **$500**

Courtesy of Heritage Auctions

▶ Beatles girls' high top Wing
Dings sneakers, never worn
(NEMS, 1964). **$500**

▲ *Beatles vintage megaphone manufactured by Yell-a-Phone in 1965, sold only at Beatles concerts in the United States.* **$500**

*"A Hard Day's Night" program (United Artists, 1964), unrestored with bright color and clean overall appearance.* **$74**

*"A Hard Day's Night" lobby card (Universal, R-1982), unrestored with bright color and clean overall appearance.* **$78**

# Books

By Noah Fleisher

**NOAH FLEISHER**
received his Bachelor of
Fine Arts degree from
New York University
and brings more than a
decade of newspaper,
magazine, book, antiques
and art experience to
his position as Public
Relations Director of
Heritage Auctions, one
of the country's foremost
auction houses. He is the
former editor of *Antique
Trader, New England
Antiques Journal* and
*Northeast Antiques Journal*,
is the author of *Warman's
Modern Furniture,* and
has been a longtime
contributor to *Warman's
Antiques & Collectibles.*

Joe Fay is the manager of the Rare Books Department at Heritage Auctions. He's a young man, a devoted husband and father of two, an obsessive film buff and VHS tape aficionado. He also has an encyclopedic knowledge of the printed word.

He can wax poetic about the mysteries of incunabula, then turn around a breath later and extol the virtues of Stephen King or Sherlock Holmes, his personal favorite, finding the common thread between them – don't ask me, ask him. He's got an eye for early copies of *The Federalist Papers* and can spot a rare first edition of J.K. Rowling's *Harry Potter and the Philosopher's Stone,* reciting from memory exactly what makes it a true first edition.

We sat down for a conversation about the current market in rare books, which proved as entertaining as it did enlightening.

**Warman's:** Give me an overview of rare books.

**Joe Fay:** As always, the top of the market is very stable. The market seems to be holding steady against a fairly violent public assault on the printed word.

I hear the question all the time: "Will the Kindle kill the printed book?" Of course not. Folks bemoan the death of the printed word, but it's not going to happen anytime soon. It seems like every new technology that transmits information has called for the death of the book, but it hasn't happened yet and I don't think it will.

I think rare books will become increasingly more precious because of their physicality. People will come to interact with books in a different, more intimate way because of their relative scarcity.

**Warman's:** Is the market improving? Where are the best buying opportunities?

**Joe Fay:** The market is improving since the rather large hiccup of 2008. There is strength in special or unique books: examples with wonderful inscriptions, association copies, fine bindings, etc. Also, with the prevailing cultural obsession with superheroes and comic book-related material, there has never been a stronger market for science fiction and genre fiction.

You can also never go wrong with incunabula, books printed before 1500, or great copies of great works in the major collecting categories.

*Marc Chagall (1887-1985), seven coffee table books:* Lithographe III, *Boston, 1969;* Chagall at the Met, *New York, 1971;* The Ballet, *New York, 1969;* Daphnis & Chloe, *New York, 1977;* Chagall by Chagall, *New York, 1979;* Ceramics – Sculptures, *Monaco, 1972; and* Chagall in Jerusalem, *New York, 1983; all with dust jackets.* **$400**

Early printed books are always strong, the incunabula I just mentioned. Important first editions in the major categories, such as history, science and medicine, natural history, travel, religion, maps and atlases, literature, economics, early American imprints, children's books, and illustrated books.

Fine press printing and artists' books seem to be on the upward trend, too, as books become more of a specialty in the face of competing technologies.

**Warman's:** Is there room for new and younger collectors in rare books right now?

**Joe Fay:** I think it's a good market to get into at any time and any age. The rule I live by when talking about book collecting, as any expert in any category will tell you: Collect what you like. Find some focus within a subject area, author, printer or publisher, and collect everything you can.

Don't limit yourself to just the books, either. For a given author, seek out autograph material, posters, artifacts, original art if applicable, and so on. It can be very rewarding to walk into a person's personal library and not only see an incredible run of first editions by Ray Bradbury, but also find a *Fahrenheit 451* poster on the wall, next to a framed letter from the author. I guess this is a disguised version of diversification, in a way.

**Warman's:** It's a huge field. How do you go about starting or bolstering a collection if you've been out for a while?

**Joe Fay:** Vigilance. It's a great time to be a buyer of rare books because they are so readily available to be bought.

Build a relationship with a reputable dealer, save keyword searches at online sites like eBay and Heritage, places where

▶ *Sir Winston Churchill (1874-1965), five volumes: My African Journey, London: Hodder & Stoughton, 1908, first edition, illustrated, in publisher's pictorial red cloth, stamped with image of Churchill beside slain rhinoceros, plastic jacket, 7 1/2" x 4 3/4"; London to Lady Smith via Pretoria, New York: Longmans, Green, & Co., 1900, first American edition, illustrated, bound in publisher's red cloth with gold lettering on spine and front board, spine sunned, board surfaces lightly rubbed, plastic jacket, 4 5/8" x 7 5/8"; Ian Hamilton's March, London: Longmans, Green, & Co., 1900, first edition, with portrait frontispiece, maps, and plans, in red publisher's binding with gilt lettering on spine and front board, and black end papers, binding bumped, scratched, spine sunned, plastic jacket, 7 1/2" x 5"; Savrola, New York: Longmans, Green, & Co., 1900, octavo, half-title, 12 leaves of publisher's advertisements after text, in publisher's blue cloth lettered in gilt on front board and spine, endcaps rubbed, bookplate removed from inside cover leaving adhesive behind, leaning slightly, 7 1/2" x 5"; Liberalism and the Social Problem, London: Hodder & Stoughton, 1909, in publisher's red cloth, blind stamp that reads "Presentation Copy" on title page.* **$1,560**

you get email reminders when material matching your interests becomes available.

**Warman's:** What is it that draws people to rare books?

**Joe Fay:** That's a really big question. I think the desire to collect rare books started with a thirst to converse with the great minds of the past, which encompasses really anything. There are practically limitless possibilities for a subject area to collect in rare books.

If you want to assemble the best collection of books bound in yellow cloth, you can do that. You want to collect signs made by homeless panhandlers? Let me introduce you to Michael Zinman, who already does that. You want to collect pamphlets and other imprints dealing with early 20th century American Communism? I hope you have a lifetime to devote to it and I would love to see your collection someday.

For me, personally, the allure of rare books comes down to both what they are, physically, and what they represent. Books are wonderful to handle. If a book is well put together, it fits nicely in the hand or lies well when opened on a table, it stimulates both the eye to flip through and the mind to read, and is a pleasure to look at on the shelf. Even the smell of a book is a unique phenomenon that evokes myriad emotions and memories.

A rare first printing of a given important novel is rare in itself, but it also represents a viewpoint and a cultural zeitgeist that is usually universal, that mattered both when the book was published and today. They are a window into the minds of people long gone, markers of our evolution as humans. This is not something you get with many other collecting categories.

**Warman's:** Looking back 10 years and looking ahead 10 years, how does/will the market look in comparison?

**Joe Fay:** A couple of generations ago everyone had books in their house. For 550 years books have been the primary method by which people learned. Now, there are so many competing delivery systems for information that print culture has obviously taken a hit.

I think the number of collectors 10 years from now will be smaller in number but more intense in terms of who is collecting. Rare books have become a bit of a niche market, but you can see the contraction markedly at regional book fairs. More people used to come to fairs than they do now. High-end fairs like the New York Antiquarian Book Fair are still going strong, and will likely continue to do so, because the top end of the market is not going anywhere. Truly valuable rarities always bring premium prices.

**Warman's:** You hear how technology has hurt books. Tell me how it has helped.

**Joe Fay:** The Internet and the eReader have certainly had an effect on the trade, no doubt – we have fewer and fewer bookstores these days – but the web has also opened up thousands upon millions of avenues for finding books, especially those that people once thought were very rare or even unique. The Internet has also had a positive effect on some titles by reinforcing their rarity.

The Internet helped to stratify the rare book world. With so much information, no one can pay – and no one will ask – unreasonable prices for common books. I talk to book dealers all the time who say something to the effect of, "I used to be able to get $500 for that book, now I can't give it away." Then they turn around and say, "You know that book I sold in your Internet weekly auction for $1,000? I've had that book on my table at book fairs for 10 years for $150 and barely anyone looked at it."

Obviously, the web can now help actually identify rarity instead of proving commonness.

**Warman's:** How much homework should a collector do before entering the category, or is it best to consult experts and let them fill in the gaps?

**Joe Fay:** Do a lot of homework. Many people have been burned by casually starting to collect books or by trusting the wrong dealer. Don't just do homework on the books; check out the dealer, the auction house, or whatever entity you might do business with.

Call other dealers and talk to them about a given dealer. Check with the Better Business Bureau. Call the auction house and talk to the book department.

Book dealers and rare books auctioneers, once trusted, can be a very important source of information for collectors, and can often "fill in gaps," as you say.

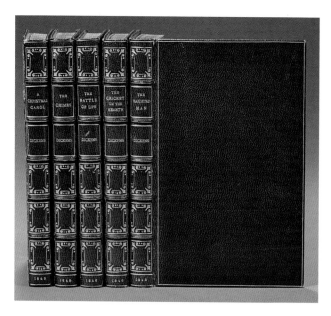

Courtesy of Skinner, Inc.; www.skinnerinc.com

*Charles Dickens (1812-1870), Christmas Tales, five volumes:* A Christmas Carol, *London: Chapman & Hall, 1843, second issue, title printed in red and blue, half-title and title verso printed in blue, "Stave One" on first page of text, one page of ads after text, hand-colored frontispiece and three plates by John Leech, four wood engravings in text by W.J. Linton;* The Chimes, *London: Chapman & Hall, 1845, engraved frontispiece and additional title after Maclise, wood engravings after Doyle, Leech, and Stanfield;* The Cricket on the Hearth, *London: for the author by Bradbury & Evans, 1846, engraved frontispiece and additional title, illustrations by Leech, et al.;* The Battle of Life, *London: Bradbury & Evans, 1846, engraved frontispiece and additional title, illustrations by Leech, et al.;* The Haunted Man, *London: Bradbury & Evans, 1848, engraved frontispiece and additional title, illustrated; all five volumes bound in uniform green Morocco by Riviere, a.e.g., cloth from original bindings bound in every volume at back; spines sunned to brown, 6 1/4" x 4".* **$2,160**

Courtesy of Skinner, Inc.; www.skinnerinc.com

▲ *Franz Kafka (1883-1924),* The Trial, *New York: Knopf, 1937, first American edition, translated by Willa and Edwin Muir, in publisher's orange cloth with black and gray lettering and illustration, in George Salter (1897-1967) designed jacket, jacket in very good condition, one corner rubbed, spine slightly sunned, 7 3/4" x 4 3/4".* **$1,200**

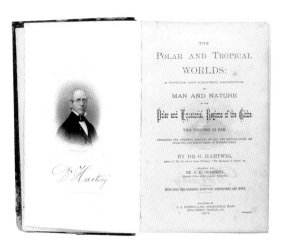

Courtesy of Heritage Auctions

◄ *Dr. Georg Hartwig,* The Polar and Tropical Worlds: A Popular and Scientific Description of Man and Nature in the Polar and Equatorial Regions of the Globe, *C. A. Nichols and Co., 1876, early printing, illustrated with engravings and maps, two volumes in one, contemporary embossed leather binding lettered in gilt, portions of leather lacking from lower portion of front board and lower spine, contents with light to moderate scattered foxing, good condition.* **$15**

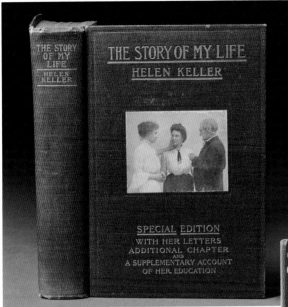

◀ *Helen Keller,* The Story of My Life, *New York: Doubleday, Page & Co., 1904, octavo, stated "Special Edition" on title, with illustrations and additional chapter by Keller, in publisher's red cloth, stamped in gilt, with black and white picture inset on front board, rubbed, foxing to tissue guard facing frontispiece and in text, 8 1/4" x 5 3/4".* **$431**

▲ *Martin Luther King, Jr.,* Strength to Love, *Harper & Row, Publishers, 1963, first edition, publisher's original binding and dust jacket, jacket scuffed, former owner's stamp on front pastedown, very good condition.* **$26**

▲ *Lewis H. Morgan,* League of the Ho-De-No-Sau-Nee, or Iroquois, *Rochester: Sage & Brother, 1851, first edition, illustrated with frontispiece, large folding map of Iroquois nation (New York State), numerous text illustrations, folding table, etc., in worn publisher's cloth, with gilt-stamped spine, sewing supports attaching back board broken, de-cased, binding worn and rubbed, head cap torn, 9 1/4" x 5 3/4";* The Pirates Own Book, or Authentic Narratives of the Lives, Exploits, and Executions of the Most Celebrated Sea Robbers, *Portland: Sanborn & Carter, 1844, octavo, illustrated with wood engravings of pirate characters and adventures, in publisher's brown blind-stamped cloth, with title blocked on spine in gold with skull and crossbones, one signature sprung, 7 1/4" x 4 1/2".* **$154**

Courtesy of Swann Auction Galleries

*Philip Miller,* The Gardeners Dictionary: Containing the Methods of Cultivating and Improving the Kitchen, Fruit and Flower Garden, as also the Physick Garden, Wilderness, Conservatory, and Vineyard, *London: printed for author and sold by C. Rivington, 1733, engraved frontispiece and four plates, 842 pages, including initial license leaf, contemporary paneled calf, rebacked, cover corners worn, hinges reinforced with cloth tape, repaired clean tear in dedication leaf, armorial bookplate of Robert Briscoe, Esq.* **$531**

Courtesy of Skinner, Inc.; www.skinnerinc.com

*Chinese illustrated manuscript on* Production of Tea, *19th century, small-format 12-leaf book with gouache paintings depicting 12 steps of tea production, single signature, paintings on rice paper and mounted, approximately half with tears or breaks, with notes alluding to associations with Commodore Perry's grandchildren inside front board, and inserted letter; bound in decorated paper over boards, worn, ties at fore edge partially detached, 5 1/4" x 3 3/4".* **$1,560**

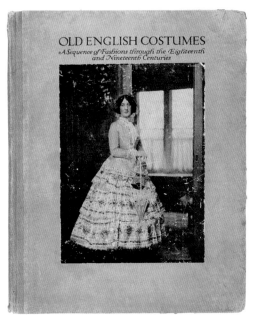

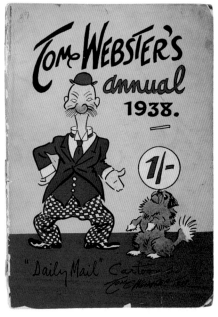

Courtesy of Heritage Auctions

Old English Costumes: A Sequence of Fashions Through the Eighteenth and Nineteenth Centuries, *London: presented to Victoria and Albert Museum by Harrods, 1913, quarto, photographic illustrations throughout, large photograph of painting laid in, publisher's binding with photographic illustration pasted to front board, boards soiled and rubbed, edges and spine worn, good condition.* **$20**

Courtesy of Heritage Auctions

Tom Webster's Annual, 1938, "Daily Mail" Cartoons, *publisher's pictorial wraps, heavily toned, pages brittle, wrapper edgeworn and heavily soiled, good condition, 7" x 10".* **$119**

Courtesy of Skinner, Inc.;
www.skinnerinc.com

*United States,* The Laws of the United States of America, *Philadelphia/Washington, D.C.: Folwell, Ross, Smith, Carey, Duane, and Weightman, 1796 (-1811), 10 octavo volumes, contemporary sheepskin bindings, worn, with losses to endcaps, four volumes with both boards detached, hinges tender on others, most labels intact, bindings dry and dusty with some interior foxing, not collated; includes original three-volume set of* Laws *from 1796, and additional volumes published in 1797, 1801, 1804, 1806, 1807, 1809, and 1811.* **$492**

# Cookbooks

*Fannie Merritt Farmer,* What to Have for Dinner: Containing Menus With the Recipes Necessary for Their Publication, *New York: Dodge Publishing Co., circa 1905, frontispiece and 13 full-page plates from photographs, original decorated cloth, first edition. Farmer is easily the best remembered and enduring of the authors of late 19th century-early 20th century American cookbooks, and her* Boston Cooking School Cook Book *continues to be issued in new editions to this day. This title is one of her less common works, offering complete menus with recipes for family dinners, company and formal dinners, and dinners for holidays and other special occasions.* **$160**

*Two 1900s litho Jell-O cookbooks, both with full-color inserts, very good condition.* **$40**

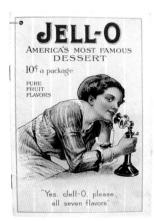

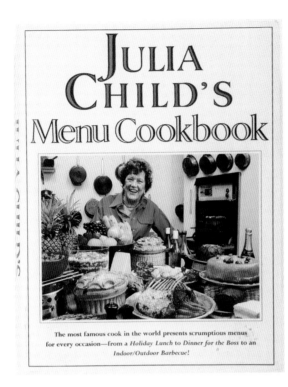

▲ *Carolyn Neithammer,* American Indian Food and Lore, *circa 1974, soft cover, 191 pages.* **$25**

▲ *Julia Child,* Julia Child's Menu Cookbook, *New York: Wings Books, 1991, later edition, signed and inscribed by author on verso of half-title page.* **$175**

▲ *Dana Crumb and Shery Cohen,* Eat It, *cover by American cartoonist Robert Crumb, 1972, first printing.* **$30**

◀ *Jane Breskin Zalben,* To Every Season: A Family Holiday Cookbook, *Simon and Schuster, 1999, first edition, signed by author and dated in year of publication, publisher's binding and dust jacket.* **$15**

# Bottles

By Michael Polak

**MICHAEL POLAK** has collected more than 3,000 bottles since entering the hobby in 1976. He is a regular contributor to a variety of antiques publications and is the author of *Antique Trader Bottles Identification & Price Guide,* 7th edition, and *Picker's Pocket Guide: Bottles.*

Glass bottles are not as new as some people believe. In fact, the glass bottle has been around for about 3,000 years. In the late first century B.C., the Romans, with the assistance of glassworker craftsmen from Syria and Egypt, began making glass vials that local doctors and pharmacists used to dispense pills, healing powders, and miscellaneous potions.

The first attempt to manufacture glass in America is thought to have taken place at the Jamestown settlement in Virginia around 1608 by the London Co. The first successful American glass house was opened in 1739 in New Jersey by Caspar Wistar, who immigrated from Germany to Philadelphia in 1717.

Throughout the 19th century, glasshouses opened and closed because of changes in demand and technological improvements. Between 1840 and 1890, an enormous demand for glass containers developed to satisfy the demands of the whiskey, beer, medical, and food-packing industries. Largely due to this steady demand, glass manufacturing in the United States evolved into a stable industry.

Unlike other businesses of the time that saw major changes in manufacturing processes, glass bottle production remained unchanged. The process gave each bottle character, producing unique shapes, imperfections, irregularities, and various colors. That all changed at the turn of the 20th century when Michael J. Owens invented the first fully automated bottle-making machine. Although many fine bottles were manufactured between 1900-1930, Owens' invention ended an era of unique bottle design that no machine process could ever duplicate.

The modern antique bottle collecting craze started in the 1960s with dump digging. Since then, interest in bottle collecting continues to grow, with new bottle clubs forming throughout the United States and Europe. More collectors are spending their free time digging through old

dumps and foraging through ghost towns, digging out old outhouses where people often tossed empty bottles, exploring abandoned mine shafts, and searching favorite bottles or antiques shows, swap meets, flea markets, and garage sales. In addition, the Internet offers collectors numerous opportunities and resources to buy and sell bottles with many new auction websites. Many bottle clubs now have websites providing even more information for the collector. These new technologies and resources have helped bottle collecting to continue to grow and gain interest.

Most collectors, however, still look beyond the type and value of a bottle to its origin and history. Researching the history of a bottle is almost as interesting as finding the bottle itself. Both pursuits have close ties to the rich history of the settling of the United States and the early methods of merchandising.

▲ *Cosmetic/hair bottle, W.A. Batchelor's / Moldavia Cream / Manufactured Only At 16 Bond Street / New York, deep cobalt blue, American 1860-1875, 2 1/8".* **$375-$500**

**RECOMMENDED READING**

**Picker's Pocket Guide: Bottles.** Professional and practical strategy on where to look for bottles, what to look for, how to negotiate, how to accurately identify, and how to flip the bottles you find. Includes top examples of bottles across the most popular categories and their record prices brought at auction. www.krausebooks.com

*Mineral bottle, I. Sutton
& Co. / Covington / KY,
medium cobalt blue,
American 1840-1860,
8 1/2".* **$800-$1,200**

*Beer bottle, E.A.
Olendorf / Sarsaparilla
Lager (in slug plate) This
Bottle / Is Never Sold,
medium orange amber,
American 1885-1895,
9 1/4".* **$250-$300**

*Bitters bottle, Celebrated
Nectar / Stomach Bitters
/ And Nerve Tonic – The
/ Nectar Bitter Co. /
Toledo, O, bright yellow
green, American 1890-
1900, 9 3/8".* **$275-$475**

Courtesy of Norm Heckler Auctions

*Rare history flask, cobalt blue
"Washington Bust / Tree in
Leaf" portrait flask (GI-35),
1845-1860.* **$24,000**

*Soda bottle, California / Natural / Seltzer Water / H&G, rare color, American 1875-1880, 7 1/2".* **$3,000-$4,000**

*Whiskey bottle, Star Whiskey / New York / W.B. Crowell Jr., American 1860-1875, 8 1/2".* **$500-$800**

*Poison bottle, Poison / The Owl Drug Co. / Aqua Ammonia Poison, deep cobalt blue, American 1890-1910, 9 5/8".* **$100-$125**

*Poison bottle, cobalt blue, American 1885-1900, 4 1/4" long.* **$1,500-$2,000**

◄ Fire grenade, Grenade / L.B., medium turquoise blue, French 1880-1900, 5 1/8". **$800-$1,200**

▼ Two fire grenades, medium green, French 1885-1900, 5 5/8". **$700-$900**

▲ Soda bottle, Carbutt & Hamilton / Manufacturers / Cincinnati, ten-pin shape, American 1855-1870, 7 7/8". **$375-$450**

► Stripe-pattern domed inkwell, clear glass with white and pink alternating stripe pattern swirled to right, Sandwich Glass Works, Sandwich, Massachusetts, 1830-1850, 2 1/4". **$1,200-$1,800**

*Target ball, C. Bogardus / Patd / Apr 10th / 1877 / Glass Ball (on base), extremely rare, English 1877-1900, 2 5/8" diameter.* **$5,000-$7,000**

 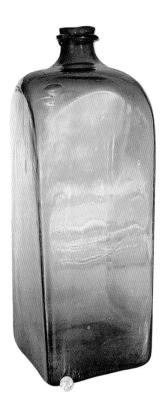 

*Hutchinson bottle, Birmingham / Coca-Cola / Bottling Co., clear, American 1885-1900, 7".* **$1,800-$2,200**

*Large case gin bottle, yellow olive green, Dutch 1740-1760, 18".* **$1,500-$2,000**

*Mineral bottle, Massena Spring / Water, golden yellow amber, quart, American 1880-1885.* **$250-$375**

*Bitters bottle, St / Drakes / 1860 / Plantation / X / Bitters – Patented / 1862, yellow green (citron), American 1862-1875, 9 3/4".* **$1,500-$2,500**

*Gin bottle, Royal Imperial Gin, London, sapphire blue, American 1860-1870, 9 7/8".* **$1,000-$1,200**

Whiskey bottle, Turner
Brothers / New York,
yellow amber, American
1855-1860, 10".
**$400-$600**

Soda bottle, Pomroy &
Hall, rare, American
1840-1860, 7 1/4".
**$500-$800**

◄ *Medicine bottle, Vaughn's / Vegetable / Lithontriptic / Mixture / Buffalo, deep blue aqua, American 1855-1865, 7 5/8".* **$400-$600**

▲ *Pattern-molded globular bottle, 24-rib pattern swirled to left, American 1820-1835, 8".* **$600-$800**

◄ *Sandwich cologne bottle, 12-sided, American 1850-1870, 4 1/2".* **$200-$300**

◄ FAR LEFT *Bunker Hill Monument cologne bottle, American 1875-1890, 11 3/4".* **$800-$1,200**

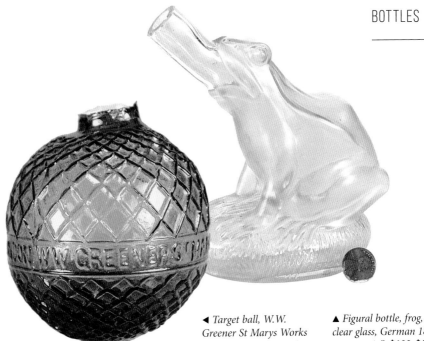

◄ Target ball, W.W. Greener St Marys Works Birmm & 68 Haymarket London, English 1880-1900, 2 5/8" diameter. **$400-$600**

▲ Figural bottle, frog, clear glass, German 1890-1915, 5 1/2". **$120-$160**

Warner bottle, Warner's Safe Cure (around shoulder), American 1880-1890, 9 3/4". **$275-$450**

Barber bottle, fiery opalescent turquoise blue, stars and stripes, American 1885-1925, 7". **$250-$350**

Blown bottle, Pitkin flask, blue green, American 1815-1825, 6 3/8". **$500-$700**

# Celebrity Memorabilia

By Noah Fleisher

**NOAH FLEISHER** received his Bachelor of Fine Arts degree from New York University and brings more than a decade of newspaper, magazine, book, antiques and art experience to his position as Public Relations Director of Heritage Auctions, one of the country's foremost auction houses. He is the former editor of *Antique Trader, New England Antiques Journal* and *Northeast Antiques Journal,* is the author of *Warman's Modern Furniture,* and has been a longtime contributor to *Warman's Antiques & Collectibles.*

As I write this, in the second decade of the 21st century, our relationship with Celebrity – with a capital "C" – is tortured. Reality TV has blurred the line between talent and fame like no other time in pop culture.

While I would like to pen a diatribe against the vapid culture of people who are famous for being famous, this is about the *collectibles*. Fortunately for us, "American Idol" has yet to influence the discussion, and "The Bachelorette" has not yielded a single thing of value.

As it is reflected in collectibles, via celebrity, talent and charisma are held in very high regard. As reflected in collectibles, the past is of intense interest and, as reflected in the material culture of fame that survives to this day – from the earliest days of modern celebrity in the 20th century – of considerable value.

There are evergreen names in celebrity memorabilia – Marilyn Monroe, John Wayne, Elvis Presley, The Beatles (who are so evergreen they have their own section in this book) – that will cost you a pretty penny. You don't have to spend a fortune to start a good collection, however, especially if you are smart about your buying and have a good idea of what you want. If you can't compete for the high profile five- and six-figure items (even millions these days), with an intrepid eye and sensible budget you might just end up surprising yourself with what you can accomplish.

There are a lot of venues to pick up interesting pieces, from eBay to major auction houses to longtime collectors divesting themselves of their treasure. It's a buyer's market right now, no question, though knowing just what to buy and when is a different story. A little luck can go a long way, but so can understanding the market.

No auction house in the world sees the level of quality and variety of celebrity memorabilia that Julien's Auctions in

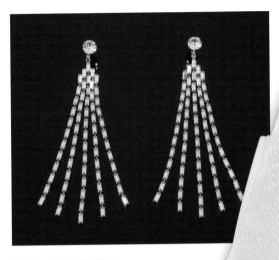

Courtesy of Julien's Auctions

*Marilyn Monroe earrings.*
**$185,000**

Beverly Hills does. From
living celebrities selling their
collections to high-end groupings based
on specific personalities from top collectors, Julien's
is in the thick of it, selling collections of material from and
relating to Elizabeth Taylor, Michael Jackson, Marilyn Monroe,
and Debbie Reynolds, among many. Whether he is on television
promoting his next major event or taking time from his busy
schedule to chat with *Warman's*, Darren Julien, the company's
president and CEO, is always working and, happily for us, willing
to share his insight.

Courtesy of Julien's Auctions

*Charlie Chaplin self-
portrait drawing and
signature.* **$4,688**

"The market is as strong as ever because of the global interest
in Western pop culture and the ease of the Internet, with live
technology for bidding available to anyone anywhere in the
world," Julien said. "Investors now look at celebrity memorabilia
as a way to increase their portfolio. This market has seen a huge
increase due to these factors, and I think it's safe to say it will
only continue to grow."

As Julien sees it, the allure of celebrity memorabilia, like so
many other collectibles, is nostalgia. As he points out, though,
with celebrity items it carries another important dimension:
intimacy with the remote.

"In many cases it's someone buying a memory or something
that reminds them of their childhood or an important/
memorable time in their life," he said. "Celebrities are just
people, too, but society makes them unobtainable objects we

Courtesy of Julien's Auctions

*"Seinfeld" cast-signed finale script.* **$8,320**

can't know or meet. That's where memorabilia comes in. It's a way to have an intimate connection with a celebrity that we otherwise might not be able to have."

Going beyond the evergreen aspect of a celebrity, other factors should be considered: Popularity and longevity – "anyone who's an A list celebrity with a global fan base," as Julien put it. If it's a performer still working, look for legends, for those who've been well-known for decades, such as Bruce Springsteen, Bob Dylan, Cher, Madonna, Barbra Streisand, and the Rolling Stones.

From there, education is key. What differentiates a good piece of memorabilia from a great one? A common piece from a Holy Grail?

"The more iconic the item as it relates to the celebrity, the greater the piece will be," said Julien. "For example, if you have an object historic to an important part of [his/her] career, then it'll be more sought after. Contrast that with an item from a famous film used or worn by an actor that is not collectible. It is also important if the piece is an important part of pop culture history."

For instance, a high-level, highly collectible celebrity can elevate a low-level piece from a failed movie. One of the least successful projects Michael Jackson did in his career was "The

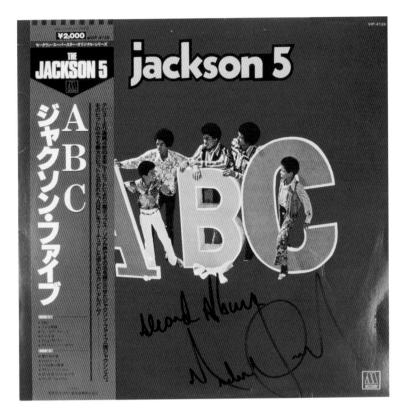

*Michael Jackson
signed and
inscribed album.*
**$1,536**

Wiz," but because he wore something in it or used it as a prop, that piece is now highly collectible because it was part of his career.

"Nothing else associated with that film would be collectible or desirable," Julien added.

All these things matter to Julien when he is evaluating a collection. He looks at the significance of a given film/celebrity/performance. He looks for the global and/or historic import, if it would be sought-after all over the world or just domestically and, most importantly, the authenticity and provenance. This is why, at a certain point in collecting, you need to move beyond an online marketplace and engage someone who can help explain the difference between good and great.

"You really need to make sure you do the research, that you're buying from a reputable source and that you're not buying a 'replica,'" Julien said. "Sometimes people sell items that they genuinely believe to be real, but they're not educated enough to know the difference. You can't just buy something based upon hearsay or a third-party story. Go to or participate in a live auction at a major auction house. There are always deals and steals in live auctions and it's just a matter of being at the

*Lady Gaga 1990 Rolls
Royce convertible.*
**$128,000**

right place at the right time."

While names like Marilyn Monroe and John Wayne are true collector obsessions, are there any celebrities of today that could have even remotely the same impact? That is indeed the million-dollar question, and the answer could be worth well more than that.

"I don't think it's something you can predict," said Julien, "so it's best that, when you're collecting, you do it out of your passion and love for an object and hope that someday it appreciates in value."

Time will tell if either the artist or the memorabilia has any stickiness to them. There is definitely a market emerging in modern celebs. Names like Lady Gaga, Rihanna, Beyoncé, Justin Bieber, and similar pop culture figures are bringing record prices, which Julien attributes to the advances of technology opening the market to a global consumer base. If Americans won't buy Justin Bieber's hat, there are buyers in many other countries happy to do just that.

Most of all, passion for the material is what still drives Julien, even after so many years in the business. His love of the object is what drives him, something we can all take note of and appreciate as collectors.

"I get really excited when I go into our warehouse and see all the historic artifacts that have been part of pop culture history," he said. "I view my job as preserving them and passing them on to owners who will care for and protect their history and value. I love my job. I'm fortunate to do something I love, especially in a great industry like this."

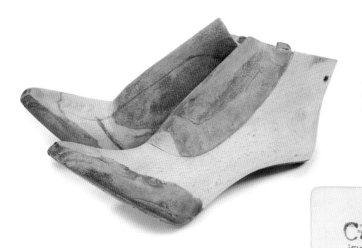

*Farrah Fawcett
custom shoe
molds.* **$128**

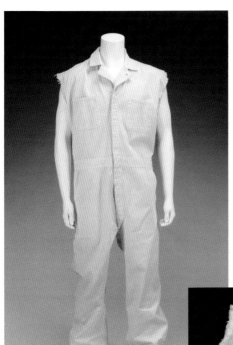

Courtesy of Julien's Auctions

*Johnny Cash passport.* **$5,625**

Courtesy of Julien's Auctions

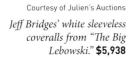

*Jeff Bridges' white sleeveless
coveralls from "The Big
Lebowski."* **$5,938**

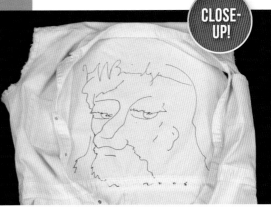

CLOSE-UP!

Courtesy of Julien's Auctions

*Claudette Colbert*
*"Zaza" gown.* **$6,400**

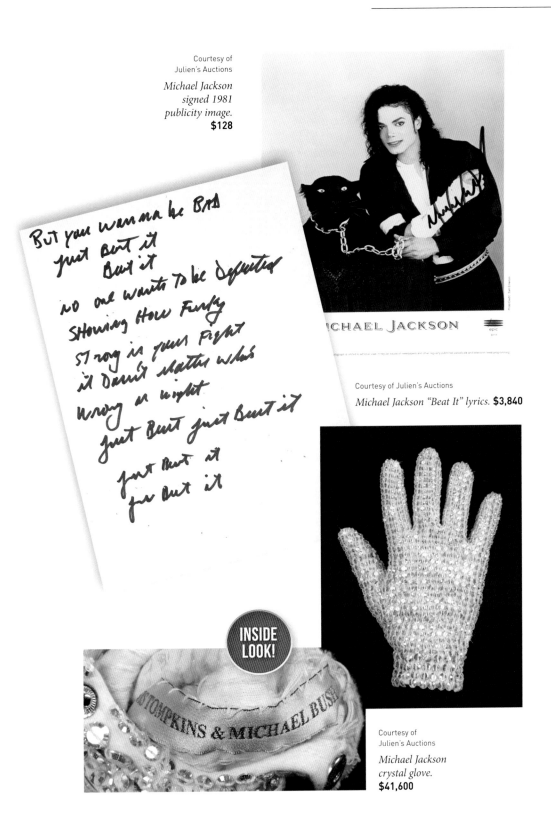

Courtesy of
Julien's Auctions

*Michael Jackson
signed 1981
publicity image.*
**$128**

ICHAEL JACKSON

Courtesy of Julien's Auctions

*Michael Jackson "Beat It" lyrics.* **$3,840**

But you wanna be Bad
just Beat it
Beat it
no one wants To be defeated
shouing How Funky
strong is your Fight
it Doesnt Matter who's
wrong or right
just Beat just Beat it
just Beat it
just Beat it

**INSIDE LOOK!**

TOMPKINS & MICHAEL BUSH

Courtesy of
Julien's Auctions

*Michael Jackson
crystal glove.*
**$41,600**

Courtesy of Julien's Auctions

*Bruce Lee "Game of Death" worn Asics sneakers.* **$12,160**

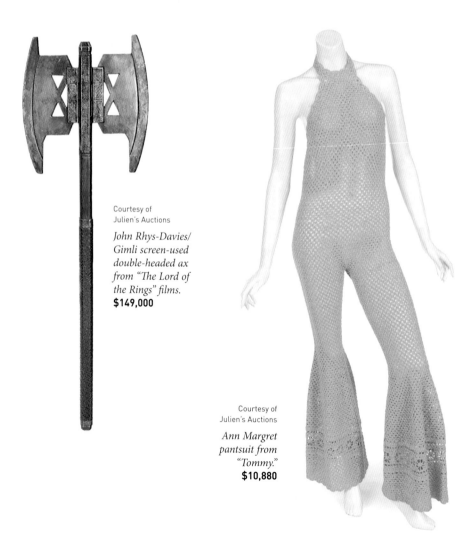

Courtesy of Julien's Auctions

*John Rhys-Davies/ Gimli screen-used double-headed ax from "The Lord of the Rings" films.* **$149,000**

Courtesy of Julien's Auctions

*Ann Margret pantsuit from "Tommy."* **$10,880**

Courtesy of Julien's Auctions
▲ *Frank Sinatra "Love" painting.*
**$8,125**

Courtesy of Julien's Auctions
◄ *Princess Diana photograph
and signature.* **$1,250**

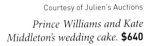

Courtesy of Julien's Auctions
*Prince Williams and Kate
Middleton's wedding cake.* **$640**

Courtesy of Julien's Auctions

*Jonathan Winters original painting.* **$4,688**

Courtesy of Julien's Auctions

*James Brown "Sex" jumpsuit.*
**$10,000**

Courtesy of Julien's Auctions

*David Bowie signed poster.* **$512**

Courtesy of Julien's Auctions

*Olivia de Havilland Broadway theater trunk.* **$2,560**

**CLOSE-UP!**

*LANA TURNER
2256*

Courtesy of Julien's Auctions

*Lana Turner "Honky Tonk" gown.* **$2,813**

Courtesy of Julien's Auctions

*Cream signed cut sheets: Clapton, Bruce and Baker.* **$250**

**CLOSE-UP!**

Courtesy of Julien's Auctions

*Justin Timberlake concert tour vest.* **$3,520.**

Courtesy of Julien's Auctions

*James Gandolfini/ Tony Soprano hospital gown.* **$448**

Courtesy of Julien's Auctions
*Jimi Hendrix's first stage-used guitar.*
**$64,000**

Courtesy of Julien's Auctions
*Bruce Lee wooden octagon nunchakus.*
**$4,160**

FRONT
VIEW

Courtesy of Julien's Auctions
*David Hasselhoff 1986 DH Pontiac Firebird two-door hatchback Kitt.* **$152,600**

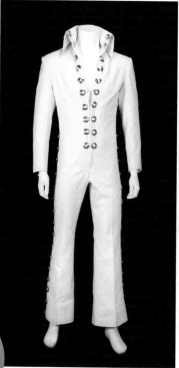

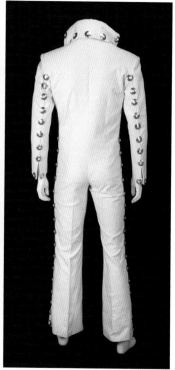

Courtesy of Julien's Auctions

▲ *Elvis Presley stage worn jumpsuit.* **$197,000**

Courtesy of Julien's Auctions

▲ *Elvis Presley stage-played Martin acoustic guitar.* **$44,800**

CLOSE-UP!

Courtesy of Julien's Auctions

*Miles Davis Emsley purple velvet jacket.* **$10,000**

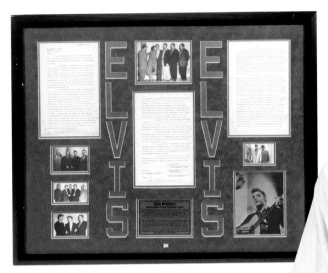

◄ *Elvis Presley 1955 contract with Col. Tom Parker.* **$96,000**

*David Hasselhoff signed "Baywatch" robe.* **$75**

*Marilyn Monroe hair roller.* **$1,125**

*Elvis Presley-owned* Autobiography of a Yogi. **$512**

Courtesy of Julien's Auctions

*Harry Houdini handcuffs.* **$3,840**

Courtesy of Heritage Auctions

*Bruce Springsteen handwritten lyrics to song "The E Street Shuffle," penned entirely by Springsteen.* **$4,113**

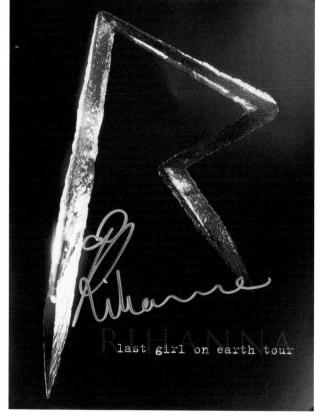

Courtesy of Julien's Auctions

*Rihanna "Last Girl on Earth" tour signed program.* **$125**

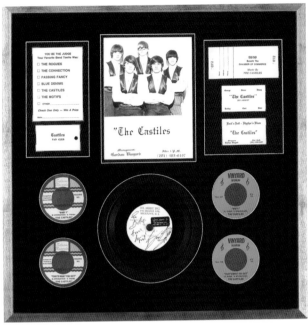

Courtesy of Julien's Auctions

*Madonna Best Video VMA Moonman.* **$20,480**

Courtesy of Heritage Auctions

*Bruce Springsteen–The Castiles signed record and memorabilia display. The band recorded a single on acetate ("Baby I" backed with "That's What You Get," written in the back of a car en route to the studio) during their brief existence, and it has never been released. Seven copies were printed and only three are believed to still exist.* **$10,755**

Courtesy of Julien's Auctions

*Cher "Will & Grace" show-worn leather jacket.* **$11,250**

Courtesy of Julien's Auctions

*Rihanna stage-worn leather playsuit.* **$10,625**

Courtesy of Julien's Auctions

*Kurt Cobain signed drawings.*
**$10,000**

Courtesy of Julien's Auctions

*The Rolling Stones signed photograph.* **$1,280**

Courtesy of Julien's Auctions

*Greta Garbo United States immigrant identification card.*
**$5,440**

Courtesy of Julien's Auctions

*Various film stars' signed checks.* **$896**

Courtesy of Julien's Auctions

*Humphrey Bogart cigarette lighter.* **$19,200**

Courtesy of Julien's Auctions

*Marilyn Monroe 1952* Photoplay *award.* **$100,000**

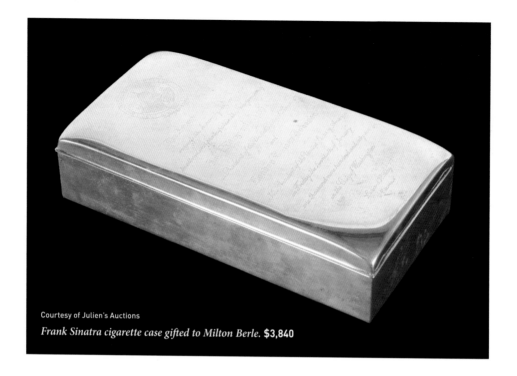

Courtesy of Julien's Auctions

*Frank Sinatra cigarette case gifted to Milton Berle.* **$3,840**

Courtesy of Julien's Auctions

*Elizabeth Taylor prescription bottle.* **$1,250**

Courtesy of Julien's Auctions

*Marilyn Monroe inscribed photograph.* **$9,600**

# CERAMICS

# American Ceramics

## Fiesta

The Homer Laughlin China Co. originated with a two-kiln pottery on the banks of the Ohio River in East Liverpool, Ohio. Built in 1873-'74 by Homer Laughlin and his brother, Shakespeare, the firm was first known as the Ohio Valley Pottery, and later Laughlin Bros. Pottery. It was one of the first whiteware plants in the country.

After a tentative beginning, the company was awarded a prize for having the best whiteware at the 1876 Centennial Exposition in Philadelphia.

Three years later, Shakespeare sold his interest in the business to Homer, who continued on until 1897. At that time, Homer Laughlin sold his interest in the newly incorporated firm to a group of investors, including Charles, Louis, and Marcus Aaron and the company bookkeeper, William E. Wells.

Under new ownership in 1907, the headquarters and a new 30-kiln plant were built across the Ohio River in Newell, West Virginia, the present manufacturing and headquarters location.

In the 1920s, two additions to the Homer Laughlin staff set the stage for the company's greatest success: the Fiesta line.

Dr. Albert V. Bleininger was hired in 1920. A scientist, author, and educator, he oversaw the conversion from bottle kilns to the more efficient tunnel kilns.

In 1927, the company hired designer Frederick Hurten Rhead, a member of a distinguished family of English ceramists. Having previously worked at Weller Pottery and Roseville Pottery, Rhead began to develop the artistic quality of the company's wares, and to experiment with shapes and glazes. In 1935, this work culminated in his designs for the Fiesta line.

▲ *Fruit bowls in original six colors, 4 3/4" diameter.* **$93**

For more information on Fiesta, see *Warman's Fiesta Identification and Price Guide* by Glen Victorey.

## Fiesta Colors

From 1936 to 1972, Fiesta was produced in 14 colors (other than special promotions). These colors are usually divided into the "original colors" of cobalt blue, light green, ivory, red, turquoise, and yellow (cobalt blue, light green, red, and yellow only on the Kitchen Kraft line, introduced in 1939); the "1950s colors" of chartreuse, forest green, gray, and rose (introduced in 1951); medium green (introduced in 1959); plus the later additions of Casuals, Amberstone, Fiesta Ironstone, and Casualstone ("Coventry") in antique gold, mango red, and turf green; and the striped, decal, and Lustre pieces. No Fiesta was produced from 1973 to 1985. The colors that make up the "original" and "1950s" groups are sometimes referred to as "the standard 11."

In many pieces, medium green is the hardest to find and the most valuable Fiesta color.

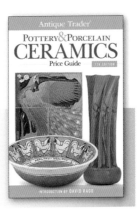

**RECOMMENDED READING**

**Antique Trader Pottery & Porcelain Ceramics Price Guide.** More than 3,000 color photos, descriptions and values for 150 companies, including Fiesta, McCoy, Roseville, Red Wing, Weller, Wedgwood, and others big and small. www.krausebooks.com

Courtesy of Strawser Auctions

▶ *Cobalt chop plate,*
*13" diameter.* **$23**

Courtesy of Strawser Auctions

▼ *Plates in all 11 colors,*
*10" diameter.* **$116**

Courtesy of Strawser Auctions

*Rose demitasse cup*
*and saucer.* **$151**

## Fiesta Colors and Years of Production to 1972

Antique Gold—dark butterscotch ................................. 1969-1972
Chartreuse—yellowish green ........................................... 1951-1959
Cobalt Blue—dark or royal blue ..................................... 1936-1951
Forest Green—dark hunter green .................................. 1951-1959
Gray—light or ash gray ..................................................... 1951-1959
Green—often called light green when comparing it to
    other green glazes; also called "Original" green ........... 1936-1951
Ivory—creamy, slightly yellowed .................................... 1936-1951
Mango Red—same as original red ................................. 1970-1972
Medium Green—bright rich green .................................. 1959-1969
Red—reddish orange ............................ 1936-1944 and 1959-1972
Rose—dusty, dark pink ...................................................... 1951-1959
Turf Green—olive ................................................................ 1969-1972
Turquoise—sky blue, like the stone ............................... 1937-1969
Yellow—golden yellow ...................................................... 1936-1969

Courtesy of Strawser Auctions

*Turquoise teapot and creamer and sugar set.* **$91**

Courtesy of Strawser Auctions

*Cobalt Kitchen Kraft platter with metal holder.* **$81**

Courtesy of Strawser Auctions

*Medium green individual salad bowl.* **$70**

Courtesy of Strawser Auctions

*Red syrup pitcher.* **$205**

Courtesy of
Strawser Auctions

*Five compartment
plates in red (some
wear), yellow, cobalt,
green, and ivory, 12"
diameter.* **$110**

Courtesy of Strawser Auctions
*Medium green platter.* **$81**

Courtesy of Strawser Auctions
◀ *Cobalt syrup pitcher.* **$232**

Courtesy of
Strawser Auctions
◀ *Chartreuse eggcup.*
**$93**

◀ *Red chop plate, 13" diameter.* **$35**

*Yellow Kitchen Kraft fork and pie server.* **$110**

*Chartreuse ashtray.* **$81**

*Utility trays in original six colors, nicks to red and cobalt trays.* **$81**

Courtesy of Strawser Auctions

▲ *Dark green chop plate, 15" diameter.* **$46**

Courtesy of Strawser Auctions

▶ *Red sweets compote.* **$110**

Courtesy of Strawser Auctions

◀ *Six eggcups in original six colors.* **$197**

▲ *Turquoise World's Fair potter plates.* **$42**

▲ *Yellow cake plate.* **$493**

▶ FAR RIGHT *Red vase, 12" high.* **$696**

▶ *Turquoise syrup pitcher.* **$230**

Courtesy of Strawser Auctions

◄ *Kitchen Kraft five-piece stack set with red lid, nick to one yellow unit.* **$220**

Courtesy of Strawser Auctions

*Yellow onion soup bowl with lid, scratch to lid.* **$435**

Courtesy of Strawser Auctions

▲ *Cobalt Kitchen Kraft medium covered jar.* **$220**

Courtesy of Strawser Auctions

*Five medium green fruit bowls, nick to one, 5 1/2" diameter.* **$128**

Courtesy of
Strawser Auctions
*Four
compartment
plates in rose,
gray, dark green,
and chartreuse,
10 1/2" diameter.*
**$197**

Courtesy of Strawser Auctions
*Mocha World's Fair potter plates.* **$36**

Courtesy of Strawser Auctions
*Turquoise bulb candle
holders.* **$81**

# Fulper

The firm that became Fulper Pottery Co. of Flemington, New Jersey, originally made stoneware pottery and utilitarian wares beginning in the early 1800s. Fulper made art pottery from about 1909 to 1935.

The company's earliest artware was called the VaseKraft line (1910-1915). Its middle period (1915-1925) included some of the earlier shapes, but it also incorporated Oriental forms. Its glazing at this time was less consistent but more diverse. The last period (1925-1935) was characterized by Art Deco forms.

FULPER in a rectangle is known as the "ink mark" and dates from 1910-1915. The second mark, which dates from 1915-1925, was incised or in black ink. The final mark, FULPER, die-stamped, dates from about 1925 to 1935.

Courtesy of Mark Mussio, Humler & Nolan

*Ribbed vase in green crystalline glaze over which white glaze has been dripped from rim, impressed on bottom with Fulper in block letters and 4031, overall crazing, 4 7/8" high; bulbous ribbed vase in blue flambé glaze over which white glaze has been dripped from rim, marked on bottom with impressed F, fine crazing, 7".* **$120**

Courtesy of Mark Mussio, Humler & Nolan

▲ *Effigy bowl with three hominoid creatures holding it aloft, glazed in combination of blue flambé over green mat, craze lines in bowl due to heavy glazing, repairs to rim and base, 7 1/8" high x 10" diameter.* **$100**

Courtesy of Rago Arts

▼ *Four vessels, 1910-1916, two crescent moon flower holders and two small vases in crystalline glazes, vertical marks, paper labels, tallest 11" x 10" high.* **$750**

Courtesy of Mark Mussio, Humler & Nolan

▲ *Pilgrim flask vase in Flemington Green glaze with blue highlights over cream high glaze, marked with Fulper vertical ink stamp, small open glaze bubbles, 10" high.* **$225**

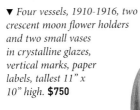

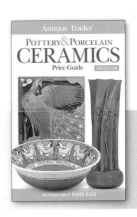

*Pair of flower frogs showing Egyptian women standing on scarabs, one in mustard flambé glaze and other in green flambé, green one marked on bottom with rectangular Fulper ink stamp, broken at waist and repaired, mustard one not marked, tight line at base, both 7 1/2" high.* **$250**

*Vase with twin ring handles in Cat's Eye flambé glaze, marked on bottom with Fulper vertical racetrack ink stamp, excellent condition, 12 1/2" high.* **$375**

*Bowl cast with five leaping fish encircling interior in frothy brown flambé over Flemington Green glaze, excellent original condition, 2 7/8" high x 11 3/8" diameter.* **$750**

Courtesy of Belhorn Auctions, LLC

*Handled vase in microcrystalline black glaze, marked with vertical Fulper ink stamp, excellent condition, 9" wide x 6" high.* **$130**

Courtesy of Mark Mussio,
Humler & Nolan

*Bullet vase in Copper Dust crystalline glaze, marked on bottom with Fulper vertical racetrack ink stamp and impressed 530, two firing separations on one handle, 6 1/2" high.* **$350**

Courtesy of Rago Arts

◀ *Two doorstops, "Bum" bull pup in mat mustard glaze and Siamese cat in Cat's Eye flambé glaze, 1910s, both with vertical marks, dog 8 1/4" x 11", cat 5 3/4" x 9 1/2" high.* **$1,125**

Courtesy of Rago Arts

*Four potpourri jars, 1910-1920, all marked, 4 3/4" x 3 1/2" high.* **$750**

Courtesy of Belhorn Auctions, LLC

*Shell vase in blue, marked Fulper 4054, excellent condition with minor roughness to rim, 11 1/2" wide.* **$25**

Courtesy of Belhorn Auctions, LLC

*Heavy and broad vase, marked with vertical ink stamp, mint condition, 10 3/4" wide x 7 1/2" high.* **$145**

Courtesy of Mark Mussio, Humler & Nolan

◀ *Twin-handled vase in Mirror Black over rose mat glaze, blue highlights where Mirror Black meets rose, marked on bottom with raised vertical oval mark and original Fulper paper label, excellent original condition, 10 3/4" high.* **$275**

Courtesy of Mark Mussio, Humler & Nolan

*Rare Norse jar in Mirror Black glaze, bottom marked with raised racetrack mark, circular firing separation, professional repairs to body of jar, one leg, and base, 10 1/4" high.* **$200**

Courtesy of Belhorn Auctions, LLC

*Matte blue vase marked with vertical Fulper ink stamp, mint condition, 6 3/4" high.* **$35**

Courtesy of Belhorn Auctions, LLC

*Broad three-handled jar in microcrystalline blue glaze, marked Fulper 4084, opposing vertical cracks, 12" wide.* **$65**

Courtesy of Mark Mussio,
Humler & Nolan

*Cat doorstop in light green crystalline glaze, impressed FULPER on base in block letters, chip on right ear, glaze misses at base, small open glaze bubbles, 6 3/4" high.* **$400**

Courtesy of Belhorn Auctions, LLC

*Vase with three squared handles, marked with vertical Fulper ink stamp, mint condition, 4 1/8" high.* **$75**

Courtesy of Belhorn Auctions, LLC

*Shouldered vase with vertical Fulper mark obscured by heavy glaze, mint condition, 4 1/4" high.* **$70**

Courtesy of Jeffrey S. Evans & Associates

▲ *Art Deco porcelain "mademoiselle" two-part lamp and powder jar, upper section formed as figure of young woman holding fan over voluminous skirt, cylindrical base painted with ribbon garland with floral bouquets, each with impressed maker's mark, jar base stamped "323" and lamp base stamped "317," circa 1925, lamp 7" high, powder jar base with light 1" diagonal hairline off rim.* **$196**

Courtesy of Belhorn Auctions, LLC

◄ *Flower holder in form of Native American Indian in canoe, marked with Fulper ink stamp, excellent condition, 7 1/4" long.* **$325**

# Grueby

William Grueby was active in the ceramic industry for several years before he developed his own method of producing matte-glazed pottery and founded the Grueby Faience Co. of Boston in 1897.

The art pottery was hand-thrown in natural shapes, hand-molded and hand-tooled. A variety of colored glazes, singly or in combinations, was produced, but green was the most popular. In 1908, the firm was divided into the Grueby Pottery Co. and the Grueby Faience and Tile Co. The Grueby Faience and Tile Co. made art tile until 1917, although its pottery production was phased out about 1910.

Courtesy of Rago Arts and Auction Center

*Spherical vase carved with leaves, circa 1905, circular pottery stamp, chip to rim, 3 3/4" x 4".* **$3,000**

*Vase in mustard-colored matte glaze, marked, impressed logo on base, overall very good condition, minor crazing, 5 1/2" wide x 3" high.* **$458**

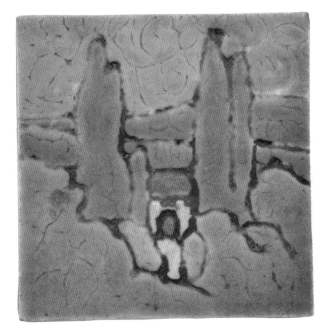

*Tile with landscape decoration of house flanked by cypress trees, polychrome glaze, marked, minor chips to corners, 4 1/4" square.* **$1,625**

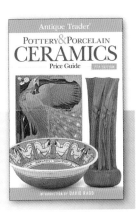

Courtesy of Mark Mussio, Humler & Nolan

*Flower form bowl in mat green glaze, marked on bottom with circular Grueby Pottery Boston USA mark and incised with initials of artist Ruth Erickson, fine crazing inside vessel and professional repair to rim, 2" high x 6" wide.* **$700**

Courtesy of Treadway/Toomey Auctions

*Vase with tapered shape and carved geometric design under suspended green matte glaze, impressed mark, minor factory imperfections, impressed logo and painted 174 on base, overall very good condition, 4" wide x 4 1/2" high.* **$671**

◄ *Bowl in unusual
cream-colored
matte glaze and
green interior,
marked, #96?,
impressed logo on
base, overall very
good condition,
minor crazing, 5"
wide x 2" high.*
**$305**

*Ovoid form vase with carved leaf
design in oatmeal-colored glaze,
incised cipher, probably for Annie
Lingley, minor crazing, 4" wide x
5" high.* **$915**

◄ *Rare, tall vase with curdled
blue glaze and carved irises, circa
1905, circular pottery stamp,
incised RE (Ruth Erickson), light
wear to widest part of vase,
14 3/4" x 9".* **$26,000**

Courtesy of Treadway/Toomey Auctions

*Vase with tapered shape and trefoil top, carved and applied leaves and buds, in suspended green matte glaze, marked, impressed logo on base, overall very good condition, 5" wide x 7" high.* **$1,342**

Courtesy of Treadway/Toomey Auctions

*Rare wall pocket, unusual shape with carved and applied leaves, suspended green matte glaze, 3 1/2" wide x 8 1/2" long.* **$1,952**

Courtesy of Treadway/
Toomey Auctions

*Scarab in light green matte glaze, marked, impressed logo on base, overall very good condition, minor crazing, 2 1/2" wide x 3 1/2" long.* **$1,830**

◀ *Tile with tulip, circa 1905, unmarked, chip to bottom right corner, restoration to areas around edges, glaze shaved off one side, 1" x 6" square.* **$550**

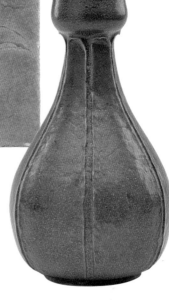

▲ *Gourd-shaped vase carved with leaves, circa 1905, circular faience stamp/101, incised MS (Marie Seaman), flecks to high points of leaves, 8 1/2" x 4 1/2".* **$5,500**

◀ *Round vase in thick, leathery green mat glaze, impressed Grueby logo on base, excellent original condition, 4 1/2" high.* **$800**

Courtesy of Belhorn Auctions, LLC

▲ *Framed tile with musician, unmarked, excellent condition, 6" square, 11 3/4" square with frame.* **$425**

Courtesy of Treadway/Toomey Auctions

▶ *Classic form vase in suspended green matte glaze, marked, impressed logo on base, restoration at rim, minor crazing, 5 1/2" wide x 8" high.* **$732**

Courtesy of Belhorn Auctions, LLC

▲ *Vase with curdled blue glaze, impressed circular Grueby mark, repaired chips to rim, 12 1/8" high.* **$1,000**

Courtesy of Rago Arts and Auction Center

*Vase with lobed rim and full-height leaves and buds, curdled green glaze, circa 1905, obscured stamp, glaze pop to body, some minor efflorescence, light wear around rim, 7 1/2" x 4 1/2".* **$1,600**

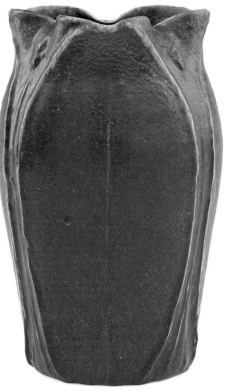

Courtesy of Skinner, Inc.; www.skinnerinc.com

▲ *Art pottery tile decorated by Kiichi Yamada, Cuenca decoration of turtle under garland of leaves in yellow, brown, and green glazes, white clay body, decorator's initials on back, chip, 1" x 6" square.* **$1,476**

Courtesy of Mark Mussio, Humler & Nolan

◄ *Low bowl in oatmeal-colored mat glaze on exterior and high glaze on interior, impressed on bottom with circular Grueby logo, grinding chips on base and heavy crazing, 1 7/8" high x 5" diameter.* **$150**

# Hull Pottery

In 1905, Addis E. Hull purchased the Acme Pottery Co. of Crooksville, Ohio. In 1917, the A.E. Hull Pottery Co. began making art pottery, novelties, stoneware and kitchenware, later including the famous Little Red Riding Hood line. Most items had a matte finish with shades of pink, blue, and brown predominating.

After a flood and fire in 1950, the factory reopened in 1952 as the Hull Pottery Co. New pieces, mostly with a glossy finish, were produced. The firm closed in 1985.

Pre-1950 vases are marked "Hull USA" or "Hull Art USA" on the bottom. Many also retain their paper labels. Post-1950 pieces are marked "Hull" in large script or "HULL" in block letters.

Each pattern has a distinctive letter or number, e.g., Wildflower has a "W" and a number; Water Lily, "L" and number; Poppy, numbers in the 600s; Orchid, numbers in the 300s. Early stoneware pieces are marked with an "H."

For more information on Hull Pottery, see *Warman's Hull Pottery Identification and Price Guide* by David Doyle.

Courtesy of Belhorn Auctions, LLC

▲ *Woodland Gloss ewer, marked Hull USA W3-5 1/2", mint condition, 6" high.* **$5**

Courtesy of Belhorn Auctions, LLC

▶ *Woodland Gloss window box, marked Hull USA W14-10", chips to rim, 10" long.* **$6**

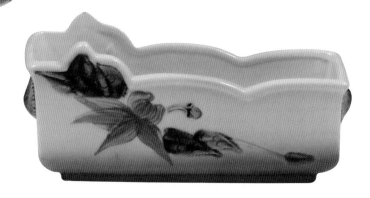

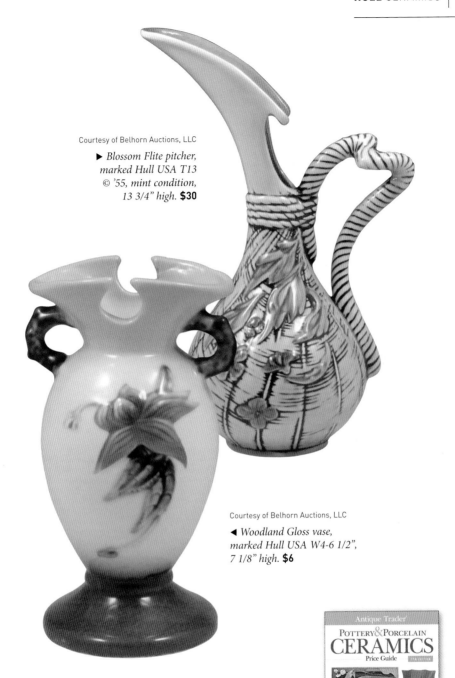

Courtesy of Belhorn Auctions, LLC

▶ *Blossom Flite pitcher,
marked Hull USA T13
© '55, mint condition,
13 3/4" high.* **$30**

Courtesy of Belhorn Auctions, LLC

◀ *Woodland Gloss vase,
marked Hull USA W4-6 1/2",
7 1/8" high.* **$6**

**RECOMMENDED
READING**

**Antique Trader Pottery & Porcelain Ceramics
Price Guide.** More than 3,000 color photos,
descriptions and values for 150 companies,
including Fiesta, McCoy, Roseville, Red Wing,
Weller, Wedgwood, and others big and small.
www.krausebooks.com

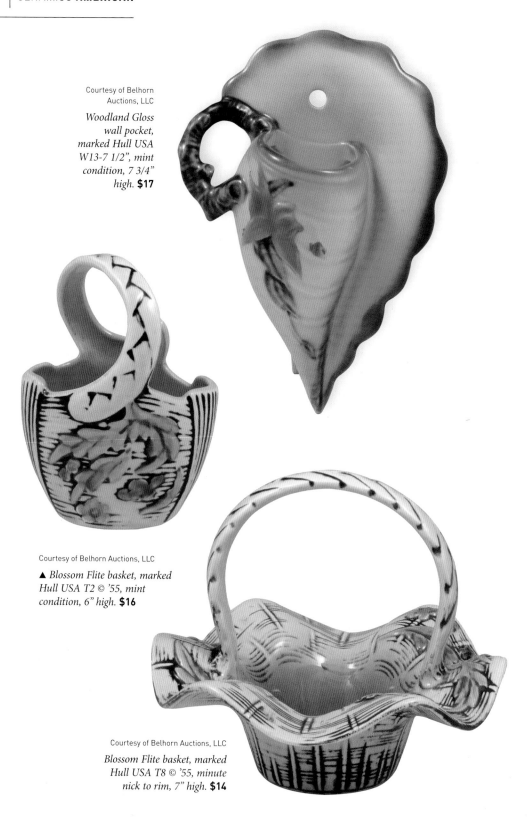

Courtesy of Belhorn Auctions, LLC

*Woodland Gloss wall pocket, marked Hull USA W13-7 1/2", mint condition, 7 3/4" high.* **$17**

Courtesy of Belhorn Auctions, LLC

▲ *Blossom Flite basket, marked Hull USA T2 © '55, mint condition, 6" high.* **$16**

Courtesy of Belhorn Auctions, LLC

*Blossom Flite basket, marked Hull USA T8 © '55, minute nick to rim, 7" high.* **$14**

Courtesy of Belhorn Auctions, LLC

*Open Rose tea set with teapot, creamer and sugar, marked Hull USA 110-8 1/2", 111-5", and 112-5", excellent condition.* **$50**

Courtesy of Belhorn Auctions, LLC

*Corky Pig Bank, marked Pat Pend Corky Pig HPCo C 1957 USA, mint condition, 7" wide.* **$20**

Courtesy of Belhorn Auctions, LLC

*Orchid bookend set, marked Hull USA 316-7x5, chip to back edge of one bookend, 7" wide.* **$50**

Courtesy of Belhorn Auctions, LLC

*Two Hull novelty hippo planters in green and brown, marked Hull USA 68, mint condition, 9" wide.* **$30**

Courtesy of Belhorn Auctions, LLC

*Little Red Riding Hood salt and pepper shakers, marked Pat. Des. No. 135889, excellent condition with slight loss to some transfers, 3 3/8" high.* **$25**

Courtesy of Belhorn Auctions, LLC

*Parchment & Pine vase and teapot, marked Hull USA S-15, excellent condition, teapot 7" high.* **$20**

*Blossom Flite
honey jug,
marked Hull
USA T1 © '55,
mint condition,
6" high.*
**$16**

*Tropicana T51 flower dish, marked Hull USA 51,
excellent condition with small factory clay blemish
on tip of rim, 15 1/4" wide.* **$60**

*Wildflower basket, marked Hull Art USA W-16-10
1/2", mint condition, 11" high.* **$30**

Courtesy of Belhorn Auctions, LLC

*Woodland Gloss cornucopia,
marked Hull USA W10-11",
mint condition, 11 1/2" long.* **$16**

Courtesy of Belhorn Auctions, LLC

*Corky Pig Bank, marked Corky
Pig C USA 1957 HPCo., mint
condition, 7 1/2" wide.* **$40**

Courtesy of Belhorn Auctions, LLC

*Woodland Gloss flowerpot with attached saucer, marked Hull USA
W11-5 3/4", large chip to rim and chip to saucer, 6" high.* **$6**

Courtesy of Belhorn Auctions, LLC

*Sitting Corky Pig Bank, marked
Hull USA 196, mint condition, 6"
high.* **$40**

# McCoy Pottery

The first McCoy with clay under his fingernails was W. Nelson McCoy. With his uncle, W.F. McCoy, he founded a pottery works in Putnam, Ohio, in 1848, making stoneware crocks and jugs.

That same year, W. Nelson's son, James W., was born in Zanesville, Ohio. James established the J.W. McCoy Pottery Co. in Roseville, Ohio, in the fall of 1899. The J.W. McCoy plant was destroyed by fire in 1903 and was rebuilt two years later.

It was at this time that the first examples of Loy-Nel-Art wares were produced. The line's distinctive title came from the names of James McCoy's three sons, Lloyd, Nelson, and Arthur.

George Brush became general manager of J.W. McCoy Pottery Co. in 1909, the company became Brush-McCoy Pottery Co. in 1911, and the name was shortened to Brush Pottery Co. in 1925. This firm remained in business until 1982.

Separately, in 1910, Nelson McCoy, Sr. founded the Nelson McCoy Sanitary and Stoneware Co., also in Roseville. By the early 1930s, production had shifted from utilitarian wares to art pottery, and the company name was changed to Nelson McCoy Pottery.

Designer Sydney Cope was hired in 1934, and was joined by his son, Leslie, in 1936. The Copes' influence on McCoy wares continued until Sydney's death in 1966. That same year, Leslie

Courtesy of
Rich Penn Auctions

*McCoy pitcher and four mugs, Frontier Family, pitcher in excellent condition, one mug in good condition, other three in excellent condition, 9 1/2" and 6 1/2" high.*
**$25-$50**

Courtesy of Mark Mussio, Humler & Nolan

▲ *Pair of Brush-McCoy Jewel candlesticks, marked only with number 030 on bottom of each, excellent original condition, 7" high.* **$275**

Courtesy of Fox Auctions

▶ *Nelson McCoy art pottery vase, relief floral with matte blue glaze, Arts & Crafts era, two glaze flakes, 8" high.* **$80**

Courtesy of Woody Auction

▲ *McCoy figural cookie jar of Native American Indian teepee, marked, chip on top of lid, 11" high.* **$40**

opened a gallery devoted to his family's design heritage and featuring his own original art.

Nelson McCoy, Sr. died in 1945, and was succeeded as company president by his nephew, Nelson McCoy Melick.

A fire destroyed the plant in 1950, but company officials – including Nelson McCoy, Jr., then 29 – decided to rebuild, and the new Nelson McCoy Pottery Co. was up and running in just six months.

Nelson Melick died in 1954. Nelson McCoy, Jr. became company president and oversaw the company's continued growth. In 1967, the operation was sold to entrepreneur David Chase. At this time, the words "Mt. Clemens Pottery" were added to the company marks. In 1974, Chase sold the company to Lancaster Colony Corp., and the company marks included a stylized "LCC" logo. Nelson, Jr. and his wife, Billie, who had served as a products supervisor, left the company in 1981.

In 1985, the company was sold again, this time to Designer Accents. The McCoy pottery factory closed in 1990.

For more information on McCoy pottery, see *Warman's McCoy Pottery,* 2nd edition, by Mark F. Moran.

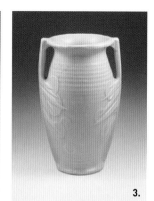

1.  2.  3.

4.  5.  6.

Images courtesy of Belhorn Auctions, LLC

**1.** *Brush McCoy Rockraft candleholders, unmarked, mint condition, 4 7/8" high.* **$210**

**2.** *Brush McCoy Onyx vase with unusual glaze treatment, marked 18, excellent condition, 6 1/4" high.* **$130**

**3.** *McCoy handled "sand dollar" vase in light green, marked USA, chip to molded design, 14" high.* **$35**

**4.** *McCoy flower planter with hand coloration, signed Leslie Cope over glaze, marked McCoy, excellent condition, 5" high x 7 1/2" long.* **$50**

**5.** *Two McCoy blended glaze jardinieres, unmarked, some small nicks, otherwise excellent condition, 8" wide x 6 1/2" high.* **$15**

**6.** *McCoy Art Deco vase in burgundy red gloss, unmarked, scratch to glaze, 10" high.* **$25**

7.

8.

9.

10.

11.

12.

Images courtesy of Belhorn Auctions, LLC

**7.** *McCoy blended glaze jardiniere, unmarked, excellent condition.* **$10**

**8.** *McCoy Art Deco vase in semi-matte periwinkle purple, unmarked, excellent condition, 10" high.* **$10**

**9.** *McCoy vase in white, unmarked, chips to base and glaze pops to body, 8" high.* **$5.50**

**10.** *McCoy fin vase in white gloss, unmarked, small spider line to body, otherwise excellent condition, 14 1/4" high.* **$65**

**11.** *McCoy four-piece train decanter set, all pieces marked, excellent condition, longest piece 13 1/2" long.* **$30**

**12.** *Brush McCoy early stoneware vase with stylized wheat, marked 526, mint condition, 6" high.* **$10**

# Red Wing Pottery

Various potteries operated in Red Wing, Minnesota, starting in 1868, the most successful being the Red Wing Stoneware Co., organized in 1877. Merged with other local potteries through the years, it became known as Red Wing Union Stoneware Co. in 1906 and was one of the largest producers of utilitarian stoneware items in the United States.

After a decline in the popularity of stoneware products, an art pottery line was introduced to compensate for the loss. This was reflected in a new name for the company, Red Wing Potteries, Inc., in 1936. Stoneware production ceased entirely in 1947, but vases, planters, cookie jars, and dinnerware of art pottery quality continued in production until 1967, when the pottery ceased operation altogether.

For more information on Red Wing pottery, see *Warman's Red Wing Pottery Identification and Price Guide* by Mark F. Moran.

Courtesy of Cedarburg Auction Co., Inc.

▲ *Signed gray line sponge-banded nesting mixing bowl set with eight bowls, two with advertising in them, one reads, "It pays to mix with C. W. Shaffer, Branch Wis.," 4 1/2" high x 7" wide; second bowl reads, "Compliments of Wetzel's Grocery, Phone 591, Fort Atkinson," 4" high x 6" wide; remainder of bowls: 5 1/2" x 11", 5" x 10", 4" x 9", 4 1/2" x 8 1/4", 3 1/2" x 5 1/4", 3 1/4" x 4".* **$791**

Courtesy of Rich Penn Auctions

▶ *Stoneware water cooler, five-gallon capacity with bar handle lid marked "W," large wing and Union Stoneware Co. oval, area of surface loss and crow's foot inside bottom, otherwise cooler and lid in excellent condition, 16 1/2" high.* **$270**

Courtesy of Cedarburg Auction Co., Inc.

*Twelve-gallon crock with bale handles, patented 1926.* **$79**

Courtesy of Cedarburg Auction Co., Inc.

▲ *Rare stoneware wall-hung saltbox with original cover and advertisement, "Compliments / of / J. J. Wolfram / 1934 / Hart, Minn.," good condition, 7 1/2" high with lid x 5 1/2" wide.* **$1,413**

Courtesy of Cedarburg Auction Co., Inc.

▲ *Rare covered blue band salt glazed butter crock or pantry jar with formed cover and Red Wing logo, minor flake to base, 6" high x 7 1/4" wide.* **$311**

Courtesy of Cedarburg Auction Co., Inc.

◄ *Paneled spongeware bowl, 5 1/2" high x 10" wide.* **$57**

*Petal-lid
stoneware crock
cover, 13" wide.* **$90**

*Three-gallon
stoneware
jug in good
condition.* **$34**

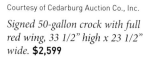

*Signed 50-gallon crock with full
red wing, 33 1/2" high x 23 1/2"
wide.* **$2,599**

*Rare salesman sample open
miniature drainpipe, "Red Wing /
Sewer Pipe / Co / Redwing Minn,"
2 1/2" high x 3" wide.* **$226**

Courtesy of Cedarburg Auction Co., Inc.

*Gray line, sponge-banded, ribbed wall-hung salt crock, no cover, 7 1/2" high x 5 1/2" wide.* **$848**

Courtesy of Cedarburg Auction Co., Inc.

*Rare signed 60-gallon crock with spout hole and full red wing, 35" high x 25" wide.* **$4,577**

Courtesy of Cedarburg Auction Co., Inc.

▲ *Twenty-five gallon stoneware leaf mark crock, insignia in blue, "Red Wing Union Stoneware Co. Redwing, Minn," 21" high x 22" wide.* **$226**

Courtesy of Cedarburg Auction Co., Inc.

◄ *Rare crock marked with large red wing, interior manufacturing line inside crock in clay and overglazed, 8" high x 7 1/2" wide.* **$339**

Courtesy of Jeffrey S. Evans & Associates

▶ *No. 1454L modern art pottery wall sconces, blue fleck, scroll wall plate supporting cone-form single-socket candleholder, back incised "RED WING / U.S.A. / 1454 / L," mid-20th century, 11 3/4" high overall x 5 3/4" wide overall.* **$108**

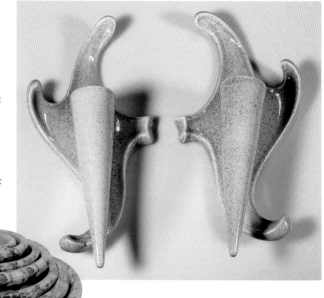

Courtesy of Cedarburg Auction Co., Inc.

▼ *Set of seven nesting spongeware paneled bowls, good condition, 6" high x 11" wide, 5 1/2" high x 10" wide, 5" high x 9" wide, 4 1/4" high x 8" wide, 4" high x 7" wide, 4" high x 6" wide, 3 1/2" high x 5" wide.* **$650**

Courtesy of Cedarburg Auction Co., Inc.

▶ *Rare signed gray line sponge-banded batter bowl with spout and original baled handle, good condition, 5" high x 9 1/2" wide to spout.* **$622**

Courtesy of Cedarburg Auction Co., Inc.

*Signed gray line sponge-banded cake stand with molded decorations, minor flake to top, 2" high x 10" wide.* **$2,260**

◄ *Miniature poultry
drinking fount and
buttermilk feeder,
minor flakes, 6 1/2"
high.* **$102**

▼ *Rare gray line sponge-
banded stoneware mug
in good condition, 4"
high x 4 1/4" wide to
handle.* **$452**

▼ *Rare gray line
sponge-banded cookie
jar signed on base,
original cover in good
condition, 4" high x
9 1/2" wide.* **$463**

► *Rare five-gallon
beehive jug with large
red wing, 17" high.*
**$170**

# Rookwood

Maria Longworth Nichols founded Rookwood Pottery in 1880. The name, she later reported, paid homage to the many crows (rooks) on her father's estate and was also designed to remind customers of Wedgwood. Production began on Thanksgiving Day 1880 when the first kiln was drawn.

Rookwood's earliest productions demonstrated a continued reliance on European precedents and the Japanese aesthetic. Although the firm offered a variety of wares (Dull Glaze, Cameo, and Limoges, for example), it lacked a clearly defined artistic identity. With the introduction of what became known as its "standard glaze" in 1884, Rookwood inaugurated a period in which the company won consistent recognition for its artistic merit and technical innovation.

Rookwood's first decade ended on a high note when the company was awarded two gold medals: one at the Exhibition of American Art Industry in Philadelphia and another later in the year at the Exposition Universelle in Paris. Significant, too, was Maria Longworth Nichols' decision to transfer her interest in the company to William W. Taylor, who had been the firm's manager since 1883. In May 1890, the board of a newly reorganized Rookwood Pottery Co. purchased "the real estate, personal property, goodwill, patents, trade-marks… now the sole property of William W. Taylor" for $40,000.

Under Taylor's leadership, Rookwood was transformed from a fledgling startup to a successful business that expanded throughout the following decades to meet rising demand.

Throughout the 1890s, Rookwood continued to attract critical notice as it kept the tradition of innovation alive. Taylor

Courtesy of Mark Mussio, Humler & Nolan

◀ *Hand-carved lamp base by Kataro Shirayamadani, 1903, dark blue mat glaze at top lightens to green mat glaze covering three fish in reticulated aquatic foliage carved into base, marks: Rookwood logo, date, shape 663Z, artist's incised Japanese cipher and cast wiring hole in center of bottom, repair to base, 13 1/4"" high.* **$1,300**

rolled out three new glaze lines—Iris, Sea Green and Aerial Blue—from late 1894 into early 1895.

At the Paris Exposition in 1900, Rookwood cemented its reputation by winning the Grand Prix, a feat largely due to the favorable reception of the new Iris glaze and its variants.

Over the next several years, Rookwood's record of achievement at domestic and international exhibitions remained unmatched.

Throughout the 1910s, Rookwood continued in a similar vein and began to more thoroughly embrace the simplified aesthetic promoted by many Arts & Crafts figures. Production of the Iris line, which had been instrumental in the firm's success at the Paris Exposition in 1900, ceased around 1912. Not only did the company abandon its older, fussier underglaze wares, but the newer lines the pottery introduced also trended toward simplicity.

Unfortunately, the collapse of the stock market in October 1929 and ensuing economic depression dealt Rookwood a blow from which it did not recover. The Great Depression eventually led to the company's bankruptcy in April 1941.

Rookwood's history might have ended there were it not for the purchase of the firm by a group of investors led by automobile dealer Walter E. Schott and his wife, Margaret. Production started once again. In the years that followed, Rookwood changed hands a number of times before being moved to Starkville, Mississippi, in 1960. It finally closed its doors there in 1967.

For more information on Rookwood, see *Warman's Rookwood Pottery Identification and Price Guide* by Denise Rago and Jonathan Clancy.

Courtesy of Cowan's Auctions, Inc.

*Garden urns and birdbath in shades of green, early 20th century, urns with deep circular wells over square bases with floral and leaf designs, birdbath with flower petals around rim and detachable three-sided base with Art Nouveau-style nudes in water, birdbath dated 1915 and marked with impressed Rookwood logo, two circled Xs, and 3051Y, pedestal marked Rookwood / Faience / 3040Y, urns with impressed Rookwood logo, circled 8s, 3041Y, and E217, largest 31" high.* **$1,800**

Courtesy of Mark Mussio, Humler & Nolan

▶ *Uncommon polychromed high glaze production vase with embossed parrot decoration, designed, glazed and signed by Sallie Toohey in 1928, marks: Rookwood logo, date, shape 6032 and artist's initials in black slip, wheel ground X due to minor glaze bleeding, blue hazing on shoulder, 11" high.* **$900**

Courtesy of Mark Mussio, Humler & Nolan

▶ FAR RIGHT *Decorated Mat Glaze vase with abstract flowers, decorated by Sallie Coyne in 1925, marks: Rookwood logo, date, shape 1882 and decorator's monogram in blue slip, no crazing, 9 3/8" high.* **$700**

Courtesy of Mark Mussio, Humler & Nolan

▶ *Vase decorated at shoulder with woodbine set against background of dark blue, light green, and peach by Elizabeth Lincoln, 1907, marks: Rookwood logo, date, shape 905D and artist's monogram, fine overall crazing, 8 1/4" high.* **$600**

Courtesy of Mark Mussio, Humler & Nolan

▶ FAR RIGHT *Blue porcelain glaze vase with parrot by Arthur Conant, 1919, marks: Rookwood logo, date and artist's monogram, no shape number and incised stylized CB, tight line running from rim and craze lines near bottom, 6 1/2" high.* **$1,300**

*Early vase decorated by Laura Fry, 1882, incised geometric pattern along rim, incised blue and green fronds with gilt outlines, 1882 Rookwood logo, artist's initials, reads 1882 Cincinnati Pottery Club, even crazing with slight loss to gilt, 6 3/4" high.* **$2,829**

*Round lidded box in blue Vellum glaze decorated with cherries and leaves by Sarah "Sallie" E. Coyne, impressed Rookwood logo, dated 1926, shape 2927, and artist's initials on underside of base and lid, 8 1/4" diameter.* **$1,680**

▼ *Black Opal glazed vase with repeating floral pattern by Lorinda Epply, 1922, marks: Rookwood logo, date, shape 1358E and artist's incised initials, uncrazed, 7" high.* **$600**

▲ *Monumental vase with grapevines, leaves, and grape clusters in blue, green, amber and brown against shaded orange to brown background, high glaze, marked on bottom with Rookwood flame mark with two flames dating piece to 1888, artist signed but signature is illegible, very good to excellent condition with minor crazing and tight hairline in underside of vase, 19" high.* **$1,944**

◄ *Rare Flying Fish bookend designed by Louise Abel, cast in 1937, cormandel glaze, marks: Rookwood logo, date, shape 6482, and designer's mark in mold, excellent original condition, 4 1/2" high.* **$600**

Courtesy of Cowan's Auctions, Inc.

◀ *Standard glaze vase with daffodils by Sadie Markland, 1893, stylized Gorham sterling silver overlay, marked R 1098 Gorham Mfg. Co., vase with impressed Rookwood seven flame mark, shape 612, and artist's initials, 4" high.* **$2,706**

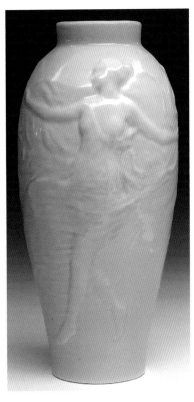

Courtesy of James D. Julia Auctioneers, Fairfield, Maine, www.jamesdjulia.com

▲ *Monumental Art Nouveau vase with high relief nudes on front and back with sheer wraps flowing around them, high glaze gray, signed on underside with Rookwood flame mark dated 1928, "2449," very good to excellent condition, 17" high.* **$1,481**

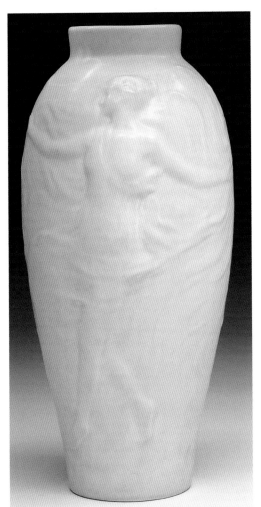

Courtesy of James D. Julia Auctioneers, Fairfield, Maine, www.jamesdjulia.com

◀ *Monumental Art Nouveau vase with high relief nudes on front and back with sheer wraps flowing around them, pale yellow glaze, signed on underside with Rookwood flame mark dated 1928, "2449," very good to excellent condition, 17" high.* **$1,458**

Cowan's Auctions, Inc.

*Baluster form matte glaze vase decorated by Louise Abel, floral design with mottled blue and green accents, impressed Rookwood logo, dated 1922, shape 604C, and artist's initials, 10" high.* **$1,320**

Courtesy of Cowan's Auctions, Inc.

◄ *Decorated matte glaze vase by Sarah "Sallie" E. Coyne, grapes and leaves against yellow background, impressed Rookwood logo, dated 1929, shape 900C, and artist's initials, 8 3/4" high.* **$1,080**

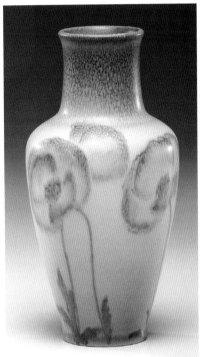

Courtesy of Cowan's Auctions, Inc.

▲ *Decorated matte glaze vase by Kataro Shirayamadani, pansies with mottled violet rim against cream and green gradient, impressed Rookwood logo, dated 1936, shape 6578, and artist's signature, 8 3/4" high.* **$1,200**

Courtesy of Mark Mussio, Humler & Nolan

◄ *Faience Bacchus decorated with white, purple, green, blue and yellow mat glazes, marked on back "Rookwood Faience," 8569 and A30, crazing and minor glaze skips and one edge chip away from glazed area,14 1/2" high x 10" wide.* **$1,300**

▶ *Standard glaze pillow vase decorated with portrait of young girl by Bruce Horsfall, impressed Rookwood logo with eight flames indicating 1894 date, shape 707 and artist's initials, fine overall crazing, 7 3/4" high.* **$1,020**

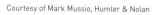

▲ *Standard glaze mug with kitten skipping rope with piece of yarn, decorated by Bruce Horsfall in 1893, marks: Rookwood logo, date, shape 587, impressed W for white clay and artist's cipher, excellent original condition with no crazing, 4 5/8" high.* **$1,400**

▶ *Hand-carved Vellum glazed advertising tile from 1908, Rookwood Pottery banner near top with three rooks sitting on carved perch below, marks: Rookwood logo, date, impressed V and incised V for Vellum, overall crazing with small glaze skips in white Vellum field, glaze skip on center rook's beak and multiple small firing separations within carving, 5 1/2" x 7 3/8".* **$2,700**

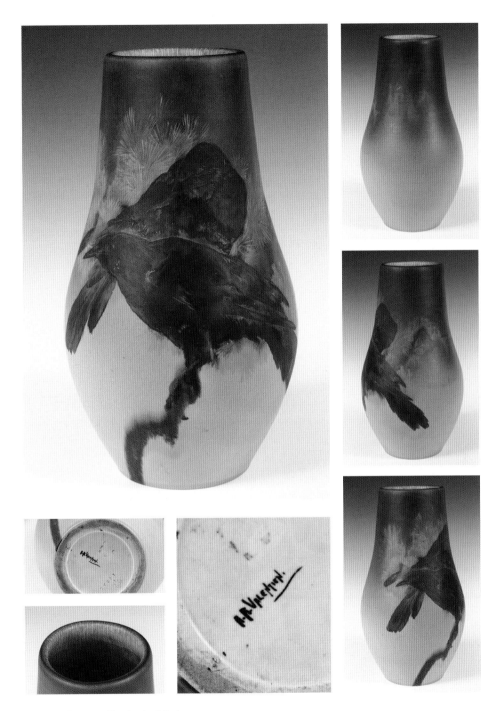

Courtesy of Thomaston Place Auction Galleries

*Large, rare Vellum glaze vase decorated by A.R. Valentien, with two carved rooks on branch, ombred green background, signed, dated 1901, and marked 198 AZ, fine condition, small scuffs inside mouth, 13" high x 7" diameter. Albert Robert Valentien or Valentine was head of the decorating department at Rookwood in Cincinnati. Namesake rooks seldom appeared on pieces, but were done by special request.* **$25,875**

# Roseville Pottery

Roseville is one of the most widely recognizable of potteries across the United States. Having been sold in flower shops and drugstores around the country, its art and production wares became a staple in American homes through the time Roseville closed in the 1950s.

The Roseville Pottery Co., located in Roseville, Ohio, was incorporated on Jan. 4, 1892, with George F. Young as general manager. The company had been producing stoneware since 1890, when it purchased the J. B. Owens Pottery, also of Roseville.

The popularity of Roseville Pottery's original lines of stoneware continued to grow. The company acquired new plants in 1892 and 1898, and production started to shift to Zanesville, just a few miles away. By about 1910, all of the work was centered in Zanesville, but the company name was unchanged.

Young hired Ross C. Purdy as artistic designer in 1900, and Purdy created Rozane—a contraction of the words "Roseville" and "Zanesville." The first Roseville artwork pieces were marked either Rozane or RPCO, both impressed or ink-stamped on the bottom.

In 1902, a line was developed called Azurean. Some pieces were marked Azurean, but more often RPCO. In 1904 at the St. Louis Exposition, Roseville's Rozane Mongol, a high-gloss oxblood red line, captured first prize, gaining recognition for the firm and its creator, John Herold.

Many Roseville lines were a response to the innovations of Weller Pottery, and in 1904 Frederick Rhead was hired away from Weller as artistic director. He created the Olympic and Della Robbia lines for Roseville. His brother, Harry, took over as artistic director in 1908, and in 1915 he introduced the popular Donatello line.

By 1908, all handcrafting ended except for Rozane Royal. Roseville was the first pottery in Ohio to install a

Courtesy of Mark Mussio, Humler & Nolan

*Sunflower handled vase, excellent original condition, 4 1/8" high.*
**$375**

Courtesy of Mark Mussio, Humler & Nolan

▶ *Wisteria handled vase, textured background, blue glaze, good condition, 9 1/4" high.* **$550**

Courtesy of Mark Mussio, Humler & Nolan

◀ *Windsor handled vase in two-tone mottled blue glaze with green stalks with triangular leaves and small yellow flowers, incised "3" and blue "8" on bottom, paint covers chip to edge of handle, 8 3/8" high.* **$225**

**RECOMMENDED READING**

**Antique Trader Pottery & Porcelain Ceramics Price Guide.** More than 3,000 color photos, descriptions and values for 150 companies, including Fiesta, McCoy, Roseville, Red Wing, Weller, Wedgwood, and others big and small. www.krausebooks.com

Courtesy of Mark Mussio, Humler & Nolan

▲ *Small Vista oblong basket, tiny glaze "zits" and small flat glaze chip to corner rim, 6 3/4" high.* **$140**

Courtesy of Mark Mussio, Humler & Nolan

▲ *Early Velmoss vase with wide green foliage surrounding round saffron yellow body with crimson mingled in, excellent condition, 8" high.* **$475**

tunnel kiln, which increased its production capacity.

Frank Ferrell, who was a top decorator at Weller Pottery by 1904, was Roseville's artistic director from 1917 until 1954. This Zanesville native created many of the most popular lines, including Pine Cone, which had scores of individual pieces.

Many collectors believe Roseville's circa 1925 glazes were the best of any Zanesville pottery. George Krause, who in 1915 became Roseville's technical supervisor responsible for glaze, remained with Roseville until the 1950s.

Company sales declined after World War II, especially in the early 1950s when cheap Japanese imports began to replace American wares, and a simpler, more modern style made many of Roseville's elaborate floral designs seem old-fashioned.

In the late 1940s, Roseville began to issue lines with glossy glazes. Roseville tried to offset its flagging artware sales by launching a dinnerware line—Raymor—in 1953. The line was a commercial failure.

Roseville issued its last new designs in 1953. On Nov. 29, 1954, the facilities of Roseville were sold to the Mosaic Tile Co.

For more information on Roseville, see *Warman's Roseville Pottery*, 2nd edition, by Denise Rago.

*Sunflower handled vase, excellent original condition, 3 3/4" high x 6 3/4" wide.* **$350**

*Large Pauleo vase decorated with life-size tulips and foliage in three colors of luster, design outlined in black enamel, chip to black outline on rim, mother-of-pearl surface, 15 1/2" high.* **$475**

*Windsor handled vase in blue, shape 551-7, marked with black paper Roseville label and marked in orange grease pencil with shape number, drilled through bottom but in excellent shape otherwise, 7 1/4" high.* **$450**

◀ *Sunflower vase in shape 487, textured background shading from yellow-brown to green to dark blue, repair to small flat chips at rim, color runs, 7 1/4" high.* **$275**

▲ *Rozane portrait vase of spaniel made for Hunter Arms Co., work of artist Mae Timberlake, signed by artist on side of vase and marked on back "Hunter Arms Co. First Prize Class A," excellent original condition with faint crazing, 13" high.* **$800**

▶ *Rozane Ware Woodland vase with stalks of hollyhocks and buds and budding stalk on back, in shiny brown and mustard glazes against matte biscuit body with needlepoint stippling, raised "Rozane Ware" logo, glaze chips at rim and base, 6 1/4" high.* **$160**

Courtesy of Mark Mussio, Humler & Nolan

◄ *Pauleo pear-shape vase covered in mottled high glaze, gold speckled with blue, excellent original condition, 7 7/8" high.* **$275**

Courtesy of Mark Mussio, Humler & Nolan

▶ *Three Rozane pieces: tankard decorated with monk pouring from stein to mug with irises on opposite side, 14" high, and two mugs with monk on one side and spring crocus on other side, 4 1/4" high, all impressed "Rozane, RPCo" with numbers, repair to rim of tankard.* **$300**

Courtesy of Mark Mussio, Humler & Nolan

▲ *Wincraft vase, shape 290, with panther leaping from tree branch, raised marks of company and numbered 290-11", overall crazing, excellent condition, 10 1/2" high.* **$550**

▶ *Victorian Art Pottery vase with cobalt blue flowers and ochre and green foliage over stippled band, chocolate glaze, stamped with company's cobalt "Rv" logo on bottom, faint crazing, 7" high.* **$300**

▲ *Windsor handled vase in blue, shape 554-10, unmarked, excellent original condition, 10 1/2" high.* **$400**

▶ *Miniature Rozane vase decorated with daffodil and leaves and signed with obscure marks of artist, accompanied by rare serrated round label reading "Hollywood Ware" attached to bottom, minor surface scratches, 5 1/8" high.* **$110**

Courtesy of Mark Mussio, Humler & Nolan

*Windsor handled vase in blue, shape 553-9, marked with silver foil Roseville label, excellent original condition, 9 1/4" high.* **$600**

Courtesy of Mark Mussio, Humler & Nolan

*Wisteria vase in blue, shape 632-5", marked with gold foil Roseville label and bearing shape number 632 in orange grease pencil, excellent original condition, 5" high.* **$400**

Courtesy of Mark Mussio, Humler & Nolan

*Woodland vase with trillium decoration, marked with Rozane Ware Woodland wafer seal, small stray color spots on one side, 6 1/8" high.* **$350**

# Weller Pottery

Weller Pottery was made from 1872 to 1945 at a pottery established originally by Samuel A. Weller at Fultonham, Ohio and moved in 1882 to Zanesville, Ohio.

Weller's famous pottery slugged it out with several other important Zanesville potteries for decades. Cross-town rivals such as Roseville, Owens, La Moro, and McCoy were all serious fish in a fairly small and well-stocked lake. While Weller occasionally landed some solid body punches with many of his better art lines, the prevailing thought was that his later production ware just wasn't up to snuff.

Samuel Weller was a notorious copier and, it is said, a bit of a scallywag. He paid designers such as William Long to bring their famous discoveries to Zanesville. He then attempted to steal their secrets, and, when successful, renamed them and made them his own.

After World War I, when the cost of materials became less expensive than the cost of labor, many companies, including the famous Rookwood Pottery, increased their output of less expensive production ware. Weller Pottery followed along in the trend of production ware by introducing scores of interesting and unique lines, the likes of which have never been created anywhere else, before or since.

In addition to a number of noteworthy production lines, Weller continued in the creation of hand-painted ware long after Roseville abandoned them. Some of the more interesting Hudson pieces, for example, are post-World War I items. Even later lines, such as Bonito, were hand painted and often signed by important artists such as Hester Pillsbury. The closer you look at Weller's output after 1920, the more obvious the fact that it was the only Zanesville company still producing both quality art ware and quality production ware.

For more information on Weller pottery, see *Warman's Weller Pottery Identification and Price Guide* by Denise Rago and David Rago.

Courtesy of Mark Mussio, Humler & Nolan

*Matt Ware reticulated floral vase in trio of mat glazes, impressed "WELLER" on bottom in small block letters, crazing, tight line extending from rim into one reticulation, 8 7/8" high.* **$600**

▲ *Clewell copper-clad corn vase on Weller L'Art Nouveau blank, Canton, Ohio, stamped L'ART NOUVEAU WELLER, 10" x 4".* **$1,625**

▲ *Coppertone trumpet vase with quatrain of frogs surrounding base, Weller half kiln ink stamp with numbers 2 and 11 in green slip, excellent original condition, 11 1/2" high.* **$1,600**

*Coppertone helmet-shaped bowl with frog seated on edge and trio of fish cast on outer portion of bowl, marked with Weller Pottery half kiln ink stamp and either 3B or 38 on bottom, excellent original condition, 5 1/2" high x 10" long.* **$425**

Courtesy of Mark Mussio, Humler & Nolan

*Hudson red and gray vase, signed by Mae Timberlake, who painted pinkish-red bird on branch with fall oak leaves, inscribed "Weller Pottery," crude drill hole in bottom, glaze chips on base edge and minor factory glaze irregularities on rim, 8 7/8" high.* **$700**

Courtesy of Mark Mussio, Humler & Nolan

*Rare monumental Hudson vase by Mae Timberlake, pair of birds perched among branches of fruit tree, marked on bottom with circular Weller Ware ink stamp and signed by artist in blue slip near base, excellent original condition, 29 3/8" high.* **$8,500**

Courtesy of Mark Mussio, Humler & Nolan

*Hudson vase by Hester Pillsbury, two hummingbirds among honeysuckle flowers, incised "Weller Pottery" on bottom and signed "Pillsbury" above foot, fine overall crazing, 12 7/8" high.* **$1,700**

Courtesy of Mark Mussio, Humler & Nolan

*Hudson vase with hollyhocks by Hester Pillsbury, impressed "WELLER" on bottom and signed by artist in white slip near base, light crazing, 11 3/4" high.* **$850**

Courtesy of Mark Mussio, Humler & Nolan

*Hudson vase with pair of black-throated warblers perched on juniper branch, Weller impression, faint line visible from inside, ivory backdrop, 9 3/8" high.* **$1,500**

Courtesy of Mark Mussio, Humler & Nolan

*Hudson cylinder vase with iris blossom and bud among leaves, painted by Mae Timberlake who signed it front and center, impressed "Weller" on bottom, excellent original condition, 9" high.* **$450**

▶ *Jap Birdimal vase decorated in Japonesque fashion with seven blue and yellow fish amid bubbles and waves, deployed by tube lining against light green ground, impressed "533 5" on base with no other markings visible, overall crazing, overspray at rim indicating professional repair and minor stilt pulls on bottom, 5 3/4" high.* **$650**

▲ *Knifewood vase with male peacock perched on fountain among rose bushes and woodland, twice impressed "Weller" on bottom, chip under vase, 8 7/8" high.* **$500**

◀ *LaSa vase with pine tree decoration and red and gold sky, unmarked, accompanied by 3" x 5" card on which is written: "The enclosed piece of pottery is given to you with compliments of THE LIMA ROTARY CLUB. This piece has been selected from the La Sl [sic] line, our latest creation. This line, which is strictly hand made, we consider the finest that we have ever produced. By reason of its artistic qualities, we hope that it will be used as a decorative piece of pottery, and not for fresh or cut flowers. Manufactured by S.A. Weller Co., Pottery Zanesville, Ohio"; scratches on lower third of body, 11 3/8" high.* **$450**

Courtesy of Mark Mussio, Humler & Nolan

*Rare Louwelsa vase in glossy red glaze, decorated by Mae Timberlake, pink orchid front and back with foliage, incised "Weller Pottery" on bottom, hairline crack extending 3" from rim, open glaze bursts inside rim, areas of base edge lack glaze, 7" high.* **$900**

Courtesy of Mark Mussio, Humler & Nolan

◀ *LaSa footed vase with summertime trees in front of lake with hills on other side, large clouds, Weller LaSa scratched in above foot, minor surface scratches, excellent condition, 9 1/8" high.* **$500**

Courtesy of Mark Mussio, Humler & Nolan

*Matt Louwelsa cylinder vase with apricot mums on serpentine stems by Frank Farrell, who signed it on the side in slip, impressed "X 437" and hand incised "CM" on bottom, excellent condition, 16" high.* **$1,300**

Courtesy of Mark Mussio, Humler & Nolan

*Matt Louwelsa or Perfecto vase slip decorated with pink flowers in Art Nouveau fashion, body glazed in mat blue with mat green applied, impressed "SA Weller X440" with other impressions, SA could be partial impression for Louwelsa, excellent original condition, 12" high.* **$1,200**

*Matt Ware vase with molded tendrils extending from rim in medium green matt glaze with lighter green and purple highlights, marked "Weller" in script on bottom, excellent original condition, 11 1/4" high.* **$800**

▲ *Matt Louwelsa vase with milkweed, impressed on bottom with circular Weller Louwelsa stamp with number 525 in middle and incised "MATT," faint crazing, 6 1/2" high.* **$450**

▶ *Louwelsa vase with lily front and back surrounded by foliage and scroll decoration, artistic design by Frank Ferrell, impressed "578-9" on bottom, minor surface scratches, 9 3/4" high.* **$650**

◄ *Matt Ware reticulated floral vase with trio of green mat glazes, unmarked, fine overall crazing and one glaze chip, 10 1/4" high.* **$850**

▲ *Matt Ware tapered form vase with beetles and oak leaves in mat glazes of green, brown, blue and red, incised "Weller" on bottom, excellent original condition, 5" high.* **$1,000**

◄ *Matt Ware vase with green oak leaves against purple ground, marked "WELLER" in small block letters on bottom, mild crazing, small glaze chips at base, 7" high.* **$550**

▶ *Rochelle vase with long-needled branch with three pine cones, painted by Hester Pillsbury whose monogram is in slip on back, "Weller" incised on bottom, 2" rim line, 7 1/4" high.* **$550**

▲ *Rare Minerva pitcher with two dancing satyrs on one side and autumnal forest on other, impressed "Weller" in large block letters on bottom, excellent original condition with no apparent crazing, 9 7/8" high. Provenance: Pitcher comes with 1977 warrant card from White Pillars Museum in Zanesville, Ohio, signed by Louise Purviance and Harold Nichols.* **$2,000**

▶ *Roma hanging chandelier, impressed "Weller" inside shade, fine overall crazing, 17 1/2" dia.* **$500**

Courtesy of Mark Mussio, Humler & Nolan

◄ *Sicard vase with mistletoe decoration in textured glaze, signed "Weller Sicard" on side, 5 3/4" high.* **$650**

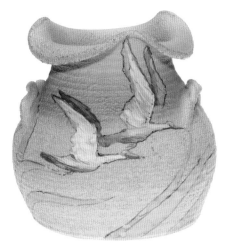

Courtesy of Mark Mussio, Humler & Nolan

▲ *Weller Ware handmade marked vase with storks in flight above reeds front and back, braided closed handles and trifold-down rim covered with textured blue glaze, glaze chips to decoration, 6 1/4" high.* **$550**

Courtesy of Mark Mussio, Humler & Nolan

◄ *Xenia vase with stencil-like design of red flowers on gray vines surrounding shoulder, impressed "Weller," 5 3/4" high.* **$600**

# European Ceramics

## Select English & European Makers

The **Amphora Porcelain Works** was one of several pottery companies located in the Teplitz-Turn region of Bohemia in the late 19th and early 20th centuries. It is best known for art pottery, especially Art Nouveau and Art Deco pieces. Several markings were used, including the name and location of the pottery and the Imperial mark, which included a crown. Prior to World War I, Bohemia was part of the Austro-Hungarian Empire, so the word "Austria" may appear as part of the mark. After World War I, the word "Czechoslovakia" may be part of the mark.

**Belleek** is thin-bodied, ivory-colored, almost iridescent porcelain first made in 1857 in County Fermanagh, Ireland. Production continued until World War I, was

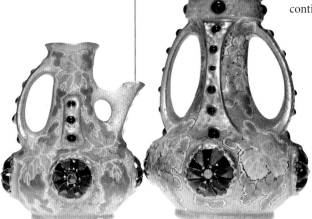

Courtesy of Mark Mussio, Humler & Nolan

*Amphora pitcher with overall grape decor with four reticulated flower heads trimmed with fired-on gold, 7 1/4" high; vase with same decorative effect, 9 1/2" high; both signed with impressed crown and "Amphora Austria" in thin ovals, both in excellent original condition.* **$300**

Courtesy of Leslie Hindman Auctioneers

▲ *Belleek porcelain covered basket, second half 20th century, reticulated form with floral encrusted and domed lift-off cover over cylindrical body with double scroll handles, underside impressed Belleek R Ireland, 5 1/4" high x 8 1/4" diameter.* **$473**

Courtesy of Mark Mussio, Humler & Nolan

▲ *Lenox Belleek vase signed and dated by artist Mattie Hursey in 1913, pair of exotic birds perched in branches of fir tree, green palette logo and artist signature with date beneath, excellent condition, 10" high.* **$2,755**

discontinued for a period of time, and then resumed. The Shamrock pattern is most familiar, but many patterns were made, including Limpet, Tridacna, and Grasses.

Several American firms made a Belleek-type porcelain. The first was Ott and Brewer Co. of Trenton, New Jersey, in 1884. Other firms producing this ware included The Ceramic Art Co. (1889), American Art China Works (1892), Columbian Art Co. (1893) and Lenox Inc. (1904). Irish Belleek bore specific marks during given time periods, which makes it relatively easy to date. Variations in mark color are important, as well as the symbols and words.

**Capo-di-Monte:** In 1743, King Charles of Naples established a soft-paste porcelain factory. The firm made figurines and dinnerware. In 1760, many of the workmen and most of the molds were moved to Buen Retiro, near Madrid, Spain. A new factory, which also made hard-paste porcelains, opened in Naples in 1771. In 1834, the Doccia factory in Florence purchased the molds and continued production in Italy.

Capo-di-Monte was copied well into the 20th century by makers in Hungary, Germany, France, and Italy.

*Capo-di-Monte*

*Spode*

*Copeland*

In 1749, **Josiah Spode** was apprenticed to Thomas Whieldon and in 1754 worked for William Banks in Stoke-on-Trent, Staffordshire, England. In the early 1760s, Spode started his own pottery, making cream-colored earthenware and blueprinted whiteware. In 1770, he returned to Banks' factory as master, purchasing it in 1776.

Spode pioneered the use of steam-powered, pottery-making machinery and mastered the art of transfer printing from copper plates. Spode opened a London shop in 1778 and sent William Copeland there in about 1784. A number of larger London locations followed. At the turn of the 18th century, Spode introduced bone china. In 1805, Josiah Spode II and William Copeland entered into a partnership for the London business. A series of partnerships between Josiah Spode II, Josiah Spode III, and William Taylor Copeland resulted.

In 1833, Copeland acquired Spode's London operations and seven years later, the Stoke plants. William Taylor Copeland managed the business until his death in 1868. The firm remained in the hands of Copeland heirs. In 1923, the plant was electrified; other modernization followed.

In 1976, Spode merged with Worcester Royal Porcelain to become Royal Worcester Spode, Ltd.

**Delftware** is pottery with a soft, red-clay body and tin-enamel glaze. The white, dense, opaque color came from adding tin ash to lead glaze. The first examples had blue designs on a white ground. Polychrome examples followed.

The name originally applied to pottery made in the region around Delft, Holland, beginning in the 16th century and ending in the late 18th century. The tin used came from the Cornish mines in England. By the 17th and 18th centuries, English potters in London, Bristol, and Liverpool were copying the glaze and designs. Some designs unique to English potters also developed.

Courtesy of Thomaston Place Auction Galleries

*Blue and white traditional Delft ginger jar, 20th century, six-sided with lion finial on domed lid, artist signed, 10 1/2" high.* **$115**

Courtesy of Cowan's Auctions, Inc.

*Six blue and white Delft plates of various sizes, Continental, 19th century, each with marks on underside, largest 14" diameter.* **$584**

**Gouda** and the surrounding areas of Holland have been principal Dutch pottery centers for centuries. Originally, the potteries produced a simple utilitarian, tin-glazed Delft-type earthenware and the famous clay smoker's pipes.

When pipe making declined in the early 1900s, Gouda turned to art pottery. Influenced by the Art Nouveau and Art Deco movements, artists expressed themselves with freeform and stylized designs in bold colors.

Gouda

In 1842, American china importer **David Haviland** moved to Limoges, France, where he began manufacturing and decorating china specifically for the U.S. market. Haviland is synonymous with fine, white, translucent porcelain, although early hand-painted patterns were generally larger and darker colored on heavier whiteware blanks than were later ones.

Haviland revolutionized French china factories by both manufacturing the whiteware blank and decorating it at the same site. In addition, Haviland and Co. pioneered the use of decals in decorating china.

Haviland's sons, Charles Edward and Theodore, split the company in 1892. In 1936, Theodore opened an American division. In 1941, Theodore bought out Charles Edward's heirs and re-combined both companies under the original name of H. and Co. The Haviland family sold the firm in 1981.

Charles Field Haviland, cousin of Charles Edward and Theodore, worked for and then, after his marriage in 1857, ran the Casseaux Works until 1882. Items continued to carry his name as decorator until 1941.

Thousands of Haviland patterns were made, but not consistently named until after 1926. The similarities in many of the patterns make identification difficult. Numbers assigned by Arlene Schleiger and illustrated in her books have become the identification standard.

**Creamware** is a cream-colored earthenware created about 1750 by the potters of Staffordshire, England, which proved ideal for domestic ware. It was also known as "tortoiseshellware" or "Prattware" depending on the color of glaze used.

The most notable producer of creamware was Josiah Wedgwood. Around 1779, he was able to lighten the cream color to a bluish white and sold this product under the name "pearl ware." Wedgwood supplied his creamware to England's Queen Charlotte

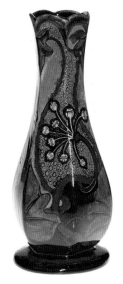

Mark Mussio, Humler & Nolan

*Gouda Distel Art Nouveau floral vase in high glaze, circa 1900, exotic flowers cover six-sided form, marked in black slip "Distel T.V.V. 62/dec. III." on bottom, 8 1/2" high.* **$375**

Haviland

*Leeds*

(1744-1818) and Russian Empress Catherine the Great (1729-1796), and used the trade name "Queen's ware."

The **Leeds** Pottery in Yorkshire, England, began production about 1758. Among its products was creamware that was competitive with that of Wedgwood. The original factory closed in 1820, but various subsequent owners continued until 1880. They made exceptional cream-colored ware, either plain, salt glazed or painted with colored enamels, and glazed and unglazed redware.

Early wares are unmarked. Later pieces are marked "Leeds Pottery," sometimes followed by "Hartley-Green and Co." or the letters "LP."

**Liverpool** is the name given to products made at several potteries in Liverpool, England, between 1750 and 1840. Seth and James Pennington and Richard Chaffers were among the early potters who made tin-enameled earthenware.

By the 1780s, tin-glazed earthenware gave way to cream-colored wares decorated with cobalt blue, enameled colors, and blue or black transfers.

Bubbles and frequent clouding under the foot rims characterize the Liverpool glaze. By 1800, about 80 potteries were working in the town producing not only creamware, but also soft paste, soapstone, and bone porcelain.

The reproduction pieces have a crackled glaze and often age cracks have been artificially produced. When compared to genuine pieces, reproductions are thicker and heavier and have weaker transfers, grayish color (not as crisp and black), ecru or gray body color instead of cream, and crazing that does not spiral upward.

*Minton*

In 1793, Thomas **Minton** joined other entrepreneurs and formed a partnership to build a small pottery at Stoke-on-Trent, Staffordshire, England. Production began in 1798 with blueprinted earthenware, mostly in

Courtesy of Doyle New York

◄ *Pair of Minton majolica jardinières with underplates en suite, third quarter 19th century, each in urn form, decorated with ram's head masks and garlands on turquoise ground, areas of restoration, 14 3/4" high x 17 1/4" diameter.* **$1,875**

Skinner, Inc.; www.skinnerinc.com

*Mocha bowl with Earthworm slip decoration, Britain, early 19th century, London-shape bowl with green rouletted rim band over wide rust band with thin black bands and ornamented with looping Earthworm slip decoration, 5 1/4" high x 9 7/8" diameter.* **$780**

Skinner, Inc.; www.skinnerinc.com

*Mocha Pearlware pint mug, Britain, early 19th century, with molded base decorated with medial rust band with zigzagging blue, brown, and white slip flanked by black and blue bands, 4 7/8" high.* **$369**

the Willow pattern. In 1798, cream-colored earthenware and bone china were introduced.

A wide range of styles and wares was produced. Minton introduced porcelain figures in 1826, Parian wares in 1846, encaustic tiles in the late 1840s, and majolica wares in 1850. In 1883, the modern company was formed and called Mintons Limited. The "s" was dropped in 1968.

Many early pieces are unmarked or have a Sèvres-type marking. The "ermine" mark was used in the early 19th century. Date codes can be found on tableware and majolica. The mark used between 1873 and 1911 was a small globe with a crown on top and the word "Minton."

**Mocha** decoration usually is found on utilitarian creamware and stoneware pieces and was produced through a simple chemical action. A color pigment of brown, blue, green or black was made acidic by an infusion of tobacco or hops. When the acidic colorant was applied in blobs to an alkaline ground, it reacted by spreading in feathery designs resembling sea plants. This type of decoration usually was supplemented with bands of light-colored slip.

Types of decoration vary greatly, from those done in a combination of motifs, such as Cat's Eye and Earthworm, to a plain pink mug decorated with green ribbed bands. Most forms of mocha are hollow, e.g., mugs, jugs, bowls and shakers.

English potters made the vast majority of the pieces. Collectors group the wares into three chronological periods: 1780-1820, 1820-1840, and 1840-1880.

*Moorcroft*

*Royal Bayreuth*

**William Moorcroft** was first employed as a potter by James Macintyre & Co., Ltd. of Burslem, Staffordshire, England, in 1897. He established the Moorcroft pottery in 1913.

The majority of the art pottery wares were hand thrown, resulting in a great variation among similarly styled pieces. Colors and marks are keys to determining age.

Walter Moorcroft, William's son, continued the business upon his father's death and made wares in the same style.

The company initially used an impressed mark, "Moorcroft, Burslem"; a signature mark, "W. Moorcroft," followed. Modern pieces are marked simply "Moorcroft," with export pieces also marked "Made in England."

In 1794, the **Royal Bayreuth** factory was founded in Tettau, Bavaria. Royal Bayreuth introduced its figural patterns in 1885. Designs of animals, people, fruits and vegetables decorated a wide array of tableware and inexpensive souvenir items.

Tapestry wares, in rose and other patterns, were made in the late 19th century. The surface of the pieces feel and look like woven cloth.

The Royal Bayreuth crest used to mark the wares varied in design and color.

**Derby Crown Porcelain Co.,** established in 1875 in Derby, England, had no connection with earlier Derby factories that operated in the late 18th and early 19th centuries. In 1890, the company was appointed "Manufacturers of Porcelain to Her Majesty" (Queen Victoria) and since that date has been known as Royal Crown Derby.

Most of these porcelains, both tableware and figural, were hand decorated. A variety of printing processes were used for additional adornment.

Derby porcelains from 1878 to 1890 carry only the standard crown printed mark. After 1891, the mark includes the "Royal Crown Derby" wording. In the 20th century, "Made in England" and "English Bone China" were added to the mark.

**Doulton** pottery began in 1815 under the direction of John Doulton at the Doulton & Watts pottery in Lambeth, England. Early output was limited to salt-glazed industrial stoneware. After John Watts retired in 1854, the firm became Doulton and Co., and production was expanded to include hand-decorated stoneware such as figurines, vases, dinnerware and flasks.

In 1878, Doulton's son, Sir Henry Doulton, purchased Pinder

*Royal Doulton*

*Royal Doulton vase, stoneware, small round foot supporting wide ovoid body tapering to short, wide and deeply rolled neck, wide body band in cream incised with cattle in meadow, cobalt blue shoulder decorated with incised pale blue scrolls, lower body and foot with lappet bands in cobalt blue, pale blue and brown, decorated by Hannah Barlow, 1887, Doulton-Lambeth, 6 3/8" high.* **$1,093**

Bourne & Co. in Burslem, Staffordshire. The companies became Doulton & Co., Ltd. in 1882. Decorated porcelain was added to Doulton's earthenware production in 1884.

Most Doulton figurines were produced at the Burslem plants, where they were made continuously from 1890 until 1978. After a short interruption, a new line of Doulton figurines was introduced in 1979.

Dickensware, in earthenware and porcelain, was introduced in 1908. The pieces were decorated with characters from Dickens' novels. Most of the line was withdrawn in the 1940s, except for plates, which continued to be made until 1974.

Character jugs, a 20th century revival of early Toby models, were designed by Charles J. Noke for Doulton in the 1930s. Character jugs are limited to bust portraits, while Royal Doulton Toby jugs are full figured. The character jugs come in four sizes and feature fictional characters from Dickens, Shakespeare, and other English and American novelists, as well as historical heroes. Marks on both character and Toby jugs must be carefully identified to determine dates and values.

Doulton's Rouge Flambé (Veined Sung) is a high-glazed, strong-colored ware.

Production of stoneware at Lambeth ceased in 1956.

Beginning in 1872, the "Royal Doulton" mark was used on all types of wares produced by the company.

Beginning in 1913, an "HN" number was assigned to each new Doulton figurine design.

*Royal Doulton vase, Rouge Flambé, wide bulbous baluster form tapering to wide flat mouth, decorated with black-silhouetted Arabian landscape with men on camels, marked on bottom "Royal Doulton Flambé," early 20th century, 11 1/2" high.* **$1,200-$1,800**

The "HN" numbers, which referred originally to Harry Nixon, a Doulton artist, were chronological until 1940, after which blocks of numbers were assigned to each modeler. From 1928 until 1954, a small number was placed to the right of the crown mark; this number, when added to 1927, gives the year of manufacture.

In 1751, the **Worcester Porcelain Co.,** led by Dr. John Wall and William Davis, acquired the Bristol pottery of Benjamin Lund and moved it to Worcester. The first wares were painted blue under the glaze; soon thereafter decorating was accomplished by painting on the glaze in enamel colors. Among the most famous 18th century decorators were James Giles and Jeffery Hamet O'Neal. Transfer-print decoration was developed by the 1760s.

A series of partnerships took place after Davis' death in 1783: Flight (1783-1793); Flight & Barr (1793-1807); Barr, Flight & Barr (1807-1813); and Flight, Barr & Barr (1813-1840). In 1840, the factory was moved to Chamberlain & Co. in Diglis, Worcester. Decorative wares were discontinued. In 1852, W.H. Kerr and R.W. Binns formed a new company and revived the production of ornamental wares.

In 1862, the firm became the Royal Worcester Porcelain Co. Among the key modelers of the late 19th century were James Hadley, his three sons, and George Owen, an expert with pierced clay pieces. Royal Worcester absorbed the Grainger factory in 1889 and the James Hadley factory in 1905. Modern designers include Dorothy Doughty and Doris Lindner.

**Spatterware** generally was made of common earthenware, although occasionally creamware was used. The earliest English examples were made about 1780. The peak period of production was from 1810 to 1840. Firms known to have made spatterware are Adams, Barlow, and Harvey and Cotton.

Courtesy of Cowan's Auctions, Inc.

*Spatterware saucer with central multicolored peafowl and green background, American, 19th century, 4 3/4" diameter.* **$215**

The amount of spatter decoration varies from piece to piece. Some objects simply have decorated borders. These often were decorated with a brush, requiring several hundred touches per square inch to achieve the spatter effect. Other pieces have the entire surface covered with spatter. Marked pieces are rare.

Collectors today focus on the patterns—Cannon, Castle, Fort, Peafowl, Rainbow, Rose, Thistle, Schoolhouse, etc. The decoration on flat ware is in the center of the piece; on hollow ware, it occurs on both sides.

Aesthetics and the colors of spatter are key to determining value. Blue and red are the most common colors; green, purple, and brown are in a middle group; black and yellow are scarce.

**Vilmos Zsolnay** (1828-1900) assumed control of his brother's factory in Pécs, Hungary, in the mid-19th century. In 1899, Vilmos' son, Miklos, became manager. The firm still produces ceramic ware.

The early wares are highly ornamental, glazed, and have a cream-colored ground. Eosin glaze, a deep, rich play of colors reminiscent of Tiffany's iridescent wares, received a gold medal at the 1900 Paris exhibition.

Originally no trademark was used, but in 1878 the company began to use a blue mark depicting the five towers of the cathedral at Pécs. The initials "TJM" represent the names of Miklos' three children.

Zsolnay Pottery

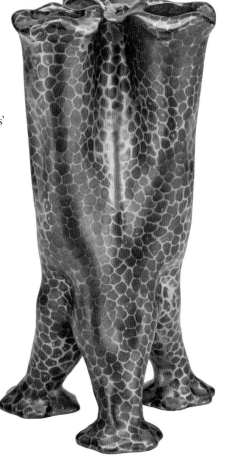

Courtesy of Rago Arts

*Three-footed Zsolnay "giraffe" vase, eosin glaze, circa 1900, stamped PECS 5879/1003, 9 1/4" x 5 1/2".* **$7,500**

# KPM

By Melody Amsel-Arieli

**MELODY AMSEI-ARIELI**
is a freelance writer and
frequent contributor to
*Antique Trader* magazine.
She is the author of
*Between Galicia and
Hungary: The Jews of
Stropkov* as well as *Jewish
Lives: Britain 1750-1950*
(Pen & Sword, 2013). She
lives in Israel.

KPM plaques are highly glazed, enamel paintings on
porcelain bases that were produced by Konigliche Porzellan
Manufaktur (KPM), the King's Porcelain Factory, in Berlin,
Germany, between 1880 and 1901.

Their secret, according to Afshine Emrani, dealer and
appraiser at www.some-of-my-favorite-things.com, is KPM's
highly superior, smooth, hard paste porcelain, which could be
fired at very high temperatures.

"The magic of a KPM plaque is that it will look as crisp
and beautiful 100 years from now as it does today," he said.
Even when they were introduced, these plaques proved highly
collectible, with art lovers, collectors, tourists, and the wealthy
acquiring them for extravagant sums.

KPM rarely marketed painted porcelain plaques itself,
however. Instead, it usually supplied white, undecorated ones to
independent artists who specialized in this genre. Not all artists
signed their KPM paintings, however.

While most KPM plaques were copies of famous paintings,
some, commissioned by wealthy Americans and Europeans
in the 1920s, bear images of actual people in contemporary
clothing. These least collectible of KPM plaques command
between $500 and $1,500 each, depending on the attractiveness
of their subjects.

Gilded, hand-painted plaques featuring Middle Eastern
or female Gypsy subjects and bearing round red "Made in
Germany" stamps were produced just before and after World
War I for export. They command between $500 and $2,000 each.
Plaques portraying religious subjects, such as the Virgin Mary
or the Flight into Egypt, command higher prices but are less
popular.

Popular scenes of hunters, merrymakers, musicians, etc.,
generally fetch less than $10,000 apiece because they have
been reproduced time and again. Rarer, more elaborate scenes,
however, like "The Dance Lesson" and "Turkish Card Players"

*Porcelain plaque, rectangle, of penitent Magdalene, set in giltwood frame, 3 1/2" high x 5 1/2" wide.* **$630**

may be worth many times more.

Highly stylized portraits copied from famous paintings – especially those of attractive children or décolleté women – allowed art lovers to own their own "masterpieces." These are currently worth between $2,000 and $20,000 each. Romanticized portrayals of cupids and women in the nude, the most desirable KPMs subjects of all, currently sell for up to $40,000 each. Portraits of men, it must be noted, are not only less popular, but also less expensive.

Size also matters. A 4" x 6" plaque, whose subject has been repeatedly reproduced, may sell for a few thousand dollars. Larger ones that portray the same subject will fetch proportionately more. A "Sistine Madonna" plaque, fashioned after the original work by Rafael and measuring 10" x 7 1/2", might cost $4,200. One featuring the identical subject, but measuring 15" x 11", might cost $7,800. A larger plaque, measuring 22" x 16", might command twice that price.

The largest KPM plaques, measuring 22" x 26", for example, often burst during production. Although no formula exists for

◄ *Framed painted porcelain plaque of woman with parasol seated on wall in carved gilt frame, circa 1900, marks: (scepter) KPM, H, O, 255 195, good condition, frame with some subbing of gilt surface, 10" high x 7 5/8" wide, 20 1/4" x 17 3/4" overall.* **$4,375**

▲ *Oval portrait plaque of young girl with whistle, late 19th century, signed "L. Sturm, Dresden, 1886" (Ludwig Sturm), impressed KPM with arrow on back, in oval frame, 13" high x 10" wide.* **$6,300**

determining prices of those that have survived, Afshine Emrani said that each may sell for as much as $250,000. Rare plaques like these are often found in museums.

The condition of a KPM plaque also affects its price. Most, since they were highly glazed and customarily hung instead of handled, have survived in perfect condition. Thus those that have sustained even minor damage, like scratches, cracks, or chips, fetch considerably lower prices. Those suffering major damage are worthless.

KPM's painted plaques arouse so much interest and command such high prices that, over the last couple of years, unscrupulous dealers have entered the market. According to dealer Balazs Benedek, KPM plaques are "the mother of all fakes. About 90 percent of KPM plaques are mid- to late-20th century reproductions. And about 70 percent are not hand painted."

Collectors should be aware that genuine KPM paintings always boast rich, shiny, glazes that preserve their colors, and though subject matter may vary, they typically feature nude scenes, indoor portraits of women, or group gatherings in lush settings. Anything wildly different should raise suspicion.

Genuine KPMs, on their backs or edges, feature small icons of scepters deeply set in the porcelain, over the letters KPM. These marks are sometimes accompanied by an "H" or some other letter, which may indicate their production date or size. Some are imprinted with the size of the plaque as well, which facilitated sorting or shipping. Shallow or crooked imprints may reveal a fake.

Courtesy of John Moran Auctioneers

◄ *Porcelain rectangular plaque, painted after Thumann with Three Fates, Clotho, Lachesis and Atropos, measuring and cutting the thread of life, late 19th/early 20th century, impressed monogram and scepter mark, further impressed "565" and "415," "W" and with incised cipher, with paper label "Mit Genehmigung / Professor / P. Thumann / Berlin," signed lower right "Wenzel," within gilt frame, 21 3/4" high x 16 1/4" wide.* **$36,000**

CLOSE-UP!

Courtesy of John Moran Auctioneers

▲ ▶ *Porcelain rectangular plaque painted after Thumann with Three Fates, Clotho, Lachesis and Atropos, measuring and cutting thread of life, late 19th/early 20th century, impressed monogram and scepter mark, further impressed "255" and "195," "W" and with incised cipher, framed, 9 3/4" high x 7 1/2" wide.* **$4,500**

Courtesy of James D. Julia Auctioneers, Fairfield, Maine, www.jamesdjulia.com

*Plaque of nude maiden hovering above lily pond with arms raised, in gold frame with blue velvet liner, frame with enclosed back with two paper labels with diagrams of marks on plaque that indicate plaque signed "KPM" with scepter mark, very good to excellent condition with some very minor wear to gilding on frame, plaque 6 1/2" x 9 1/2", frame 12 3/4" x 16".* **$11,850**

Courtesy of Kaminski Auctions

*Plaque of cherub, 19th century, 12" high x 9" wide (view), 19" high x 16" wide overall.* **$2,200**

Courtesy of Kaminski Auctions

*Porcelain plaque of girl with basket, 19th century, 7 1/2" high x 9 1/2" wide (view), 15" high x 17" wide overall.* **$1,300**

Courtesy of Kaminski Auctions

*Plaque of woman playing instrument, 19th century, 13" x 10" (view), 16 7/8" x 13 5/8" overall.* **$1,600**

Courtesy of Kaminski Auctions

*Porcelain plaque of woman in pink with butterfly, 19th century, 8" high x 8 1/2" wide (view), 11" high x 16" wide overall.* **$1,800**

Courtesy of Heritage Auctions

Courtesy of Skinner, Inc.; www.skinnerinc.com

*Painted porcelain and enamel ewer, circa 1880, ewer with blue ground, painted medallion under scalloped spout of classical scene of young man watching girl stringing flowers, body decorated with painted and enameled sphinxes, stylized floral and foliated motifs, leading to trifurcated C-scroll handle, resting on four scroll and shell feet, marks: KPM, (orb and cross), (scepter), D, 28.2, impressed P, S2; with expected minor rubbing of gilt and minor surface wear commensurate with age, 20 3/4" high.* **$9,375**

*Hand-painted porcelain plaque of seated woman in black dress holding Bible, 19th century, polychrome enamel-decorated, signed "J. Matthews," with impressed factory mark, in modern brown Lucite frame, plaque 7 7/8" x 5 1/2", 13 7/8" x 11 1/2" overall.* **$308**

Courtesy of Heritage Auctions

▶ *Framed Hausmaler painted porcelain plaque of Jesus in temple with elders, circa 1890, marks: (scepter), KPM, H, 9 3/4-7 3/8 (incised), very good condition, 9 3/4" high x 7 3/8" wide.* **$3,375**

Courtesy of Mark Mussio, Humler & Nolan

*Figure of Westphalian Buckeburgerian, woman in native dress sitting on basket of apples, designed by Karl Himmelstoss, signed "KPM" with scepter, orb and cross and Iron Cross, also marked "140/320" in brown slip, excellent original condition, small areas of glaze loss in green and black fabric of skirt and blouse, 10" high.* **$550**

Courtesy of Heritage Auctions

*Porcelain plaque of nobleman with weapon, circa 1880, painted by Hans Kundmuller (1837-1893, Germany), marked "KPM" verso, good condition with wear commensurate with age and no visible repairs, 19 1/4" x 16".* **$8,125**

Courtesy of Heritage Auctions

*Painted porcelain plaque of seated woman with oil lamp in Rococo-style giltwood frame, circa 1900, marks: (scepter), KPM, 11, 9" high x 6 1/2" wide, 18" high x 13" wide overall.* **$1,500**

# Limoges

"Limoges" has become the generic identifier for porcelain produced in Limoges, France, and the surrounding vicinity. Over 40 manufacturers in the area have, at some point, used the term as a descriptor of their work, and there are at least 400 different Limoges identification marks. The common denominator is the product itself – fine hard paste porcelain created from the necessary components found in abundance in the Limoges region: kaolin and feldspar.

Until the 1700s, porcelain was exclusively a product of China, introduced to the Western world by Marco Polo and imported at great expense. In 1765, the discovery of kaolin in St. Yrieixin, a small town near Limoges, made French production of porcelain possible. (The chemist's wife credited with the kaolin discovery thought at first that it would prove useful in making soap.)

Limoges entrepreneurs quickly capitalized on the find. Adding to the area's allure were expansive forests providing fuel for wood-burning kilns; the nearby Vienne River, with water for working clay; and a workforce eager to trade farming for a (hopefully) more lucrative pursuit. Additionally, as the companies would be operating outside metropolitan Paris, labor and production costs would be significantly less.

By the early 1770s, numerous porcelain manufacturers were at work in Limoges and its environs. Demand for the porcelain was high because it was both useful and decorative. To meet that demand, firms employed trained, as well as untrained, artisans for the detailed hand painting required. (Although nearly every type of Limoges has its fans, the most sought-after—and valuable—are those pieces decorated by a company's professional artists.) At its industrial peak in 1900, Limoges factories employed over 8,000 workers in some aspect of porcelain production.

Courtesy of Skinner, Inc.;
www.skinnerinc.com

*Arts & Crafts silver and Limoges enamel box, Frank Gardner Hale, enamel panel depicting butterfly and mounted into silver box, box marked F.G. HALE, enamel approximately 3 3/4" x 3 1/4", box 6 1/4" x 4 1/4" x 1 7/8".*
**$6,765**

A myriad of products classified as Limoges flooded the marketplace from the late 1700s onward. Among them were tableware pieces, such as tea and punch sets, trays, pitchers, compotes, bowls and plates. Also popular were vases and flower baskets, dresser sets, trinket boxes, ash receivers, figural busts, and decorative plaques.

Although produced in France, Limoges porcelain was soon destined for export overseas; eventually over 80 percent of Limoges porcelain was exported. The United States proved a particularly reliable customer. Notable among the importers was the Haviland China Co.; until the 1940s, its superior, exquisitely decorated china was produced in Limoges and then distributed in the United States.

By the early 20th century, many exporters in the United States were purchasing porcelain blanks from the Limoges factories for decoration stateside. The base product was authentically made in France, but production costs were significantly lower: Thousands of untrained porcelain painters put their skills to work for a minimal wage. Domestic decoration of the blanks also meant that importers could select designs suited to the specific tastes of target audiences.

Because Limoges was a regional designation rather than the identifier of a specific manufacturer, imported pieces were often marked with the name of the exporting firm, followed by the word "Limoges." Beginning in 1891, "France" was added. Some confusion has arisen from products marked "Limoges China Co." (aka "American Limoges"). This Ohio-based firm, in business from 1902-1955, has absolutely no connection to the porcelain produced in France.

The heyday of quality French Limoges lasted roughly into the 1930s. Production continues today, but after World War II, designs and painting techniques became much more standardized.

Vintage Limoges is highly sought-after by today's collectors. They're drawn to the delicacy of the porcelain as well as the colors and skill of decoration. Viewing a well-conceived Limoges piece is like seeing a painting in a new form. Valuation is based on age, decorative execution and, as with any collectible, individual visual appeal.

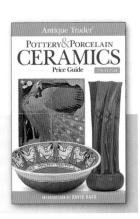

Courtesy of Mark Mussio, Humler & Nolan

Courtesy of Heritage Auctions

*Bernardaud porcelain vase hand-decorated with tall stalks of columbine in blue against gold band, gold around rim, green stamped "B & Co France" on bottom, excellent condition, 15" high.* **$150**

*Three-piece Art Nouveau-style hand-painted porcelain tea service, 20th century, marks: LIMOGES, FRANCE, HANDPAINTED, CHINA, W PICKARD A, 9 3/4" high.* **$406**

Courtesy of Skinner, Inc.; www.skinnerinc.com

▲ *Enamel portrait plate depicting Elisabeth of Austria, Queen of France, 19th century, circular, with portrait of woman in jeweled purple hat and blue dress against black ground, signed "RP Limoges," 9 1/2" diameter.* **$246**

Courtesy of Leslie Hindman Auctioneers

◀ *Porcelain vase, William Guerin & Co., elongated ovoid form and decorated with portrait of woman, 14 1/8" high.* **$252**

Courtesy of Skinner, Inc.; www.skinnerinc.com

*Eight pieces of hand-painted Limoges porcelain, grapevine-decorated punch bowl, tray, and five sherbets, and iris-decorated vase with gilt elements, imperfections, height to 9 1/4", diameter to 13".* **$431**

Courtesy of Skinner, Inc.; www.skinnerinc.com

*Porcelain desk set, 19th century, ovoid tray with scrolled and pierced foliate handles, polychrome enameled floral bouquets, 8 5/8" long, together with two covered inkpots and candlestick, 2 5/8" high.* **$300-$500**

Courtesy of Skinner, Inc.; www.skinnerinc.com

*Hand-painted porcelain partial breakfast service, early 20th century, retailed by Delvaux, Paris, each piece enamel-decorated with red poppies, blue cornflowers, yellow crocuses, and gilt accents: covered chocolate pot, 6 1/2" high; covered hot milk jug; covered sugar bowl; kidney-shaped dish; sugar caster; salt and pepper casters; two cups; saucer; dish, 6 5/8" diameter; dish, 7 1/4" diameter; small bowl; and small creamer, 2 7/8" high; together with similar Limoges sugar caster retailed by Delvaux and decorated with strawberries and cornflowers.* **$277**

Courtesy of Skinner, Inc.; www.skinnerinc.com

*Pair of porcelain hand-painted vases, 19th century, molded with flowers and foliage, gilded and polychrome enamel decorated central cartouches of maidens, 18 3/4" high.* **$300**

Courtesy of Skinner, Inc.; www.skinnerinc.com

*Six Ancienne Manufacture Royale de Limoges Pompeian-style porcelain plates, 20th century, each with different classical vignette on iron red ground, and variant borders of grape leaves and anthemions with gilt accents, 10 1/4" diameter.* **$400**

Courtesy of Skinner, Inc.; www.skinnerinc.com

*Enamel vase, 20th century, textured relief over purple ground, artist signed, paper label for E. Pillorget Darnat Cognac, hairline along footrim, 9 1/4" high.* **$600-$800**

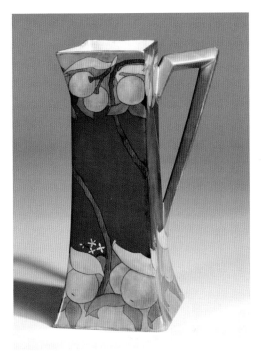

Courtesy of Skinner, Inc.; www.skinnerinc.com

*Hand-painted porcelain pitcher with matte black ground, gilt rim and handle, and bands of oranges along top and bottom of body, underglaze green "D & Co France" and impressed "F" marks to base, 13 3/4" high.* **$185**

Courtesy of Skinner, Inc.; www.skinnerinc.com

*Art Nouveau porcelain vase, body with opalescent and copper luster, decorated with irises, 12 3/4" high x 7" diameter.* **$338**

Courtesy of Skinner, Inc.; www.skinnerinc.com

*Porcelain potpourri vase and cover, 19th century, oval shape heavily pierced with gilded borders to pink ground and polychrome floral cartouches to either side, paneled cover with colored flowers and gilded flower finial, 10 3/4" high.* **$500-$700**

*Enamel portrait plaque,
early 20th century,
rectangular, with
polychrome enameled
depiction of Titian,
artist signed "C. Faure,"
in wood frame, 8 1/2" x
12".* **$308**

*Pair of Rutherford B. Hayes presidential oyster plates, circa
1880, each of Haviland Limoges porcelain and designed
by Theodore Russell Davis, gilded and polychrome enamel
decorated, reverse with eagle to border, artist signed and
printed factory marks, 8 5/8" diameter.* **$1,680**

*French Barbotine De Marcel
Chaufriasse pate-sur-pate vase,
circa 1900, marks: BARBOTINE
DE MARCEL CHAUFRIASSE,
LIMOGES, rubbing to gilt,
surface wear commensurate with
age, 6" high.* **$375**

Courtesy of
Heritage Auctions

*Set of 12 Charles Ahrenfeldt porcelain plates, circa 1900, gilt rim and border of stylized scrolling foliate and painted floral medallions, marks: CA (interlaced), C. AHRENFELDT LIMOGES pour C. REIZENSTEIN, PITTSBURGH-ALLEGHENY, Patented, 9 3/4" diameter.* **$275**

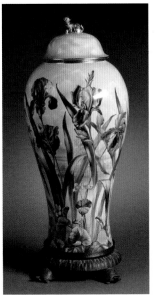

Courtesy of Skinner, Inc.; www.skinnerinc.com

*Limoges-style porcelain covered floor vase on stand, early 20th century, domed cover with foo dog finial, baluster body polychrome painted with irises with lake in background, unmarked, 29" high, together with circular bronze base cast with leaftips on four turtle-form feet.* **$2,952**

Courtesy of Skinner, Inc.; www.skinnerinc.com

*Pair of pink porcelain vases, late 19th century, gilded scrolled trim, pierced neck and cover, polychrome-enamel decorated with flowers, 12 3/4" high.* **$180**

# Majolica

In 1851, an English potter was hoping that his new interpretation of a centuries-old style of ceramics would be well received at the "Great Exhibition of the Industries of All Nations" set to open May 1 in London's Hyde Park.

Potter Herbert Minton had high hopes for his display. His father, Thomas Minton, founded a pottery works in the mid-1790s in Stoke-on-Trent, Staffordshire. Herbert Minton had designed a "new" line of pottery, and his chemist, Leon Arnoux, had developed a process that resulted in vibrant, colorful glazes that came to be called "majolica."

Trained as an engineer, Arnoux also studied the making of encaustic tiles, and had been appointed art director at Minton's works in 1848. His job was to introduce and promote new products. Victorian fascination with the natural world prompted Arnoux to reintroduce the work of Bernard Palissy, whose naturalistic, bright-colored "maiolica" wares had been created in the 16th century. But Arnoux used a thicker body to make pieces sturdier. This body was given a coating of opaque white glaze, which provided a surface for decoration.

Pieces were modeled in high relief, featuring butterflies and other insects, flowers and leaves, fruit, shells, animals, and fish. Queen Victoria's endorsement of the new pottery prompted its acceptance by the general public.

When Minton introduced his wares at Philadelphia's 1876 Centennial Exhibition, American potters also began to produce majolica.

For more information on majolica, see *Warman's Majolica Identification and Price Guide* by Mark F. Moran.

Courtesy of Strawser Auctions

◄ *Monumental Sarreguemines (attributed) majolica two-piece jardiniere with four lion heads, paw feet, repair to lower jaws of lions, hairline to jardiniere, 48" high x 20" wide.* **$1,624**

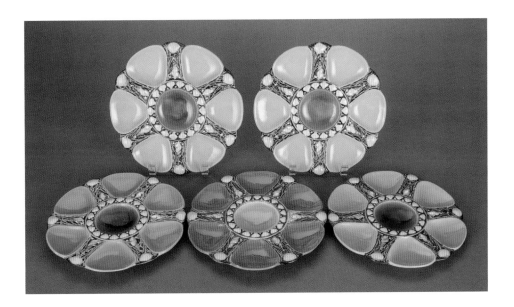

## Other Majolica Makers

**John Adams & Co.,** Hanley, Stoke-on-Trent, Staffordshire, England, operated the Victoria Works, producing earthenware, jasperware, Parian, majolica, 1864-1873.

Another Staffordshire pottery, **Samuel Alcock & Co.,** Cobridge, 1828-1853; Burslem, 1830-1859, produced earthenware, china and Parian.

The **W. & J.A. Bailey Alloa Pottery** was founded in Alloa, the principal town in Clackmannanshire, located near Edinburgh, Scotland.

The **Bevington** family of potters worked in Hanley, Staffordshire, England in the late 19th century.

**W. Brownfield & Son** operated in Burslem and Cobridge, Staffordshire, England from 1850-1891.

**T.C. Brown-Westhead, Moore & Co.** produced earthenware and porcelain at Hanley, Stoke-on-Trent, Staffordshire, from about 1862 to 1904.

The **Choisy-le-Roi** faience factory of Choisy-le-Roi, France, produced majolica from 1860 until 1910. The firm's wares are not always marked. The common mark is usually a black ink stamp "Choisy-le-Roi" pictured to the right with a large "HBm," which stands for Hippolyte Boulenger, a director at the pottery.

**William T. Copeland & Sons** pottery of Stoke-on-Trent, Staffordshire, England, began producing porcelain and earthenware in 1847. (Josiah Spode established a pottery at Stoke-on-Trent in 1770. In 1833, the firm was purchased by William Copeland and Thomas Garrett. In 1847, Copeland became the sole owner. W.T.

Courtesy of Heritage Auctions

*Five English majolica oyster plates, Minton, Stoke-on-Trent, Staffordshire, England, 19th century, marks: MINTON, TWR4 IV (in diamond), M, (arrow), 1323, 9 1/2" diameter.*
**$1,375**

*Large majolica figural centerpiece with faience bowl, seated nude female mermaid figure with double serpent-like tails straddling dolphin with tail raised above her head, she holds golden ribbon as reins steering dolphin, figural putti with arms stretched to left side seated on dolphin's head, round raised base decorated with tall reeds and lily pads, exterior of bowl decorated with griffins and swirling filigree on yellow background with signature for A. Jean, single hairline in base with chips to leaves, 19 1/2" diameter, 30" high overall.* **$1,452**

Copeland & Sons continued until a 1976 merger when it became Royal Worcester Spode. Copeland majolica pieces are sometimes marked with an impressed "COPELAND," but many are unmarked.)

**Jose A. Cunha,** Caldas da Rainha, southern Portugal, also worked in the style of Bernard Palissy, the great French Renaissance potter.

**Julius Dressler,** Bela, Czech Republic, was founded 1888, producing faience, majolica and porcelain. In 1920, the name was changed to EPIAG. The firm closed about 1945.

**Eureka Pottery** was located in Trenton, New Jersey, circa 1883-1887.

**Railway Pottery** was established by S. Fielding & Co., Stoke-on-Trent, Staffordshire, England, 1879.

There were two **Thomas Forester** potteries active in the late 19th century in Staffordshire, England. Some sources list the more famous of the two as Thomas Forester & Sons, Ltd. at the Phoenix Works, Longton.

Established in the early 19th century, the **Gien** pottery works is located on the banks of France's Loire River near Orleans.

**Joseph Holdcroft** majolica ware was produced at Daisy Bank in Longton, Staffordshire, England, from 1870 to 1885. Items can be found marked with "J HOLDCROFT," but many pieces can only be attributed by the patterns and colors that are documented to have come from the Holdcroft potteries.

**George Jones & Sons, Ltd.,** Stoke, Staffordshire, started operation in about 1864 as George Jones and in 1873 became George Jones & Sons, Ltd. The firm operated the Trent Potteries in Stoke-on-Trent (renamed "Crescent Potteries" in about 1907).

In about 1877, **Samuel Lear** erected a small china works in Hanley, Staffordshire. Lear produced domestic china and, in addition, decorated all kinds of earthenware made by other manufacturers, including "spirit kegs." In 1882, the firm expanded to include production of majolica, ivory-body earthenware, and Wedgwood-type jasperware. The business closed in 1886.

Robert Charbonnier founded the **Longchamp** tile works in 1847 to make red clay tiles, but the factory soon started to produce majolica. Longchamp is known for its "barbotine" pieces (a paste of clay used in decorating coarse pottery in relief) made with vivid colors, especially oyster plates.

**Hugo Lonitz** operated in Haldensleben, Germany, from 1868-1886, and later Hugo Lonitz & Co., 1886-1904, producing household and decorative porcelain, earthenware, and metalwares. Look for a mark of two entwined fish.

The **Lunéville** pottery was founded about 1728 by Jacques Chambrette in the city that bears its name, in the Alsace-Lorraine region of northeastern France. The firm became famous for its blue monochromatic and floral patterns. Around 1750, ceramist Paul-

Louis Cyfflé introduced a pattern with animals and historical figures. Lunéville products range from hand-painted faience and majolica to pieces influenced by the Art Deco movement.

The **Massier** family began producing ceramics in Vallauris, France, in the mid-18th century.

**François Maurice,** School of Paris, was active from 1875-1885 and also worked in the style of Bernard Palissy.

**George Morley & Co.** was located in East Liverpool, Ohio, 1884-1891.

**Morley & Co. Pottery** was founded in 1879, Wellsville, Ohio, making graniteware and majolica.

**Orchies,** a majolica manufacturer in northern France near Lille, is also known under the mark "Moulin des Loups & Hamage," 1920s.

**Faïencerie de Pornic** is located near Quimper, France.

**Quimper** pottery has a long history. Tin-glazed, hand-painted pottery has been made in Quimper, France, since the late 17th century. The earliest firm, founded in 1685 by Jean Baptiste Bousquet, was known as HB Quimper. Another firm, founded in 1772 by Francois Eloury, was known as Porquier. A third firm, founded by Guillaume Dumaine in 1778, was known as HR or Henriot Quimper. All three companies made similar pottery decorated with designs of Breton peasants, and sea and flower motifs.

The **Rörstrand** factory made the first faience (tin-glazed earthenware) produced in Sweden. It was established in 1725 by Johann Wolff, near Stockholm.

The earthenware factory of **Salins** was established in 1857 in Salins-les-Bains, near the French border with Switzerland. Salins was awarded the gold medal at the International Exhibition of Decorative Arts in Paris in 1912.

**Sarreguemines** wares are named for the city in the Lorraine region of northeastern France. The pottery was founded in 1790 by Nicholas-Henri Jacobi. For more than 100 years, it flourished under the direction of the Utzschneider family.

**Wilhelm Schiller and Sons,** Bodenbach, Bohemia, was established 1885.

**Thomas-Victor Sergent** was one of the School of Paris ceramists of the late 19th century who was influenced by the works of Bernard Palissy.

**St. Clement** was founded by Jacques Chambrette in Saint-Clément, France, in 1758. Chambrette also established works in Lunéville.

The **St. Jean de Bretagne** pottery works are located near Quimper, France.

**Vallauris** is a pottery center in southeastern

Courtesy of Strawser Auctions

*Monumental Minton majolica floor jardiniere in form of cherub riding dolphin terminating in turquoise trumpet-shaped flower vase, designed by Hughes Protat, shape No. 808, professional repairs to base, 27 1/2" high x 24" long x 17 1/2" wide.* **$1,856**

*Minton majolica "gun dog" game tureen with hunting dog on cover and rabbit and pheasant on base with basketweave ground, holly and berry motif, paw feet, 14" long.*
**$2,784**

France, near Cannes. Companies in production there include Massier and Foucard-Jourdan.

**Victoria Pottery Co.** was located in Hanley, Staffordshire, England from 1895-1927.

**Wardle & Co.** was established 1871 at Hanley, Staffordshire, England.

**Josiah Wedgwood** was born in Burslem, Staffordshire, England, on July 12, 1730, into a family with a long pottery tradition. At the age of nine, after the death of his father, he joined the family business. In 1759, he set up his own pottery works in Burslem. There he produced cream-colored earthenware that found favor with Queen Charlotte. In 1762, she appointed him royal supplier of dinnerware. From the public sale of "Queen's Ware," as it came to be known, Wedgwood was able to build a production community in 1768, which he named Etruria, near Stoke-on-Trent, and a second factory equipped with tools and ovens of his own design. (Etruria is the ancient land of the Etruscans, in what is now northern Italy.)

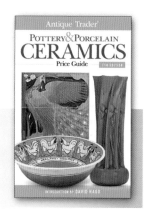

Courtesy of Skinner, Inc.; www.skinnerinc.com

*George Jones majolica cheese dish, England, late 19th century, cover molded with flowering cherry blossoms spreading from double-branch handle on cobalt ground, above band of molded basketweave repeated as border on rim of dish, pad mark, 12" high.* **$1,200**

Courtesy of Heritage Auctions

*Boch Freres majolica rooster, 20th century, marks: Boch Freres, La Louvier, 32" high.* **$3,125**

Courtesy of Strawser Auctions

◀ *George Jones majolica stag and doe comport with rabbit, professional repair to doe's ear and stag's antler, 10" high x 10 1/2" diameter.* **$5,452**

Courtesy of Strawser Auctions

▲ *Minton majolica fruit plate with oranges and lemons, rim repair, 8" diameter.* **$170**

*Two Minton
majolica parrots,
12 1/8" high.*
**$504**

*Minton majolica garden seat, England, circa 1870,
shaped seat with central flowerhead over hexagonal
baluster-form body decorated with polychrome
arabesques, with impressed factory and cipher
marks, 19 3/4" high.* **$2,040**

*Minton majolica Palissy ewer, England, circa 1860,
modeled by Hamlet Bourne after Palissy design, with
head of triton below spout, mermaid draped along
handle and Renaissance-style cartouches and motifs
across body, all on cobalt ground, 10 1/2" high.*
**$1,422**

*Large majolica seated musician figure in colorful attire playing guitar, legs crossed, impressed numbers on bottom 1825 over 22, stress hairlines along base with minor glaze slips, small edge chips and break and repair at top of guitar neck, 28" high x 20" wide x 19" deep.* **$666**

*Monumental Continental majolica floor vase with milk maiden and cow, various professional repairs, 35" high.* **$580**

*Etruscan majolica swan and water lily cheese keeper, rim nick to underside of rim on base, 8".* **$928**

Courtesy of Heritage Auctions

*Pair of Minton majolica snake handle jardinières, circa 1843, 10 1/2" high x 16 3/4" wide.* **$4,375**

Courtesy of
Kaminski Auctions

*Two Ginori majolica
handled urns, circa
1900, 11" high.* **$750**

Courtesy of Strawser Auctions

*Rare Minton majolica cat with
mouse figural pitcher, shape
No. 1924, calico cat 10" high.*
**$6,960**

Courtesy of
Strawser Auctions

*Monumental
Continental majolica
shell compote, 16"
wide x 12" high.* **$638**

Courtesy of Skinner, Inc.; www.skinnerinc.com

*Fifteen-piece Wedgwood majolica fruit service, England, circa 1872, each with polychrome decoration of pierced basket border to leaf and berry trim, impressed marks, 12 plates (8 7/8" diameter) and three compotes set on four hoofed feet (two circular, 9 1/8" and 9 1/4" diameter, and one oval, 11" long).* **$1,230**

Courtesy of Skinner, Inc.; www.skinnerinc.com

*Wedgwood majolica game pie dish and cover, England, circa 1878, oval shape with molded relief of dead game between fruiting grapevine festoons, hare finial, impressed mark, 8 1/8" long.* **$360**

Courtesy of Skinner, Inc.; www.skinnerinc.com

*Griffen, Smith & Hill Etruscan majolica compote, Phoenixville, Pennsylvania, circa 1880, polychrome enamel decorated and molded in shell and seaweed pattern, impressed mark, 6 1/4" high.* **$330**

# Meissen

Augustus II, Elector of Saxony and King of Poland, founded the Royal Saxon Porcelain Manufactory in Albrechtsburg, Meissen, in 1710. Johann Friedrich Bottger, an alchemist, and Tschirnhaus, a nobleman, experimented with kaolin from the Dresden area to produce porcelain. By 1720, the factory produced a whiter hard-paste porcelain than that from the Far East.

The Meissen factory experienced its golden age from the 1730s to the 1750s. By the 1730s, Meissen employed nearly 100 workers. It became known for its porcelain sculptures; Meissen dinnerware also won acclaim.

The Meissen factory was destroyed and looted by the forces of Frederick the Great during the Seven Years' War (1756-1763). It was reopened but never achieved its former greatness.

By the early 1800s, Meissen's popularity began to wane. In the 19th century, the factory reissued some of its earlier forms.

Many marks were used by the Meissen factory. The famous crossed swords mark was adopted in 1724. The swords mark with a small dot between the hilts was used from 1763 to 1774, and a star between the hilts from 1774 to 1814.

Courtesy of Leslie Hindman Auctioneers

*Porcelain figural group, probably 20th century, woman with duck and swan on circular base, bearing blue crossed swords mark to underside, 9 3/4" high.* **$536**

Courtesy of Skinner, Inc.; www.skinnerinc.com

▲ *Two porcelain figures, late 19th century, each polychrome enamel-decorated and gilt-accented, with first quality crossed swords mark, boy with watering can and shovel, incised "C69," and girl with birdcage resting on her shoulder and lamb at her feet, incised "F73," height to 7 5/8".* **$1,230**

Courtesy of Skinner, Inc.; www.skinnerinc.com

▲ *Porcelain figure of Scaramouch with lute, 20th century, polychrome enamel-decorated, Commedia dell'arte character standing on freeform base with applied flowers, with first quality crossed swords mark and incised "215," 7 1/4" high.* **$492**

Courtesy of Leslie Hindman Auctioneers

▼ *Porcelain schneeballen cup and saucer with allover floral encrusted exterior and leafy branches and gilt banding, cup with crossed swords in underglaze blue, saucer 5 1/4" diameter.* **$882**

Courtesy of Bonham's

*Oval reticulated bowl surmounted by maiden holding cornucopia and bacchanalian putto holding aloft wine glass, raised on tree form support, trunk flanked by putto blowing horn for hunt, dead game at his feet, and putto pulling in fishing net, his catch at his feet, on scroll feet, late 19th century, underglaze blue crossed swords, incised P.102 and impressed 137, 29 1/4" high.* **$50,000**

Courtesy of Skinner, Inc.; www.skinnerinc.com

▲ *Three porcelain figures of children, late 19th to 20th century, all polychrome enamel-decorated and gilt-accented, with first quality crossed swords mark, group with four putti gathered around fire set on pedestal, incised "2453," girl selecting flower sprays from basket resting on tree stump, impressed "1213," and boy carrying basket of grapes on his back, incised "G5," height to 4 5/8".* **$984**

Courtesy of Skinner, Inc.; www.skinnerinc.com

◄ *Porcelain figure group of putti with cannon, late 19th century, polychrome enamel-decorated with gilded accents, one figure with shield, other holding fuse, on naturalistic base adorned with scrollwork, with first quality crossed swords mark and incised "639," 5 1/4" high.* **$738**

*Centerpiece, rocaille-molded pierced oval basket applied with floral garland, interior with insects and floral sprays, over Beauty and her gallant in 18th century dress, encircling tree-form standard further applied with flowering vines, rising from waisted rocaille base, late 19th/early 20th century, underglaze blue crossed swords mark, incised "2772" and impressed "110," 19 3/4" high x 13 3/4" wide x 10 3/4" deep.* **$3,000**

*Pair of German urns, cobalt blue porcelain, 19th century, 15 1/2" high x 9 1/2" wide at handles.* **$950**

*Porcelain figure group, late 19th/20th century, polychrome enamel-decorated and gilt-accented, molded as two standing figures, man holding carafe of wine and glass, and woman with baskets of fruit and flowers, on ovoid naturalistic base, with first quality crossed swords mark and incised "C 60," 6 1/4" high.* **$615**

Courtesy of Elite Decorative Arts

*Figurine of woman with geese, signed in blue underglaze, 9 1/2" high.* **$850**

Courtesy of Elite Decorative Arts

*Large figurine, Leda & Swan, signed in blue underglaze, 10" high.* **$1,100**

Courtesy of Skinner, Inc.; www.skinnerinc.com

▲ *Two porcelain figures of putti, 20th century, each polychrome enamel-decorated and gilt-accented, and with first quality crossed swords marks, one modeled as putto working in garden and personifying earth from "Elements" series, incised "C100," other modeled with two putti writing in book, incised "C36," height to 4 5/8".* **$800**

Courtesy of Skinner, Inc.; www.skinnerinc.com

▶ *Two porcelain figures, late 19th century, each polychrome enamel-decorated, with first quality crossed swords marks, one boy with shovel and watering can, incised "C69," and girl with applied flower garland, incised "F69," height to 7 1/2".* **$1,230**

Courtesy of Skinner, Inc.; www.skinnerinc.com

▶ *Pair of porcelain figures of children with fowl, late 19th century, each polychrome enamel-decorated, gilt-accented, molded seated, and with first quality crossed swords mark, girl with hen and basket of eggs, incised "2281," and boy with rooster and basket of flowers, incised "2923," height to 4 1/8".* **$738**

*Porcelain group of revelers, standing man with basket of grapes and woman and man with barrel, crossed swords in underglaze blue, incised C65, 9 1/8" high.* **$882**

Courtesy of Skinner, Inc.; www.skinnerinc.com

▲ *Pair of porcelain hand-painted cabinet plates, late 19th/early 20th century, each with central circular unsigned polychrome enamel-decorated scene of courting couple in landscape, set within rococo-style gilded reserve to deep blue ground, reticulated border decorated with pale blue flower heads and further gilding, with first quality crossed swords mark and various impressed numbers, 10 1/8" diameter.* **$2,583**

Courtesy of Skinner, Inc.; www.skinnerinc.com

*Two porcelain figures of garden children, late 19th century, each polychrome enamel-decorated and gilt-accented, and with first quality crossed swords mark, girl carrying sickle and basket of flowers, incised "4," and boy removing single flower from basket, indistinctly incised, height to 5 3/8".* **$492**

Courtesy of Leslie Hindman Auctioneers

▲ *Two porcelain figural master salts in Blue Onion pattern, modeled as reclining woman and man, with crossed swords mark in underglaze blue, wider salt 11 1/2".* **$1,260**

Courtesy of Skinner, Inc.; www.skinnerinc.com

*Porcelain figure group of Broken Bridge, 20th century, polychrome enamel-decorated and molded with two putti and man assisting distraught woman over stream covered by plank, on oval naturalistic base with fluted border, with first quality crossed swords mark and incised "F63," 9 3/4" high.* **$1,476**

Courtesy of Leslie Hindman Auctioneers

▲ *Pair of porcelain cabinet plates, each with reticulated rim and painted cartouche depicting figures with horses on cobalt field, with crossed swords in underglaze blue and other impressed marks, 9 1/4" diameter.* **$2,142**

Courtesy of Skinner, Inc.; www.skinnerinc.com

▲ *Porcelain figure of Cupid as beggar, 20th century, figure in tattered clothing and supported on crutches, on circular base, with first quality crossed swords mark and incised "L112," 8 3/8" high.* **$492**

Courtesy of John Moran Auctioneers

▲ *Candelabra, each with shaped rocaille-molded base painted with birds and butterflies, surmounted by two figures (one with man and child, other with woman and child), issuing cornucopia-form stem fitted with detachable top section comprising central light and three S-form candle arms encrusted with flowers and fruit, late 19th/early 20th century, underglaze blue crossed swords marks, two pieces, each 19" high x 10" diameter.* **$3,998**

Courtesy of Skinner, Inc.; www.skinnerinc.com

▲ Three porcelain figures of women, late 19th to 20th century, each polychrome enamel-decorated and gilt-accented, with first quality crossed swords mark, standing figure collecting flowers in basket, incised "C72," seated woman with dog on her lap, dog looking in mirror, incised "F50," and seated woman feeding milk to cat on her lap, incised "B94," height to 6". **$1,476**

Courtesy of Leslie Hindman Auctioneers

◄ Porcelain urn and cover, cover modeled with bird perched on branch, urn of baluster form with white ground painted to show bouquet of flowers on one side and figures in landscape on reverse, with applied flowers and vines bearing fruit throughout, base overpainted with crossed swords, possibly second, 16 5/8" high overall. **$536**

# Sèvres

Some of the most desirable porcelain ever produced was made at the Sèvres factory, originally established at Vincennes, France, and transferred, through permission of Madame de Pompadour, to Sèvres as the Royal Manufactory about the middle of the 18th century. King Louis XV took sole responsibility for the works in 1759, when production of hard paste wares began. Between 1850 and 1900, many biscuit and soft-paste pieces were made again. Fine early pieces are scarce and high-priced. Many of those available today are late productions. The various Sèvres marks have been copied, and pieces in the "Sèvres style" are similar to actual Sèvres wares but not necessarily from that factory.

Courtesy of Rago Arts and Auction Center

*Large framed earthenware charger with pheasant, 1881, Emile Belet (d. 1896), Felix Optat Milet (1838-1911), signed Belet to front, Sèvres stamp and date to back, original lacquered wood frame 30 1/2" square, charger 23" diameter.* **$1,500**

Courtesy of Elite
Decorative Arts

*Large tray plaque
with hand-painted
floral still life titled
"Philippine Jeune,"
dated 1823, signed
lower left and dated
by listed French
artist of period, old
staple repair to back
of plaque, 20" x 17",
frame 25 1/2" x
22 1/2".* **$6,750**

Courtesy of J. Garrett Auctioneers

▲ *Plate in bronze stand, 19th century,
courting couple with gold overlay border,
signed R. Pelib, with Sèvres mark, 9 1/2"
wide, frame 12 1/2" wide.* **$600**

Courtesy of Rago Arts and Auction Center

◄ *Enamel-decorated porcelain cabinet vase,
circa 1900, Taxile Doat (1851-1939), signed,
chip to foot ring, 5" x 2 3/4".* **$650**

Courtesy of Mark Mussio,
Humler & Nolan

*Monumental centerpiece mounted within elaborate bronze doré frame, porcelain oval body with Victorian courting scene near lake, obverse of castle-like house on far banks, floral sprigs and spear designs in Roman gold within bowl, metalwork of bearded men masks adorning each end with foliage, rim trimmed with leaves, gilt base with acanthus leaf collar, ribbon motif, beadwork and four squared buttresses with raised flowers, signed by P. Robin, excellent original condition, porcelain body 4" x 13 1/2", 17 1/2" handle to handle, 11" high.* **$2,100**

Courtesy of Skinner, Inc.;
www.skinnerinc.com

*Porcelain jeweled coffee cup and saucer, date letter for 1758, cup with polychrome hand-painted portraits of Gabrielle d'Estrees, Henry IV, and Marie de Medici, saucer with bouquet of flowers, both with gilt-decorated blue ground set with enameled "jewels," with underglaze blue factory marks, cup 2 7/8" high.* **$960**

Courtesy of Skinner, Inc.; www.skinnerinc.com

*Pair of porcelain hand-painted three-light candelabra, 19th century, polychrome enameled and gilded, dark blue ground with foliate framed cartouches of nymph with cherubs to one side, landscape to reverse, 16 1/4" high.* **$1,599**

Courtesy of Leslie Hindman Auctioneers

*Gilt bronze mounted porcelain urn of baluster form with cobalt ground and gilt inscription at neck commemorating 1884 Paris shooting competition, with applied foliate and scroll handles, iron red Decore Sèvres mark and green 2.73 lozenge mark to base, 27" high.* **$1,890**

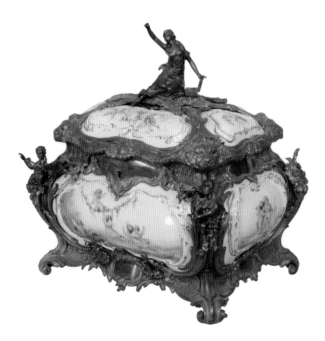

Courtesy of Fontaines Auction Gallery

◄ *Porcelain and bronze Bombay casket with four large painted porcelain panels with winged putti figures, four floral-decorated panels in lid, gilt bronze filigree framework with figural maidens on front corners with silvered finish, lion heads on corners of lid, seated figure of maiden on top beside trinket box with coins inside, sitting on large lion's pelt carpet draped across top, panels in very good condition with no breaks, cracks, chips or repairs, 16 1/2" high x 16" wide x 11 1/2" deep.* **$13,000**

Courtesy of Fine Arts
Auctions LLC

*Pair of 19th century
porcelain and champleve
enamel and bronze vases,
14 1/2" high.* **$1,000**

Courtesy of Rago Arts and Auction Center

*Pair of porcelain vases with pâte-sur-pâte
medallions, circa 1890, Taxile Doat (1851-
1939), one signed TD to body, other signed
T DOAT to body, HD-86-2-PN to base of
one, HD-86-4-PN on other, post-factory drill
hole to base of each, 14" x 5" each.* **$4,500**

Courtesy of Elite Decorative Arts

*Potpourri centerpiece, hand-painted, in brass frame,
Bares Sèvres mark under glaze to base, early to mid-20th
century, frame 8" wide x 4" high.* **$275**

Courtesy of Skinner, Inc.;
www.skinnerinc.com

*Cloisonné garniture
set, each with hand-
painted romantic
scenes within central
cartouches, on blue
ground, signed "Paul,"
height to 12 1/2",
width to 10 1/2",
depth to 5 1/4".* **$369**

Courtesy of Leslie Hindman Auctioneers

▲ *Pair of porcelain vases, 19th century, each of baluster form with faux lapis ground and gilt highlights, with iron red Dore Sèvres mark and blue S.85 lozenge marks to bases, 8 3/4" high.* **$441**

Courtesy of Mark Mussio, Humler & Nolan

◄ *Vase with blue, green, and yellow crystalline glaze and metal mounts, circa 1920, Paul Milet, marked on bottom with circular MP Sèvres and France ink stamps, crazing and chip to foot ring on ceramic portion of piece, 9 3/8" high.* **$350**

Courtesy of Courtesy of Clements

*Porcelain figural grouping of two seated women, one holding cherub, other feeding birds, marked on reserve with blue interlocking l's underglaze, piece missing off bow on ground in front of younger female, 9" high x 10" wide x 6" deep.* **$400**

Courtesy of Elite Decorative Arts

*Vintage porcelain covered box with hand-painted floral design on heavy gilt brass feet, circa mid-19th century, Sèvres mark to base, 7" wide x 4" high.* **$300-$500**

Courtesy of Skinner, Inc.; www.skinnerinc.com

*Three porcelain tea wares, 18th and 19th century, each gilded and with polychrome enamel decoration, globular miniature teapot and cover with floral sprays, 2 3/4" high; cylindrical single-cup teapot and cover with green ground and cartouches to either side, one with mountain landscape, one with fruit still life, 3 3/8" high; and handleless cup or bowl with floral sprays, 2 3/4" high.* **$800**

*Pair of porcelain and bronze urns, signed, 27 1/4" high.* **$650**

*Pair of 18th/early 19th century vases, heavily gilt, each bearing portraits of women signed "ds David Sèvres," with eagle emblems on opposite sides, 20" high.* **$3,750**

*Pair of 19th century porcelain ormolu mounted vases, 18 1/4" high.* **$1,500-$2,000**

*Pair of 19th century vases with bronze doré, decorated with satyr masks and painted scenes of flowers and couples in countryside on other side, 19 1/2" high x 5 5/8" wide.* **$1,500**

*Inkwell/pot, circa 1780,
hand-painted, removable
inkpot, 3 1/2" high.* **$110**

◀ *Porcelain box with
raised gold overlay, 19th
century, 13" wide x 9"
deep x 5" high.* **$5,500**

*Pair of Continental
porcelain capped urns,
circa 19th century, white
ground with pink borders,
decorated with birds and
flowers and gold overlays,
possibly Old Paris or
Sèvres, not marked,
14" high x 7" diameter.*
**$1,600**

Courtesy of World of Antiques, Inc.

*Pair of bronze mounted urns,
15 1/2" high x 7" wide.*
**$2,400-$4,800**

# Wedgwood

In 1754, Josiah Wedgwood and Thomas Whieldon of Fenton Vivian, Staffordshire, England, became partners in a pottery enterprise. Their products included marbled, agate, tortoiseshell, green glaze, and Egyptian black wares.

In 1759, Wedgwood opened his own pottery at the Ivy House works, Burslem. In 1764, he moved to the Brick House (Bell Works) at Burslem. The pottery concentrated on utilitarian pieces.

Between 1766 and 1769, Wedgwood built the famous works at Etruria. Among the most-renowned products of this plant were the Empress Catherina of Russia dinner service (1774) and the Portland Vase (1790s). The firm also made caneware, unglazed earthenwares (drabwares), piecrust wares, variegated and marbled wares, black basalt (developed in 1768), Queen's or creamware, and Jasperware (perfected in 1774).

Bone china was produced under the direction of Josiah Wedgwood II between 1812 and 1822, and was revived in 1878. Moonlight Lustre was made from 1805 to 1815. Fairyland Lustre began in 1920. All Lustre production ended in 1932.

A museum was established at the Etruria pottery in 1906. When Wedgwood moved to its modern plant at Barlaston, North Staffordshire, the museum was expanded.

Courtesy of Skinner, Inc.;
www.skinnerinc.com

*Pair of solid light blue Jasper roundels, England, 19th century, each with applied white classical figures from "Achilles in Scyros Among Daughters of Lycomedes," impressed marks, set in contemporary giltwood frames, one with slight surface pit and hairline, 9" diameter.* **$1,800**

Courtesy of James D. Julia Auctioneers, Fairfield, Maine, www.jamesdjulia.com

*Fairyland Lustre plaque decorated in "Picnic By River" design of orange and green elves against lavender background with green river, green roc bird and Flame Lustre sky, signed on reverse with gold Portland vase mark, "Wedgwood Made in England" and housed in black lacquered frame, very good to excellent condition, plaque 4 1/2" x 10", 7" x 12 3/4" overall.* **$5,333**

Courtesy of James D. Julia Auctioneers, Fairfield, Maine, www.jamesdjulia.com

*Fairyland Lustre punch bowl decorated on exterior with poplar trees against flame background, interior decorated in Woodland Elves V pattern and center mermaid medallion, signed on underside with Portland vase mark "WEDGWOOD MADE IN ENGLAND Z-5360," signed on interior in five places with initials MJ, very good to excellent condition with minor scratches to mermaid medallion, 11" diameter.* **$11,850**

Courtesy of James D. Julia Auctioneers, Fairfield, Maine, www.jamesdjulia.com

*Fairyland Lustre lily tray decorated with Celtic Ornaments II in gold and brown against mottled flame background, exterior of bowl trimmed with Celt pattern against flat black ground, signed on underside with Portland vase mark "WEDGWOOD ENGLAND," numerous scratches to bottom interior of bowl, otherwise very good condition, 13" diameter.* **$474**

Courtesy of Thomaston Place
Auction Galleries

*Dark blue Jasperware covered cheese dish decorated with Greek figures, oak leaf and acorn, palmette design around inverted acorn knop, small flake to foot, 6 3/4" x 11 1/2" diameter.*
**$173**

Courtesy of Skinner, Inc.;
www.skinnerinc.com

▲ *Dark blue Jasper dip
Portland vase, England,
19th century, applied white
classical figures in relief and
with man wearing Phrygian
cap under base, impressed
mark, very good condition,
10" high.* **$2,760**

Courtesy of Cowan's Auctions, Inc.

◄ *Jasperware bolted urns,
English, early 20th century,
with contrasting white
paste sprigged decoration,
11 1/2" high.* **$615**

*Fairyland Lustre vase, England, circa 1920, pattern Z5244 with black Firbolgs to dark blue ground, printed mark, neck with scattered gilt wear and glaze blemish, 7 3/4" high.* **$3,240**

*Fairyland Lustre Candlemas vase, England, circa 1920, pattern Z5157 with striped panels of candle figures to black ground alternating with goblins climbing bell ropes to blue ground, printed factory mark, very good condition, 8 5/8" high.* **$5,100**

*Fairyland Lustre Daventry vase, England, circa 1925, rose red ground body with panels of flowers and butterflies and mountain landscapes, printed factory mark, very good condition, 10 1/2" high.* **$1,200**

*Fairyland Lustre vase and cover, England, circa 1920, pattern Z5200 with black Firbolgs to ruby-colored ground, printed mark, very good condition, 9 1/2" high.* **$9,000**

*Fairyland Lustre Malfrey pot in Sycamore Tree pattern against pink sky, lid decorated on top with fairy caught in spiderweb against midnight background, interior of lid decorated with two imps against light blue slightly iridescent background, signed on underside with Portland vase mark "WEDGWOOD MADE IN ENGLAND Z-4968," very good to excellent condition, 10" high.* **$14,813**

*Green Jasper dip oval plaque, England, 19th century, applied white relief depiction of Hercules in Garden of Hesperides within fruiting grapevine border, impressed mark, very good condition, 15" long.* **$960**

*Lustre fish bowl, England, circa 1915, exterior polychrome enameled and gilded with fish and aquatic vegetation, mottled pale blue ground interior with gilded stiff leaf border and black printed with fish, printed factory mark, area of gilt wear to interior rim, no evidence of any cracks, chips or restorations, 10 1/2" diameter.* **$5,700**

*Pair of three-color Jasper vases, England, circa 1870, solid white ground, applied lilac medallions with white classical figures and columns with lion masks and paw feet, green foliage and floral festoons, impressed mark, one vase with rim chip and spider hairline under base, 5 1/4" high.* **$960**

Courtesy of Skinner, Inc.; www.skinnerinc.com

*Three-color Jasper brooch, England, 19th century, oval form with solid white ground, central lilac motif of classical putti within scrolled green foliate border, impressed mark, set in 14kt gold mount, very good condition, 3 1/4" long.* **$492**

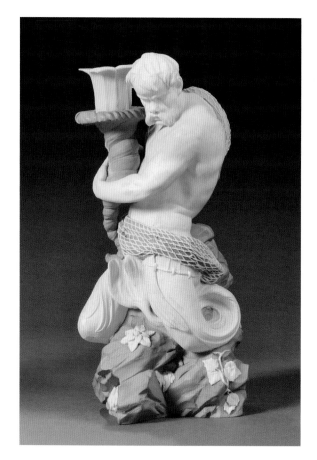

Courtesy of Skinner, Inc.; www.skinnerinc.com

*Blue and white Jasper triton candlestick, England, circa 1800, typically modeled figure kneeling on rocky base and holding cornucopia form stem and foliate candle nozzle, fishnet draped about his waist and over one shoulder, impressed mark, professionally restored to entire nozzle and cornucopia, shoulders through at neck, to hairlines along footrim, chips along footrim, 10 3/4" high.* **$3,690**

*Crimson Jasper dip jug, England, circa 1920, applied white classical figures in relief below floral festoon border, impressed mark, firing line to tree in relief below spout, 5 1/8" high.* **$960**

▼ *Three-color Jasper dip Diceware eggcup, England, late 18th century, black engine-turned cut to white with applied green quatrefoils and applied white foliate borders, impressed mark, spider lines to interior center and under base, 2 3/8" high.* **$3,900**

▲ *Three-color Jasper dip biscuit jar and cover, England, late 19th century, applied white classical figures to black ground bordered with yellow, silver-plated rim, handle, and cover, urn finial, impressed mark, very good condition, plating well worn, 6 3/4" high.* **$360**

# Children's Literature

## First Editions

By Noah Fleisher

**NOAH FLEISHER** received his Bachelor of Fine Arts degree from New York University and brings more than a decade of newspaper, magazine, book, antiques and art experience to his position as Public Relations Director of Heritage Auctions, one of the country's foremost auction houses. He is the former editor of *Antique Trader, New England Antiques Journal* and *Northeast Antiques Journal,* is the author of *Warman's Modern Furniture,* and has been a longtime contributor to *Warman's Antiques & Collectibles.*

When my daughter was born in early 2006, my wife and I bought her three books: *The Very Hungry Caterpillar* by Eric Carle, *Goodnight Moon* by Margaret Wise Brown, and *Guess How Much I Love You* by Sam McBrantney. We read to her from the moment we brought her home. We followed these standbys with more classic kids' lit, with not-so classic kids' lit, with anything appropriate we could find. Now, more than nine years later as of the publishing of this edition of *Warman's,* she still devours books by the dozens. Chapter books, kids' magazines, comic books, picture books, you name it.

While the bonus of this is that our daughter loves the written word and reads like a champ, the reason we really did it was the sheer joy of reading all the classic titles and authors from our childhoods again. The journey has been amazing. We marveled at the compelling simplicity of Eric Carle's various animals, fish, birds and bugs, and we loved the messages in Margaret Wise Brown's direct and lovely prose. A. A. Milne's Winnie the Pooh proved every bit as lovely and deep as he did when we were little, and the rhymes and lessons of Russell Hoban's Frances the Badger are the axiomatic backdrop against which we measured her social progress.

The journey has been long and delightful and it pleases me to no end that our child, at nine, still likes to read with her parents before bed. I know it will end someday soon, but the connection has been made.

I don't mean just the connection between our daughter and us, I mean between her and a good book. Her childhood books will form the basis of what, I hope, is a lifelong relationship with the printed page. I know that the books we read with her, from the classics to the modern contenders, has shown me the wisdom in great children's literature, a sagacity that I had forgotten.

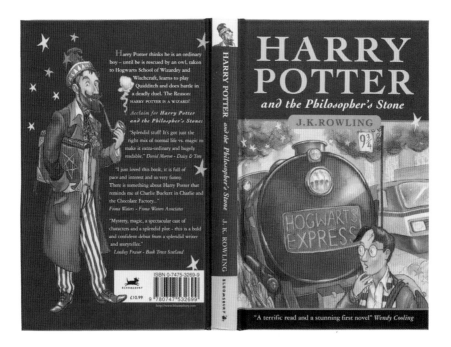

Given my position with *Warman's* and my history in the antiques and collectibles business, then, it is a short leap to the collecting side of the equation. These are great books, many of them, and timeless. It's easy to covet the first editions, to see these tales in their original glory as the publishers first presented them and readers of whatever era first enjoyed them.

Putting aside the emotional connection, however, is it a good time to start collecting first edition children's literature? This is a question we must ask at *Warman's* and a question best-answered by James Gannon, the Director of Rare Books at Heritage Auctions in Dallas, and a man who has sold thousands of first editions in his day, positioning him uniquely to see the big picture in the modern day market for first edition children's lit.

"As with any collectible, you have to love what you're buying or you shouldn't be spending your money," Gannon said. "The best examples of first edition children's literature, where the biggest names are concerned, is still a competitive market and requires a solid foundation to make the right choices."

If a collector is focused, willing to invest the time to learn what's out there and what to pay for it, there's a broad world of charming books awaiting.

"Being willing to learn is key in this hobby," Gannon added. "When you know what you're after, and what it's really worth, the overall market benefits."

As important as it is to define "children's literature" – any reading

Courtesy of Heritage Auctions

*J. K. Rowling. Harry Potter and the Philosopher's Stone. London: Bloomsbury, 1997, first edition, first issue, book and jacket as new. Although this book was not issued with a dust jacket, this copy is now housed in a first edition, later printing dust jacket. This copy was issued in a very small print run, around 500 copies, most of which went to libraries or into the hands of children.* **$43,750**

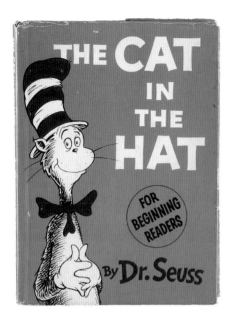

*Dr. Seuss,* The Cat in the Hat *first edition in first issue dust jacket, and* The Cat in the Hat Comes Back *first printing in dust jacket.* **$2,868**

material enjoyed by children, including stories, books, magazines and poetry or, in the modern era, genre or age specific – it's also quite difficult to pin down. We know that the late 19th century is considered the Golden Age of children's literature, but we also know that there has been a huge surge in the popularity of genre fiction in the last 15 years. For the sake of this argument, then, and of the images that follow, let's keep the age range we are shooting for between two years old and 15 years old.

Easy enough, right? We can't forget the massive sea changes there have been in technology in the last decade. That doesn't complicate the issue, does it?

"For the current or prospective collectors sitting and reading this book with money in their pockets and a desire to get that first edition *Where the Wild Things Are,* no," said Gannon. "The future, however, is not so easy to discern. It's hard to tell whether any category will be healthy 30-40 years from now, but few face the challenges that books do."

What Gannon is getting at is the main question that has to be asked of any collectible category: Has the massive shift toward digital everything hurt the hobby?

As far as children's lit goes in specific, and books in general, if we're hesitant in this business to use the word "hurt," the iPad, Amazon, and the proliferation of video games has certainly punched the rare book market in the gut.

"You're working on a second generation now that has been raised

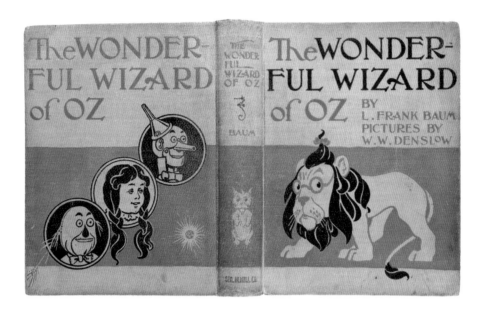

in an almost exclusively digital manner," said Gannon. "There's bound to be a fall-off not only in the amount of people actually reading physical books, but also in the amount of people seeking out the classics for their kids in any format."

This may not bode well for our grandkids and great-grandkids to treasure our first edition Johnny Gruelle *Raggedy Ann and Andy* books, but it may not bode ill, either. Collectors are born with the gene to collect and, with the right exposure, they will gravitate toward books.

"Book collecting hasn't collapsed since the advent of the Internet," said Gannon. "In many ways it's expanded. We've been able to get a much better idea of what exactly is out there. This has, in turn, led to a leveling of the playing field in that prices are much more uniform."

It's also not hard to see a backlash movement against digital life in a few generations, much the same as pop culture is undergoing a shift in eating habits right now – stick with me – as people are cutting back on processed foods and looking for fresh, not to mention the "slow food movement," defined by farm-to-table eating, which formed against the prevalence of fast food in our lives. So too could there be a movement back to the printed page in the mid-21st century as digital media prepares to pronounce the printed page dead.

What are we looking for, then, in our first edition kids' lit? Besides the titles we loved, I mean.

"Three words: Condition, condition, condition," said Gannon. "Does it have its original dust jacket? Is it signed or inscribed? Is it in

Courtesy of Heritage Auctions

*L. Frank Baum.* The Wonderful Wizard of Oz. *Chicago and New York: George M. Hill Co., 1900, first edition, first state of text.*
**$9,375**

good shape or it torn? Is the hardback cover in good condition? Are the corners bent or shredded? Are the pages dog-eared? Does it have all the pages in it and, most importantly, does it say 'first printing' on that title page?"

The Auction Archives at Heritage Auctions (HA.com) are a good place to start searching specifically by author to get a good sense of price and condition. Mainstream booksellers like Barnes & Noble, Half-Price Books, and Powell's Books (out of Portland, Oregon) all feature good first edition children's lit and can give you a good idea of what retail is on a given title.

Smart collectors, or would-be collectors, are all also well-served to check out online booksellers like Alibris.com, Biblio.com, and Abebooks.com.

All and any of the above are enough to give you a sense of what's out there and, hopefully, a good bead on that signed first-edition *Harry Potter* you've been coveting since your kids starting reading the books.

A last word of advice from Gannon to the neophyte: This is a true buyer's market right now.

"In the end, I would urge any new collector to find a dealer or an auctioneer that you trust and have a good rapport with," said Gannon. "There has been and will continue to be a proliferation of small auction houses selling collections of good books. This is a side effect of the closing of so many brick and mortar stores due to current market conditions."

This means patience, it means not rushing out immediately and buying from the top auctioneers and dealers in the field as they tend toward the expensive side. A good relationship with a reputable dealer is very desirable, but there are many tools available to speed along an education.

"Go find offerings that others are missing," said Gannon. "With a computer you can do this from home mostly by looking at auctions and specialty sites and using want lists and keywords to get what you want. The fun comes in getting a great kid's book before anyone else and paying much less for the effort."

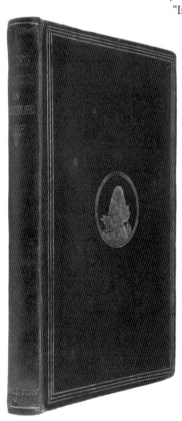

Courtesy of Heritage Auctions

◀ *Lewis Carroll.* Alice's Adventures in Wonderland. *New York: D. Appleton and Co., 1866, first American edition (i.e., first edition, second issue), comprising pages from 1865* Alice *with new title, with 42 wood engravings and wood-engraved frontispiece after illustrations by John Tenniel.* **$5,975**

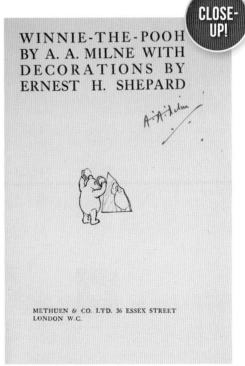

Courtesy of Heritage Auctions

*A. A. Milne. First edition set of four Pooh Books, each signed by author, near fine condition in original dust jackets.*
**$23,900**

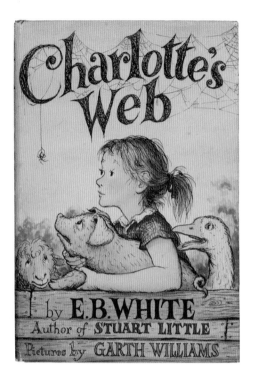

Courtesy of Heritage Auctions

*E. B. White.* Charlotte's Web. *New York: Harper & Brothers, Publishers, 1952, first edition, 184 pages, illustrations by Garth Williams.* **$3,250**

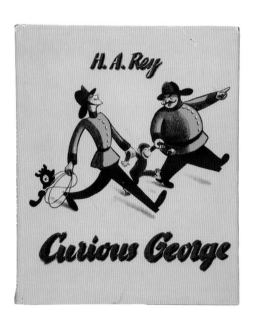

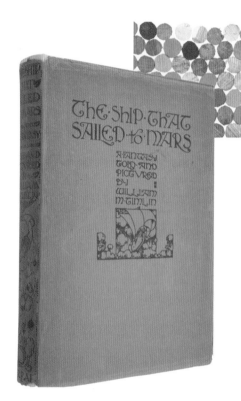

Courtesy of Heritage Auctions

▲ *William M. Timlin.* The Ship That Sailed to Mars, A Fantasy Told and Pictured by William M. Timlin. *London: George G. Harrap & Co. Limited, 1923, 48 pages of calligraphic text lithographed in blue, black, and gray and 48 color plates.* **$2,988**

Courtesy of Heritage Auctions

◄ *H. A. Rey.* Curious George. *Boston: Houghton Mifflin, 1941, first edition, original dust jacket with $1.75 price, near fine condition, extremely scarce.* **$26,290**

# THE VERY HUNGRY CATERPILLAR

by Eric Carle

The World Publishing Company / New York and Cleveland

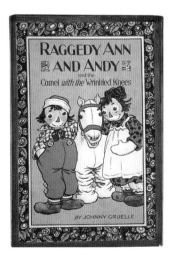

Courtesy of Heritage Auctions

*Eric Carle.* The Very Hungry Caterpillar. *New York: The World Publishing Co., 1969, first edition signed by Carle on page facing title page. While more than 30 million copies of this title have been printed, very few first editions have survived, especially with the extremely rare dust jacket and signature.* **$11,250**

Courtesy of Heritage Auctions

*Johnny Gruelle.* Raggedy Ann and Andy and the Camel with the Wrinkled Knees. *Joliet: P. F. Volland Co., 1924.* **$717**

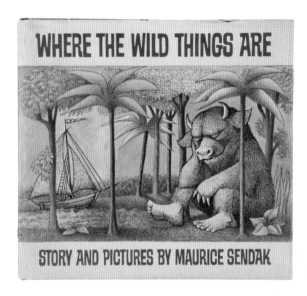

Courtesy of Heritage Auctions

*Maurice Sendak.* Where the Wild Things Are. *New York: Harper & Row, 1963, first edition, first issue jacket with $3.50 price intact and no mention of Caldecott Award on jacket flaps, no metallic medal sticker on front of jacket.* **$4,063**

Courtesy of Heritage Auctions

*Madeleine L'Engle.* A Wrinkle in Time. *New York: Ariel Books/Farrar, Straus and Cudahy, 1962, first edition, first printing stated, with bookplate signed by author placed inside.* **$3,500**

Courtesy of Heritage Auctions

*E. B. White.* Stuart Little. *New York: Harper & Brothers, 1945, first edition, first printing, inscribed by White on half-title page, "For Max / from E B White," illustrated by Garth Williams and signed by him in pencil on lower margin of frontispiece.* **$3,500**

CLOSE-UP!

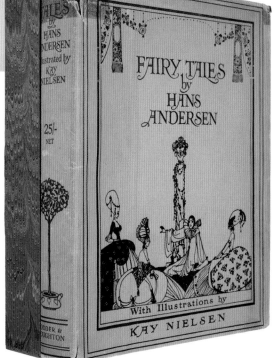

This Edition de Luxe is limited to Five hundred copies,
signed by the Artist, and numbered,
of which this is

No. 412

*INSIDE LOOK!*

*CLOSE-UP!*

Courtesy of Heritage Auctions

▲ ▶ *Hans Andersen, Kay Nielsen, illustrator.* Fairy Tales by Hans Andersen. *London: Hodder & Stoughton, no date, 1924, first limited edition, one of 500 numbered copies signed by Nielsen.* **$2,250**

Courtesy of Heritage Auctions

▲ *Kay Thompson.* Eloise. *New York: Simon and Schuster, 1955, first edition, first printing, inscribed and signed by author and illustrator on front endpapers.* **$1,375**

Courtesy of Heritage Auctions

▶ *Felix Salten.* Bambi, A Life in the Woods. *New York: Simon and Schuster, 1928, first American edition, first printing, and first English-language edition.* **$1,625**

*J. M. Barrie Arthur Rackham, illustrator.* The Peter Pan Portfolio. *New York: Brentano's, 1914, first edition, American issue, number 9 of 300 limited edition copies.* **$2,125**

*Dr. Seuss.* Thidwick the Big-Hearted Moose. *New York: Random House, 1948, first edition.* **$1,434**

*A.A. Milne.* When We Were Very Young. *New York: E. P. Dutton & Co., 1924, first American edition, one of 100 copies signed by Milne from total edition of 500.* **$2,000**

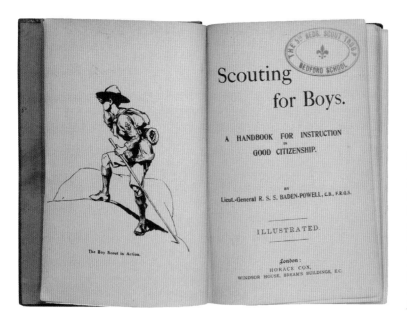

Courtesy of
Heritage Auctions

*Lieut.-General R. S. S. Baden Powell.* Scouting for Boys. A Handbook for Instruction in Good Citizenship. *London: Published by Horace Cox, 1908, first edition, first issue.* **$10,000**

Courtesy of Heritage Auctions

*Roald Dahl.* Charlie and the Chocolate Factory. *New York: Knopf, 1964, first edition, first issue, illustrated by Joseph Schindelman.* **$1,375**

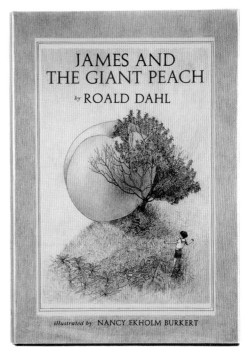

Courtesy of Heritage Auctions

*Roald Dahl.* James and the Giant Peach, A Children's Story. *New York: Alfred A. Knopf, 1961, illustrated by Nancy Ekholm Burkert.* **$1,195**

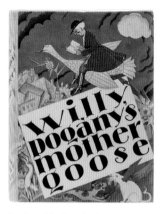

Courtesy of Heritage Auctions

*Willy Pogany.* Willy Pogany's Mother Goose. *New York: Thomas Nelson and Sons, 1928, first edition.* **$325**

Courtesy of Heritage Auctions

*Joel Chandler Harris.* Uncle Remus Returns. *Boston and New York: Houghton Mifflin, 1918, first edition, in scarce dust jacket.* **$688**

Courtesy of Heritage Auctions

*Maurice Sendak.* In der Nachtkuche (In the Night Kitchen). *Diogenes, 1971, first edition in German of* In The Night Kitchen, *signed with original drawing by Sendak.* **$896**

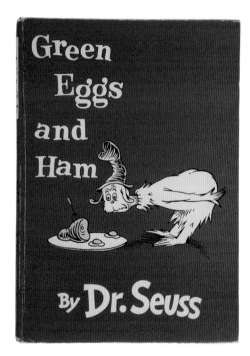

Courtesy of Heritage Auctions

*Dr. Seuss.* Green Eggs and Ham. *First London edition.* **$938**

Courtesy of Heritage Auctions

*Walt Disney Studios.* Mickey Mouse Waddle Book. *New York: Blue Ribbon Books, 1934, first edition, with two folding pages of unpunched waddlers, rarest of any Disney book.* **$3,750**

Courtesy of Heritage Auctions

*Margaret Wise Brown.* Little Fur Family. *New York: Harper & Brothers Publishers, 1946, original fur slipcover over boards in fine condition, with original illustrated box, illustrated by Garth Williams.* **$657**

Courtesy of Heritage Auctions

*George Selden.* The Cricket in Times Square. *New York: Ariel Books/Farrar, Straus and Cudahy, 1960, first edition, first printing, illustrations by Garth Williams.* **$388**

Courtesy of Heritage Auctions

*P. L. Travers.* Mary Poppins. *New York: Reynal & Hitchcock, 1934, first American edition of author's first book (published same year as first English edition), illustrated by Mary Shepard.* **$239**

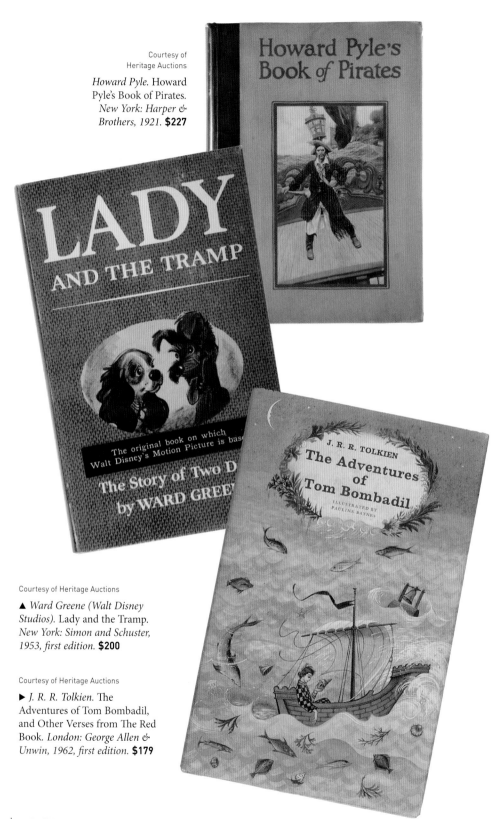

Courtesy of
Heritage Auctions

*Howard Pyle.* Howard Pyle's Book of Pirates. *New York: Harper & Brothers, 1921.* **$227**

Courtesy of Heritage Auctions

▲ *Ward Greene (Walt Disney Studios).* Lady and the Tramp. *New York: Simon and Schuster, 1953, first edition.* **$200**

Courtesy of Heritage Auctions

▶ *J. R. R. Tolkien.* The Adventures of Tom Bombadil, and Other Verses from The Red Book. *London: George Allen & Unwin, 1962, first edition.* **$179**

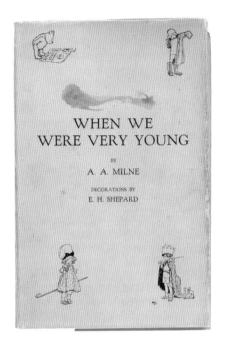

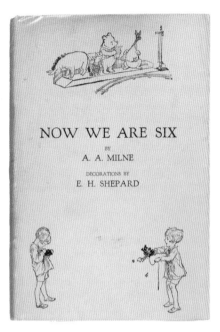

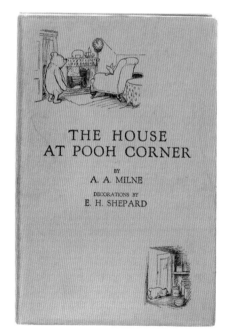

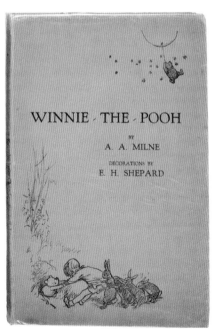

Courtesy of Heritage Auctions

*A. A. Milne. First edition set of Winnie-the-Pooh books, unsigned. London: Methuen & Co., 1924-1928,* When We Were Very Young, Winnie-the-Pooh, Now We Are Six, *and* The House at Pooh Corner. **$5,938**

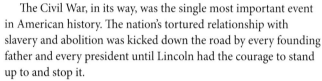

# Civil War Collectibles

By Noah Fleisher

**NOAH FLEISHER**
received his Bachelor of
Fine Arts degree from
New York University
and brings more than a
decade of newspaper,
magazine, book, antiques
and art experience to
his position as Public
Relations Director of
Heritage Auctions, one
of the country's foremost
auction houses. He is the
former editor of *Antique
Trader, New England
Antiques Journal* and
*Northeast Antiques Journal,*
is the author of *Warman's
Modern Furniture,* and
has been a longtime
contributor to *Warman's
Antiques & Collectibles.*

The Civil War, in its way, was the single most important event in American history. The nation's tortured relationship with slavery and abolition was kicked down the road by every founding father and every president until Lincoln had the courage to stand up to and stop it.

The ramifications of the conflict still play out today, though an increasingly large segment of the population has less and less familiarity with the particulars. Films like Spielberg's 2012 epic *Lincoln* help keep the conflict current in the broadest sense, but the true scope of the war, its players and battles, its massive reach and devastating effects, requires a healthy intellectual curiosity and the time to nurture it.

The War Between the States also left behind a rich material history to bolster any study of the era. From uniforms to guns to photographs, writings and various printed ephemera, the field of Civil War collecting is vast and intricate, with pieces from most every corner of the war available to serious collecting.

The market of Civil War collecting is a market, however, that is somewhat in flux.

Prices are down from a decade or two ago, when common and mid-range pieces were bringing high prices, respective to their previous comparables, and the very best material – those things tied to big names in the war, or important regiments, with impeccable provenance – were simply exorbitant.

Things seemed to reach a bottom of sorts a few years ago and now, as we approach the sesquicentennial of the war's end, the best material is experiencing a balancing out, perhaps even a comeback. No matter how you come at it, there are good opportunities if you know where to look.

"The Civil War market is evolving to meet the demands of a changing collector base," said Eric Smylie, noted historian and an

*Civil War grouping pertaining to Company E, 15th Regiment, New Jersey Volunteers, originally gathered by Union Capt. John H. Vandeveer, included with 8" x 9" photo of unit in field at rest with each member identified below image, and Vandeveer's Tiffany sword and scabbard.* **$2,825**

expert in Civil War and Arms & Militaria at Heritage Auctions. "Most dealers and collectors have finally realized that if the market is going to grow and thrive, they need to cultivate a new generation of collectors to follow the current generation. The prospects for that happening are very good, even if it will be a smaller number of collectors. I've seen movement in the last few years of collectors from other areas moving into the Civil War market. They're generally buying high-quality, identified, and unique pieces."

The exuberance of a decade ago has worn off and with it, for several years, the exuberance of collectors, which – as Smylie points out – has led to a contracted market and a generation of collectors that was almost passed over altogether. As current trends at auction seem to indicate, however, there is a younger generation of collectors (men and women in their 30s and 40s) beginning to show interest in the history. The prices also support Smylie's observation that the pool is smaller and that they are interested in paying good money for top-level material and let the bottom fall away.

"The market shows sustained strength of late led by high quality, well-provenanced weapons, uniforms, and more showy equipment," Smylie said. "The more common material, bullets, run-of-the mill cartridge boxes, U.S. belt plates, and ephemera have suffered in recent years."

The prices realized on the images that follow certainly seem to bear this out.

While the overall market, at the top end, follows the truism that quality will always sell, smart collectors would indeed do well to look at the more generic parts of the market because there are sure to be good deals on the areas that have "suffered," plenty of which are more than sufficient to start a collection, bolster an existing grouping, or hook a beginner who doesn't have the discretionary income yet to go after the big stuff.

"Indeed there are always opportunities," said Smylie. "There are many older collections coming on the market right now. You'll often see the large collections accompanied by fanfare, but there are smaller collections, with good material, coming out of rural attics and suburban cellars and quietly slipping onto the market. Finding that hidden or overlooked treasure is often a matter of knowledge and lots of luck."

Most any Civil War dealer or auctioneer worth his salt is going to be happy to spend some time with you if you are new to the market, or thinking of getting back in after staying away for a while, and neophyte collectors should find someone they like and trust. That, coupled with some time spent in self-erudition on what you like – North? South? Uniforms? Correspondence? Battlefield artifacts? – should lead you into a very rewarding and infinitely fascinating area.

"Study the items that interest you before you buy," said Smylie. "Go to shows, touch the material, ask questions, carefully read auction catalogs, and follow the prices realized. Buy from well-established and reputable dealers and auction houses, as they will stand by the material they sell. In time, you will recognize a genuine piece from a reproduction in a booth bulging with items."

"To all collectors, perhaps the best advice is to buy the best you can afford," added Smylie. "Don't try to save a few dollars by purchasing a faded or repaired item if a better one is available. Buying quality is always better than settling for something less."

More than 650,000 soldiers died in the brutal bloodshed of the Civil War, in fighting that was obviously horrifying to endure and still shocking to learn about. The war nearly destroyed America and helped forge the Union as it is today – infinitely diverse and prone to disagreement, as ever, but decidedly united when push comes to shove.

The artifacts of the conflict carry that heavy history; the rifle a soldier carried into battle, or the coarse wool tunic that provided scant protection from cold and was suffocating in the heat, they tie us to our past and thrill us with their immediacy to such a charged and important moment in time.

The important material is out there, waiting to be appreciated, almost 250 years after its intended purpose expired. Now it is waiting for a new generation to make it new again.

Courtesy of Heritage Auctions

▼ *American eagle-decorated snare drum, circa 1810-1830, very large, commensurate with early date of manufacture, original ink script paper label inside, across from air hole, "M.A. BAKER / No. 10," high seam with seven brass tacks, maple body, fine condition, retaining 95% of original paint, some crazing, back side with possible bullet hole, likely regular U.S. Army, 17 1/2" diameter x 19 3/4" high.* **$3,750**

Courtesy of Morphy Auctions

*Colt Walker Dragoons (Third Model) with consecutive serial Nos. 15601 and 15602 ordered/purchased circa 1856-1857 from Colt Manufacturing by Lambert B. Wolfe near Hanover, Pennsylvania; excellent condition, clear Colt markings, address and serial number markings strong and clean, guns solid and lock up tightly, cylinders move smoothly and actions are crisp, cylinder scene faint, both show typical black powder wear and rifling is prominent. Wolfe served as captain in 142nd Ohio Infantry Regiment, 100-day service regiment formed to assist with Gen. Ulysses Grant's 1864 Overland Campaign to take Confederate capital of Richmond, Virginia. Provenance: Passed down through Wolfe family for 150 years.* **$56,400**

**CLOSE-UP!**

FLAG OF THE 55th VIRGINIA CAVALRY

This flag was made for Co. A 55th V. in 1858. It was carried at the capture of John Brown at Harpers Ferry in 1859.

Courtesy of Heritage Auctions

*Blue silk 33-star flag of 55th Virginia Cavalry carried at Harpers Ferry, 1859, white stars pierced through blue silk and bound around edges with silk thread, silk ties attached to both leading edge corners, silk with expected minor splits and tears, centered on flag is type-written note stating flag was made in 1858 and carried by Co. A 55 Virginia Cavalry at capture of John Brown at Harpers Ferry in 1859; includes detailed analysis by noted textile expert Fonda Thomsen; flag 25" x 26 1/2".* **$10,625**

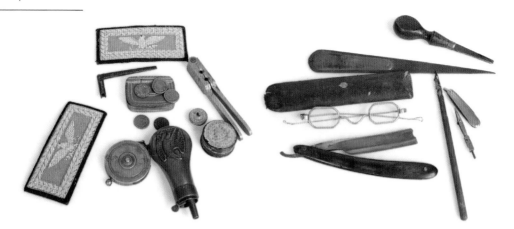

*Civil War officer's writing desk with cased 1849 Colt Iron Guard pocket revolver, desk and firearm inscribed C. (Chapman) Biddle; mahogany lap writing desk with red velvet writing surface with interior lids concealing storage compartment, hinges stamped P.M. & Co. Patent, desk filled with period accessories including officer's shoulder boards, brass letter opener, inkwells, stamp in slot, writing utensils, straight edge razor, white gold-filled pocket knife, reading glasses, Hamilton open-faced gold-filled 17 jewel model 956 pocket watch (serial no. 1171194), button and pillbox containing Civil War period Indian Head cents; main compartment contains 1849 Colt Iron Guard pocket revolver and effects, 4" long octagonal barrel with .31 caliber rifled boar, hinged ramrod, iron triggerguard and strap, walnut grips and five-shot cylinder with stagecoach holdup scene; signed on top of barrel in two lines Address Sam Colt, New-York City, matching serial number 152300 (circa 1859) on all parts including barrel, frame, cylinder, wedge, guard and strap; strap inscribed C. Biddle 121st P.V.I.; overall good condition, bore, barrel and cylinder show minor pitting and dings; box 4" high x 14" wide x 9" deep.* **$7,865**

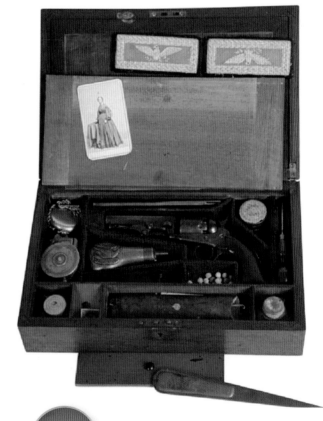

CLOSE-UP!

"Union Prisoners at Salisbury, N.C." Civil War baseball lithograph, 1863, one of earliest color representations of baseball. **$26,680**

▲ *Leech & Rigdon Confederate field and staff officer's sword, slightly curved blade with unstopped fuller, smooth gray patina with darker spots, etched for two-thirds of length on obverse with floral and scroll motifs with arms/flag panoply terminating in pointed projections, reverse with floral scroll decorations centered with large Old English "C.S," etching clear with highlights, hilt of classic form with deeply cast scroll and rose decorations, large "CS" centered on upper guard, plain pommel, original leather grip with twisted brass wire with minor wear, leather scabbard with minor crazing, plain brass mounts with undisturbed patina, mounts attached by brass screws, blade 31 3/8" long.* **$16,250**

◄ *1861-O $20 gold coin, AU55 PCGS, strong date, die crack from rim near star 2 to obverse field, struck at New Orleans Mint; the Civil War closed the New Orleans Mint to coinage after 1861, when the facility was alternately held by three entities: U.S. government, State of Louisiana, and Confederate States of America; Confederate troops occupied the New Orleans Mint in April 1861.* **$70,500**

Courtesy of Heritage Auctions

*Civil War Cavalry Officer's grouping, Maj. William H. Dunn, 5th & 10th Michigan Cavalry: Civil War officer's cavalry short jacket, nine-button front with matching Goddard & Bro. Waterbury eagle "C" buttons, matching six cuff buttons, 9 1/2" elbows tapering to 4 1/2" cuff, tufted shoulder, 1 1/4" high standing collar, cuffs with black quatrefoil, shoulders with double border Cavalry captains shoulder straps showing wear to outer borders, interior body quilted black polished cotton, left breast pocket, velvet collar lining, white cotton sleeve lining, jacket with scattered mothing and service wear to inner cuffs; Civil War officer's tarred linen haversack with embossed scroll, flower and Federal shield motif, body soft and pliable, strap torn from body on one side; leather cap box in poor condition; Civil War officer's scarlet silk sash, faded, worn fringe and few holes; gold hat cord; Model 1858 bull's-eye canteen with brown cover and strap showing wear; post-Civil War veteran's kepi with Michigan side buttons and double gold cord chin strap, body with mothing, interior with label "Frank Henderson Regalia Kalamazoo Mich"; broken white leather belt with cast brass GAR belt buckle; red silk fringed tie; post-Civil War leather mittens and leather holster; 2 1/2" china GAR Gettysburg souvenir canteen; group of 1/6 plate ambrotypes and daguerreotypes of family members and daguerreotype of house.* **$13,750**

▶ *Abraham Lincoln, Ulysses
S. Grant, and Edwin Stanton
endorsed field pass, signed and
issued to Frederick Tompkins,
secretary of National Freedmen's
Aid Society of London,
from War Department on
Feb. 27, 1865; pass allowed
Tompkins to travel to "Norfolk,
Va., Charleston, S.C., and
Savannah, Ga. and return with
transportation at half rates
on Govt. transport." On verso,
Secretary of War Edwin Stanton
wrote: "Transportation free [signed] E M Stanton
Sec of War." Directly below Stanton, President
Abraham Lincoln placed his endorsement: "I
heartily commend Dr. Tomkin's object, and bid him
Godspeed in it. [signed] A. Lincoln Feb. 27, 1865."
To allow ease of travel, Gen. Ulysses S. Grant,
commander of all Union forces, writes directly
below Lincoln: "Pass Mr. F. Tompkins through all
parts of Armies of U. States. [signed] U.S. Grant Lt.
Gen. City Point, Va. March 2d 1865"; two punch
cancellations on verso, staining along edges touches
date in Grant's inscription, 5 1/4" x 3".* **$20,000**

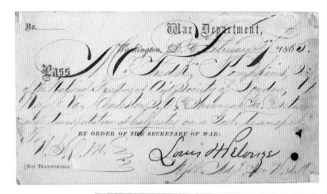

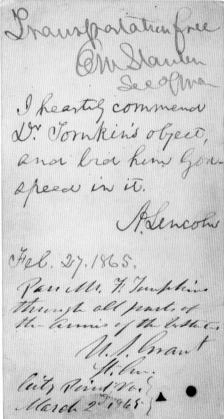

◀ *Five-gallon stoneware churn with cobalt marching
Civil War soldier decoration, New York State origin,
possibly Fort Edward, circa 1861-1865, ovoid churn
with tooled shoulder, rounded rim, and applied lug
handles, decorated with large slip-trailed design of
four marching Union soldiers, faint surface lines
to shoulder at handle on left side and other minor
flaws, 15 1/2" high; one of most important stoneware
discoveries of past several years.* **$430,500**

## Most Thoroughly Documented Civil War Soldiers' Baseball

Text and image courtesy of Heritage Auctions

"Famous War-Time Baseball Will Be Shown at Banquet," reads the headline of the news clipping from the Feb. 18, 1911 edition of the *Los Angeles Express*. "Members of Loyal Legion Will Fondle Old Sphere and Hear Story of the Part It Took in Army Sport During the Stirring Days of '64." The article's text tells the story best:

"Captain France was a member of the Seventeenth New York zouaves, who were attached to the Sixteenth corps under the command of N.S. Granger. There were a number of good ballplayers in the Seventeenth and when, in May '64, the corps was encamped at Decatur, Ala., the baseball enthusiasts conceived the plan of sending to Nashville, 130 miles north, for a ball and bat.

"The plan was executed and many a hot game of baseball was played on the parade grounds. When the call for dress parade came and a game was in progress, it was customary for the man having the ball in his hand at the time to keep it until the next game was played.

"In this manner the ball was carried on Sherman's march to the sea, through the Atlanta campaign, its siege and capture, then through the Carolinas campaign to Raleigh, Richmond and finally to Washington. At Washington, while the soldiers were waiting to be mustered out, the last game of ball was played. When it was over Lieutenant Barnett was walking off the field with Captain France. 'Here, France,' he called, and gave the ball an underhand toss into France's waiting hands."

The trail of the provenance picks up shortly after the printing of the newspaper

## FAMOUS WAR-TIME BASEBALL WILL BE SHOWN AT BANQUET

Members of Loyal Legion Will Fondle Old Sphere and Hear Story of the Part It Took in Army Sport During the Stirring Days of '64.

*Los Angeles Express. Feb 18th 1911*

It was Gen. Adna R. Chaffee's idea, this "play ball" banquet program of the Loyal Legion tonight at Hotel Alexandria. General Chaffee had it in mind for a long time and it is put into execution on this occasion.

However, General Chaffee had no previous knowledge that a baseball with a history—one that is, perhaps, the oldest ball in Los Angeles, was to be produced at the banquet and its story told.

That was the idea of Capt. James S. France of Eagle Rock and here is the story of a baseball with a history:

Captain France was a member of the Seventeenth New York zouaves, who were attached to the Sixteenth corps under the command of N. S. Granger. There were a number of good ballplayers in the Seventeenth and when, in May, '64, the corps was encamped at Decatur, Ala., the baseball enthusiasts conceived the plan of sending to Nashville, 130 miles north, for a ball and bat.

#### Many Games Played

The plan was executed and many a hot game of baseball was played on the parade grounds. When the call for dress parade came and a game was in progress, it was customary for the man having the ball in his hand at the time to keep it until the next game was played.

In this manner the ball was carried on Sherman's march to the sea, through the Atlanta campaign; its siege and capture, then through the Carolinas campaign to Raleigh, Richmond and finally to Washington.

At Washington, while the soldiers were waiting to be mustered out, the last game of ball was played. When it was over Lieutenant Barnett was walking off the field with Captain France.

"Here, France," he called, and gave the ball an underhand toss into France's waiting hands.

Numerous inquiries afterwards were made for that ball, but it never could be found. Captain France, even, had forgotten about it until he arrived home and found it stowed away in his knapsack. He has it yet. He wouldn't part with it for any money.

**CAPT. JAMES S. FRANCE**

#### Will Watch Ball

During the progress of the banquet tonight Captain France will keep a watchful eye on it lest, among the visitors, there might be some other member of that famous war-time baseball team with envious eyes and an 1864 conception of the spoils of war.

The speakers at the banquet tonight will include Lieutenant-General Chaffee, U. S. A., toastmaster, who is senior vice-commander of the commandery of California and president of the Los Angeles association; Rev. Robert J. Burdette, Rear Admiral O. W. Farenholt, U. S. N., Perry W. Weldner, Maj. John A. Donnell and Colonel Smedberg. Old army songs will be sung by the assemblage.

17th N.Y. at Decatur, Ala in '62 during the ocupation (sic) by Federal troops and when the 17th received marching orders to go to the front at Atlanta Ga it was in possession of Capt. James S. France who kept it long after the war and finally gave it to my son Harry France Pease in 1915." Pease signs below. The close relationship between these former brothers in arms is apparent in the middle name of Pease's son.

The ball itself is crafted in the lemon peel style typical of the Civil War-era and bears vintage handwritten block-lettered text that reads, "Zouave B.B.C." and "Officers 17th N.Y.V.V.I." The ball is deeply toned but text remains bold and the structural integrity of the sphere is strong with no loose stitching or major defects to the leather. Also there is a modern printed transcript of many

article with an undated but clearly very old handwritten letter from Charles H. Pease, a captain with the 17th New York Veteran Volunteers (Zouaves), who served with France. He writes:

"This ball was used by the Officers of the of Capt. Pease's letters home from the war and a 2011 letter of appraisal from noted Civil War historian Will Gorges. The ball was consigned by the great-great grandson of Capt. Charles H. Pease, with his letter of provenance. **$41,825**

*Bowie knife and book of Psalms of Confederate soldier Joseph Kent Ewing, 2nd Lieutenant in Company G of 4th Virginia Infantry (CSA), part of "Stonewall Brigade" under command of Brig. Gen. James A. Walker; bone handle inscribed "J.K. Ewing" on one side and "4th Virginia" on other, with Psalm book presented to him by his mother.* **$5,156**

*Civil War Confederate rectangular CSA belt plate with original three mounting hooks, letters evenly centered, excellent condition, approximately 48 mm x 70 mm, approximately 3 ounces.* **$3,250**

*Civil War Union colonel's frock coat, blue wool with black polished cotton lining quilted on upper body with draped skirt, period sleeve cut, 8 1/2" elbows tapering to 5" cuff, raw cut skirt edge, white cotton sleeve lining, brown polished cotton tail lining, 1 1/2" black velvet standup collar, double-breasted nine-button front with mixed backmarked staff buttons, 13 marked Extra Quality, four rear pleat buttons backmarked Waterbury Button Co., original staff colonel's shoulder straps, 2" wide with matching silver bullion eagles, one with wear to brass wire edge, fine condition overall.* **$4,531**

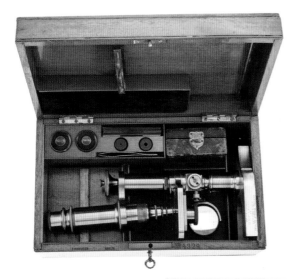

Courtesy of Heritage Auctions

◀ *Medal of Honor winner Dr. Mary Edwards Walker presentation microscope and medal, steel base of microscope inscribed "Presented To Dr. Mary E. Walker By American Women Syracuse Medical College," case includes two lenses, two eyepieces, tweezer, seven glass slides and small wooden box with three additional eyepieces (marked 4, 7 and 10) and gold and enamel G.A.R. lapel badge accompanied by boxed medal with one bar with name, hanger marked W.C.U. and metal drop with religious symbols and inscription that roughly translates to "St. John's Association Rock Island, Ill. 1880," inside lid of box with photo of unidentified building and engraved copper plaque that reads: "Honorable Guest / Presented To / Dr. Mary E. Walker / For her / Distinguished Service / To Men of the / Union Army."*
*Dr. Walker (1832-1919) is famous primarily for her efforts during the Civil War to give medical treatment to the wounded. She was captured by Confederate forces after crossing enemy lines to treat wounded civilians, was accused of being a Union spy and sent to the POW facility in Richmond, Virginia prior to being exchanged. After the war she was awarded the Congressional Medal of Honor, the only woman to receive the award and only one of eight civilians. Her post-war efforts centered on promoting prohibition and women's suffrage.* **$5,000**

Courtesy of Heritage Auctions

*Large mounted albumen of Gen. Philip Sheridan and members of his staff, Sheridan at extreme left next to table where his generals study map, left to right: James Forsyth, Wesley Merritt, Thomas C. Devin, and George Armstrong Custer; mount unevenly toned, spots of foxing on mount and image, 17 1/4" x 10 1/2", affixed to mount to overall size of 21" x 14 1/2".* **$4,375**

*Scarce B Kittredge & Co copper cartridge box, untouched example with dark patina and crisp markings on lid, including patent dates of Jan. 27 and April 14, 1863, iron spring for lid, mounted on reverse, with dark patina and old surface rust, works well.* **$1,750**

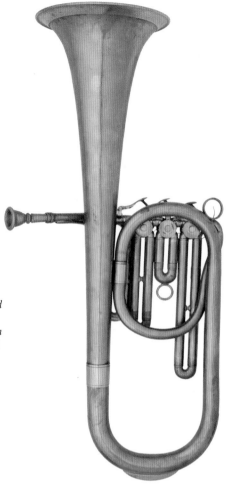

▲ *Civil War rotary valve Eb alto sax horn by "E. Seltmann & Co./ Phila." marked on bell, body of brass with nickel silver trim and rotary valves that function well, excellent overall condition with scattered small light dents, dovetailed seam evident, 23" overall with 6 3/4" diameter bell and 5/8" nickel silver floating rim, scarce.* **$2,500**

◀ *Confederate Brig. Gen. William Ruffin Cox presentation Masonic 14k gold fob on chain and signet ring, fob engraved on reverse "Presented by Grand Lodge of North Carolina to William R. Cox P.G.M 1878-1879," front of fob with blue enamel accents and small diamond accent, suspended via 12" long 18k gold chain, opposing fob with oval bloodstone on one side and carnelian on other; narrow wooden signet ring with initials "W.R.C." in script; both pieces in excellent condition, fob approximately 1 1/2" x 1 3/4".* **$2,750**

Courtesy of Heritage Auctions

▲ Civil War Union Model 1859 forage cap, body in fine condition with no damage, leather chinstrap stiff and crazed, leather visor with moderate crazing, chin strap with two matching Federal eagle buttons, interior sweatband missing, brown cotton lining torn and shows losses, crown displays what appears to be original insignia for Company B 22nd Infantry, horn reverse loops held in place with leather thong, burlap reinforced band 1 1/2". **$3,250**

Courtesy of Heritage Auctions

▶ Civil War Corps Badge belonging to Capt. Frank Baldwin, two-time Medal of Honor recipient; silver, approximately 1" x 4" with five suspended bars, each engraved with engagements Baldwin participated in including (from top to bottom): "Frank D. Baldwin / Lt. Col. 19th Mich. Inft."; "Resaca Cassville / Dallas Woods"; "New Hope Church / Golgotha Church"; "Culp's Farm / Kenesaw Mt."; and "Peach Tree Creek / Averysboro [sic] / Bentonville"; drop approximately 1 3/4" diameter with cloth-backed voided star motif, additional battles engraved around rim of drop include Atlanta, Milledgeville, Savannah, Columbia, Raleigh and Stockade Stone River. **$3,750**

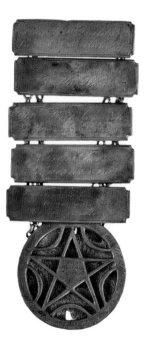

Courtesy of Heritage Auctions

▲ White canvas/cotton Civil War haversack of Congressional Medal of Honor winner Samuel Wright, 29th Massachusetts Infantry, reinforcing on one side where sling attaches and heavy wear where sling attaches on other side, closure with two bone buttons, original rice bag affixed by two bone buttons, printed in heavy black ink on inside edge of front flap "Samuel Wright," stenciled on front of haversack is "E / 29." Wright was awarded the Congressional Medal of Honor for action at Antietam, when he volunteered to tear down a fence amidst enemy fire. **$2,375**

# Clocks

The clock is one of the oldest human inventions. The word "clock" (from the Latin word *clocca*, "bell") suggests that it was the sound of bells that also characterized early timepieces.

The first mechanical clocks to be driven by weights and gears were invented by medieval Muslim engineers. The first geared mechanical clock was invented by an 11th century Arab engineer in Islamic Spain. The knowledge of weight-driven mechanical clocks produced by Muslim engineers was transmitted to other parts of Europe through Latin translations of Arabic and Spanish texts.

In the early 14th century, existing clock mechanisms that used water power were being adapted to take their driving power from falling weights. This power was controlled by some form of oscillating mechanism. This controlled release of power – the escapement – marks the beginning of the true mechanical clock.

Courtesy of Dreweatts & Bloomsbury

*Victorian lacquered brass Litchfield Cathedral hour-striking skeleton clock with trip repeat, John Smith and Sons, London, mid-19th century, front with pierced silvered Roman cartouche numeral chapter ring engraved RHODES BRADFORD to lower margin, with shaped outer minute track and blued steel moon hands, on rectangular brass base plate, 13" high; mounted on original inlaid rosewood stand with symmetrical rococo scroll decoration within line borders to front, rounded angles and bell shaped feet, upper surface cut with rebate for original glass dome cover, 16 1/4" high overall.* **$3,270**

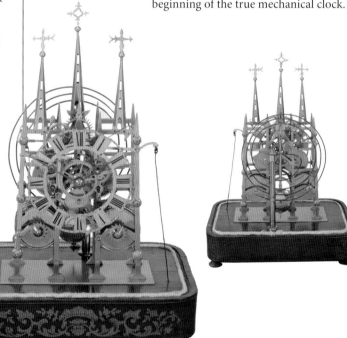

◀ *French gilt brass mounted ebony religieuse table clock, movement signed for Charles Champion, Paris, circa 1675, two train movement with rectangular scroll-top plates united by five tapered baluster pillars pinned at rear and signed Charles Champion AParis to lower margin of backplate, black velvet-covered dial with gilt collets to winding squares and foliate-pierced and engraved hands within applied Roman numeral chapter ring with tied starburst half-hour markers and each minute numbered to outer track, upper angles applied with symmetrical scroll cast spandrel mounts, lower with larger conforming mounts flanking hinged rococo cartouche engraved Charles Champion, AParis, ebony veneered case with cartouche-centered symmetrical leafy scroll cast arched crest with dolphins and armorial lion terms above rectangular glazed door applied with further cast mounts to angles and rails, sides with break-arch lozenge-shaped windows, rear with walnut panel-veneered door, on shallow molded skirt base with cast lion's paw feet, case with worm damage, 18" high.* **$2,610**

*Tiffany marble mantle clock with gilded bronze mounts of rearing horses with men, applied scrolled panels and surmounted by putti with staff, gilt metal and porcelain dial with Roman numerals, marked "Tiffany & Co. Made in France," brass movement marked "9.2," missing pendulum, not running, wear to gilding, 22" wide x 20" high.* **$2,185**

Courtesy of Dreweatts & Bloomsbury

*Victorian carved oak fusee dial wall timepiece, Lund and Blockley, London, circa 1875, four pillar single-chain fusee movement with anchor escapement and pivoted beam rise/fall pendulum regulation, backplate signed LUND & BLOCKLEY, (TO QUEEN), 42 PALL MALL, LONDON, 2/852, 12" circular silvered brass Roman numeral dial with repeat signature Lund & Blockley, TO THE QUEEN, 42 Pall Mall, LONDON to center, with regulation square at 12 o'clock and blued steel hands set behind deep convex glazed hinged cast brass bezel within concentric deep repeating foliate scroll-carved cushion surround fronting cylindrical case with curved access flaps to right-hand side and base, rear with rectangular door, 17 1/2" diameter.* **$1,230**

Courtesy of Dreweatts & Bloomsbury

*Regency brass inlaid ebonized bracket clock with enamel dial, Grant, London, early 19th century, five pillar twin fusee bell striking movement signed Grant, Fleet Street, LONDON and with arrow-shaped strike/silent lever to lancet-shaped backplate, 6 1/2" fired white enamel circular Roman numeral dial signed GRANT Fleet Street LONDON, No. 602 to center and with blued steel hands set behind hinged convex glazed cast brass bezel, lancet-shaped case with brass parquetry star motif within circular panel above dial and recessed brass fillet bordered shaped panel enclosing inlaid stylized tulip-form motif beneath, front edges with cast Gothic column mounts continuing to form molded lancet-arch above, sides with brass fruiting vine leaf ring handles above lancet arch-shaped brass fishscale sound frets, rear with conforming lancet-glazed door, on brass bound stepped fillet molded skirt base with brass ball feet, 15 3/4" high.* **$3,920**

Courtesy of Fontaines Auction Gallery

◀ FAR LEFT *No. 47 wall-hanging astronomical regulator clock, circa 1876, E. Howard & Co., one of only three known examples, hand-carved American walnut with carved finials and incised burled trim, carved bust of Christopher Columbus, and original 16 1/2" reverse-painted glass dial in excellent condition, 8' 3" high.* **$200,000-$300,000**

Courtesy of Cordier Auctions

◀ *Dutch baroque marquetry tall case clock, 18th century.* **$4,250**

Courtesy of Dreweatts & Bloomsbury

*French Sèvres-style porcelain inset ormolu mantel clock, Jean-Baptiste Delettrez, Paris, circa 1865, circular eight-day bell striking movement with Brocot-type pendulum regulation and stamped with oval J.B.D trademark above serial number 31209, 21-9 to backplate, circular porcelain dial painted with cherub to center within gilt bordered pink ground Roman numeral cartouche chapter ring and bead cast bezel, arch-shaped case with cylindrical molded upstand supporting twin-handled urn surmount applied with porcelain plaque portrait of woman in 18th century dress and flanked by cast floral trails and swags applied to sides of arch, front with arched gilt-edged floral trail decorated panel over dial flanked by female portraits and conforming floral inserts with shaped panel of cherub in flight beneath dial between, sides with bowed porcelain panels painted with musical trophies within pink ground gilt borders, elaborate skirt base with chased foliate top molding and inset with arrangement of further porcelain panels, on cast toupe feet with foliate apron to front, gilt-painted wood stand applied with engraved brass presentation plaque dated 1869, 21 1/4" high overall.* **$4,090**

Courtesy of Dreweatts & Bloomsbury

CLOSE-UP!

*French gilt brass and champleve enamel mounted green onyx four-glass mantel clock garniture, movement by S. Marti and Cie, Paris, late 19th century, eight-day circular gong striking movement stamped with S. Marti et Cie, MEDAILLE D'ARGENT 1889 roundel, oval A.1 trademark and numbers 4486, 5 and 2 to backplate and with polychrome enameled gilt brass twin glass capsule mercury compensated pendulum, gilt dial with rosette-decorated center, Arabic cartouche numerals and steel hands within conforming enameled bezel, bevel-glazed case with humped onyx pediment applied with winged motif above leaf cast cornice and twin putto caryatid mounts with sky and cobalt blue ground polychrome enameled panels and molded bases to canted front angles, on skirt base with further band of enamel decoration forming canted top molding and foliate case squab feet, 13 1/2" high; with pair of ovoid urn side pieces en suite, each with gilt flared neck applied with scroll cast lion's mask side handles and on stepped skirt base with canted polychrome enameled band and foliate cast squab feet, 10 1/2" high.* **$2,120**

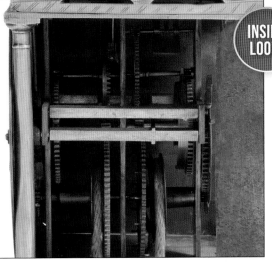

Courtesy of Dreweatts & Bloomsbury

▲ *Rare Charles II brass lantern clock, Thomas Knifton, London, circa 1665, dial signed Thomas Knifton at (crossed keys) in Lothbury, London toward upper margin of dial center and with engraved flowering tulip scrolling infill beneath, center with alarm disc and sculpted iron arrowhead hand within applied circular silvered Roman numeral chapter ring with fleur-de-lis half-hour markers and leafy infill to spandrel areas, large Lothbury-type frame with column-turned corner posts beneath openwork gallery and foliate pierced and engraved frets set between multi-knop vase-shaped finials with domed bell bearer with decorative pierced lobes and fitted with further central finial above, sides with brass doors, rear with iron hanging hoop and short spurs, on turned ball feet, 19 3/4" high.* **$16,300**

Courtesy of Dreweatts & Bloomsbury

◄ *Rare Black Forest carved walnut weight-driven Angelus cuckoo wall clock, Johann Baptist Beha, Eisenbach, circa 1875, cuckoo automaton announces hour with two-note call followed by hour repeated on gong, monk appears within arched recess beneath dial, circular wooden dial applied with bone Gothic Roman numerals and with pierced hands set within Gothic tracery to front of architectural case with arched recess beneath dial and flanked by projecting spiral twist columns to canted angles, top with pierced spire containing pivoted church bell above gable with circular doors for cuckoo automaton flanked by spire finials and castellated parapet to sides, base with inverted crotchet finials to shaped pendant apron, 32 1/4" high, excluding pendulum.* **$7,840**

BACK VIEW!

Courtesy of Dreweatts & Bloomsbury

*Rare German Renaissance gilt brass astronomical monstrance table clock case originally fitted with Universal Astrolabe, in manner of Jeremiah Metzger, Augsburg, circa 1570, movement and dial center later, English single fusee movement dating to around 1830, dial with later center engraved with foliate scrolls on matted ground with banner bearing inscription Reighs, Dresden, 1536, set within original 24-hour chapter ring with asterisk half-hour markers, button touch pieces and outer track engraved for each minute, case with ovoid urn finial to disc-shaped upstand engraved with subsidiary day-of-the-week dial annotated with planets to rear opposing foliate scroll cast and pierced rosette within molded surround to front with chased open strapwork fret to circumference, rear with center cut-out to accommodate later movement, border engraved with lines for stereographic projection around celestial equator stamped POLUS, MITNECHTLICH to upper margin opposing MITLEGLICH, POLUS at base, left- and right-hand margins with series of horizontal lines annotated with symbols for signs of zodiac, edge of shallow drum casing with continuous border etched in low relief with Arabesque strapwork within molded bands, whole raised on patinated bronze figure cast as Atlas seated on pieced and chased strapwork dome with molded collar over shallow ogee-shaped foot, 15 1/2" high overall.* **$5,720**

CLOSE-UP!

CLOCKS C

Courtesy of Dreweatts & Bloomsbury

*George III mahogany long case clock, Alexander Cumming, London, circa 1790, five pillar rack and bell striking movement with deadbeat escapement and 12" silvered brass Roman numeral ogee-arch top dial with large subsidiary seconds dial and calendar aperture to center, pierced steel hands and Arabic five minutes to outer track beneath N/S strike/silent lever at 12 o'clock and signed Alexander Cumming, LONDON to arch, case with ogee-arch shaped cavetto cornice over brass stop-fluted columns and rectangular foliate-pierced side frets to hood and flame figured block top door to trunk, on raised panel fronted plinth base with molded double skirt, 86 1/4" high.* **$10,600**

Courtesy of Dreweatts & Bloomsbury

*George III mahogany domestic long case regulator clock, James Vigne, London, circa 1790, 12" silvered brass Roman numeral ogee-arch top dial with subsidiary seconds dial and calendar aperture to center, pierced blued steel hands and Arabic five minutes to outer track beneath N/S strike/silent lever at 12 o'clock and signed James Vigne, London to arch, in case with ogee-arch shaped cavetto cornice, brass stop-fluted canted angles and rectangular side windows to hood above conforming shaped-top caddy molded flame figured door to trunk, on raised panel fronted plinth base with molded double skirt and later ogee bracket feet, 77" high excluding later feet, 80" high overall.* **$6,540**

Courtesy of Dreweatts & Bloomsbury

*Victorian mahogany hour-striking long case regulator clock, Francis Smith, Blandford, circa 1845, 12" square silvered brass dial with subsidiary seconds over hour dials and signed Francis, Smith to center within outer minute track annotated with Arabic five minutes, in case with ogee-arch cavetto molded pediment over plain frieze and reeded canted angles to hood above conforming shaped-arch caddy molded flame figured door flanked by quarter columns to trunk, on raised shaped panel fronted plinth base with shallow skirt, 76" high.* **$4,250**

*Warman's* Antiques & Collectibles | **363**

Courtesy of Dreweatts & Bloomsbury

▶ *Rare Queen Anne verge pocket watch movement, Thomas Tompion and George Graham, London, number 4650, circa 1713, full plate gilt verge movement with four Egyptian pillars pinned through frontplate and three-arm sprung steel balance, backplate with leaf-bordered symmetrical foliate scroll pierced and engraved balance cock with female mask decoration at base and conforming pierced broad foot flanked by silvered regulation disc with adjacent applied foliate scroll infill opposing signature Tho: Tompion, Geo: Graham, LONDON and engraved serial number 4560, frontplate stamped with repeat serial number, fitted to late 18th century circular white enamel Roman numeral sedan timepiece dial with blued steel spade hands, case contemporary to dial with hinged cast brass bezel fitted with convex glass within molded cavetto surround, rear with circular hinged brass cover and brass suspension ring fitted to upper margin, 5 3/4" diameter.* **$9,800**

Courtesy of Direct Auction Galleries

▶ *Ornate floral designed Ansonia porcelain mantel clock, 11 1/2" high.* **$460**

Courtesy of Thomaston Place Auction Galleries

▶ *French mantel clock with garnitures, hour eight-day time and strike, circa 1890, in gilt bronze and crystal with cloisonné decoration, concave architectural form of clock surmounted by large urn with two hand-painted concave Sèvres porcelain portrait panels signed "H. Poitevin," matching urns with painted allegories for art and music by same decorator, marked "A-1" and "Ch. Hour, France," faux mercury pendulum cracked, clock 19" x 15" x 7 1/2", urns 15" x 5" x 5".* **$7,280**

Courtesy of Dreweatts & Bloomsbury

*French patinated metal and gilt brass sculptural mystery timepiece, Guilmet, Paris, circa 1900, eight-day back-wound movement with tic-tac escapement and short bob pendulum swinging behind frontplate, backplate fitted with counterpoise for hour hand and stamped with circular trademark GLT, BTE, SGDG, MEDAILLE D OR, PARIS above serial number 4886, circular white enamel Roman numeral dial with scroll-pierced gilt hands and Arabic five-minutes to outer track, cylindrical case with Greek-key decoration to silvered drum housing surmounted by gilt foliate crest above conforming side scrolls flanking sprung pivot support, with triple-rod gridiron pendulum shaft terminating with gilt cartouche with regulation screw beneath, figural stand cast as semi naked male holding aloft timepiece via sprung pivot in left hand and cradling money box draped with banner inscribed EPARGNE-PREVOYANCE in right, cast base with beehive, cornucopia and inscribed Pour la MUTALITE, with impressed indistinct signature and applied with MADE IN FRANCE roundel to left hand side, on circular molded foot, 27 1/4" high.* **$1,310**

Courtesy of Dreweatts & Bloomsbury

*Rare George II Louis XV-style ormolu mantel timepiece with year calendar dial, Clay, London, mid-18th century, 4 1/4" circular enameled dial with cobalt blue center within small diameter Roman numeral chapter ring with Arabic five minutes and concentric bands annotated with painted signs of Zodiac, sunrise for each sign and date-of-the-month with months named to outer track, with sculpted steel hour and minute hands to center and calendar hand issuing from gilt solar mask within narrow canted gilt bezel surround, in waisted asymmetric rococo scroll and leafy spray cast and chased case with surmount cast with eagle on dragon above hinged convex glazed bezel and scroll pierced and engraved brass shaped frets to sides, rear with circular glazed aperture, on asymmetric scroll cast feet with scallop shell detail, 15 1/4" high.* **$10,600**

*Rare Charles II paneled oak quarter-chiming 30-hour long case clock, John Williamson, London, movement circa 1683, case circa 1672, square brass dial with applied silvered seconds ring to engraved symmetrical flowering tulip and foliate decorated center with drapery cartouche signed John Williamson, Near Temple Barr, Londini Fecit toward lower margin within applied silvered Roman numeral chapter ring with fleur-de-lis half-hour markers and Arabic five minutes within outer minute track, with sculpted blued steel hands and applied winged cherub head cast brass spandrels to angles, in paneled oak case with molded triangular pediment and tall scroll-lattice pierced frieze to both front and sides above glazed dial aperture and large side windows to hood, trunk with convex throat over 46" full-width single fielded panel door, base of same width with waist molding above conforming fixed shorter fielded panel and molded skirt, 92 1/2" high.* **$18,800**

**CLOSE-UP!**

Courtesy of Dreweatts & Bloomsbury

*Charles II architectural key-wound 30-hour hooded wall clock, Jonathan Chambers, Shefford, circa 1670, four finned pillar single-handed movement latched at front and originally pinned to rear with plates with integral cast extensions for strike detents to left-hand side, rounded-arch shaped lower edge, square brass dial centered with engraved rose motif above drapery lambrequin signed Jonathan Chambers, Fecit to lower margin within silvered Roman numeral chapter ring with fleur-de-lis half-hour markers, pierced steel hand and spandrel areas engraved with symmetrical decoration with dog rose over pomegranate and other fruit, in wall-mounted pedimented case veneered in padouk-like timber with ebonized moldings, rising hood with applied gilt brass cherub mount to tympanum above raised moldings to glazed dial aperture and rectangular side windows, backboard fitted with latch to hold hood in raised position above horizontal table applied with pair of tall blocks to support movement, underside with ebonized shaped apron flanked by conforming side brackets with short rectangular veneered back panel behind, case probably later, 28" high.* **$ 20,500**

INSIDE LOOK!

# Coca-Cola

By Allan Petretti

**ALLAN PETRETTI** is one of the world's top authorities on Coca-Cola memorabilia. He conducts seminars for Coca-Cola collector groups and has been interviewed by the *Wall Street Journal*, *USA Today*, *London Times*, and *New York Times*, and has appeared on many television shows, including *"History Detectives."*

Organized Coca-Cola collecting began in the early 1970s. The advertising art of The Coca-Cola Co., which used to be thought of as a simple area of collecting, has reached a whole new level of appreciation. Because of their artistic quality, these images deserve to be considered true Americana.

Coca-Cola art is more than bottles and trays, more than calendars and signage, more than trinkets, giveaways, and displays. It incorporates all the best that America has to offer. The Coca-Cola Co., since its conception in 1886, has taken advertising to a whole new level. So much so that it has been studied and dissected by scholars as to why it has proved to be so successful for more than 120 years.

Can soda pop advertising be considered true art? Without a doubt! The very best artists in America were an integral part of that honorary place in art history. Renowned artists like Rockwell, Sundbloom, Elvgren, and Wyeth helped take a quality product and advance it to the status of an American icon and all that exemplifies the very best about America.

This beautiful advertising directly reflects the history of our country: its styles and fashion, patriotism, family life, the best of times, and the worst of times. Everything this country has gone through since 1886 can be seen in these wonderful images.

For more information on Coca-Cola collectibles, see *Petretti's Coca-Cola Collectibles Price Guide,* 12th edition, by Allan Petretti.

Courtesy of Morphy Auctions

◀ *Lighted counter sign, 1930, made by Brunhoff, very good condition, 14" high.* **$20,400**

Courtesy of Morphy Auctions

▲ *Cardboard sign, 1940s-1950s, excellent condition, 15" x 12".* **$210**

Courtesy of Morphy Auctions

▲ *1930s Coca-Cola lamp.* **$4,200**

Courtesy of Morphy Auctions

◄ *1930s Dura-Products glass sign.* **$9,000**

**RECOMMENDED READING**

**Petretti's Coca-Cola Collectibles Price Guide, 12th edition.** "The Encyclopedia of Coca-Cola Collectibles." The definitive source for identifying and valuing nearly a century of Coca-Cola treasures.
www.krausebooks.com

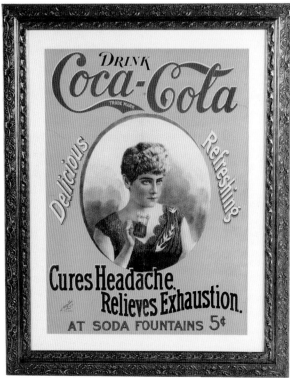

Courtesy of Richard Opfer Auctioneering, Inc.

▲ *Blinking marquee sign, circa 1930s-1940s, in Asheville, North Carolina, original metal framework, Plexiglas cover, refurbished as excellent condition, 5' x 18'.* **$39,000**

Courtesy of Richard Opfer Auctioneering, Inc.

▲ *Cameo paper sign, 1896, produced by J. Ottmann Litho Co. in New York, excellent condition as restored, 30" x 40".* **$105,000**

Courtesy of Morphy Auctions

▶ *Pick up 12 sign, 1956, near mint-plus condition, 54 1/4" x 16".* **$14,400**

*Cardboard sign, 1952, featuring Sugar Ray Robinson, 12" x 15".* **$896**

*Porcelain double-sided sign, circa 1950s, original base and brackets, never used, planned for use outdoors at service stations, outstanding condition.* **$16,000**

*Embossed tin sign, 1933, good color and appearance, very good condition, 27 1/4" x 19 1/4".* **$1,920**

Courtesy of Morphy Auctions

▲ *Whirligig sign, 1950s, eight panel surfaces, original base mount, near mint condition, 13" high.* **$11,400**

Courtesy of Richard Opfer Auctioneering, Inc.

▲ *Neon building clock and sign, circa mid-to-late 1930s, once adorned Piqua, Ohio, bottling plant, clock face, hands and silver bezel and trim of metal, remainder of sign embossed porcelain with neon tubing and highlights, neon tubing replaced, excellent condition, 14' x 7'.* **$50,000**

Courtesy of Bertoia Auctions

▶ *Sonja Henie Coca-Cola advertising sign, circa mid-1930s, one of only two known, heavy lithographed cardboard with added graphic, lettering printed in French, 40" high x 36" wide.* **$11,500**

◄ *1896 Coca-Cola calendar, reportedly the only existing example.* **$105,000**

*Circa 1970s Coca-Cola sign crafted into bench, 60" long.* **$795**

▼ *1910 Coca-Cola embossed tin sign.* **$2,400**

Courtesy of Ron Garrett

*Double-sided "Drink Coca Cola" tin drug store sign, excellent condition, 63" x 42".* **$2,000-$3,000**

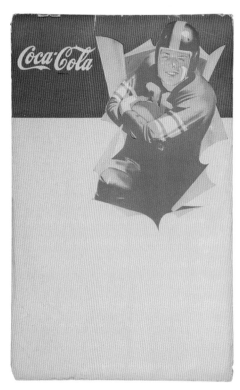

Courtesy of Heritage Auctions

*Paper football sign, 1950s, unknown football player, 13 1/2" x 21".* **$24**

Courtesy of Morphy Auctions

*Tin and wood sign, 1948, near mint condition, 35 1/2" x 17 3/4".* **$390**

BACK VIEW!

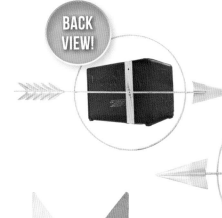

Courtesy of Heritage Auctions

▲ *Arrow sign, 1940, aluminum, die cut embossed with cooler, "Kay Displays / Grand Rapids Michigan" marked on back, very good condition, 16" diameter.* **$567**

Courtesy of Morphy Auctions

*Cooler sign, 1940s to 1950s, featuring famous Sprite Boy, near mint condition, 31" long.* **$1,200**

Courtesy of Morphy Auctions

*Early Baird clock, "Coca-Cola / The Ideal Brain Tonic / Relieves / Exhaustion."* **$3,000**

Courtesy of Morphy Auctions

*1905 cardboard poster, "Coca-Cola At Soda Fountains 5¢."* **$20,400**

Courtesy of Morphy Auctions

*1900 calendar with actress Hilda Clark, near mint condition.* **$210,000**

Courtesy of Morphy Auctions

*Tin sign, 1936, bold graphic with bottle, excellent condition, 45 1/2" diameter.* **$540**

Courtesy of Heritage Auctions

*Lithographed sign, circa 1904, picturing singer Lillian Nordica, aka the "Yankee Diva" of American opera scene, metal hanging strips, excellent condition, 14 1/2" x 19 1/2".*
**$7,170**

Courtesy of Richard Opfer Auctioneering, Inc.

*Porcelain double-sided triangle sign, strong unfaded color, strong shine and no surface scratches, near mint condition, 22" x 24".*
**$16,000**

# Coin-Operated Devices

Coin-operated devices fall into three main categories: amusement or arcade games, trade stimulators, and vending machines.

Vending machines have been around longer than any other kind of coin-op, and the 1880s witnessed the invention of many varieties. Gambling devices and amusement machines soon followed suit. The industry swelled during the 1890s and early 1900s but slowed during World War I. It rebounded in the 1920s and 1930s, which is considered the "Golden Age" of coin-ops.

Coin-ops reflect the prevailing art form of the era in which they were produced. Early machines exhibit designs ranging from Victorian to Art Nouveau and Art Deco, while later devices manufactured from 1940 on feature modernism.

For more information on coin-operated devices, visit the website of the Coin Operated Collectors Association at http://coinopclub.org.

Courtesy of Victorian Casino Antiques/Morphy Auctions

*Rare Mills/Hoke 5¢ "Trap the Snake Futurity" three-reel table model revamp escalator bell slot machine with working skill stops, circa 1939, original condition, fully operational, excellent condition, with key.*
**$46,800**

Courtesy of Morphy Auctions

▲ *Callie double upright floor model slot machine, 5¢ Centaur, 25¢ Big Six, oak case, all plating in gold, Big Six wheel with repaint of original, both marquees with new plays, restored.* **$90,000**

Courtesy of Morphy Auctions

◀ *Mills Novelty Co. Imperial Shocker Electric Treatment machine, circa early 1900s, jolt of electricity was believed to be therapeutic and attracted patrons who wanted to test their endurance, 1¢, cast metal top, wood base, new side door for battery compartment, 23" high.* **$11,400**

BACK VIEW!

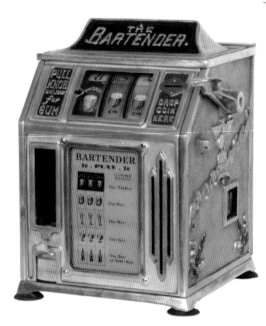

Courtesy of Fontaine's Auction Gallery

*The Bartender 1¢ three-reel-type trade stimulator slot machine by Groetchen Tool Mfg. Co., Chicago, cast aluminum case with bell and eagle on sides and banners with years of nation's independence and year that Groetchen Co. started, 1776 and 1930; top banner reads "The Bartender" with beer and whiskey labels, banner below displays payout in beer or whiskey for matching spins, machine also dispenses gumball with each play; working condition with key, 12" high x 8 1/2" wide x 8 1/2" deep.* **$514**

Courtesy of Fontaine's Auction Gallery

◀ *Beach-Nut Gum + Fruit Drops + Mints 5¢ coin-operated countertop vending machine, green and gold metal case with crest display, Beech-Nut displays on front and sides, glass body with seven columns for packets of gum/candy/mints with coin chutes above and push-button selector levers in front, good working condition, original paint with minor flaking, 15" high x 10 3/4" wide x 6" deep.* **$544**

Courtesy of Morphy Auctions

▲ *Pace Deluxe Gold Cherry Bell Harrah's Lake Tahoe Resort Casino gooseneck bell slot machine with top candle change light, counters, side bell and Harrah's jackpot club reels, missing parts, circa 1945, not in working condition, with key.* **$720**

Courtesy of James D. Julia Auctioneers, Fairfield, Maine, www.jamesdjulia.com

*Rare Goo Goo penny gum vendor with decorated front, iron casting over wooden case with images of brownie-type characters on sides, one side shows man on roller skates, other side shows country woman chewing piece of straw.* **$42,660**

Courtesy of Victorian Casino Antiques/ Morphy Auctions

◄ *Floor model Midget Derby 25¢ horse race gambling machine, manufacturer unknown, only one known to exist, condition excellent, with keys and museum information placard on stand.* **$37,200**

ORIGINAL PACKAGE!

Courtesy of James D. Julia Auctioneers, Fairfield, Maine, www.jamesdjulia.com

*Ad-Lee E-Z 5¢ gumball vendor with original box, probably all-original with original fortune balls, cardboard box for machine, boxes for ball gum fortunes, and marquee holder with card; probably never on location, no wear, boxes containing ball gum intact, approximately 23" to top of marquee.* **$4,147**

Courtesy of Morphy Auctions

*Chuck-O-Luck dice gambling machine with domed glass, 5¢ turn, circa 1920s, manufactured by Southern Novelty of Atlanta, satin finish aluminum base, 14 1/2" high.* **$6,600**

Courtesy of Victorian Casino Antiques/
Morphy Auctions

◀ *1904 Caille roulette floor
machine, mahogany with
ornate repoussé, nickel-plated
embellishments. Provenance:
William F. Harrah collection.*
**$213,600**

Courtesy of James D. Julia Auctioneers,
Fairfield, Maine, www.jamesdjulia.com

*Climax 10 1¢ vendor enameled in
dark red with yellow pinstriping,
very fine-plus all-original condition
including paper label within glass
globe, functional and filled for
display, minimal wear overall,
approximately 20" high.*
**$2,470**

Courtesy of James D. Julia Auctioneers, Fairfield, Maine, www.jamesdjulia.com

*Honey Breath mint dispenser manufactured by Gravity Vending
Machine Co. in early 20th century, Wagner & Miller sole agents
in eastern Ohio; four cascading glass tubes hold breath mints that
roll to bottom and dispense through front; large original decal on
front glass of women holding draped banner with "CHEW HONEY
BREATH BALLS 4 for 1¢," cast iron base and top with four nickel-
plated columns and plate glass windows, nickel plated castings, all
original machine, darkening and loss to nickel plating, chipping to
bottom of plate glass panels on front and left side, approximately
7 1/4" x 8 1/2" x 13 1/2" high.* **$6,075**

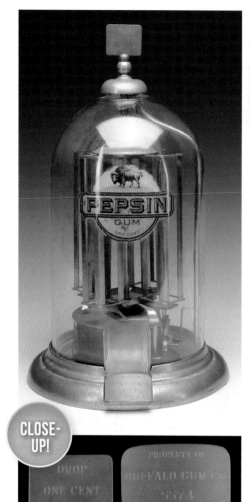

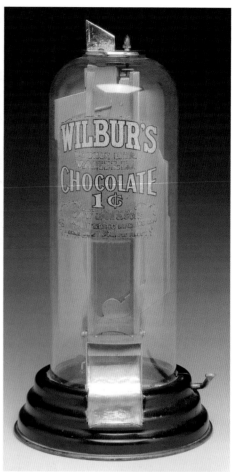

**CLOSE-UP!**

*Rare Buffalo Gum Co. Pepsin Gum vendor manufactured by White Vending Co., when coin is deposited, exposed clockwork mechanism trips and four gum columns turn a quarter revolution, dispensing gum; original decal on front and side of globe in very good condition with minimal lifting in gold background, slotted ball on top of machine probably held signage, original signage missing, one side says, "DROP ONE CENT HERE" and reverse side says, "PROPERTY OF BUFFALO GUM CO.," approximately 14 1/2" high.* **$9,000-$11,000**

*Rare Wilbur's chocolate 1¢ vendor by National Vending Co., cast dome contains column of chocolate confections, large original decal with some loss applied to inside front of dome, exceptional original condition, mechanism intact and working; penny dropped in slot at top of dome falls into position and when lever is pressed, penny pushes out chocolate, then drops into coin reservoir below; approximately 14 1/2" high.* **$4,500-$6,500**

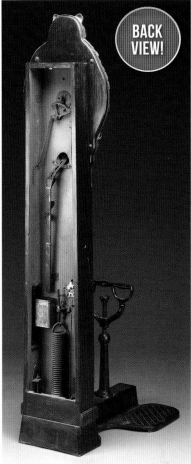

BACK VIEW!

Courtesy of James D. Julia Auctioneers,
Fairfield, Maine, www.jamesdjulia.com

▲ *Mills Novelty Co. Perfect Muscle Developer strength tester arcade machine, early 20th century, elaborate top casting with trademark Mills owl cast at center, tin dial of man flexing muscles in center, porcelain plaque on front details operation of machine, which could be altered from 1¢ to 5¢ by adjustment to coin mechanism, overall restoration to cabinet and castings, missing lock for wooden back door, 68" high.* **$8,000-$12,000**

Courtesy of Morphy Auctions

◄ *Callie 5¢ Busy Bee cast iron trade stimulator, paper wheel, restored nickel finish, iron replacement, back door excellent condition, 13" long.* **$16,800**

Courtesy of Morphy Auctions

◄ *Custom Coinola Nickelodeon Orchestrion light-up music machine in upright oak case with three leaded stained glass doors, one-of-a-kind piece with flute pipes, xylophone, cymbal, triangle, and self-playing piano, with keys, schematic manual and four type "o" multi-play music rolls, approximately 76" x 59" x 25".* **$6,600**

Courtesy of Fontaine's Auction Gallery

*Marvel's Pop-Up 1¢ trade stimulator, baseball pinball-type skill game in oak case with reverse-painted glass panel and painted wood panel playing field, right knob has batter hit ball to field where it bounces off pins, left knob moves fielder left and right to catch ball, working condition, with key, some flaking to paint, 19" high x 12 1/2" wide x 10" deep.* **$695**

Courtesy of Fontaine's Auction Gallery

*Jennings Rockaway 1¢ trade stimulator, pressed aluminum polychrome case with oak sides, base and backboard, coin drops into rocking pinned wheel with incised scene of two children on seesaw, five receiver slots at bottom of game board feed into jackpot wells, working condition, signed with Jennings decal on side, missing key, 23" high x 15" wide x 12" deep.* **$665**

TOP VIEW!

Courtesy of James D. Julia Auctioneers, Fairfield, Maine, www.jamesdjulia.com

▲ *Carris Novelty cigar cutter and match dispenser, also marked "Roundy Peckham & Dexter / Co. / ParFay / General Good / Sir Hector," cast iron with bronze highlights, dispenser holds wooden matches that dispense with lever action, cigar cutter activated with same lever, Cpt. JAN. 1905, base 6" x 8".* **$679**

Courtesy of Morphy Auctions

◀ *Mills Novelty Co. Double Dewey upright slot machine, 5¢ and 25¢, with original music, mechanics in untouched original condition with original wheels, oak case refinished, Watts nickel plating refinished, both silver glasses are newer replacements, small crack at lock hole on face plate of quarter side, 70" long.* **$114,000**

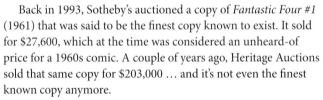

# Comics

By Barry Sandoval

**BARRY SANDOVAL** is Director of Operations for Comics and Comic Art, Heritage Auctions. In addition to managing Heritage's Comics division, which sells some $20 million worth of comics and original comic art each year, Sandoval is a noted comic book evaluator and serves as an advisor to the *Overstreet Comic Book Price Guide.*

Back in 1993, Sotheby's auctioned a copy of *Fantastic Four #1* (1961) that was said to be the finest copy known to exist. It sold for $27,600, which at the time was considered an unheard-of price for a 1960s comic. A couple of years ago, Heritage Auctions sold that same copy for $203,000 ... and it's not even the finest known copy anymore.

It used to be that only comics from the 1930s or 1940s could be worth thousands of dollars. Now, truly high-grade copies of comics from the Silver Age (1956-1969 by most people's reckoning) can sell for four, five, or even six figures. Note I said truly high-grade. Long gone are the days when a near mint condition copy was only worth triple the price of a good condition copy. Now near mint is more like 10-20 times good, and sometimes it's as much as a factor of 1,000.

A trend of the last couple of years has been that the "key" issues have separated even further from the pack, value-wise. Note that not every key is a "#1" issue – if you have *Amazing Fantasy #15, Tales of Suspense #39,* and *Journey into Mystery #83,* you've got the first appearances of Spider-Man, Iron Man, and Thor. (Beware of reprints and replica editions, however.)

The most expensive comics of all remain the Golden Age (1938-1949) first appearances, like Superman's 1938 debut in *Action Comics #1,* several copies of which have sold for $1 million or more. However, not every single comic from the old days is going up in value. Take western-themed comics. Values are actually going down in this genre as the generation that grew up watching westerns is at the age where they're looking to sell, and there are more sellers than potential buyers.

Comics from the 1970s and later, while increasing in value, rarely garner anywhere near the same value as 1960s issues, primarily because in the 1970s comics were increasingly seen as a potentially valuable collectible. People took better care of them, and in many cases hoarded multiple copies.

What about 1980s favorites like *The Dark Knight Returns* and

*The Flash #105 (DC, 1959), CGC VF+ 8.5; the Golden Age series ended in 1949, 10 years before this premiere issue of the Silver Age version; artist Carmine Infantino rendered both versions; origin of Flash is retold, and story features origin and first appearance of Mirror Master.* **$11,353**

*Watchmen*? Here the demand is high, but the supply is really high. These series were heavily hyped at the time and were done by well-known creators, so copies were socked away in great quantities. We've come across more than one dealer who has 20-30 mint copies of every single 1980s comic socked away in a warehouse, waiting for the day when they're worth selling.

I should mention one surprise hit of the last couple of years. When Image Comics published *The Walking Dead #1* in 2003, it had a low print run and made no particular splash in the comics world. Once AMC made it into a television series, however, it was a whole different story. High-grade copies of #1 have been fetching $1,000 and up lately.

If you've bought comics at an auction house or on eBay, you might have seen some in CGC holders. Certified Guaranty Co., or CGC, is a third-party grading service that grades a comic book on a scale from 0.5 to 10. These numbers correspond with traditional descriptive grades of good, very fine, near mint, and mint, with the higher numbers indicating a better grade. Once graded, CGC encapsulates the comic book in plastic. The grade remains valid as long as the plastic holder is not broken open. CGC has been a boon to the hobby, allowing people to buy comics with more confidence and with the subjectivity of grading taken out of the equation. Unless extremely rare, it's usually only high-grade comics that are worth certifying.

One aspect of collecting that has absolutely exploded in the last 20 years has been original comic art, and not just art for the vintage stuff. In fact, the most expensive piece Heritage Auctions has ever sold was from 1990: Todd McFarlane's cover art for *Amazing Spider-Man #328*, which sold for more than $650,000. It's not unusual for a page that was bought for $20 in the 1980s to be worth $5,000 now.

If you want to get into collecting original comic art, McFarlane

Photo via eBay

## Record-Breaking Comic

The first comic book ever to feature Superman, *Action Comics #1* (1938), broke the record price for a comic when it sold in an eBay auction in August for just over $3.2 million.

The comic is only one of 50 originals of *Action Comics #1* that has not been restored. It received a near-perfect 9/10 rating by Certified Guaranty Co., a collectibles rating agency.

Forty-eight people placed bids on the item over the course of the sale. It was consigned by Darren Adams, the owner of Pristine Comics in Federal Way, Washington. According to a photo posted to Instagram, New York's Metropolis Comics and Collectibles entered the winning bid of $3,207,852, according to eBay.

Metropolis' owner, Stephen Fishler, told the AP that the piece was "just too good of an opportunity to pass up." Pointing out that the original sold for only 10 cents in 1938, he said that the comic's worth is almost unbelievable, "but it is Superman. That's an iconic thing. It's the first time anybody saw what a superhero was like."

This latest copy of *Action Comics #1* (1938) to sell beats the previous record for a comic book at auction set by another copy of the same comic, which sold for $2.16 million in 2011, and belonged to actor Nicolas Cage.

would not be the place to start unless you've got a really fat wallet. I suggest picking a current comic artist you like who isn't yet a major "name." Chances are his originals will be a lot more affordable. Another idea is to collect the original art for comic strips. You can find originals for as little as $20, as long as you're not expecting a Peanuts or a Prince Valiant. Heritage Auctions (HA.com) maintains a free online archive of every piece of art they've sold and it is an excellent research tool.

As expensive as both comic books and comic art can be at the high end of the spectrum, in many ways this is a buyer's market. In the old days you might search for years to find a given issue of a comic; now you can often search eBay and see 10 different copies for sale. Also, comics conventions seem to be thriving in almost every major city – and while the people in crazy costumes get all the publicity, you can also find plenty of vintage comics dealers at these shows. From that point of view, it's a great time to be a comics collector.

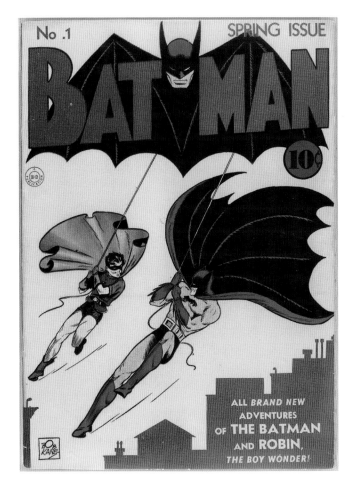

Courtesy of Heritage Auctions

*Batman #1 (DC, 1940), CGC Apparent FN/VF 7.0, one of the most sought-after issues in the comic book hobby with first appearances of two major characters, the Joker and Catwoman; Bob Kane and Jerry Robinson cover and art.* **$38,838**

Courtesy of Heritage Auctions

Funnies on Parade #nn *(Eastern Color, 1933),*
*CGC VF- 7.5, first comic book ever published,*
*promotional book produced for Procter &*
*Gamble, with print run of 10,000 copies.* **$8,962**

Courtesy of Heritage Auctions

Detective Comics #8 *(DC, 1937), CGC FN 6.0,*
*"classic" Creig Flessel cover with Mister Chang,*
*Joe Shuster art; it is estimated that fewer than*
*50 copies exist today.* **$5,079**

Courtesy of Heritage Auctions

Detective Comics #7 *(DC, 1937), CGC FN-*
*5.5, crime cover courtesy of artist Creig Flessel,*
*who also drew Speed Saunders feature inside;*
*Jerry Siegel and Joe Shuster provided stories*
*and art for both the Spy and Slam Bradley*
*features.* **$5,079**

Courtesy of Heritage Auctions

Famous Funnies #1 *(Eastern Color, 1934), CGC*
*FN+ 6.5, first comic book sold to general public*
*through newsstand distribution, contains comic*
*strip reprints with characters including Mutt and*
*Jeff, Tailspin Tommy, and Joe Palooka.* **$7,768**

Courtesy of Heritage Auctions

Fantastic Four #1 *(Marvel, 1961), CGC FN/VF 7.0, first appearance of Fantastic Four, Marvel's first superhero team, origin and first appearance of Mole Man; written by Stan Lee, art by Jack Kirby.* **$19,120**

Courtesy of Heritage Auctions

▲ The Avengers #1 (Marvel, 1963), CGC NM 9.4, brought in the highest price for an item in the Don and Maggie Thompson Pedigree Collection when it sold for **$89,625**. The issue features the origin and first appearance of the Avengers (Thor, Iron Man, Hulk, Ant-Man, and Wasp), plus appearances by the Fantastic Four, Loki, and the Teen Brigade. The Jack Kirby cover also doesn't hurt.

Courtesy of Heritage Auctions

▲ Besides comic books, the Thompson collection included original comic art, including this Barry Smith Conan the Barbarian #4 "The Tower of the Elephant" cover (Marvel, 1971). **$87,235**

Courtesy of Heritage Auctions

▲ Green Lantern #76, Don/Maggie Thompson Collection pedigree (DC, 1970), CGC NM+ 9.6. Considered by some to be the comic book that started the Bronze Age of comics, this is Neal Adams' first issue as penciler of the title and the first time Green Arrow received co-star billing. **$6,274**

Courtesy of Heritage Auctions

*Tales of Suspense #39, Don/Maggie Thompson Collection pedigree (Marvel, 1963), CGC NM 9.4. First appearance and origin of Iron Man (Tony Stark); Jack Kirby's cover is complemented by interior art from Don Heck, Steve Ditko, and Gene Colan.* **$83,650**

## Pedigree Collection

The Don and Maggie Thompson Pedigree Collection is a classic example of the time and care so many people put into their collections, and the payoff can be huge when it comes time to sell them.

In November 2013, the first selections of comic books and original comic art from the Thompson collection hit a combined $835,384 to lead $5.8+ million in comic books and original comic art at Heritage Auctions. In a February 2014 auction, another comic in their collection, *Tales of Suspense #39*, sold for $83,650.

According to Heritage Auctions, the Don and Maggie Thompson Pedigree Collection has garnered headlines worldwide due to its quality and the passion of its owners. The Thompsons were responsible for launching, as well as participating in, several publications that brought readers closer to creators, characters, and fellow fans. Starting with a mimeographed one-sheet called *Harbinger* in 1960, the two produced a variety of other publications until both jointly edited *Comics Buyer's Guide*, published by Krause Publications/F+W, until Don's passing in 1994. Maggie then served in an editorial role until the end of the publication's run in 2013.

"(The) first installment of what I'm calling 'My Pedigreed Adventure' has been rewarding in more ways than one," Maggie Thompson said. "Heritage Auctions has consistently displayed unvarying kindness and knowledge. Its experts permitted me to profit from my hobby without ever treating my treasures solely in terms of their market value."

Courtesy of Heritage Auctions

Daredevil Comics #1 Daredevil Battles Hitler, *Vancouver pedigree (Lev Gleason, 1941), CGC NM+ 9.6.* **$50,788**

Courtesy of Heritage Auctions

Amazing-Man Comics #5 (#1), *Mile High pedigree (Centaur, 1939), CGC NM 9.4.* **$56,763**

Courtesy of Heritage Auctions

All-American Comics #16 *(DC, 1940), CGC VG- 3.5; Sheldon Moldoff's most famous cover introduces Green Lantern in 1940.* **$44,813**

Courtesy of Heritage Auctions

Detective Comics #31 *(DC, 1939), CGC GD 2.0, with one of the most classic covers in the history of comics, with fifth appearance of Batman; cover art by Bob Kane and Jerry Robinson.* **$34,655**

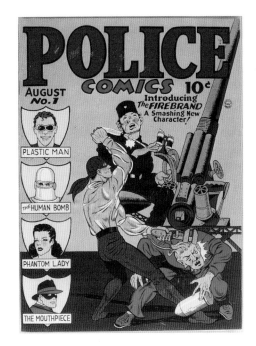

◄ Police Comics #1, *Mile High pedigree (Quality, 1941), CGC NM 9.4, premiere issue of Quality's flagship title of 1940s with origin and first appearance of Plastic Man by Jack Cole, Phantom Lady, Firebrand, and Human Bomb, with art by Fred Guardineer and Paul Gustavson.* **$38,838**

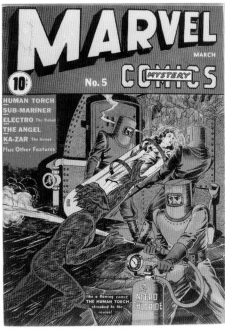

▲ Marvel Mystery Comics #5, *Larson pedigree (Timely, 1940), CGC VF 8.0, Human Torch on classic Schomburg cover (his first Torch cover and only second Torch cover ever), Human Torch story inside drawn by Carl Burgos, Angel story done by Paul Gustavson, and Sub-Mariner story by Bill Everett. Provenance: From the collection of actor Nicolas Cage.* **$28,680**

◄ X-Men #1 *(Marvel, 1963), CGC VF+ 8.5, first appearances of Professor Xavier's X-Men, by Jack Kirby, with archetypal arch-villain Magneto.*
**$22,705**

Courtesy of Heritage Auctions

Superman #1 *(DC, 1939), CGC Apparent VF- 7.5, famous cover by Joe Shuster.* **$32,265**

Courtesy of Heritage Auctions

Amazing Fantasy #15 *(Marvel, 1962), CGC VF/ NM 9.0, Spider-Man's dramatic entrance on cover, his first appearance and origin.* **$191,200**

Courtesy of Heritage Auctions

Strange Tales #110, *Northland pedigree (Marvel, 1963), CGC NM 9.4, contains first appearances of Doctor Strange, Ancient One, Nightmare, and Wong, first Paste-Pot Pete and Wizard team-up; cover by Jack Kirby, interior art by Dick Ayers and Steve Ditko.* **$50,788**

Courtesy of Heritage Auctions

The Incredible Hulk #1 *(Marvel, 1962), CGC VF- 7.5, first issue with first appearance and origin of hero-villain, who wages war against terrors of governmental society; Rick Jones, Betty Ross, and Thunderbolt Ross also make first appearances; classic cover art by Jack Kirby, interior art by George Roussos.* **$26,290**

Courtesy of Heritage Auctions

Wonder Comics #1 *(Fox, 1939), CGC NM 9.4, debut of Wonder Man, first hero to ride Superman's coattails.* **$68,712**

Journey Into Mystery #83 *(Marvel, 1962), CGC VF 8.0, origin and first appearance of Thor, with cover and interior art by Jack Kirby.* **$16,730**

The Incredible Hulk #181 *(Marvel, 1974), CGC NM/MT 9.8, with first full appearance of X-Men's Wolverine.* **$11,950**

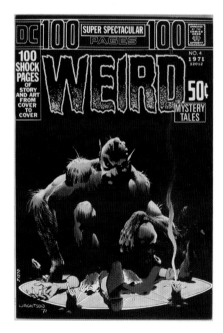

DC 100-Page Super Spectacular #4 Weird Mystery Tales *(DC, 1971), CGC NM+ 9.6.* **$5,079**

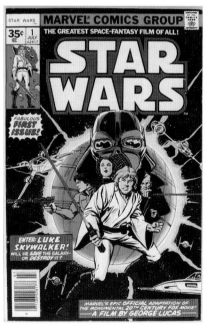

Star Wars #1 *(Marvel, 1977), CGC NM 9.4, rare 35¢ variant, part 1 of Star Wars movie adaptation, Howard Chaykin cover and art.* **$9,859**

*Tales to Astonish #27 (Marvel, 1962), CGC VF- 7.5, first appearance of Henry Pym, who shows up as Ant-Man eight issues later; cover and art by Jack Kirby, backup features by Steve Ditko and Don Heck.*
**$11,950**

# Cookie Jars

Cookie jars, colorful and often whimsical, are popular with collectors. They were made by almost every manufacturer in all types of materials. Figural character cookie jars are the most popular with collectors.

Cookie jars often were redesigned to reflect newer tastes. Hence, the same jar may be found in several different variations, and these variations can affect the price.

Many cookie-jar shapes were manufactured by more than one company and, as a result, can be found with different marks. This often happened because of mergers. Molds also were traded and sold among companies.

Some cookie jars by American Bisque were enhanced with flashers – a plastic piece, technically known as a lenticular image, that changes when the item is moved back and forth.

For more information on cookie jars, see *Warman's Cookie Jars Identification and Price Guide* by Mark F. Moran.

Photo courtesy Hake's Americana & Collectibles

*Abingdon Halloween-themed china cookie jar with relief image on each side of witch flying on broomstick by light of crescent moon with bat nearby, jar lid handle of cat with arched back, circa 1950s, incised "692" on underside, with Abingdon stamp, handle with professional repair at both feet, 8 1/4" x 11 1/4" x 4 1/2".* **$494**

Photo courtesy Skinner Inc.; www.skinnerinc.com

*American Bisque Popeye figural cookie jar with corncob pipe, 10 1/2" high x 7" wide x 7" deep.* **$277**

Photo courtesy Heritage Auctions

▲ *Three items related to ballooning: U.S.-made pottery cookie jar, octagonal cookie jar with printed historic balloon images, and American liquor decanter, all in fine condition.* **$47**

Photo courtesy Skinner Inc.; www.skinnerinc.com

▲ *Edmands & Co. Albany-glazed pottery cookie jar, Charlestown, Massachusetts, in molded cylindrical form with narrow paneled sides and molded rope-ring handles, base impressed "Edmands & Co.," rim chips on cover, 6 3/4", with Bennington Potters flint enamel teapot, Bennington, Vermont (not shown).* **$83**

Photo courtesy Hake's Americana & Collectibles

◄ *Glazed ceramic cookie jar in shape of Kentucky Fried Chicken founder Col. Harland Sanders holding bucket of KFC chicken, inside lid marked "73/250 Wolfe Studio," very limited production, bottom with KFC copyright, 1998, excellent condition, 15 1/2" high.* **$127**

*Bisque cookie jar designed as classic flying saucer, 1960s, underside with sticker reading "Handmade Exclusively For Silvestri, Chicago Ill.," top of saucer lifts off, underside of base with scuffs, very fine condition, all-over even aging with light scattered wear to gold paint accent on saucer's rim edge, scarce and desirable, 12 1/2" diameter x 6" high.* **$316**

◀ *Batman Batmobile limited edition cookie jar, no. 1608/3600 (Vandor/Warner Bros. Studio Store, 2002), excellent condition, in box, approximately 14 1/2" long x 7" wide x 5" high.* **$74**

▼ *Two Austrian glass vases with brass-mounted Austrian glass cookie jar (center), circa 1900, tallest piece 7 3/8" high, all in fine condition.* **$531**

Photo courtesy O'Gallerie

*Brush Pottery Co. cookie jar of red-maned white circus horse with blue-trimmed bridle, saddle and reins, small dog seated on horse's saddle as handle to lid, unmarked, 8 1/2" high.* **$120**

Photo courtesy Jeffrey S. Evans & Associates

*Twentieth-century black Americana-themed cold-painted pottery cookie jar, unmarked porcelain grease jar, and plastic salt and pepper shakers, cookie jar with heavy wear to paint, 5" to 12 1/2" high.* **$150**

Courtesy of Strawser Auction

▲ *Roseville Clematis pattern cookie jar in green.* **$90**

Photo courtesy Heritage Auctions

◄ *Superman in Phone Booth cookie jar, 1978, rectangular, removable top, excellent condition, approximately 13 1/4" high (with lid) x 6 1/2" wide. Provenance: From the Kirk Alyn Archives Collection. This was the "Superman" actor's personal cookie jar, as seen in a snapshot taken of his office with the porcelain jar sitting on a shelf.* **$313**

*Male and female African-American figural cookie jars, American, second quarter 20th century, marked "U.S.A.," 10 1/4" high and 9 1/4" high, respectively.* **$180**

*Five American ceramic figural cookie jars and two shakers, Dutch Girl (Regal China), Jocko the Monkey (Rowsbottom Pottery), Umbrella Kids (American Bisque), Boy With Butter Churn (Regal China), and three-piece Goldilocks cookie jar and shakers set (Regal China), jars and shakers in good overall condition, minimal wear, 4 1/4" to 12" high.* **$100**

*Four American ceramic figural cookie jars, Dutch girl, clown, Dutch boy, and early car.* **$130**

*Four ceramic cookie jars and mug, Formal Pig #W7 (Brush Pottery), Clown #W22 (Brush Pottery), Davy Crockett (Brush-McCoy), Humpty Dumpty #W18, and Davy Crockett mug (Brush Pottery), good condition with minimal wear, Humpty Dumpty jar with interior chip on rim of hat, cookie jars 9 3/4" to 12" high.* **$50**

Courtesy of Woody Auction

*Two Red Wing figural cookie jars, Dutch Woman, 10" high, and Fat Chef, 11" high, both with green coloring, good condition, no chips, cracks or repairs.* **$125**

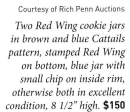

Courtesy of Rich Penn Auctions

*Two Red Wing cookie jars in brown and blue Cattails pattern, stamped Red Wing on bottom, blue jar with small chip on inside rim, otherwise both in excellent condition, 8 1/2" high.* **$150**

Photo courtesy William Bunch Auctions and Appraisals

▲ *Two ceramic cookie jars, Superman emerging from silver telephone booth, 13" high, and Cookie Can figural jar showing animal peeking out beneath lid of trash can, 10" high.* **$50**

Photo courtesy Thomaston Place Auction Galleries

◄ *Mammy figural cookie jar by McCoy, marked on underside, loss to paint, 11" high.* **$50**

# Folk Art & Americana

Folk art generally refers to items that originated among the common people of a region and usually reflect their traditional culture, especially regarding everyday or festive items. Unlike fine art, folk art is primarily utilitarian and decorative rather than purely aesthetic.

Exactly what constitutes the genre is a question that continues to be vigorously debated among collectors, dealers, museum curators, and scholars. Some want to confine folk art to non-academic, handmade objects. Others are willing to include manufactured material.

Folk art can range from crude drawings by children to academically trained artists' paintings of "common" people and scenery. It encompasses items made from a variety of materials, from wood and metal to cloth and paper.

The accepted timetable for folk art runs from its earliest origins up to the mid-20th century.

Americana applies to items representing key figures and times in American history.

Courtesy of Sotheby's

*William Dentzel rare carved basswood carousel giraffe, circa 1900, Philadelphia, full-sized giraffe with glass eyes, original leather reins, standing on oval base inscribed "Wm. H. Dentzel, Phila. Pa.," 70" high x 52" long x 10 1/2" wide.*
**$22,500**

◀ *United States Capitol Building centennial birdcage, late 19th century, polychrome painted pierced and embossed metal, 21" high x 17 1/4" wide x 10 7/8" deep.* **$2,460**

▲ *Rare carved and painted pine 23-bird "Adirondack-style" bird tree, probably New York state, circa 1900, 37 1/2" high with base, base 12" wide, 22" overall diameter.* **$25,000**

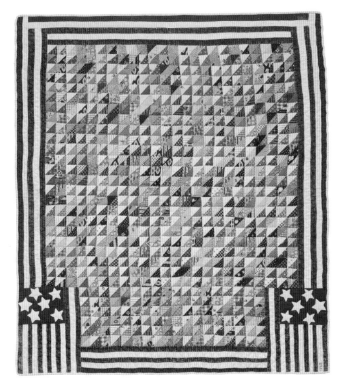

◀ *Rare Civil War flag crib quilt, American, dated 1862, composed of tiny triangles hand-pieced together, six white stars appliquéd on both flags, stripes form border, some loss in dark brown patches, mounted on stretcher, 38 1/4" x 32 1/4".* **$5,938**

Courtesy of Sotheby's

▶ *Charles Looff outside jumper carousel horse from Whalom Park Carousel, Lunenberg, Massachusetts, carved and painted basswood with carved eagle saddle and jewels, circa 1890, Rhode Island, 63 1/2" high x 51" long.* **$4,063**

Courtesy of Sotheby's

▲ *Dark green, red and white paint-decorated maple and poplar yarn reeler, southeastern Pennsylvania, dated 1821, inscribed on top of base, paint: 1821 x N 45, 37 1/2" x 24" x 14".* **$31,250**

Courtesy of Sotheby's

▶ *Rare needlework sampler, "Adam and Eve in Paradice," Lydia Hart, Boston, 1744, inscribed recto, silk thread "Adam and Eve in Paradice That Was The / ir Pedigree They Had A Grant Never To / Die Would They Obedient Be," 11 1/2" x 9".* **$233,000**

Courtesy of Sotheby's

*Rare needlework sampler,
Elizabeth Sheffield (1771-?),
Newport, Rhode Island, dated
1784, worked in silk on linen,
inscribed recto, silk thread
"[alphabet] / ELIZABETH
SHEFFIELD / BORN JULY 20
177[?] / [alphabet] ELIZABETH
SHEFFI / Now in thy youth take
hold on truth / Let Jesus be thy
Guide / Be allway mindfull of the
Lord / Prepare to be his Bride /
Elizabeth / Sheffield/ October /
11 /1784," 13" x 11".* **$25,000**

Courtesy of Sotheby's

*Needlework sampler, Ann Amelia
Matilda Borden, Pennsylvania,
dated 1839, signed "Ann Amelia
Matilda Borden was born Jan 1
year 1825, mark'd this in 1839,"
approximately 16 1/2" x 16".*
**$8,750**

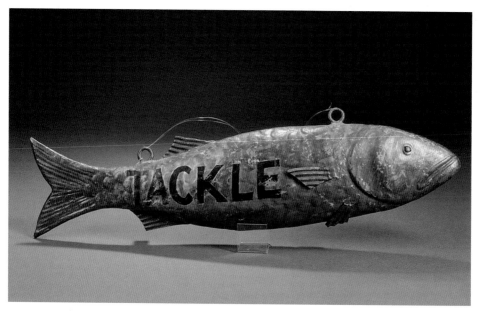

*Molded copper codfish-form "TACKLE" sign, American, late 19th century, likely former weathervane, with crimped sheet metal fins, both sides gold-painted with applied black lettering, overall 30" long.* **$2,829**

*Four Shaker paintings depicting four seasons, Canterbury, New Hampshire, mid-20th century, each inscribed on reverse "C Helena Searle / Authenticated by / Bertha Lindsay," with original price tags, each oil on Masonite, unframed, 4" x 6".* **$2,706**

*Gray-painted cast iron face of bearded man, America, late 19th century, man wearing elaborate headdress, 22 1/2" high.* **$1,722**

*Polychrome carved ship's figurehead purportedly from ship Cynthia Watkins, American, 1830-1840, female figure with brown hair looks skyward, in dark dress with pink lacy collar, 22 1/8" x 13" x 9 1/8".* **$7,995**

*Carved polychrome mermaid figure wall chandelier, early 20th century, mermaid's long flowing hair pulled back and adorned with flower, her lower body wrapped in plaid robe with flanking elk horn candle arms, 55" wide x 14 1/2" high.* **$6,765**

*Polychrome painted "Ice Cold" watermelon-form sign, American, early 20th century, with chain hanger, 14" high x 31" wide.* **$2,460**

*Copper and zinc running horse weathervane, American, late 19th/early 20th century, flattened full-body figure with cast zinc head, applied sheet copper mane, mounted on black-painted copper rod with bronze directionals, verdigris surface with traces of earlier gilding, no stand, 15 3/4" high x 27" long.* **$1,046**

*Large white-painted sheet iron and wood three-masted ship weathervane, American, early 20th century, with sheet iron sails and pennants, wire rigging, turned wood masts, and carved wood bowsprit and hull, on custom stand, 81" high x 69" long.* **$3,321**

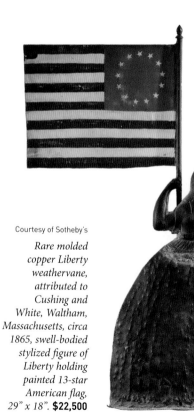

*Rare molded copper Liberty weathervane, attributed to Cushing and White, Waltham, Massachusetts, circa 1865, swell-bodied stylized figure of Liberty holding painted 13-star American flag, 29" x 18".* **$22,500**

▲ *Rare canvaswork Bible cover, Sarah Saunders (1741-1789), Philadelphia, 1753, worked in colored wool threads on linen ground with open blossoms, leafage and buds, inscribed along spine "Sarah Saunders, 1753," together with rare needlework sampler (not shown), Hannah Douglass, Baltimore or Virginia, dated 1805, 21" x 15 1/2" and 15" x 22 1/2".* **$12,500**

Courtesy of Bright Star Antiques Co.

*Four carved heads from AM&A Store, Buffalo, New York, 11", 11 1/2", 12", and 13" high. AM&A was a chain of department stores based in Buffalo and founded in 1867, well known for elaborate window displays.* **$3,800**

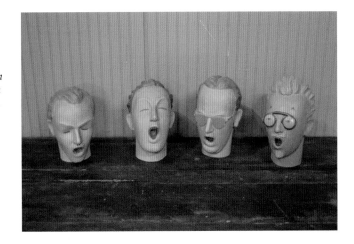

Courtesy of Sotheby's

*Red, white, and black paint-decorated pine child's blanket chest, possibly Rhode Island or New York, circa 1830, 16 1/4" x 20 3/4" x 11 1/4".* **$81,250**

Courtesy of Sotheby's

*Rare polychrome painted pine and maple round box with heart decorations, George Robert Lawton (1813-1885), Providence County, Rhode Island, circa 1845, 2 1/4" x 7 1/2" diameter.* **$209,000**

*Union Academy wool-on-linen needlework sampler, Williamson County, Tennessee, by Sarah Elizabeth Angeline "Sallie" Andrews, five alphabetic bands above identifying register, "Sarah E. A. Sampler 1850," urn filled with flowers next to verse: "The words of a man's / mouth are as deep waters / and the wellspring of wis / dom as a flowing brook. / Miss IS. Wallis / Union Academy," flanked on three sides by floral vine border, 23 5/8" high x 25 1/2" wide, framed 29 1/2" high x 31 5/8" wide.* **$3,800**

*American hooked rug of prancing horse set against striated background, circa 1890-1910, wool on burlap, bound and mounted on frame for display, discovered in Shenandoah Valley of Virginia, 40" x 42".* **$2,800**

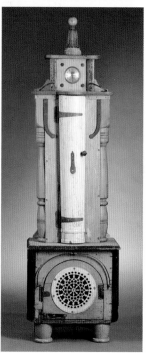

*Tall case clock made by Richard Dunbrack, 1995, Martha's Vineyard, Massachusetts, made of found materials including architectural elements and iron hardware in various colors, 79" high.* **$738**

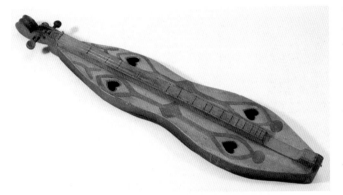

*Appalachian carved and painted dulcimer, double-bouted style with three strings, scrolled head, and heart-shaped cutouts in soundboard, original yellow, green, and red paint decoration, with custom iron display stand, attributed to Charles N. Prichard, Huntington, West Virginia, fourth quarter 19th century, 35 1/2" long x 8" wide.* **$4,000**

◄ *American painting of Mount Vernon, oil on canvas, mid-19th century, depiction of Washington's home perched on bluff overlooking Potomac River with figures in foreground, African-American servant entering rear of home, circling birds above weathervane set atop cupola, likely influenced by contemporaneous printed depictions of Washington home, pencil markings outlining home and figures, no signature located, label verso reads "Bicentennial Inventory / 'Mount Vernon, View of' / Loan of Mrs. George Neal" along with inventory label from Smithsonian Institution, 19th century walnut frame with gilt liner, 22 3/4" x 28 3/4", unframed 17 1/2" x 23 1/2".* **$6,000**

*Painting of couple under arbor, watercolor and ink on paper, probably Pennsylvania, circa 1800, 11 3/4" x 14".* **$106,250**

Courtesy of Heritage Auctions

▲ *Lincoln and Hamlin banner, hand-painted glazed or polished cotton banner produced in pivotal election of 1860, names of candidates "Lincoln and Hamlin" as centerpiece of display, framed by monuments topped with books and columns decorated with wrap-around ribbons, wreaths and baskets of flowers, 17" x 22".* **$9,375**

Courtesy of Heritage Auctions

*American powder horn, circa 1850, depicts hunter packing down powder in musket with ramrod, with dog and three trees populated with doves and serpent, unsigned, likely of Pennsylvania origin, approximately 12" high.* **$625**

Courtesy of Heritage Auctions

▶ *Engraved polychrome walrus tusk with scrimshawed images, including mother and child embracing, woman with shawl and handbag, woman with peacock fan and apron, and man holding flintlock rifle, circa 1850-1860, 22".* **$875**

CLOSE-UP!

Courtesy of California Auctioneers

*Antique Sicilian carved cart, metalwork figures include approximately 60 faces, hand-painted, 96" long, wheels 31 1/2", 41" high, bed 36" x 30" wide, side boards 10 1/2" high, wheels 42" apart.* **$3,750**

Courtesy of
Heritage Auctions

*Benjamin Franklin pre-1850 tavern sign, polychrome painted wood, two-sided hanging trade sign, American, with stylized portrait of thoughtful Franklin holding newspaper in oval format with painted lettering "FRANKLIN INN" and "J.H. WINGERT" above and below, applied molded frame, original wrought iron hardware, painted decoration on reverse side is dark and worn, 62 1/2" x 34".* **$11,250**

Courtesy of Skinner, Inc.; www.skinnerinc.com

*Carved and painted easel, probably New England, late 19th century, black-painted frame with allover geometric carving and six applied carved hearts, 65 1/2" high x 22 1/2" wide.* **$215**

Courtesy of Jeffrey S. Evans & Associates

*Fine and rare diminutive stoneware canning jar, salt-glazed, approximately one-quart capacity, shouldered cylindrical form with flared neck and nearly flat rim, Albany-slip glazed interior, brushed cobalt decoration of seated squirrel eating a nut below arch, attributed to Thompson Pottery (active circa 1810-1890), Morgantown, West Virginia, circa 1860-1870, 7 3/4" high x 3 1/2" diameter rim.* **$42,500**

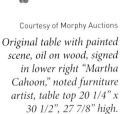

TOP VIEW!

Courtesy of Morphy Auctions

*Original table with painted scene, oil on wood, signed in lower right "Martha Cahoon," noted furniture artist, table top 20 1/4" x 30 1/2", 27 7/8" high.* **$6,000**

Courtesy of Jeffrey S. Evans & Associates

*Rare Richmond, Virginia, needlework picture, circa 1892, wool, enigmatic work of Old Stone House, currently the Poe Museum, inscriptions include "Gen. G. Washingtons / Head - Quarters 1781" at top and "Old Stone House Main St. Richmond, VA / M. E. M. / 1892" at bottom, 20 1/2" x 18".* **$4,000**

Courtesy of Jeffrey S. Evans & Associates

*S. L. Brown (American, 19th century) portrait, 19th century, oil on canvas, young woman outfitted with tortoiseshell comb, lace shawl, and gold jewelry, signed "S. L. Brown Pr. / A.N. '62 (sic)" lower left in possibly later hand, and "By S. L. Brown / A. N. ????" verso in what appears to be period hand, modern frame, 31" x 25 1/4", unframed 27 1/2" x 21 1/4".* **$2,500**

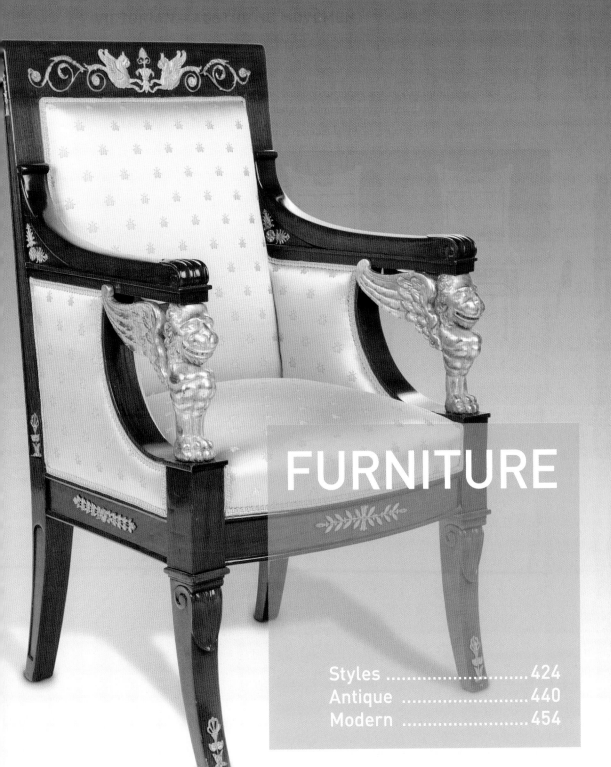

# FURNITURE

# Furniture Styles

AMERICAN

## PILGRIM CENTURY 1620–1700

**MAJOR WOOD(S):** Oak

**GENERAL CHARACTERISTICS:**

- **Case pieces:** Rectilinear low-relief carved panels; blocky and bulbous turnings; splint-spindle trim

- **Seating pieces:** Shallow carved panels; spindle turnings

## WILLIAM AND MARY 1685–1720

**MAJOR WOOD(S):** Maple and walnut

**GENERAL CHARACTERISTICS:**

- **Case pieces:** Paint-decorated chests on ball feet; chests on frames; chests with two-part construction; trumpet-turned legs; slant-front desks

- **Seating pieces:** Molded, carved crest rails; banister backs; cane, rush (leather) seats; baluster, ball and block turnings; ball and Spanish feet

## QUEEN ANNE 1720-1750

**MAJOR WOOD(S):** Walnut

**GENERAL CHARACTERISTICS:**

- **Case pieces:** Mathematical proportions of elements; use of the cyma or S-curve broken-arch pediments; arched panels, shell carving, star inlay; blocked fronts; cabriole legs and pad feet

- **Seating pieces:** Molded yoke-shaped crest rails; solid vase-shaped splats; rush or upholstered seats; cabriole legs; baluster, ring, ball and block-turned stretchers; pad and slipper feet

## CHIPPENDALE 1750-1785

**MAJOR WOOD(S):** Mahogany and walnut

**GENERAL CHARACTERISTICS:**

- **Case pieces:** Relief-carved broken-arch pediments; foliate, scroll, shell, fretwork carving; straight, bow or serpentine fronts; carved cabriole legs; claw and ball, bracket or ogee feet

- **Seating pieces:** Carved, shaped crest rails with out-turned ears; pierced, shaped splats; ladder (ribbon) backs; upholstered seats; scrolled arms; carved cabriole legs or straight (Marlboro) legs; claw and ball feet

## FEDERAL (HEPPLEWHITE)  1785–1800

**MAJOR WOOD(S):** Mahogany and light inlays

**GENERAL CHARACTERISTICS:**

- **Case pieces:** More delicate rectilinear forms; inlay with eagle and classical motifs; bow, serpentine or tambour fronts; reeded quarter columns at sides; flared bracket feet

- **Seating pieces:** Shield backs; upholstered seats; tapered square legs

## FEDERAL (SHERATON)  1800–1820

**MAJOR WOOD(S):** Mahogany, mahogany veneer, and maple

**GENERAL CHARACTERISTICS:**

- **Case pieces:** Architectural pediments; acanthus carving; outset (cookie or ovolu) corners and reeded columns; paneled sides; tapered, turned, reeded or spiral-turned legs; bow or tambour fronts; mirrors on dressing tables

- **Seating pieces:** Rectangular or square backs; slender carved banisters; tapered, turned or reeded legs

## CLASSICAL (AMERICAN EMPIRE) 1815–1850

**MAJOR WOOD(S):** Mahogany, mahogany veneer, and rosewood

**GENERAL CHARACTERISTICS:**

- **Case pieces:** Increasingly heavy proportions; pillar and scroll construction; lyre, eagle, Greco-Roman and Egyptian motifs; marble tops; projecting top drawer; large ball feet, tapered fluted feet or hairy paw feet; brass, ormolu decoration

- **Seating pieces:** High-relief carving; curved backs; out-scrolled arms; ring turnings; sabre legs, curule (scrolled-S) legs; brass-capped feet, casters

## VICTORIAN – EARLY VICTORIAN 1840–1850

**MAJOR WOOD(S):** Mahogany veneer, black walnut, and rosewood

**GENERAL CHARACTERISTICS:**

- **Case pieces:** Pieces tend to carry over the Classical style with the beginnings of the Rococo substyle, especially in seating pieces.

## VICTORIAN – GOTHIC REVIVAL 1840–1890

**MAJOR WOOD(S):** Black walnut, mahogany, and rosewood

**GENERAL CHARACTERISTICS:**

- **Case pieces:** Architectural motifs; triangular arched pediments; arched panels; marble tops; paneled or molded drawer fronts; cluster columns; bracket feet, block feet or plinth bases

- **Seating pieces:** Tall backs; pierced arabesque backs with trefoils or quatrefoils; spool turning; drop pendants

## VICTORIAN – ROCOCO (LOUIS XV) 1845–1870

**MAJOR WOOD(S):** Black walnut, mahogany, and rosewood

**GENERAL CHARACTERISTICS:**

- **Case pieces:** Arched carved pediments; high-relief carving, S- and C-scrolls, floral, fruit motifs, busts and cartouches; mirror panels; carved slender cabriole legs; scroll feet; bedroom suites (bed, dresser, commode)

- **Seating pieces:** High-relief carved crest rails; balloon-shaped backs; urn-shaped splats; upholstery (tufting); demi-cabriole legs; laminated, pierced and carved construction (Belter and Meeks); parlor suites (sets of chairs, love seats, sofas)

## VICTORIAN – RENAISSANCE REVIVAL 1860–1885

**MAJOR WOOD(S):** Black walnut, burl veneer, painted and grained pine

**GENERAL CHARACTERISTICS:**

- **Case pieces:** Rectilinear arched pediments; arched panels; burl veneer; applied moldings; bracket feet, block feet, plinth bases; medium and high-relief carving, floral and fruit, cartouches, masks and animal heads; cyma-curve brackets; Wooton patent desks

- **Seating pieces:** Oval or rectangular backs with floral or figural cresting; upholstery outlined with brass tacks; padded armrests; tapered turned front legs, flared square rear legs

## VICTORIAN – LOUIS XVI 1865–1875

**MAJOR WOOD(S):** Black walnut and ebonized maple

**GENERAL CHARACTERISTICS:**

- **Case pieces:** Gilt decoration, marquetry, inlay; egg and dart carving; tapered turned legs, fluted

- **Seating pieces:** Molded, slightly arched crest rails; keystone-shaped backs; circular seats; fluted tapered legs

## VICTORIAN – EASTLAKE 1870–1895

**MAJOR WOOD(S):** Black walnut, burl veneer, cherry, and oak

**GENERAL CHARACTERISTICS:**

- **Case pieces:** Flat cornices; stile and rail construction; burl veneer panels; low-relief geometric and floral machine carving; incised horizontal lines

- **Seating pieces:** Rectilinear; spindles; tapered, turned legs, trumpet-shaped legs

## VICTORIAN JACOBEAN AND TURKISH REVIVAL 1870–1890

**MAJOR WOOD(S):** Black walnut and maple

**GENERAL CHARACTERISTICS:**

- **Case pieces:** A revival of some heavy 17th century forms, most commonly in dining room pieces

- **Seating pieces:** Turkish Revival style features: oversized, low forms; overstuffed upholstery; padded arms; short baluster, vase-turned legs; ottomans, circular sofas

- **Jacobean Revival style features:** heavy bold carving; spool and spiral turnings

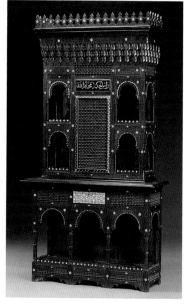

## VICTORIAN – AESTHETIC MOVEMENT  1880–1900

**MAJOR WOOD(S):** Painted hardwoods, black walnut, ebonized finishes

**GENERAL CHARACTERISTICS:**

- **Case pieces:** Rectilinear forms; bamboo turnings, spaced ball turnings; incised stylized geometric and floral designs, sometimes highlighted with gilt

- **Seating pieces:** Bamboo turning; rectangular backs; patented folding chairs

## ART NOUVEAU  1895–1918

**MAJOR WOOD(S):** Ebonized hardwoods, fruitwoods

**GENERAL CHARACTERISTICS:**

- **Case pieces:** Curvilinear shapes; floral marquetry; whiplash curves

- **Seating pieces:** Elongated forms; relief-carved floral decoration; spindle backs, pierced floral backs; cabriole legs

## TURN-OF-THE-CENTURY (EARLY 20TH CENTURY) 1895–1910

**MAJOR WOOD(S):** Golden (quarter-sawn) oak, mahogany, hardwood stained to resemble mahogany

**GENERAL CHARACTERISTICS:**

- **Case pieces:** Rectilinear and bulky forms; applied scroll carving or machine-pressed designs; some Colonial and Classical Revival detailing

- **Seating pieces:** Heavy framing or high spindle-trimmed backs; applied carved or machine-pressed back designs; heavy scrolled or slender turned legs; Colonial Revival or Classical Revival detailing such as claw and ball feet

## MISSION (ARTS & CRAFTS MOVEMENT) 1900–1915

**MAJOR WOOD(S):** Oak

**GENERAL CHARACTERISTICS:**

- **Case pieces:** Rectilinear through-tenon construction; copper decoration, hand-hammered hardware; square legs

- **Seating pieces:** Rectangular splats; medial and side stretchers; exposed pegs; corbel supports

## COLONIAL REVIVAL  1890–1930

**MAJOR WOOD(S):** Oak, walnut and walnut veneer, mahogany veneer

**GENERAL CHARACTERISTICS:**

- **Case pieces:** Forms generally following designs of the 17th, 18th, and early 19th centuries; details for the styles such as William and Mary, Federal, Queen Anne, Chippendale, or early Classical were used but often in a simplified or stylized form; mass-production in the early 20th century flooded the market with pieces that often mixed and matched design details and used a great deal of thin veneering to dress up designs; dining room and bedroom suites were especially popular.

- **Seating pieces:** Designs again generally followed early period designs with some mixing of design elements.

## ART DECO  1925–1940

**MAJOR WOOD(S):** Bleached woods, exotic woods, steel, and chrome

**GENERAL CHARACTERISTICS:**

- **Case pieces:** Heavy geometric forms
- **Seating pieces:** Streamlined, attenuated geometric forms; overstuffed upholstery

## MODERNIST OR MID-CENTURY 1945–1970

**MAJOR WOOD(S):** Plywood, hardwood, or metal frames

**GENERAL CHARACTERISTICS:** Modernistic designers such as the Eames, Vladimir Kagan, George Nelson, and Isamu Noguchi led the way in post-war design. Carrying on the tradition of Modernist designers of the 1920s and 1930s, they focused on designs for the machine age that could be mass-produced for the popular market. By the late 1950s many of their pieces were used in commercial office spaces and schools as well as in private homes.

- **Case pieces:** Streamlined or curvilinear abstract designs with simple detailing; plain round or flattened legs and arms; mixed materials including wood, plywood, metal, glass, and molded plastics

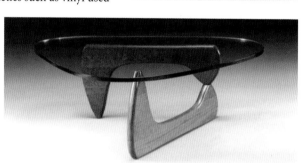

- **Seating pieces:** Streamlined or abstract curvilinear designs generally using newer materials such as plywood or simple hardwood framing; fabric and synthetics such as vinyl used for upholstery with finer fabrics and real leather featured on more expensive pieces; seating made of molded plastic shells on metal frames and legs used on many mass-produced designs

## DANISH MODERN 1950–1970

**MAJOR WOOD(S):** Teak

**GENERAL CHARACTERISTICS:**

- **Case and seating pieces:** This variation of Modernistic post-war design originated in Scandinavia, hence the name; designs were simple and restrained with case pieces often having simple boxy forms with short rounded tapering legs; seating pieces have a simple teak framework with lines coordinating with case pieces; vinyl or natural fabric were most often used for upholstery; in the United States dining room suites were the most popular use for this style although some bedroom suites and general seating pieces were available.

ENGLISH

## JACOBEAN MID-17TH CENTURY

**MAJOR WOOD(S):** Oak, walnut

**GENERAL CHARACTERISTICS:**

- **Case pieces:** Low-relief carving; geometrics and florals; panel, rail and stile construction; applied split balusters
- **Seating pieces:** Rectangular backs; carved and pierced crests; spiral turnings ball feet

## WILLIAM AND MARY 1689–1702

**MAJOR WOOD(S):** Walnut, burl walnut veneer

**GENERAL CHARACTERISTICS:**

- **Case pieces:** Marquetry, veneering; shaped aprons; 6-8 trumpet-form legs; curved flat stretchers
- **Seating pieces:** Carved, pierced crests; tall caned backs and seats; trumpet-form legs; Spanish feet

## QUEEN ANNE 1702–1714

**MAJOR WOOD(S):** Walnut, mahogany, veneer

**GENERAL CHARACTERISTICS:**

- **Case pieces:** Cyma curves; broken arch pediments and finials; bracket feet

- **Seating pieces:** Carved crest rails; high, rounded backs; solid vase-shaped splats; cabriole legs; pad feet

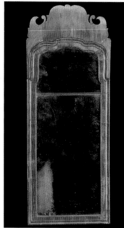

## GEORGE I 1714–1727

**MAJOR WOOD(S):** Walnut, mahogany, veneer, and yew wood

**GENERAL CHARACTERISTICS:**

- **Case pieces:** Broken arch pediments; gilt decoration, japanning; bracket feet

- **Seating pieces:** Curvilinear forms; yoke-shaped crests; shaped solid splats; shell carving; upholstered seats; carved cabriole legs; claw and ball feet, pad feet

## GEORGE II 1727–1760

**MAJOR WOOD(S):** Mahogany

**GENERAL CHARACTERISTICS:**

- **Case pieces:** Broken arch pediments; relief-carved foliate, scroll and shell carving; carved cabriole legs; claw and ball feet, bracket feet, ogee bracket feet

- **Seating pieces:** Carved, shaped crest rails, out-turned ears; pierced shaped splats; ladder (ribbon) backs; upholstered seats; scrolled arms; carved cabriole legs or straight (Marlboro) legs; claw and ball feet

## GEORGE III 1760–1820

**MAJOR WOOD(S):** Mahogany, veneer, satinwood

**GENERAL CHARACTERISTICS:**

- **Case pieces:** Rectilinear forms; parcel gilt decoration; inlaid ovals, circles, banding or marquetry; carved columns, urns; tambour fronts or bow fronts; plinth bases

- **Seating pieces:** Shield backs; upholstered seats; tapered square legs, square legs

## REGENCY 1811–1820

**MAJOR WOOD(S):** Mahogany, mahogany veneer, satinwood, and rosewood

**GENERAL CHARACTERISTICS:**

- **Case pieces:** Greco-Roman and Egyptian motifs; inlay, ormolu mounts; marble tops; round columns, pilasters; mirrored backs; scroll feet

- **Seating pieces:** Straight backs; latticework; caned seats; sabre legs, tapered turned legs, flared turned legs; parcel gilt, ebonizing

## GEORGE IV 1820–1830

**MAJOR WOOD(S):** Mahogany, mahogany veneer, and rosewood

**GENERAL CHARACTERISTICS:** Continuation of Regency designs

## WILLIAM IV 1830–1837

**MAJOR WOOD(S):** Mahogany, mahogany veneer

**GENERAL CHARACTERISTICS:**

- **Case pieces:** Rectilinear; brass mounts, grillwork; carved moldings; plinth bases
- **Seating pieces:** Rectangular backs; carved straight crest rails; acanthus, animal carving; carved cabriole legs; paw feet

## VICTORIAN 1837–1901

**MAJOR WOOD(S):** Black walnut, mahogany, veneers, and rosewood

**GENERAL CHARACTERISTICS:**

- **Case pieces:** Applied floral carving; surmounting mirrors, drawers, candle shelves; marble tops
- **Seating pieces:** High-relief carved crest rails; floral and fruit carving; balloon backs, oval backs; upholstered seats, backs; spool, spiral turnings; cabriole legs, fluted tapered legs; scrolled feet

## EDWARDIAN 1901–1910

**MAJOR WOOD(S):** Mahogany, mahogany veneer, and satinwood

**GENERAL CHARACTERISTICS:** Neo-Classical motifs and revivals of earlier 18th century and early 19th century styles

# Antique Furniture

Courtesy of Neal Auction Co.

*Antique American Federal inlaid mahogany and églomisé breakfront bookcase, Boston, shaped cornice with flame birch panels surmounted by brass spreadwing eagle and spire finials, center doors with oval mirrors and églomisé panels of floral urns, two drawers below, each side door with églomisé panel of classical maiden in garden, short drawer and cabinet below, drawer bails stamped "W.J.," likely for William Jenkins, Birmingham, turned, tapered, reeded legs, bearing T.G. Buckley Co., Boston, Massachusetts, inventory labels, 91" high x 67" wide.*
**$6,500**

Courtesy of Sotheby's

*Carved and gessoed beechwood gilded and blue satin upholstered borne de salon, France or England, late 19th century, 67" wide x 51" deep.* **$7,500**

*George III mahogany breakfront secretaire bookcase, circa 1800, 103 1/2" high x 94 1/2" wide x 24" deep.* **$22,500**

▲ *Louis XV-style jasper top ormolu mounted tulipwood and mahogany cabinet by Francoise Linke, circa 1903, signed F. Linke in script on right side of right chute, top of right door impressed with number 7440 and stamped Linke beneath lock plate of door, brown and white striated jasper top above open-shelved compartment, back board veneered with cube parquetry above pair of doors inlaid with floral marquetry, whole mounted with ormolu borders, chutes and sabots, 46" high x 21" wide x 16 1/2" deep.* **$13,000**

◄ *Empire-style upholstered mahogany and gilt bronze bergère, early 20th century, 42 1/2" x 25 1/8" x 25".* **$1,375**

INSIDE LOOK!

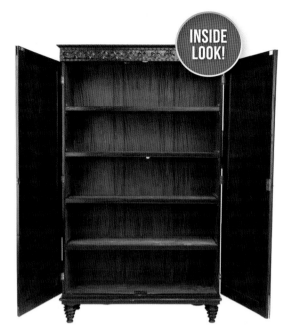

Courtesy of Heritage Auctions

▲ *Italian mahogany armoire, circa 1900, fleur-de-lis carved architectural crest, patera carved double doors, five shelves to interior, resting on turned feet, retains partial label, 78 3/4" x 47 1/4" x 17 1/2".* **$4,679**

Courtesy of California Historical Design

*L. & J.G. Stickley heavy strap-hinged sideboard, signed with branded mark inside drawer, 54" wide x 48 1/4" high x 24 1/2" deep.* **$4,250**

Courtesy of California Historical Design

*Classic Gustav Stickley bentarm Morris chair, #369, signed on back rail, 41" high x 32 1/2" wide x 37 1/2" deep.* **$5,000**

Courtesy of Skinner, Inc.; www.skinnerinc.com

*Shaker butternut and pine herb cupboard, circa 1860, top with overhanging rounded edges above two hinged cupboard doors with recessed panels and beveled edges fitted with brass and porcelain hardware opening to three shelves, on projecting base of four drawers with divided interiors, turned pulls and printed paper labels applied to drawer fronts indicating one-time contents, feet extension of case sides, old surface, 66" high x 46" wide x 18 3/4" deep.* **$123,000**

Courtesy of Heritage Auctions

*Tuscan carved walnut armoire, 19th century, with carved pierced crest over stepped cornice above frieze of grotesque masks issuing scrolling foliate and centering vertical double doors, caryatid atop stylized foliate columns to either side and separating doors, each door centered with framed dancing nude figure holding sash and surrounded by scrolling foliate and flowers, apron mirroring masks to cornice and divided further with naturalistic face flanked by lion masks, whole raised on square legs to reverse and masks bisecting scrolled feet to front, 95 1/2" x 55" x 22".* **$7,500**

Courtesy of Case Antiques, Inc. Auctions & Appraisals

◀ *Southern Chippendale chest of drawers or bureau, circa 1795-1805, cherry and poplar with molded rectangular top, two deep drawers flanking prospect or cupboard door over three graduated drawers with molded edges, nailed and dovetailed construction, full dustboards, Museum of Early Southern Decorative Arts documentation label in top left drawer (Sept. 11, 1982, #11590), 38 1/2" high (including feet) x 41 1/2" wide x 19 1/8" deep.* **$4,600**

◄ *Regency rosewood and satinwood mirror back side cabinet, circa 1815, mirror with scrolling reeded columns headed by Egyptian masks, breakfront base incorporating pair of grille fronted doors flanked by further columns headed by masks, opening to shelves, on turned feet, 71 1/2" high x 42 1/2" wide x 20" deep.* **$7,639**

*Pair of Gothic Revival mahogany upholstered hall chairs, circa 1865, 36 5/8" x 17" x 16".* **$1,375**

▶ *Chest of drawers dated 1856 (inside top upper left drawer), Philippine-made, barley-twist colonnettes with spool-turned bases and capitals, made entirely of narra, turned urn-shaped feet support base with elaborately shaped skirt outlined with lanite line-inlay, colonnettes flank four large drawers atop each other and pair of smaller drawers above, all large drawers line-inlaid with strips of lanite enclosing kamagong with pair of turned kamagong drawer pulls and brass keyhole shield, smaller drawers inlaid with same and with brass handles and keyhole shields of same, 51" high x 47 1/2" long x 22 1/2" wide.* **$94,318**

Sotheby's

*Pair of Louis XV-style Napoléon III Aubusson upholstered fauteuils, third quarter 19th century, Aubusson tapestry 18th century, each cushioned, 39 1/2" high x 29" wide.* **$11,825**

Courtesy of Dreweatts Donnington Priory

*Black lacquer and parcel gilt cabinet on stand, late 17th/early 18th century, rectangular top above pair of cupboard doors opening to arrangement of small drawers, with side carrying handles, raised on giltwood rectangular stand, circa 1720 and later, with plain frieze, above central anthemion terminal and scroll and leaf decorated legs with hairy hoof feet, 59" high x 39 1/3" wide x 23" deep.* **$7,474**

Courtesy of Neal Auction Co.

*American Late Classical mahogany mixing cabinet, circa 1835, Anthony G. Quervelle, Philadelphia, stenciled label, rectangular marble top over paneled frieze drawer above volute brackets, pedestal case with mirrored cupboard door with pointed arches, molded plinth, disc feet, 38" high x 33 3/4" wide x 18" deep.* **$8,500**

Courtesy of Case Antiques, Inc. Auctions & Appraisals

*East Tennessee cherry corner cupboard, attributed to McMinn County, second quarter 19th century, ogee cornice with incised diamond design over two doors with 12 glazed panes, straight back side returns, ring-turned molding to case corners, center drawer flanked by foliate carved designs on each side and panels with diamond incised moldings flanking central drawer, lower paneled doors with diamond incised moldings, diamond incised base molding, diamond incised turned feet, secondary wood is tulip poplar, 94 1/8" high x 47 3/4" wide x 20" deep.* **$11,500**

Courtesy of Heritage Auctions

*Pair of Georgian-style mahogany pedestal cabinets, 20th century, 43" x 18 1/2" x 18 1/2".* **$2,000**

Courtesy of Heritage Auctions

*Italian upholstered blackamoor window seat, 19th century, 24" x 14" x 14".* **$4,375**

Courtesy of Dreweatts Donnington Priory

◄ *Charles I oak and inlaid hanging mural cupboard,
circa 1630, molded cornice above chevron inlaid
frieze interspersed by mask terminals and above
pair of spindle doors flanked by turned and square
section pilasters with cabochon decoration, lower
section with central paneled door carved with foliate
motifs, flanked by parquetry and molding-decorated
panels and surrounds, 39" high x 35" wide x 12 1/2"
deep.* **$16,319**

Courtesy of Jeffrey S. Evans & Associates

*Painted yellow pine wall cupboard, circa 1780-
1800, unusually small example with cornice over
single nine-pane glazed door opening to three
shaped, fixed shelves, above applied waist molding
and single split-panel door, raised on applied base
with cut-out bracket feet, scraped to early blue-and
white-painted surface, 68" high 33" wide 18" deep.*
**$16,000**

Courtesy of Sotheby's

*Painted pine hanging cupboard with spoon shelf,
attributed to John Drissel, Milford Township, Bucks
County, Pennsylvania, dated 1800, front door
inscribed "Abraham Stauffer / 1800," 19" x 10" x
5 3/8".* **$209,000**

Courtesy of Heritage Auctions

*American upholstered sofa, 20th century, down-filled bench seat with red and gold jacquard fabric, marks: Custom Upholstery Mart, 32" x 87 1/2" x 35".* **$1,625**

Courtesy of Heritage Auctions

*George II burled walnut double bonnet top secretary bookcase, 18th century, 88 5/8" x 39 3/4" x 20 1/4".* **$7,500**

Courtesy of Roland New York

*Italian entrance, 15th century, walnut, with pair of doors, each with three panels of carved architectural motifs, each door flanked by second fixed panel, large rectangular panel with flanking seahorses above series of four carved panels, doors with arched panels, carved with two coat of arms contained within wreath, 15' high x 7' 7" wide.* **$10,000**

*Shaker maple and cherry stand, Hancock, Massachusetts or Enfield, Connecticut, circa 1850, rectangular top with slightly rounded edge above two dovetail-constructed drawers mounted on channels that open in both directions, with turned wooden pulls, underside of one drawer with blue printed label reading, "THE BERKSHIRE MUSEUM / ANDREWS / #15," all on turned pedestal and tripod base of spider legs, old finish, 26 1/4" high x 22" wide x 18 3/4" deep.* **$52,275**

*Italian Renaissance-style walnut writing desk, circa 1900, 39" high x 55 1/2" wide x 26 3/4" deep.*
**$2,875**

*Victorian Gothic
Revival upholstered
oak settee, circa 1865,
53 1/4" x 61" x 22".*
**$1,063**

*East Tennessee walnut blanket chest attributed
to cabinet maker Jacob Fisher who lived and
worked in McMinn County (working 1837-
1843), rectangular form with inlaid light wood
escutcheon and applied molding to top and
base with double incised lines, continuous stiles
forming splayed French feet, possibly original
iron hinges, 21" high x 37 5/8" long x 14 5/8"
deep.* **$5,200**

*Gallé marquetry lady's writing desk, Émile
Gallé, Nancy, France, circa 1890, desk and
over cabinet with reticulation to sides and
top of crest with marquetry scene to shelves
and locking cabinet, sitting on shaped
rectangular desk with chrysanthemum
marquetry design to top and drawer, resting
on four fluted legs with reticulated
marquetry stretcher, marks: Gallé,
60" x 30 1/2" x 22".* **$13,750**

▲ *Federal yellow paint-decorated pine footstool, probably New England or Pennsylvania, circa 1835, 4 7/8" x 8 13/16" x 4 3/8".* **$17,500**

◄ *Rare mahogany and exotic wood footstool with scrimshaw decoration, probably eastern United States, circa 1850, 7 5/8" x 12 1/2" x 7 1/8".* **$10,625**

*English Empire rosewood and gilt bronze mounted table, circa 1820, 27 1/2" x 59" x 26 3/4".* **$2,500**

Courtesy of Heritage Auctions

*Edwardian mahogany circular staircase, circa 1905, spiral-form with eight stairs covered in brown carpet, stairs terminating in circular platform with swivel seat and hinged reading easel, whole supported by columns ending in brass caps and wheels, joined with cross braces and spiral base, 106" high x 54" wide.* **$19,375**

Courtesy of Pook & Pook, Inc.

*Pennsylvania child's pine stepback cupboard, 19th century, old varnished surface, 30" high x 14 1/2" wide.* **$800**

Courtesy of Skinner, Inc.;
www.skinnerinc.com

*Pair of Louis XV-style marquetry marble-top side tables, three-drawer ormolu-mounted case with lower inlaid platform, on cabriole legs and cast paw feet, 29 1/4" high x 15 1/2" wide x 11 1/2" deep.* **$923**

CLOSE-UP!

Courtesy of Sotheby's

*Louis VX-style gilt-bronze mounted stained fruitwood and marquetry inlaid table, France, late 19th century, fitted with one frieze drawer, 28" high x 24 1/2" wide x 17" deep.* **$5,313**

# Modern Furniture

Courtesy of Skinner, Inc.;
www.skinnerinc.com

*Charles and Ray Eames ESU 270-C birch plywood desk, enameled steel, lacquered Masonite, laminate, rubber, circa 1950, three drawers in red, black, and white case panels over perforated metal screen and black laminate shelf, 32 1/2" high x 24" wide x 16" deep.* **$9,600**

Courtesy of Palm Beach
Modern Auctions

*Eames-era "Cloud" sofa, metal and upholstery, 32" high x 96" wide x 44" deep.* **$1,700**

INSIDE LOOK!

Courtesy of Austin Auction Gallery

*Bookcase designed by Osvaldo Borsani (Swiss, Italian, 1911-1985) for Atelier Borsani, Varedo, Italy, late 1940s, rectangular teakwood cabinet with ebonized perimeter, central paneled door opens to 10 drawers, two paneled doors at either side open to adjustable shelves, wide angular legs, 61" high x 98 1/2" wide x 16 1/4" deep.* **$9,500**

Courtesy of Skinner, Inc.; www.skinnerinc.com

*Charles and Ray Eames lounge chair, model no. 670, and ottoman, model no. 671, walnut, leather, enameled aluminum, steel, rubber, black-tufted leather and bent plywood construction, chair with silver Herman Miller label, ottoman with black label, chair 30" high, ottoman 17".* **$2,400**

*Charles and Ray Eames ESU 240-K birch plywood cabinet, zinc-plated steel, pylon fiberglass, enameled Masonite, Herman Miller, Zeeland, Michigan, circa 1950, natural top over two black laminated shelves in white case panels with double sliding doors, 32 1/2" high x 47" wide x 17" deep.* **$6,150**

*Erwine and Estelle Laverne Lotus dining chairs, set of four, Laverne Originals USA, 1958, lacquered fiberglass, chrome-plated steel, 23 1/4" wide x 22" deep x 30" high.* **$2,400**

*Norwegian rosewood-framed Siesta lounge chairs, circa 1960, buttoned leather cushions, design by Ingmar Anton Relling (Norway, 1920-2002) for Westnofa Furniture, 38 3/4" high x 24 1/4" wide x 29" deep.* **$1,100**

Courtesy of Sotheby's

*Charles and Ray Eames special-order lounge chair, model no. 670, and ottoman, model no. 671, circa 1956, with firm's foil label, rosewood, enameled aluminum, rubber, original leather upholstery, chair 32 1/2" x 33 1/4" x 34 3/4", ottoman 16 1/8" x 26" x 21 1/2".* **$12,500**

Courtesy of Austin Auction Gallery

*Italian desk made by Olivetti Synthesis, circa 1960s, two-drawer single floating pedestal with laminated steel top on black metal frame, 63" wide x 31 3/4" deep.* **$1,400**

Courtesy of Austin Auction Gallery

*Writing desk or library table, circa late 1940s/ early 1950s, design by Gio Ponti (Italy, 1891-1979), rectangular with teak finish, two frieze drawers, inset pulls, shaped and angled legs joined by H-form stretcher, 31" high x 55" wide x 27" deep.* **$3,500**

*J. R. Davidson articulated wall light, custom designed, circa 1946, steel, 26" reach x 16" diameter shade.* **$2,000**

*Italian dressing table, circa 1955, design by Silvio Cavatorta, long horizontal tilting mirror over glass shelf, open top dresser below with six drawers, tapered angular gilded supports at each side, chip on glass shelf, 46 1/2" high x 73 1/2" wide x 20" deep.* **$6,500**

*Rare "Pharaoh" coffee table by Philip and Kelvin LaVerne, circa 1965, acid-etched and enameled brass over wood, 18 1/8" high x 44" deep.* **$23,750**

*Mushroom-form table
lamp, teak veneer,
ceramic, glass, cylindrical
base fitted with single
ceramic socket with
frosted glass domed
shade, 12" high x 12"
deep.* **$369**

*◀ Pair of "Janus" occasional tables by Edward
Wormley, circa 1960, model No. 6047, each
with firm's label, mahogany and glazed
earthenware tiles executed by Gertrud and
Otto Nazler, manufactured by Dunbar, Berne,
Indiana, 23 3/4" x 15" x 13 1/2".* **$22,500**

*Danish Modern sideboard,
rosewood, case with two
sliding doors fitted over two
outer compartments each with
interior adjustable shelf, central
compartment fitted with five
drawers, tapered legs, unmarked,
31 1/2" high x 86" wide x 18 1/2"
deep.* **$2,706**

*Sideboard, teak, circa 1950, case
with lip to back edge and fitted
with central bank of two shallow
and two deep drawers flanked
by two cabinets each with single
adjustable shelf, all with recessed
lozenge pulls, turned legs, back
and base with branded mark
Made in Denmark, George Tanier
Selection, Sibast Møbler, 30" high
x 72" wide x 19 1/2" deep.* **$3,690**

*Cork dining table designed by Paul Frankl (Austrian/American, 1886-1958) for Johnson Furniture Co., Grand Rapids, Michigan, shaped enameled top raised on two pierced carved wood supports of diamond form, enamel loss, wear to edges, with two leaves 94 1/4" long, without leaves 29 1/2" high x 72" long x 42" deep.* **$2,000**

*Shell sofa, teak plywood, beech, Denmark, Hans Wegner (1914-2007), circa 1948, model 1936, original paper label and faded manufacturer's stamp, 27 1/2" high x 48" wide x 21" deep.* **$5,535**

*George Nakashima sideboard, circa 1960, American black walnut and pandanus cloth, 31 1/2" x 70 1/2" x 22".* **$15,000**

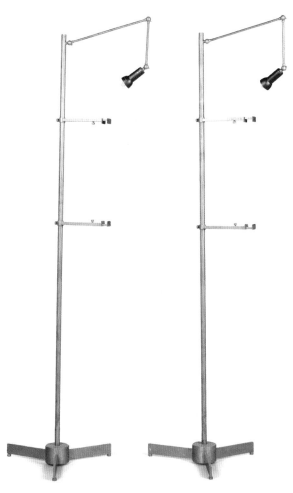

*Pair of easel floor lamps, circa 1958, brass and black enameled steel, 82 1/4" high.* **$18,810**

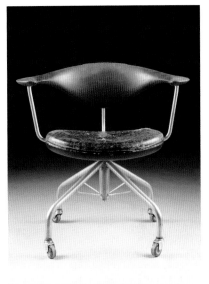

*Johannes Hansen swivel arm chair, Copenhagen, Denmark, circa 1955, designed by H. J. Wegner, wide wood carved backrest with conforming elbow rests, held to seat on chrome armature, distressed black leather seat, four chrome rolling legs on casters, one of the most sought-after pieces of furniture produced during the golden era of mid-century Danish design, 28 3/4" high x 28 3/4" wide x 21 1/2" deep.* **$12,000**

*Rosewood sideboard server, Italian, circa 1960, designed by Gianfranco Frattini (Italian, 1926-2004) for Bernini Furniture, rectangular, front with half in four drawers, other half with tambour front opening to interior shelf, shaped legs, 28 1/2" high x 55 1/2" wide x 20 3/4" deep.* **$1,900**

INSIDE LOOK!

Courtesy of Austin Auction Gallery

*China cabinet, circa 1950, with label "Widdicomb Modern Original," Widdicomb Furniture Co., Grand Rapids, Michigan, design by Terence Harold Robsjohn-Gibbings (British, 1905-1976), upper cupboard with sliding glass doors set back on lower rectangular base with five front drawers with circular brass pulls, on set-back base with castors, crazing on painted finish, 62" high x 54" wide x 20 1/4" deep.* **$2,500**

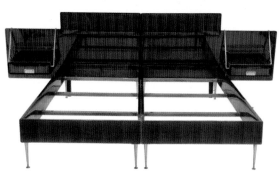

Courtesy of Austin Auction Gallery

*Gloss finish bed with attached nightstands, Italian, circa 1955, design by Silvio Cavatorta, gloss finish, paneled headboard with attached brass-supported single drawer nightstands at each side, raised on tapered wood and steel supports, headboard 36 1/2" high x 117 3/4" wide, bed section 76" long x 69" wide.* **$5,500**

Courtesy of Sotheby's

*Bar and three barstools, European, circa 1950, some elements added later, lacquered bamboo, lacquered wood, each stool with colored vinyl seat, bar 40 1/2" x 42" x 21 5/8", stools 31 7/8" high.* **$3,553**

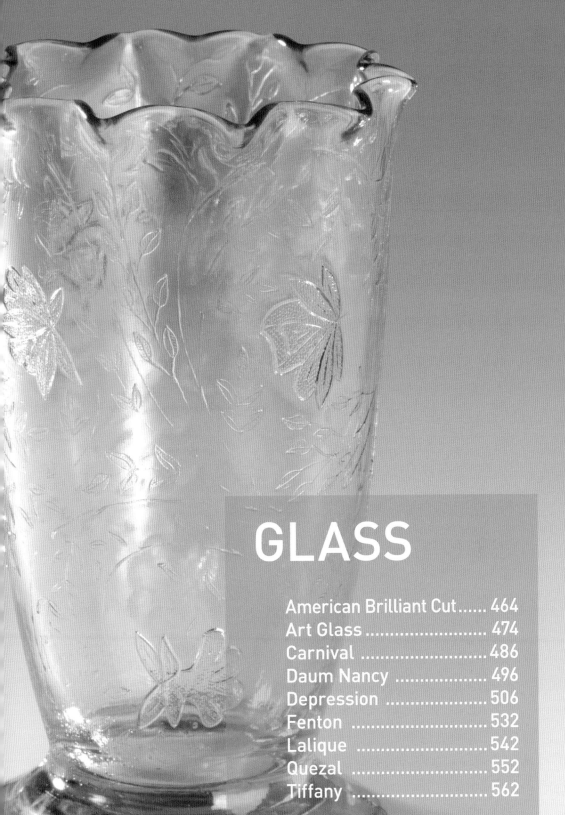

# GLASS

# American Brilliant Cut Glass

Cut glass is made by grinding decorations into glass by means of abrasive-carrying metal or stone wheels. An ancient craft, it was revived in 1600 by the Bohemians and spread through Europe to Great Britain and America. American cut glass came of age at the Centennial Exposition in 1876 and the World Columbian Exposition in 1893. America's most significant output of high-quality glass occurred from 1880 to 1917, a period now known as the Brilliant Period. Glass from this period is the most eagerly sought by collectors.

Courtesy of Woody Auction

*Wine glass, cranberry cut to clear, pattern #210 by Dorflinger, pattern cut foot, good condition, no chips, cracks or repairs, 4 1/2".* **$1,600**

Courtesy of Woody Auction

*Rare tray attributed to Shotton Cut Glass Works, Hobstar, Cane, Strawberry Diamond, Vesica and Fan motif, thick clear blank, good condition, no chips, cracks or repairs, 15 1/2".* **$2,600**

Courtesy of Woody Auction

*Water set, pitcher and six pattern-matched tumblers, signed Libbey, Mignon pattern, clear blank, good condition, no chips, cracks or repairs, pitcher 10 1/4".* **$500**

Courtesy of Woody Auction

▲ *Covered casserole, footed, Hobstar, Strawberry Diamond and Fan motif, Hobstar base, steeple finial, fine blank, good condition, no chips, cracks or repairs, 8 1/2" x 8 1/2".* **$2,500**

Courtesy of Woody Auction

▶ *Tumble-up, cranberry cut to clear, Hobstar, Cane and Fan motif, very rare, good condition, no chips, cracks or repairs, 7".* **$2,300**

Courtesy of Woody Auction

*Tray, round, Oasis pattern by W.C. Anderson, thick blank, good condition, no chips, cracks or repairs, 13 1/2".* **$500**

Courtesy of Woody Auction

*Punch bowl, two-part, Vintage and Hobstar pattern, signed Sinclaire, excellent blank, good condition, no chips, cracks or repairs, 13 1/2" x 14 1/2".* **$1,900**

Courtesy of Woody Auction

*Creamer and covered sugar on pedestal, Hobstar, Strawberry Diamond, Vesica and Fan motif, pattern cut lid on sugar, scalloped Hobstar base, double-notched handles, facet-cut teardrop stem.* **$2,200**

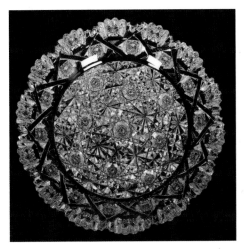

Courtesy of Woody Auction

*Bowl, low, Russian pattern center with Trellis pattern border, good condition, no chips, cracks or repairs, 2 3/4" x 8 3/4".* **$4,700**

Courtesy of Woody Auction

*Plate, Brunswick pattern, signed Hawkes, clear blank, good condition, no chips, cracks or repairs, 10".* **$600**

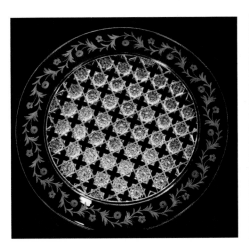

Courtesy of Woody Auction

*Tray, round, signed Sinclaire, Assyrian and Floral pattern, good condition, no chips, cracks or repairs, 10".* **$2,000**

Courtesy of Woody Auction

*Bowl, San Salvador pattern by Straus, pattern also known as Tassel, good condition, no chips, cracks or repairs, 4" x 9 1/4".* **$550**

Courtesy of Woody Auction

*Cider pitcher and three matching tumblers, fully cut Russian pattern with star cut buttons, ray cut base, triple-notched handle, good condition, no chips, cracks or repairs, pitcher 6".* **$400**

Courtesy of Woody Auction

*Punch bowl, one piece, Hobstar, Modified Hobstar, Crosscut Diamond, Strawberry Diamond, Star and Fan motif, rolled rim, signed Libbey, good condition, no chips, cracks or repairs, 7 1/2" x 12 1/2".* **$400**

Courtesy of Woody Auction

◄ *Punch bowl, two-part, Hobstar, File, Prism and Hobstar Chain motif, pattern cut base, good condition, no chips, cracks or repairs, 9 3/4" x 9 3/4".* **$550**

Courtesy of Woody Auction

▼ *Tray, eight-sided, four-point Russian pattern, star center with Hobstar, Prism and Fan border, good condition, no chips, cracks or repairs, 12".* **$1,400**

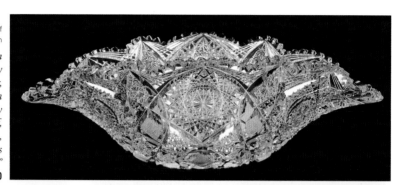

*Bowl, Napoleon hat shape, fully cut with Hobstar, Cane, Vesica and Strawberry Diamond motif, good condition, no chips, cracks or repairs, 4 1/4" x 13 3/4".* **$650**

*Pedestal vase, Prism and Bullseye motif, petticoat flared base, extra clear blank, good condition, no chips, cracks or repairs, 13 3/4".* **$600**

*Vase, two-handled, Monarch pattern by J. Hoare, triple-notched handles, step cut neck, good condition, no chips, cracks or repairs, 11 3/4".* **$400**

Courtesy of Woody Auction

*Bowl, square, Star pattern by Meriden, sharply cut, good condition, no chips, cracks or repairs, 2 1/2" x 8".* **$1,000**

Courtesy of Woody Auction

*Vase, massive, bulbous, with feathered prism and crescent moon shapes with Hobstar and File highlights, good condition, no chips, cracks or repairs, 14" high, nearly 15 pounds.* **$1,700**

Courtesy of Woody Auction

*Two matching decanters, Hobstar, Cane, Prism and Fan motif, faceted cut ring necks, six-sided teardrop stoppers with zipper highlights, very heavy blanks, good condition, no chips, cracks or repairs, 17" and 15 1/2".* **$3,250**

Courtesy of Woody Auction

*Rare handled jug, signed J. Hoare, Carolyn pattern hourglass shape with triple-notched applied handle, good condition, no chips, cracks or repairs, 8 3/4".* **$1,600**

Courtesy of Woody Auction

*Plate, signed Tuthill, five-point star in center with engraved floral highlights, Hobstar Chain border, good condition, no chips, cracks or repairs, 9 3/4".* **$500**

Courtesy of Woody Auction

*Bowl, signed J. Hoare, Trellis block design with Hobstar and Strawberry Diamond alternating blocks, Hobstar center, clear blank, good condition, no chips, cracks or repairs, 3 3/4" x 8".* **$450**

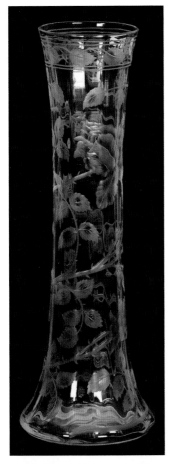

Courtesy of Woody Auction

◀ *Vase, signed J. Hoare, engraved rose branch decor, good condition, no chips, cracks or repairs, 13 3/4".* **$600**

Courtesy of Woody Auction

▼ *Pair of handled whiskey jugs, rock crystal engraved tusks with flowers and scrollwork, pattern cut stoppers, attributed to Stevens and Williams, fine quality, 8 1/2".* **$1,500**

Courtesy of Woody Auction

*Tray, round, Beverly pattern by Meriden, thick heavy blank, good condition, no chips, cracks or repairs, 14 1/2".* **$2,250**

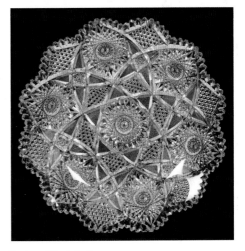

Courtesy of Woody Auction

*Round tray, Hobstar, Diamond and Nailhead Diamond motif, thick heavy blank, good condition, no chips, cracks or repairs, 13 1/2".* **$1,200**

# Art Glass

Art glass is artistic novelty glassware created for decorative purposes. Types of art glass include leaded glass, molded glass, blown glass, and sandblasted glass. Tiffany, Lalique, and Steuben are some of the best-known types of art glass. Daum Nancy, Baccarat, Gallé, Moser, Mt. Washington, Fenton, and Quezal are a few others.

Courtesy of Rago Arts

▼ *Murano glass vase and bowl, Anzolo Fuga (attr.), possible A.V.E.M., with murrine and gold foil, Murano, Italy, second half 20th century, unmarked, , 13 1/2" x 8 1/4", 3 1/4" x 16".* **$8,750**

Courtesy of James D. Julia Auctioneers, Fairfield, Maine, www.jamesdjulia.com

▲ *Four Moser cameo and intaglio stems of green cameo glass cut to clear with woodland scene of trees, meadows and ponds with intaglio carved birds and stags, unsigned, very good to excellent condition, 5 1/2" and 8 1/4" high.* **$1,185**

*Steuben plum jade bowl with flaring sides and rolled lip, translucent, polished pontil, unsigned, very good condition with light staining to interior and minor scratches to exterior sides, 8 1/4" diameter.* **$351**

*Steuben atomizer in gold iridescence with blue and green highlights with brass-colored collar and spray tip and brown hose and ball, unsigned, very good condition with some minor scratches to aurene finish on foot, 7" high.* **$237**

*Pair of Steuben Ivorene triple vases, opal iridescent, shape 7566, second quarter 20th century, each with central lily flanked by jack-in-the-pulpit, each with engraved signature and polished pontil mark, one with silver paper label, undamaged, 12" and 12 1/4" high.* **$1,035**

Courtesy of Mark Mussio,
Humler & Nolan

*Four Steuben plates in ivory,
edges in Nubian black, one plate
with polished areas in center to
possibly remove impurities in glass,
otherwise excellent condition,
8 1/2" diameter.* **$300**

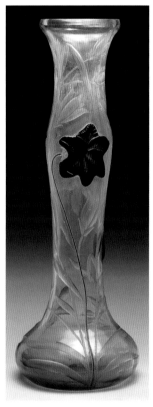

Courtesy of James D. Julia Auctioneers,
Fairfield, Maine,
www.jamesdjulia.com

*Monumental Moser vase with
wheel-carved dark red marquetry
flower on front and two green wheel-
carved marquetry buds on back,
applied green thread forming stem
to marquetry flower, rest of vase
intaglio carved with flowers, stems
and leaves, very good to excellent
condition, 19 1/2" high.* **$4,148**

Courtesy of Jeffrey S. Evans & Associates

*Thomas Webb & Sons English cameo cabinet vase, white to deep red, fully
carved with flowers and scrolls, factory polished rim, table ring and concave
base, Thomas Webb & Sons, fourth quarter 19th century, undamaged,
4" high.* **$3,450**

*Moser three-piece garniture set, rare amethyst glass decorated with gold enamel rococo motifs with applied red jewels to gilded bands on each piece, very good to excellent condition with one missing red jewel on center piece, tallest 13 3/4" high.* **$7,821**

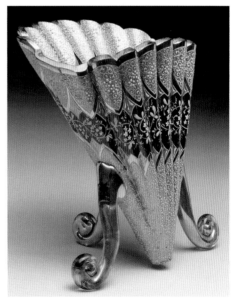

*Rare Moser vase with vertically ribbed cranberry glass body with gilded decoration at bottom and top of each rib with cream-colored enamel scrolls and blue stylized flowers, center section of each rib with cranberry glass background and enameled white and yellow flowers with cream-colored leaves and gold stems, three applied gilded scroll feet, unsigned, very good to excellent condition with minor wear to gilding, 7 1/4" high.* **$2,666**

*Moser cranberry pitcher heavily decorated with enameled flowers, stems, leaves and butterflies with applied and gilded rigaree, applied feet and ornate handle, heavy gilded rigaree around lip and handle, very good to excellent condition with chip to tip of one foot, 14 1/2" high.* **$8,295**

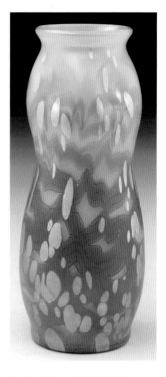

Courtesy of Thomaston Place
Auction Galleries

◄ *Steuben Aurene glass Chinese form vase in blue with ground pontil, unmarked, circa 1910, fine condition, 6 1/2" high x 6" diameter.* **$1,000-1,500**

Courtesy of James D. Julia Auctioneers,
Fairfield, Maine,
www.jamesdjulia.com

▲ *Loetz vase with pale green body and reddish-brown Cytisus pattern shading to light amber at top with random spots of gold iridescence, five indentations around shoulder, unsigned, very good to excellent condition, 8" high.* **$4,444**

Courtesy of Rago Arts

◄ *Thomas Webb & Sons cameo glass vase with flowering branches and butterfly, England, circa 1890, molded THOMAS WEBB & SONS, 10" x 7".* **$2,500**

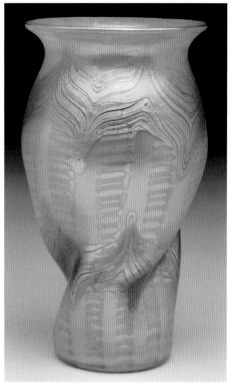

Courtesy of James D. Julia Auctioneers, Fairfield, Maine,
www.jamesdjulia.com

*Rare Loetz vase in Phanomen pattern with blue
iridescent waves against gold iridescent background,
strong purple highlights, gold iridescent stylized
leaves extending vertically up body, unsigned, very
good to excellent condition, 7" high.* **$11,258**

Courtesy of James D. Julia Auctioneers, Fairfield, Maine,
www.jamesdjulia.com

*Loetz Phanomen vase with twisted gold body and
platinum iridescent wavy pulled bands at shoulder
and waist with platinum iridescent vertical zipper
designs, blue and purple highlights, unsigned, very
good to excellent condition, 7" high.* **$7,110**

Courtesy of Woody Auction

◄ *Thomas Webb & Sons vase
with blue background with pink
and white carved cameo overlay,
flowering trees, flying birds,
three panel scenes of birds and
floral décor, signed "Thomas
Webb & Sons Gem Cameo," good
condition, 6 3/4" x 7".* **$35,000**

*Steuben Rosaline & Alabaster 6 1/4" goblet with rope twist stem, 4 1/4" wine with twist stem, two parfaits, 2 5/8" and 2 3/4", each with gold stickers from Rockwell Gallery in Corning, New York, all in excellent condition.* **$300**

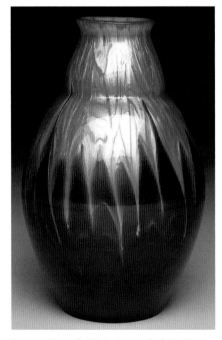

*Loetz Flammarion vase with red decoration resembling flames extending from foot toward shoulder against green background, clear glass outer layer, unsigned, minor imperfection in outer layer of glass from making, otherwise very good to excellent condition, 8 1/4" high.* **$3,259**

*Pair of Murano glass Vaseline lamps with brass fittings, Murano, Italy, 20th century, foil label to one, 32 1/4" high to finial.* **$406**

◄ *Thomas Webb & Sons cameo glass vase, Stourbridge, England, late 19th/early 20th century, inverted baluster form with squat collar with incised white cameo bands, body with apple blossom motif, moth, and maidenhair fern on red ground, marked THOMAS WEBB & SONS/CAMEO in banner to underside, slight surface abrasions, good overall condition, 8 3/8" high.* **$3,000**

*Steuben Pomona green covered jar, circa 1935, urn-form with scale pattern decoration, raised on hexagonal foot, interior of lid acid-stamped Steuben, minor fleabites to interior rim of lid, 13 1/4" high.* **$1,020**

*Murano glass vases, Anzolo Fuga (attr.), possible A.V.E.M., pink and green with murrine and lattimo decoration, Murano, Italy, second half 20th century, unmarked, 16 1/2" x 5 1/4" high each.* **$6,875**

▶ FAR RIGHT *Rare Thomas Webb & Sons signed English cameo "ivory" vase carved with Oriental portraits with extensive floral design, two figural snake handles, good condition, 7 3/4" high.* **$13,000**

▶ *Mt. Washington Crown Milano stick vase with autumnal English ivy with raised gold outlines in painted ringlet patterns over biscuit-color body, 7 3/8" high.* **$170**

*Moser water set, pitcher with ruby glass body with vertical gilded panels with scrolled outline and applied and layered enameled flowers, six matching tumblers, very good to excellent condition with minor flower petal loss and minor wear to gold, pitcher 11" high, tumblers 5 1/2" high.* **$1,067**

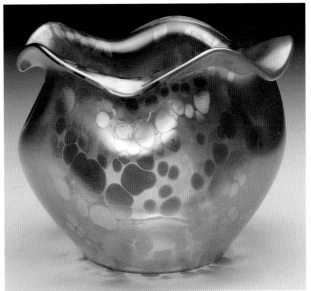

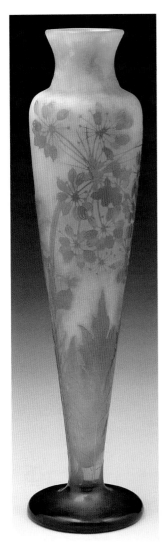

▲ *Loetz vase with vertical translucent panels of lavender, pink and gold with random spots of gold iridescence, signed in polished pontil "Loetz Austria," very good to excellent condition, 5 1/2" high x 7" diameter.* **$5,925**

◄ *Mt. Washington Royal Flemish vase with gold enameled lion standing by shield with double-headed eagle carrying large banner, gold flowers, stems and leaves on neck against frosted background, signed on underside "RF" within diamond and "574," very good to excellent condition, 14 1/2" high.* **$2,666**

▲ *Gallé glass vase with translucent amber cameo leaves, stems and flowers against frosted background of green and cream shading to pink at top, signed on top of foot with engraved signature "Gallé," very good to excellent condition, 17" high.* **$1,185**

*Czechoslovakia stem vase in flame red with black painted decoration of ducks in flight over cattails, unmarked, circa 1925, fine condition, 13" high.* **$144**

*Murano glass vase, Anzolo Fuga (attr.), possible A.V.E.M., with lattimo glass, Murano, Italy, second half 20th century, unmarked, 21" high x 6" diameter.* **$5,000**

*Murano glass tall bandiere vase, Anzolo Fuga (attr.), possible A.V.E.M., Murano, Italy, second half 20th century, polychrome and lattimo glass, 18 3/4" high x 8 1/2" diameter.* **$5,000**

*Gallé chalice with brown cameo of river flanked with trees on each shore against shaded green background, signed on side in cameo "Gallé," very good to excellent condition, 6 3/4" high.* **$911**

Courtesy of James D. Julia Auctioneers,
Fairfield, Maine,
www.jamesdjulia.com

*Two Mt. Washington vases,
each with daisies encircling body
and shoulder with gilded lip,
unsigned, very good to excellent
condition, 10" high.* **$2,607**

Courtesy of Woody Auction

▼ *Thomas Webb & Sons English
cameo art glass vase, cranberry
background with blue and white
floral decor carved overlay, two
butterflies on reverse, signed
"Thomas Webb & Sons," good
condition, 9 1/2" high.* **$19,000**

Courtesy of James D. Julia Auctioneers, Fairfield, Maine,
www.jamesdjulia.com

*Moser vase with enameled flowers, stems and
leaves against blue background with three
handles pulled from lip and attached to side,
each blue handle with applied clear glass leaf
decoration, unsigned, very good to excellent
condition, minor wear to gilding on edge,
10" high.* **$3,792**

# Carnival Glass

By Ellen T. Schroy

**ELLEN T. SCHROY**, one of the leading experts in her field, is the author of *Warman's Carnival Glass Identification and Price Guide* and other books on collectible glass. Her books are the definitive references for glass collectors.

Carnival glass is what is fondly called mass-produced iridescent glassware. The term "carnival glass" has evolved through the years as glass collectors have responded to the idea that much of this beautiful glassware was made as giveaway glass at local carnivals and fairs. However, more of it was made and sold through the same channels as pattern glass and Depression glass. Some patterns were indeed giveaways, and others were used as advertising premiums, souvenirs, etc. Whatever the origin, the term "carnival glass" today encompasses glassware that is usually pattern molded and treated with metallic salts, creating that unique coloration that is so desirable to collectors.

Early names for iridescent glassware, which early 20th century consumers believed to have all come from foreign manufacturers, include Pompeiian Iridescent, Venetian Art, and Mexican Aurora. Another popular early name was "Nancy Glass," as some patterns were believed to have come from the Daum, Nancy, glassmaking area in France. This was at a time when artistic cameo glass was enjoying great success. While the iridescent glassware being made by such European glassmakers as Loetz influenced the American marketplace, it was Louis Tiffany's Favrile glass that really caught the eye of glass consumers of the early 1900s. It seems an easy leap to transform Tiffany's shimmering glassware to something that could be mass-produced, allowing what we call carnival glass today to become "poor man's Tiffany."

Carnival glass is iridized glassware that is created by pressing hot molten glass into molds, just as pattern glass had evolved. Some forms are hand finished, while others are completely formed by molds. To achieve the marvelous iridescent colors that carnival glass collectors seek, a process was developed where a liquid solution of metallic salts was put onto the still hot glass form after it was unmolded. As the liquid evaporated, a fine metallic surface was left, which refracts light into wonderful colors. The name given to the iridescent spray by early glassmakers was "dope."

◄ *Dugan Glass Co. peach opal Persian Garden pattern bowl, six-point crimp, 12".* **$94**

▼ *Rare Fenton Art Glass Co. green Butterfly pattern ornament, 3" wingspan.* **$3,300**

Many of the forms created by carnival glass manufacturers were accessories to the china American housewives so loved. By the early 1900s, consumers could find carnival glassware at such popular stores as F. W. Woolworth and McCrory's. To capitalize on the popular fancy for these colored wares, some other industries bought large quantities of carnival glass and turned them into "packers." This term reflects the practice where baking powder, mustard, or other household products were packed into a special piece of glass that could take on another life after the original product was used. Lee Manufacturing Co. used iridized carnival glass as premiums for its baking powder and other products, causing some early carnival glass to be known by the generic term "baking powder glass."

Classic carnival glass production began in the early 1900s and continued for about 20 years. Fenton Art Glass Co. became the top producer with more than 150 patterns. No one seriously documented or researched production until the first collecting wave struck in 1960.

It is important to remember that carnival glasswares were sold in department stores as well as mass merchants rather than through the general store often associated with a young America. Glassware by this time was mass-produced and sold in large quantities by such enterprising companies as Butler Brothers. When the economics of the country soured in the 1920s, those interested in purchasing iridized glassware were not spared. Many of the leftover inventories of glasshouses that hoped to sell this mass-produced glassware found their way to wholesalers who, in turn, sold the wares to those who offered the glittering glass as prizes at carnivals, fairs, circuses, etc. Possibly because this was the last venue people associated with the iridized glassware, it became known as "carnival glass."

For more information on carnival glass, see *Warman's Carnival Glass Identification and Price Guide,* 2nd edition, by Ellen T. Schroy.

Courtesy of Randy Clark/Dexter City
Auction Gallery

▲ *Exceptionally rare Fenton Art Glass Co. amethyst Goddess of Harvest pattern bowl, plain exterior, 3/1 crimp, 9".* **$17,600**

Courtesy of Randy Clark/Dexter City
Auction Gallery

▶ *Fenton Art Glass Co. green Waterlily and Cattails pattern No. 1120 oval four-toed bowl, Thistle pattern interior, 10".* **$73**

◄ *Fenton Art Glass Co. blue Dragon and Strawberry pattern bowl, 9".* **$825**

▶ *Fenton Art Glass Co. amethyst "Season's Greetings Eat Paradise Sodas" plate, some damage, 6".* **$39**

◄ *Fenton Art Glass Co. green Peacock and Grape pattern bowl, eight-point crimp, 8 1/2".* **$50**

▶ *Rare Fenton Art Glass Co. marigold "State House of Indiana" plate, Berry and Leaf Circle pattern exterior, 7 1/2".* **$6,380**

◀ *Millersburg Glass Co. amethyst Detroit Elks shallow bowl, lettered "Detroit 1910 B. P. O. E.," 7".* **$2,640**

▶ *Fenton Art Glass Co. green Captive Rose pattern plate, 9 1/2".* **$143**

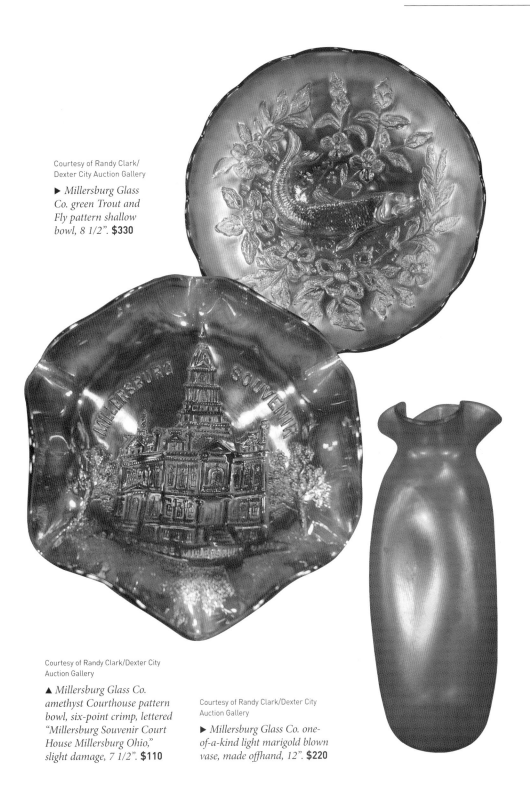

Courtesy of Randy Clark/
Dexter City Auction Gallery

▶ *Millersburg Glass Co. green Trout and Fly pattern shallow bowl, 8 1/2".* **$330**

Courtesy of Randy Clark/Dexter City Auction Gallery

▲ *Millersburg Glass Co. amethyst Courthouse pattern bowl, six-point crimp, lettered "Millersburg Souvenir Court House Millersburg Ohio," slight damage, 7 1/2".* **$110**

Courtesy of Randy Clark/Dexter City Auction Gallery

▶ *Millersburg Glass Co. one-of-a-kind light marigold blown vase, made offhand, 12".* **$220**

▲ *Fenton Art Glass Co. amethyst Peacock and Urn bowl, six-point crimp, 9".* **$132**

◄ *Very rare Fenton Art Glass Co. blue Starflower pattern pitcher.* **$1,870**

▲ *Fenton Art Glass Co. blue Peter Rabbit plate with Bearded Berry pattern exterior, 9".* **$1,980**

◄ *Fenton Art Glass Co. amethyst Thistle pattern plate, 9 1/4".* **$1,320**

Courtesy of Randy Clark/Dexter City Auction Gallery

▲ *Fenton Art Glass Co. blue Parkersburg Elks plate, lettered "1914 Parkersburg B. P. O. E.," 7 1/2".* **$1,870**

Courtesy of Randy Clark/Dexter City Auction Gallery

◄ *Fenton Art Glass Co. blue "Illinois Soldiers and Sailors Home" plate, 7 1/2".* **$935**

◀ *Fenton Art Glass Co. blue Heart and Vine pattern plate, outstanding iridescence, 9".* **$330**

▶ *Northwood Glass Co. amethyst Peacocks on the Fence pattern bowl, outstanding iridescence, 8 1/2".* **$440**

◀ **FAR LEFT** *Rare Fenton Art Glass Co. blue Lily of the Valley pattern pitcher, some damage.* **$770**

◀ *Fenton Art Glass Co. blue Parkersburg Elks bell, lettered "1914 Parkersburg B. P. O. E."* **$1,100**

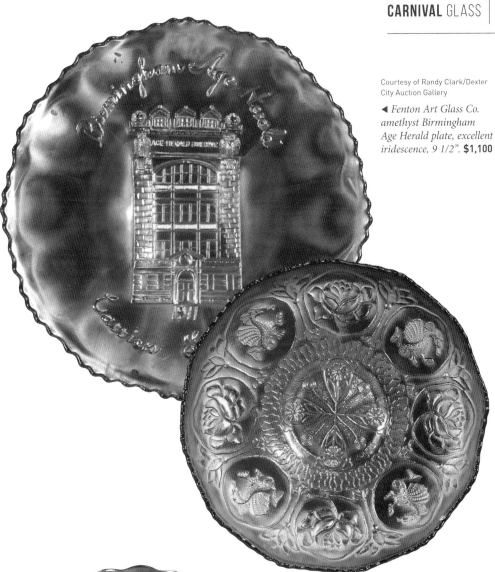

◄ *Fenton Art Glass Co. amethyst Birmingham Age Herald plate, excellent iridescence, 9 1/2".* **$1,100**

▲ *Fenton Art Glass Co. red Dragon and Lotus pattern shallow bowl, 8 1/2".* **$660**

◄ *Millersburg Glass Co. amethyst Blackberry Wreath pattern flared bowl, six-point crimp, chipped.* **$28**

# Daum Nancy

Daum Nancy fine glass, much of it cameo, was made by Auguste and Antonin Daum, who founded a factory in 1875 in Nancy, France. Most of their cameo and enameled glass was made from the 1890s into the early 20th century.

Cameo glass is made by carving into multiple layers of colored glass to create a design in relief. It is at least as old as the Romans.

Courtesy of James D. Julia Auctioneers, Fairfield, Maine, www.jamesdjulia.com

*Pate de verre parrot in blue, teal and green, signed "7-HS," very good to excellent condition with minor roughness to side of pedestal, 11 1/2" high.* **$889**

Courtesy of James D. Julia Auctioneers, Fairfield, Maine, www.jamesdjulia.com

*Vase with cameo and enameled seagulls flying over ocean with setting sun in background, sea turtle looking at a seagull, gray enameled details to feathers and turtle shell, cameo decoration set against opalescent shading to white background, gilded lip, foot and sun rays, signed on underside in gold "Daum Nancy" with Cross of Lorraine, very good to excellent condition, 7 1/2" high.* **$11,850**

*Miniature tumbler with cameo decoration of yellow flowers and shaded green and amber leaves and stems against internally decorated mottled yellow background, signed on side in black enamel "Daum Nancy France" with Cross of Lorraine, very good to excellent condition, 2" high.* **$770**

*Vase with deep purple blown out tree trunks encircling vase, area between tree trunks decorated with acid carved trees and leaves with wheel-carved vegetation and ferns against mottled yellow, green and cream background, signed on underside with engraved signature "Daum Nancy" with Cross of Lorraine, very good to excellent condition, 11 1/2" high.* **$7,110**

◄ *Autumn leaf box decorated with vitrified glass cameo leaves surrounding body and lid of box in green, yellow, orange and red against mottled frosted background, signed on side with engraved signature "Daum Nancy" with Cross of Lorraine, very good to excellent condition, 5 1/2 diameter x 3" high.* **$3,555**

*Tumbler with black cameo sailboats on water against green and orange mottled background, signed on side in cameo "Daum Nancy" with Cross of Lorraine, very good to excellent condition, 4 3/4" high.* **$770**

*Large vase with cameo and enameled winter scene with barren trees rising from enameled snowy ground, tree trunks enameled in brown, cameo decoration set against mottled yellow shading to orange background, signed on underside in black enamel "Daum Nancy" with Cross of Lorraine, very good to excellent condition, 14" high.* **$10,665**

Courtesy of James D. Julia Auctioneers, Fairfield, Maine, www.jamesdjulia.com

*Vase with cameo flowers, stems and leaves extending from applied stem upward, stems and leaves enameled in shaded green, flowers enameled in shaded red, cameo spiderwebs throughout flowers, applied foot and stem with brown cameo stylized leaves against frosted brown background, signed on side in cameo "Daum Nancy" with Cross of Lorraine, very good to excellent condition, 8 1/8" high.* **$7,703**

Courtesy of James D. Julia Auctioneers, Fairfield, Maine, www.jamesdjulia.com

*Vase with tall oval body decorated with white cameo swan in pond with white cameo trees and grasses extending around to back of vase, cameo with gray enamel shading with white cameo leaves and grasses with random green spattering, signed on underside in black enamel "Daum Nancy" with Cross of Lorraine, very good to excellent condition, 8 3/4" high.* **$11,850**

*Cameo and enameled vase with cameo decoration of barren trees rising from snowy ground against light blue frosted background sky with snow in air, trees enameled in mottled gray with four enameled blackbirds perched on tree limbs with three blackbirds in flight, signed on underside in black enamel "Daum Nancy" with Cross of Lorraine, very good to excellent condition, 2 3/4" high.* **$10,665**

*Nautical vase with brown cameo decoration of numerous sailboats in harbor, boats set against green shading to mottled yellow and orange background, signed on side in cameo "Daum Nancy" with Cross of Lorraine, very good to excellent condition, 7 3/4" high.* **$1,778**

*Tumbler with cameo bleeding heart flowers, stems and leaves against mottled purple to yellow background, enameled red flowers and shaded green stems and leaves, signed on side in cameo "Daum Nancy" with Cross of Lorraine, very good to excellent condition, 4 3/4" high.* **$1,718**

Courtesy of James D. Julia Auctioneers, Fairfield, Maine, www.jamesdjulia.com

*Cabinet vase, square with clear cameo money tree decoration and cameo bird perched on limb, mottled gilding, mottled green shading to salmon background, interior cased with thin layer of opalescence, signed on underside "Daum Nancy" with Cross of Lorraine, very good to excellent condition, 4 1/2" high.* **$1,458**

Courtesy of Jeffrey S. Evans & Associates

*Cameo vase, deep red to green, cylindrical form with acid cut-back iris decoration on feathered leaf textured ground, engraved "Daum (cross) Nancy" script signature under base of unknown association, France, probably Baccarat, late 19th/early 20th century, undamaged, 9 7/8" high x 3 3/4" diameter.* **$748**

Courtesy of James D. Julia Auctioneers, Fairfield, Maine, www.jamesdjulia.com

*Lamp with cameo and enameled decoration of barren trees rising above enameled snow-covered ground against mottled yellow shading to orange background, signed on underside of base in black enamel "Daum Nancy" with Cross of Lorraine, very good to excellent condition, lamp rewired, shade 4" diameter, lamp 3 1/4" high.* **$15,405**

Courtesy of James D. Julia Auctioneers, Fairfield, Maine, www.jamesdjulia.com

*Vase with wheel-carved blue flowers set against mottled yellow, white, and blue background, applied foot with green stylized cameo leaves and flowers against gray background, signed on top of foot with engraved signature "Daum Nancy" with Cross of Lorraine, very good to excellent condition, 17 1/4" high.* **$3,555**

◀ *Cameo and enameled table lamp, cased mottled rose and yellow vasiform body acid-cutback with flowers and leaves, signed "Daum / Nancy / France," original gilt-bronze neo-classical mounts marked for Crest Co., Chicago, early 20th century, excellent condition, later switch added to shoulder of top mount, glass 11 1/2" high, lamp 21" high to top of sockets.* **$1,495**

▲ *Miniature vase with cameo trees surrounding body, one tree extending to lip, trees enameled with brown mottled tree bark and green leaves with foreground enameled in brown, acid-textured frosted pink background, signed on underside in black enamel "Daum Nancy" with Cross of Lorraine, flake to outside edge of lip, otherwise good condition, 2" high.* **$711**

◀ *Vase in red and yellow, framework of two horizontal bands of wavy lines and dots, upper row with dots with bronze overlay, marked "Daum / Nancy / France / L. Majorelle" on base, early 20th century, chips around lip, 7" high.* **$338**

Courtesy of Jeffrey S. Evans & Associates

*Cameo and enameled table lamp, cased mottled rose and yellow urn-form body acid-cutback with flowers and leaves, signed "Daum / Nancy / France," non-original metal and wood mounts, early 20th century, glass appears undamaged, wear to finishes of mounts, 14 1/2" high overall, glass 9 1/4" high.* **$690**

Courtesy of James D. Julia Auctioneers, Fairfield, Maine, www.jamesdjulia.com

*Tumbler with cameo and enamel decoration of brown stems, green leaves, and red berries against mottled brown/orange shading to yellow/white background, signed on side in cameo "Daum Nancy" with Cross of Lorraine and "France," very good to excellent condition with minor enamel loss, 4 3/8" high.* **$711**

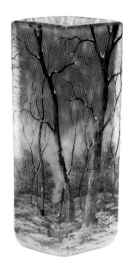

Courtesy of Mark Mussio, Humler & Nolan

*Cameo vase with panoramic view of woodland after snowfall, enamel signed "Daum Nancy" with Cross of Lorraine beneath, excellent original condition, 7 1/4" high.* **$2,800**

*Rib-optic decanter and two wine glasses, pink and colorless with gilt decorations, decanter with applied handle and original cut stopper, each wine with thistle-shape bowl engraved with fleur-de-lis, ribbed stem and foot with polished pontil mark, circa 1891, wines undamaged, decanter with small chip and associated short crack to rim at upper handle terminal, 9 1/2" high and 4 7/8" high.* **$173**

*Jar decorated on side and lid with cameo tulips against green shading to pink acid-textured background, tulips enameled in purple, orange and yellow, leaves and stems enameled in green with gilded highlights, lid with stylized cameo and enameled floral border against gilded background, handle with matching border at bottom with tulip leaves enameled to sides, signed on underside in gold "Daum Nancy" with Cross of Lorraine, very good to excellent condition, 4" high x 3 1/2" diameter.* **$5,333**

*Vase with cameo decoration of white swan swimming in pond, backside with swan with neck outstretched eating vegetation, swans framed by white cameo trees and grasses, against light blue mottled background, signed on underside in black enamel "Daum Nancy" with Cross of Lorraine, very good to excellent condition, 3 1/2" high.* **$8,295**

# Depression Glass

By Ellen T. Schroy

Depression glass is the name of the colorful glassware mass-produced during the years surrounding the Great Depression in America. Homemakers of the era enjoyed this new inexpensive dinnerware because they received pieces of their favorite patterns and colors packed in boxes of soap or as premiums on "dish night" at the local movie theater. Merchandisers, such as Sears & Roebuck and F. W. Woolworth, enticed young brides with the colorful wares that they could afford even when economic times were harsh.

Because of advancements in glassware technology, Depression-era patterns were mass-produced and could be purchased for a fraction of what cut glass or lead crystal cost. As one manufacturer found a pattern that was pleasing to the buying public, other companies soon followed with their adaptations of a similar design. Hundreds of patterns exist and include several design motifs, such as florals, geometrics, and even patterns that looked back to Early American patterns like Sandwich glass.

As America emerged from the Great Depression and life became more leisure-oriented again, new glassware patterns were created to reflect the new tastes of this generation. More elegant shapes and forms were designed, leading to what is sometimes called "Elegant Glass." Today's collectors often include these more elegant patterns when they talk about Depression glass.

Depression glass researchers have many accurate sources, including company records, catalogs, magazine advertisements, and oral and written histories from sales staff, factory workers, etc. It is one of the best-researched collecting areas available to the American marketplace. This is due in large part to the careful research of several people, including Hazel Marie Weatherman, Gene Florence, Barbara Mauzy, Carl F. Luckey, and Kent Washburn, whose books are held in high regard by researchers and collectors today.

Regarding values for Depression glass, rarity does not always equate to a high dollar amount. Some more readily found items command lofty prices because of high demand or other factors, not because they are necessarily rare. As collectors' tastes range from the simple patterns to the more elaborate patterns, so does the ability of

**ELLEN T. SCHROY,** one of the leading experts in her field, is the author of *Warman's Depression Glass Identification and Price Guide* and *Warman's Depression Glass Field Guide.* Her books are the definitive references for Depression glass collectors.

*Doric green sugar.* **$20**

*Harp crystal vase.* **$30**

*Anniversary pink sherbet.* **$12**

his/her budget to invest in inexpensive patterns to multi-hundreds of dollars per form patterns.

For more information on Depression glass, see *Warman's Depression Glass Identification and Price Guide, 6th Edition,* or *Warman's Depression Glass Field Guide, 5th Edition,* both by Ellen T. Schroy.

**RECOMMENDED READING**

**Warman's Depression Glass Identification and Price Guide, 6th edition:** 600+ color images, many featuring prized collections of the National Glass Museum; 170+ different patterns; current values; line drawings for each pattern; glass histories. **www.krausebooks.com**

# PATTERN SILHOUETTE Identification Guide

Depression-era glassware can be confusing. Many times a manufacturer came up with a neat new design and as soon as it was successful, other companies started to make patterns that were similar. To help you figure out what patteran you might be trying to research, here's a quick identification guide. The patterns are broken down into several different classifications by design elements.

### ART DECO

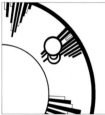

*Ovide*

### BASKETS

*Lorain*

### BEADED EDGES

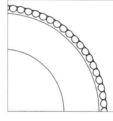

*Beaded Edge*

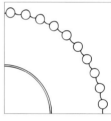

*Candlewick*

### BIRDS

*Delilah*

*Georgian*

*Parrot*

*Peacock & Wild Rose*

### BLOCKS

*Beaded Block*

*Colonial Block*

### BOWS

*Bowknot*

## COINS

## CUBES

*Coin*

*American*

*Cube*

## DIAMONDS

*Cape Cod*

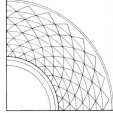

*Diamond Quilted*

*English Hobnail*

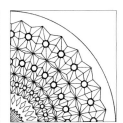

*Holiday*

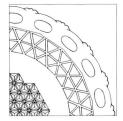

*Laced Edge*

*Miss America*

*Peanut Butter*

*Waterford*

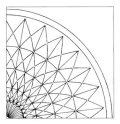

*Windsor*

## ELLIPSES (FANS)

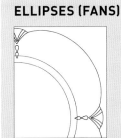

*Crow's Foot*

*Newport*

*Romanesque*

# G

GLASS

## FIGURES

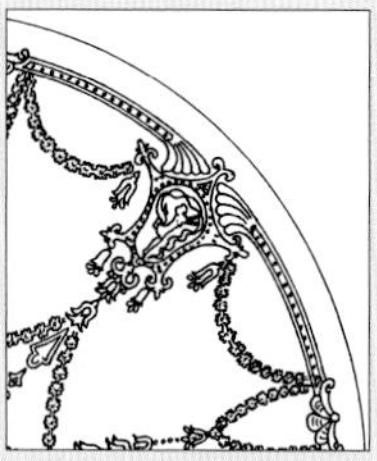

Cameo

Cupid

## FLORALS

Alice

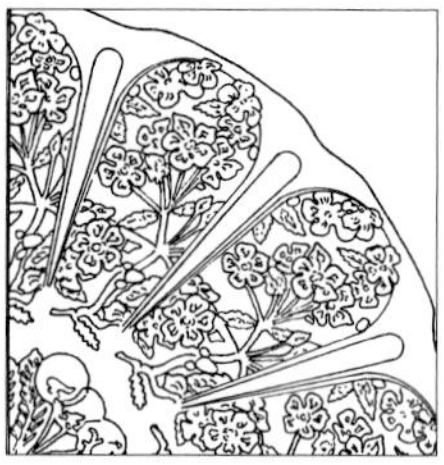

Cherry Blossom

Cloverleaf

Daisy

Dogwood

Doric

Doric & Pansy

Floragold

Floral

Floral and Diamond Band

Flower Garden with
Butterflies

Indiana Custard

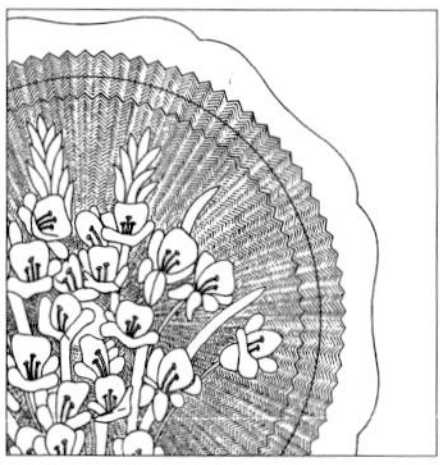

Iris

Jubilee

## FLORALS *continued*

*Mayfair (Federal)*

*Mayfair (Open Rose)*

*Normandie*

*Orange Blossom*

*Pineapple & Floral*

*Primrose*

*Rosemary*

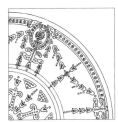
*Rose Cameo*

*Royal Lace*

*Seville*

*Sharon*

*Sunflower*

*Thistle*

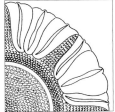
*Tulip*

*Vitrock*

*Wild Rose*

## FRUITS

Avocado

Cherryberry

Della Robbia

Fruits

Paneled Grape

Strawberry

## GEOMETIC & LINE DESIGNS

Cracked Ice

Cape Cod

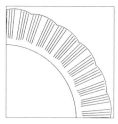
Cremax

Early American Prescut

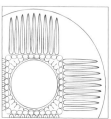
Park Avenue

Pioneer

Sierra

Star

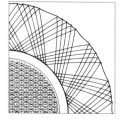
Starlight

Tea Room

## HONEYCOMB

*Aunt Polly*

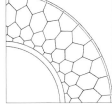

*Hex Optic*

## HORSESHOE

*Horseshoe*

## LEAVES

*Laurel Leaf*

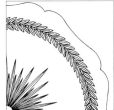

*Sunburst*

## LACY DESIGNS

*Harp*

*Heritage*

*S-Pattern*

*Sandwich (Duncan Miller)*

*Sandwich (Hocking)*

*Sandwich (Indiana)*

## LOOPS

*Christmas Candy*

*Crocheted Crystal*

*Pretzel*

## PETALS

*Aurora*

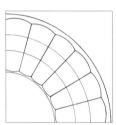
*Block Optic*

*Circle*

*Colonial*

*National*

*New Century*

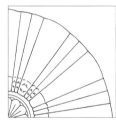
*Old Café*

*Ribbon*

*Roulette*

*Round Robin*

*Victory*

## PETALS/RIDGES WITH DIAMOND ACCENTS

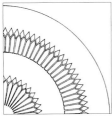

*Anniversary*

*Coronation*

*Fortune*

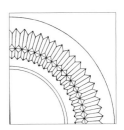

*Lincoln Inn*

*Petalware*

*Queen Mary*

## PLAIN

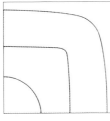

*Charm*

*Mt. Pleasant*

## PYRAMIDS

*Pyramid*

## RAISED BAND

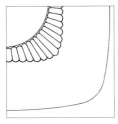

*Charm*

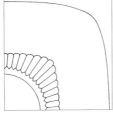

*Forest Green*

*Jane Ray*

*Royal Ruby*

## RAISED CIRCLES

*American Pioneer*

*Bubble*

*Columbia*

*Dewdrop*

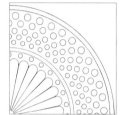

*Hobnail*

*Moonstone*

*Oyster & Pearl*

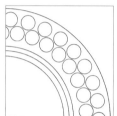

*Raindrops*

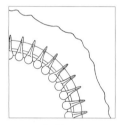

*Radiance*

*Ships*

*Teardrop*

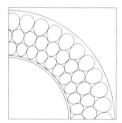

*Thumbprint*

## RIBS

*Homespun*

## RINGS (CIRCLES)

*Manhattan*

*Moderntone*

*Moondrops*

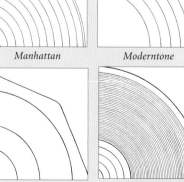

*Moroccan Amethyst*

*Old English*

*Ring*

## SCENES

*Chinex Classic*

*Lake Como*

## SCROLLING DESIGNS

*Adam*

*American Sweetheart*

*Florentine No. 1*

*Florentine No. 2*

*Madrid*

*Patrick*

*Philbe*

*Primo*

*Princess*

*Rock Crystal*

*Roxana*

*Vernon*

## SWIRLS

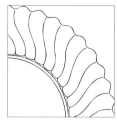

*Colony*

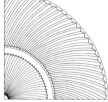

*Diana*

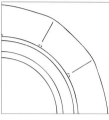

*Fairfax*

*Jamestown*

*Spiral*

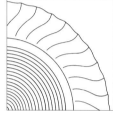

*Swirl*

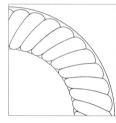

*Swirl (Fire King)*

*Twisted Optic*

## TEXTURED

*U.S. Swirl*

*By Cracky*

*Twiggy*

*Bowknot green cereal bowl.* **$30**

*Candlewick crystal wine glass.* **$25**

*By Cracky green candleholders, round base, pr.* **$10**

*Capri azure blue cup.* **$5**

*Cherry Blossom pink platter.* **$44**

*Crocheted Crystal candlesticks.* **$19.50**

*Crow's Foot 10 1/4"
ruby red vase.* **$70**

*Daisy amber cream soup bowl.* **$12.50**

*Dogwood thin pink creamer.* **$20** *Dogwood thin pink sugar.* **$20**

*Della Robbia luster stain water tumbler.* **$40**

*English Hobnail green candy dish.* **$50**

*Fairfax topaz footed creamer.* **$16** *Fairfax topaz footed sugar.* **$10**

*Floral and Diamond Band green berry bowl.* **$12**

*Floragold iridescent vase.* **$395**

*Florentine No. 2 yellow cup.* **$10**

*Flower Garden With Butterflies blue compote.* **$70**

*Homespun pink cereal bowl with handles.* **$42**

*American Pioneer green lamp.* **$115**

*Horseshoe green sugar bowl.* **$30**

*Laurel jade green dinner plate.* **$25**

*Mayfair Federal amber tumbler.* **$32.50**

*Madrid amber tumbler.* **$30**

*Mayfair Open Rose ice blue salt and pepper shakers.* **$295**

*Miss America green 6 1/4" diameter cereal bowl.* **$38**

*Moondrops red bowl with ruffled edge.* **$60**

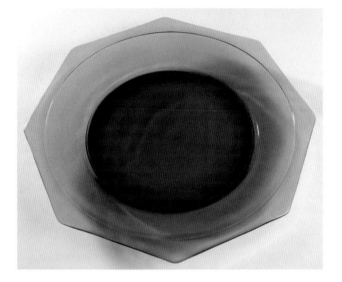

*Moroccan Amethyst 9 3/4" diameter dinner plate.* **$24**

*New Century cobalt blue tumbler.* **$30**

*Normandie amber salt and pepper shakers.* **$40**

*Old Colony pink cookie jar.* **$125**

*Paneled Grape white condiment set.* **$130**

*Peacock & Wild Rose green 12"
diameter cake plate.* **$195**

*Pineapple & Floral amber cream
soup bowl.* **$18.50**

*Princess green bowl.* **$60**

*Pyramid pink pitcher.* **$400**

*Radiance emerald green comport.* **$50**

*Rock Crystal red bowl with center
handle, silver overlay rim.* **$175**

*Rosemary pink berry bowl.* **$17.50**

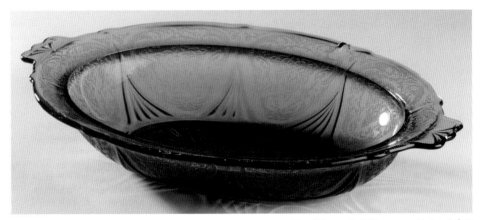

*Royal Lace cobalt blue vegetable bowl.* **$70**

*Sandwich, Hocking forest green juice tumbler.* **$8.50**

*Sharon amber candy dish.* **$30**

# Fenton Art Glass

The Fenton Art Glass Co. was founded in 1905 by Frank L. Fenton and his brother, John W., in Martins Ferry, Ohio. They initially sold hand-painted glass made by other manufacturers, but it wasn't long before they decided to produce their own glass.

The new Fenton factory in Williamstown, West Virginia opened on Jan. 2, 1907. From that point on, the company expanded by developing unusual colors and continued to decorate glassware in innovative ways. Two more brothers, James and Robert, joined the firm.

But despite the company's initial success, John W. left to establish the Millersburg Glass Co. of Millersburg, Ohio, in 1909. The first months of the new operation were devoted to the production of crystal glass only. Later iridized glass was called "Radium Glass." After only two years, Millersburg filed for bankruptcy.

Fenton's iridescent glass had a metallic luster over a colored, pressed pattern and was sold in dime stores. It was only after the sales of this glass decreased and it was sold in bulk as carnival prizes that it came to be known as carnival glass. Fenton became the top producer of carnival glass, with more than 150 patterns. The quality of the glass and its popularity with the public enabled the new company to be profitable through the late 1920s. As interest in carnival glass subsided, Fenton moved on to stretch glass and opalescent patterns. A line of colorful blown glass (called "off-hand" by Fenton) was also produced in the mid-1920s.

During the Great Depression, Fenton survived by producing functional colored glass tableware and other household items, including water sets, table sets, bowls, mugs, plates, perfume bottles, and vases.

Restrictions on European imports during World War II ushered in the arrival of Fenton's opaque colored glass, and the lines of "Crest" pieces soon followed.

In the 1950s, production continued to diversify with a focus on milk glass, particularly in Hobnail patterns.

In the third quarter of Fenton's history, the company returned

Courtesy of Randy Clark/
Dexter City Auction Gallery

▼ *Karnak red No. 3024 vase with applied Hanging Vine decoration, 18 1/2" high.* **$16,500**

Courtesy of Randy Clark/
Dexter City Auction Gallery

▲ *Lime opalescent rib optic ivy ball and black base, circa 1952.* **$220**

Courtesy of Randy Clark/
Dexter City Auction Gallery

◀ *Karnak red footed bowl with Hanging Vine decoration and random threading, cobalt blue edge and cobalt blue stem and foot, iridescent finish, mid-1920s, 8 1/2" diameter.* **$2,630**

to themes that had proved popular to preceding generations and began adding special lines, such as the Bicentennial series.

Innovations included the line of Colonial colors that debuted in 1963, including amber, blue, green, orange, and ruby. Based on a special order for an Ohio museum, Fenton in 1969 revisited its early success with "Original Formula Carnival Glass." Fenton also started marking its glass in the molds for the first time.

The star of the 1970s was the yellow and blushing pink creation known as Burmese, which remains popular today. This was followed closely by a menagerie of animals, birds, and children.

In 1975, Robert Barber was hired by Fenton to begin an artist-in-residence program, producing a limited line of art glass vases in a return to the off-hand, blown-glass creations of the mid-1920s.

Shopping at home via television was a phenomenon in the late 1980s when the "Birthstone Bears" became the first Fenton product to appear on QVC (established in 1986 by Joseph Segel, founder of The Franklin Mint).

In August 2007, Fenton discontinued all but a few of its more popular lines, and in 2011 ceased production entirely.

For more information on Fenton Art Glass, see *Warman's Fenton Glass Identification and Price Guide, 2nd edition,* by Mark F. Moran.

*See the "Carnival Glass" section for more information about Fenton.*

Courtesy of Randy Clark/Dexter City Auction Gallery

▶ *Robert Barber/Louise Piper black vase, signed "Robert Barber 1975" and "Hand Painted Louise Piper," 10 1/2" high.* **$440**

Courtesy of Randy Clark/Dexter City Auction Gallery

▶ FAR RIGHT *Mandarin red Peacock flared vase, circa early 1930s, 8" high.* **$220**

Courtesy of Randy Clark/Dexter City Auction Gallery

▲ *Flame No. 636 one-pound candy jar, circa 1926.* **$578**

Courtesy of Randy Clark/Dexter City Auction Gallery

▶ *Mosaic inlaid long oval comport with threading and applied cobalt blue foot and shiny iridescent finish, mid-1920s, 7" high.* **$2,310**

◄ *Rare ginger jar, royal blue cased with opaque periwinkle blue, crackle glass effect, circa 1935, with black base and cap.* **$1,980**

*Rare Amberina No. 222 ice tea set: pitcher with applied cobalt blue handle, four matching tumblers (one shown) and four cobalt blue coasters (one shown), circa mid-1920s.* **$2,750**

*Mosaic inlaid No. 3051 vase, ground and polished pontil, shiny finish, mid-1920s, 10 1/2" high.* **$2,750**

▶ *Victoria topaz Drapery Optic
ice tea pitcher with applied topaz
handle, circa mid-1920s.* **$1,320**

▲ *Pulled Feather offhand vase in
rainbow colors, Fenton oval logo
on underside, designed by Robert
Barber, circa 1975, 7 1/4" high.*
**$880**

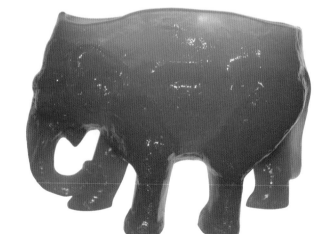

▶ *Jade green elephant planter,
circa 1930.* **$4,950**

◀ *Milk glass Silver Crest tri-crimped
vase with hand-painted bluebirds
and tree branches, signed "Fenton
Hand Painted By Louise Piper Oct.
1976," 7 1/2" high.* **$275**

▶ *Turquoise vase with applied
Hanging Vine decoration, mid-
1920s, 11" high.* **$2,750**

◀ *Mongolian green Dancing
Ladies vase, eight-point crimp,
circa 1933.* **$715**

Courtesy of Randy Clark/
Dexter City Auction Gallery

▲ *Mandarin
red No. 1093
Basketweave Open
Edge vase, circa
1933, 5 1/2" high.*
**$935**

Courtesy of Randy Clark/Dexter
City Auction Gallery

▶ *Milk glass No. 5156
fish vase, black eyes/tail,
designed by Stan Fistick,
circa 1953.* **$495**

Courtesy of Randy Clark/
Dexter City Auction Gallery

▲ *Rare periwinkle
blue Chanticleer,
circa 2004.* **$605**

Courtesy of Randy Clark/
Dexter City Auction Gallery

▶ *Flame candlestick
with royal blue foot,
circa 1925, 8 1/2" high.*
**$1,540**

Courtesy of Randy Clark/
Dexter City Auction Gallery

▶ *Green turtle base
and green opalescent
Buttons/Braids pattern
aquarium bowl, circa
1928.* **$1,760**

◄ *Satin finished Favrene tall vase with sand-carved motif, inscribed "Fenton National Sales Meeting 2004," 11" high.* **$220**

◄ *Dark green Snowcrest flowerpot and saucer, circa 1952.* **$83**

▲ *Rare light antique green 12" candlestick with pulled feather decoration, cobalt blue candle cup and cobalt blue foot, mid-1920s.* **$3,850**

▶ *Amberina Grape and Cable pattern bowl, Persian Medallion pattern interior, circa late 1920s.* **$605**

Courtesy of Randy Clark/Dexter City Auction Gallery

◄ *Mulberry Diamond Optic pitcher and matching tumbler, circa 1942.* **$358**

Courtesy of Randy Clark/Dexter City Auction Gallery

▼ *Cranberry opalescent Coin Dot two-handled vase, circa 1948, 11" high.* **$303**

Courtesy of Randy Clark/Dexter City Auction Gallery

◄ *Plated Amberina satin finished courting lamp, circa 1962.* **$303**

Courtesy of Randy Clark/Dexter City Auction Gallery

◀ *Moonstone vase with hand-painted Oriental-style decoration by decorating foreman Otto Goertler, five-toed black base, circa 1933, 6 1/2" high.* **$248**

Courtesy of Randy Clark/Dexter City Auction Gallery

▼ *Goldenrod Teardrop condiment set, circa 1956.* **$2,310**

Courtesy of Randy Clark/Dexter City Auction Gallery

◀ *Flame Grape and Cable pattern crimped bowl, circa 1925, 10 1/2" diameter.* **$2,750**

# Lalique

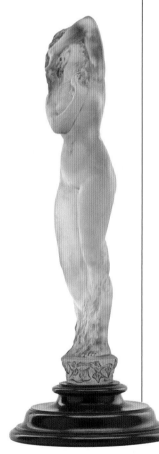

*Grande Nue Socle Lierre statuette, frosted glass with brown patina on wood base, circa 1919, etched "R. Lalique France no. 836," 16 1/4" x 6 1/4".* **$17,500**

René Jules Lalique was born on April 6, 1860, in the village of Ay, in the Champagne region of France. In 1862, his family moved to the suburbs of Paris.

In 1872, Lalique began attending College Turgot where he began studying drawing with Justin-Marie Lequien. After the death of his father in 1876, Lalique began working as an apprentice to Louis Aucoc, who was a prominent jeweler and goldsmith in Paris.

Lalique moved to London in 1878 to continue his studies. He spent two years attending Sydenham College, developing his graphic design skills. He returned to Paris in 1880 and worked as an illustrator of jewelry, creating designs for Cartier, among others. In 1884, Lalique's drawings were displayed at the National Exhibition of Industrial Arts, organized at the Louvre.

At the end of 1885, Lalique took over Jules Destapes' jewelry workshop. Lalique's design began to incorporate translucent enamels, semiprecious stones, ivory, and hard stones. In 1889, at the Universal Exhibition in Paris, the jewelry firms of Vever and Boucheron included collaborative works by Lalique in their displays.

In the early 1890s, Lalique began to incorporate glass into his jewelry, and in 1893 he took part in a competition organized by the Union Centrale des Arts Decoratifs to design a drinking vessel. He won second prize.

Lalique opened his first Paris retail shop in 1905, near the perfume business of François Coty. Coty commissioned Lalique to design his perfume labels in 1907, and he also created his first perfume bottles for Coty.

In the first decade of the 20th century, Lalique continued to experiment with glass manufacturing techniques, and mounted his first show devoted entirely to glass in 1911.

During World War I, Lalique's first factory was forced to close, but the construction of a new factory was soon begun in Wingen-sur-Moder, in the Alsace region. It was completed in 1921, and still produces Lalique crystal today.

In 1925, Lalique designed the first car mascot (hood ornament) for Citroën, the French automobile company. For the

next six years, Lalique would design 29 models for companies such as Bentley, Bugatti, Delage, Hispano-Suiza, Rolls Royce, and Voisin.

Lalique's second boutique opened in 1931, and this location continues to serve as the main Lalique showroom today.

René Lalique died on May 5, 1945, at the age of 85. His son, Marc, took over the business at that time, and when Marc died in 1977, his daughter, Marie-Claude Lalique Dedouvre, assumed control of the company. She sold her interest in the firm and retired in 1994.

For more information on Lalique, see *Warman's Lalique Identification and Price Guide* by Mark F. Moran.

Courtesy of James D. Julia Auctioneers, Fairfield, Maine, www.jamesdjulia.com

▲ *Mascot in Victoire pattern in light amethyst tinted glass with frosted head and neck and clear headdress, signed on side in raised block letters "R. Lalique," contemporary stand marked "Breves Galleries Knightsbridge S.W.3 Pat. No. 309301," very good to excellent condition, 10" long x 8 7/8" high in stand.* **$23,700**

Courtesy of Rago Arts

▲ *Rare perfume bottle "Leurs Ames" for D'Orsay, designed 1913, molded "LALIQUE," etched "France," 5" x 4 1/4".* **$9,375**

Courtesy of Rago Arts

▲ UPPER RIGHT *Formose vase, cased gray glass, designed 1924, impressed "R. LALIQUE," etched "France, no. 934," 6 3/4" x 6 1/2".* **$8,125**

Courtesy of James D. Julia Auctioneers, Fairfield, Maine, www.jamesdjulia.com

▶ *Chrysis mascot shading from amethyst at base to light blue at head and hair, signed on underside in etched block letters "R. Lalique France," silver-plated stand, very good to excellent condition, mascot 5 1/2" high, 7" high with stand.* **$5,000-$7,000**

◄ *Bacchantes vase with opalescent nude women set against textured clear glass background with gray patination, signed on underside with engraved block letters "R. Lalique France," very good to excellent condition with two fleabites to inside lip, 9 7/8" high.* **$27,848**

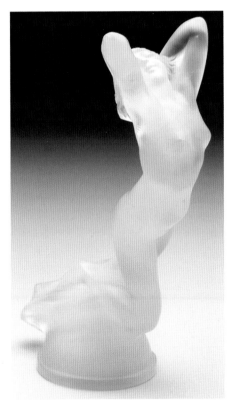

*Vittesse mascot in opalescent glass, nude figure of woman with head thrown back, signed on side "R. Lalique" in raised block letters, very good to excellent condition, 7 1/8" high.* **$17,775**

*Coq Nain mascot in form of rooster with tail raised high in green glass, signed on underside in etched block letters "R. Lalique France," contemporary stand marked "Breves Galleries Knightsbridge S.W.3 Pat. No. 309301," very good to excellent condition with one fleabite on edge of top tail feather, mascot 8 1/4" high, 11 1/2" high with stand.* **$5,000-$7,000**

Courtesy of Rago Arts

*Archers vase, amber glass with white patina, designed 1921, etched at shoulder "R. LALIQUE FRANCE," 10 1/2" x 9".* **$11,250**

Courtesy of James D. Julia Auctioneers, Fairfield, Maine, www.jamesdjulia.com

*Levrier mascot in amethyst tinted glass with impressed frosted running greyhound and signed in raised block letters "R. Lalique France," contemporary stand marked "Breves Galleries Knightsbridge S.W.3 Pat. No 309301," very good to excellent condition, 7 3/4" long x 6 1/4" high in stand.* **$15,000-$20,000**

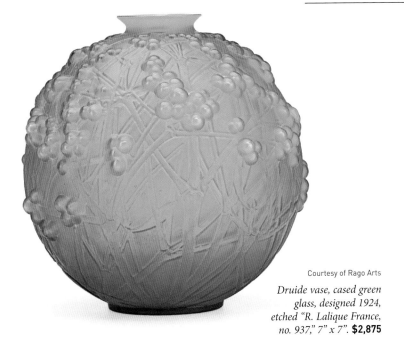

Courtesy of Rago Arts

*Druide vase, cased green glass, designed 1924, etched "R. Lalique France, no. 937," 7" x 7".* **$2,875**

Courtesy of James D. Julia Auctioneers, Fairfield, Maine, www.jamesdjulia.com

*Libellule mascot of perched dragonfly with folded wings, frosted body, clear wings with frosted texture, contemporary chrome stand marked "Breves Galleries Knightsbridge S.W.3 Pat. No. 309301," very good to excellent condition, 6 1/4" long x 4" high, including stand.* **$7,110**

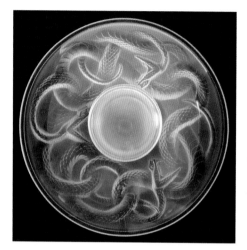

Courtesy of James D. Julia Auctioneers, Fairfield, Maine, www.jamesdjulia.com

*Inkwell impressed with entwined serpents, original domed glass lid, light brown patination, signed on side with engraved block letters "R. Lalique," very good to excellent condition with slight roughness to bottom inside edge of foot, 6 1/4" diameter.* **$9,113**

Courtesy of James D. Julia Auctioneers, Fairfield, Maine, www.jamesdjulia.com

*Hirondelle mascot in form of swallow made of amethyst tinted glass in contemporary stand, mascot marked "R. Lalique" in raised block letters and stand marked "Breves Galleries Knightsbridge S.W.3 Pat. No. 309301," very good to excellent condition, 9 1/4" high including stand.* **$5,000-$7,000**

Courtesy of James D. Julia Auctioneers, Fairfield, Maine, www.jamesdjulia.com

◄ *Cinq Chevaux mascot, rare, five rearing horses in amethyst tinted glass, signed on side below tail with raised block letters "R. Lalique" and engraved block letters "France," contemporary stand, very good to excellent condition, 9" high in stand.* **$15,000-20,000**

Courtesy of James D. Julia Auctioneers, Fairfield, Maine, www.jamesdjulia.com

▲ *Rare Chrysis mascot in fiery opalescent glass, signed on base with engraved block letters "R. Lalique France," in contemporary holder marked "Breves Galleries Knightsbridge S.W.3 Pat. No. 309301," very good to excellent condition, figure 5" high, 9" high with stand.* **$41,000**

Courtesy of Rago Arts

▲ *Gaillon plafonnier, frosted and patinated glass, circa 1927, engraved "R. LALIQUE," glass only 5" x 17 3/4" diameter.* **$4,375**

Courtesy of Rago Arts

▶ *Sophora vase, amber glass, designed 1926, etched "R. Lalique France," 10 1/2" x 10 1/4".* **$6,250**

◄ *Mascot impressed with frosted archer within clear glass disc, signed on side with engraved block letters "R. Lalique France," contemporary stand marked "Breves Galleries Knightsbridge S.W.3 Pat. No. 309301," very good to excellent condition, mascot 4 3/4" high, 8" high with stand.* **$2,000-$3,000**

▼ *Malesherbes vase, amber glass with white patina, designed 1927, etched "R. Lalique France no. 1014," 9" x 7".* **$5,625**

*Formose vase, cased gray glass, designed 1924, molded "R. LALIQUE," 7" x 6 1/2".* **$8,125**

Courtesy of Rago Arts

◄ *Le Baiser du Faune perfume bottle with original presentation box, for Molinard, Paris, France, circa 1928, molded "R. LALIQUE," base etched "MOLINARD/PARIS FRANCE," box with gilded Molinard insignia, bottle 5 3/4" x 4 1/4" x 1", box 7 1/2" high.* **$5,313**

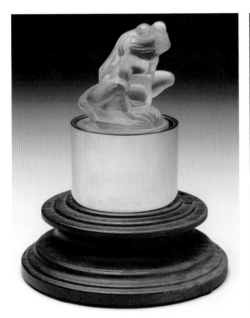

Courtesy of James D. Julia Auctioneers, Fairfield, Maine, www.jamesdjulia.com

*Grenouille mascot in form of frog in light amethyst tinted glass and signed on edge of foot with etched script signature "R. Lalique France," contemporary stand marked "Breves Galleries Knightsbridge S.W.3 Pat. No. 309301," very good to excellent condition, mascot 2 1/2" high, 5 1/2" high with stand.* **$12,000-$15,000**

Courtesy of James D. Julia Auctioneers, Fairfield, Maine, www.jamesdjulia.com

*Pintade mascot in form of Guinea hen in amethyst glass and signed with engraved block letters below tail "R. Lalique France," contemporary stand marked "Breves Galleries Knightsbridge S.W.3 Pat. No. 309301," very good to excellent condition, small scuff mark on top of glass base, 7 1/4" high including stand.* **$9,480**

# Quezal

The Quezal Art Glass Decorating Co., named for the quetzal – a bird with brilliantly colored feathers found in tropical regions of the Americas – was organized in 1901 in Brooklyn, New York, by Martin Bach and Thomas Johnson, two disgruntled Tiffany workers. They soon hired Percy Britton and William Wiedebine, two more former Tiffany employees. The first products, unmarked, were exact Tiffany imitations.

Quezal pieces differ from Tiffany pieces in that they are more defined and the decorations are more visible and brighter. No new techniques were developed by Quezal.

Johnson left in 1905. T. Conrad Vahlsing, Bach's son-in-law, joined the firm in 1918, but left with Paul Frank in 1920 to form Lustre Art Glass Co., which in turn copied Quezal pieces. Martin Bach died in 1924, and by 1925, Quezal had ceased operations.

The "Quezal" trademark was first used in 1902 and was placed on the base of vases and bowls and the rims of shades. The acid-etched or engraved letters vary in size and may be found in amber, black, or gold. A printed label that includes an illustration of a quetzal was used briefly in 1907.

Courtesy of James D. Julia Auctioneers, Fairfield, Maine, www.jamesdjulia.com

*Three shades with green pulled feather design descending from lip against cream-colored, lightly iridescent background, interior in gold iridescence, signed in fitter rim "Quezal," very good to excellent condition, 6 1/4" high.*
**$593**

Courtesy of James D. Julia Auctioneers, Fairfield, Maine, www.jamesdjulia.com

*Shades with gold double pulled feather design encircling white iridescent body, interior in gold iridescence, each signed on fitter "Quezal," each shade with minor flakes to fitter, 4 3/4" high.* **$474**

Courtesy of James D. Julia Auctioneers, Fairfield, Maine, www.jamesdjulia.com

*Three-sided flowerform vase with green pulled feather design ascending from foot, each pulled feather outlined in gold iridescence and set against white background, yellow interior, signed on underside "Quezal," very good to excellent condition, 10" high.* **$2,074**

Courtesy of James D. Julia Auctioneers, Fairfield, Maine, www.jamesdjulia.com

*Compote with white pulled feather design on exterior against white opalescent background, interior in gold iridescence with stretched rim, applied inverted saucer foot with white pulled feather design and blue iridescent zipper design against slightly iridescent clear shading to opalescent background, signed in polished pontil "Quezal P 523," very good to excellent condition, 6 1/4" high.* **$1,896**

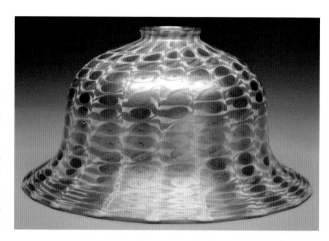

*Helmet shade with gold iridescent fishnet design against cream-colored background with platinum iridescent zipper design running vertically over fishnet, interior in gold iridescence, signed on inside of fitter "Quezal," very good to excellent condition, 10 1/4" diameter, 2 1/4" fitter.* **$2,133**

*Covered jar with orange/gold iridescent finish on body and lid with three applied gold iridescent loop feet, signed in polished pontil "Quezal," very good to excellent condition, 12" high.* **$1,701**

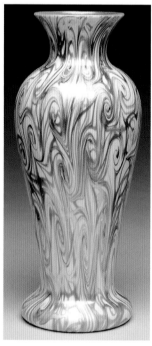

*Vase with blue and gold iridescent King Tut design against white background, interior of mouth in gold iridescence, signed in polished pontil "Quezal," very good to excellent condition, 12 3/4" high.* **$2,074**

*Vase with gold iridescent hooked feather design extending upward from foot against white background, neck and lip of vase finished in gold iridescence and end with green iridescent hooked outline at shoulder, interior of mouth in gold iridescence, signed in polished pontil "Quezal C276," very good to excellent condition, 11" high.* **$2,963**

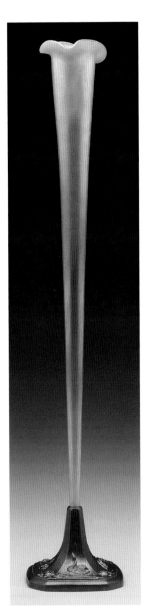

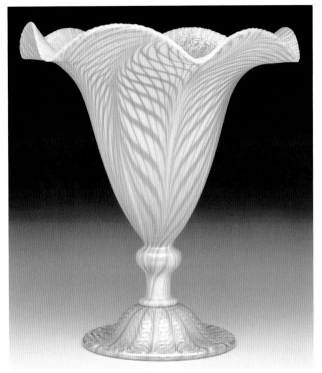

Courtesy of James D. Julia Auctioneers, Fairfield, Maine, www.jamesdjulia.com

*Vase with green pulled feather design covering body set against cream-colored background, applied inverted saucer foot with matching pulled feather design and gold iridescent zipper decoration, interior with gold iridescence with stretched rim and pink highlights, signed on underside "Quezal M 792," very good to excellent condition, 8 1/2" high.* **$2,370**

Courtesy of James D. Julia Auctioneers, Fairfield, Maine, www.jamesdjulia.com

*Tall slender lily vase with ruffled and rolled rim with gold iridescence showing bands of pink, blue and green highlights, signed on bottom side "Quezal," cast bronze foot with swans and pond lilies surrounding bottom, foot unsigned, very good to excellent condition, 20" high.* **$668**

Courtesy of James D. Julia Auctioneers, Fairfield, Maine, www.jamesdjulia.com

*Helmet shade with white pulled feather design descending from fitter rim against gold iridescent background, each feather outlined in green, interior in gold iridescence with stretched rim, signed on inside of fitter "Quezal," very good to excellent condition, 10 1/4" diameter.* **$1,896**

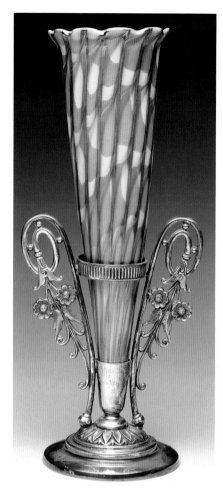

Courtesy of James D. Julia Auctioneers,
Fairfield, Maine, www.jamesdjulia.com

*Mantel lamps with shades decorated with gold iridescent fishnet design against cream-colored background, sterling silver circular stepped foot finished with sterling silver lip stamped "Sterling," very good to excellent condition, each 7 1/2" high.* **$1,067**

Courtesy of James D. Julia Auctioneers, Fairfield, Maine,
www.jamesdjulia.com

*Vase decorated with green and gold iridescent random pattern against light green background, interior in gold iridescence, silver-plated holder with floral design handles, vase marked on side at bottom "Quezal," holder marked "James W. Tufts Boston Quadruple Plate," very good condition, 8 1/2" high.* **$2,066**

Courtesy of James D. Julia Auctioneers,
Fairfield, Maine, www.jamesdjulia.com

*Five matching shades with gold iridescent pulled feather design descending from fitter against white iridescent background, signed on fitter "Quezal," very good to excellent condition, 6" high.* **$889**

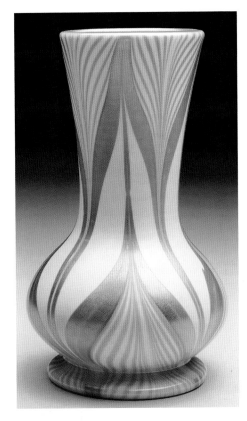

◄ *Vase with alternating green pulled feather design ascending from foot and descending from lip, each feather outlined in gold iridescence and set against cream-colored background, interior with gold/orange iridescence, signed in polished pontil "Quezal," very good to excellent condition, 6" high.* **$889**

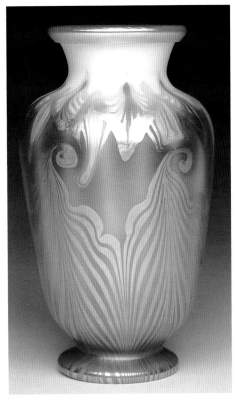

*Vase with platinum iridescent hooked feather design extending upward from foot against green shaded background, shading to gold iridescent pulled feather design at shoulder against white neck with applied gold iridescent lip, signed in polished pontil "Quezal C937," very good to excellent condition, 5 1/4" high.* **$3,555**

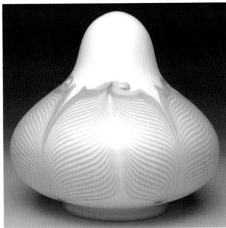

*Shade with green hooked feather decoration surrounding shoulder against white background, each feather outlined in gold iridescence, shade signed on inside of fitter "Quezal," very good to excellent condition, 8 1/2" high x 9" diameter, 5" fitter.* **$1,422**

Courtesy of James D. Julia Auctioneers, Fairfield, Maine, www.jamesdjulia.com

*Five shades with white fishnet pattern against gold iridescent background and gold iridescent zipper pattern, each shade with blue and purple flashes in iridescence, each signed in fitter "Quezal," very good to excellent condition, each shade 5 1/4" high, four shades with 2 1/4" fitters and one with 3 1/4" fitter.* **$1,185**

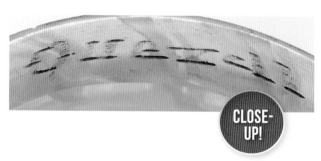

CLOSE-UP!

*Four shades with cream-colored pulled feather design descending from fitter against gold iridescent background with pink, blue and green highlights, interior in gold iridescence with green and pink highlights, all shades signed on inside of fitter "Quezal," very good to excellent condition, 5 3/8" high, 2 1/4" fitter.* **$770**

*Four pulled feather shades, two Quezal shades with green pulled feather design ascending from lip with gold iridescent outline set against white, lightly iridescent background, interior with gold iridescence, signed on fitter "Quezal"; pair of tall shades with tapered body and ruffled lip, each shade with green pulled feather decoration descending from lip with gold iridescent outline against white, lightly iridescent background and gold iridescent interior, unsigned; all very good to excellent condition, 5" and 7" high, respectively.* **$948**

Courtesy of Thomaston Place
Auction Galleries

*Feather-dragged shades
in white over celery green
with golden interior,
notched rim, signed, 5"
high, fits 2 1/4" ring.* **$374**

CLOSE-
UP!

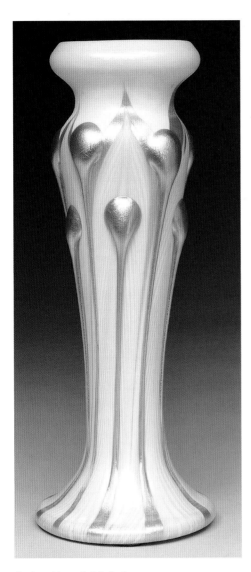

Courtesy of James D. Julia Auctioneers,
Fairfield, Maine, www.jamesdjulia.com

*Hanging lamps with bronze ceiling caps with single turned stem leading to flowerform shade holders that house long flaring vertically ribs, shades with gold iridescent hooked feather design descending from fitter against cream-colored background, each shade finished in interior with light gold iridescence and signed on inside of fitter "Quezal," brown-shaded patina, unsigned, one shade with long tight hairline in fitter, otherwise very good to excellent condition, shades 7 3/4" long, with hangers 21" long.* **$4,740**

Courtesy of James D. Julia Auctioneers,
Fairfield, Maine, www.jamesdjulia.com

*Art glass vase attributed to Quezal, green pulled feather design extending upward from foot against white slightly iridescent background, each pulled feather outlined in bright gold iridescence, vase finished with two vertical rows of applied gold iridescent tendrils, unsigned, very good to excellent condition, 10" high.* **$3,555**

# Tiffany Glass

Tiffany & Co. was founded by Charles Lewis Tiffany (1812-1902) and Teddy Young in New York City in 1837 as a "stationery and fancy goods emporium." The store initially sold a wide variety of stationery items, and operated as Tiffany, Young and Ellis in lower Manhattan. The name was shortened to Tiffany & Co. in 1853, and the firm's emphasis on jewelry was established.

The first Tiffany catalog, known as the "Blue Book," was published in 1845. It is still being published today.

In 1862 Tiffany & Co. supplied the Union Army with swords, flags and surgical implements.

Charles' son, Louis Comfort Tiffany (1848-1933), was an American artist and designer who worked in the decorative arts and is best known for his work in stained glass. Louis established Tiffany Glass Co. in 1885, and in 1902 it became known as Tiffany Studios. America's outstanding glass designer of the Art Nouveau period produced glass from the last quarter of the 19th century until the early 1930s. Tiffany revived early techniques and devised many new ones.

*More information on Tiffany is located in "Lamps & Lighting."*

Courtesy of James D. Julia Auctioneers, Fairfield, Maine, www.jamesdjulia.com

*Favrile center bowl with green leaf and vine design in interior, green leaves intaglio carved, decoration set against gold iridescence with pink and green highlights, bowl finished with gold iridescent double row flower frog insert and signed on underside "6354L L.C. Tiffany Favrile," frog signed "9894K L.C. Tiffany Favrile," very good to excellent condition, bowl 12 1/2" diameter.* **$3,555**

*Two candelabras with jeweled feet and stylized leaf design leading to four curved arms supporting reticulated glass candle cups with bobeches, bronze with reddish-brown patina with green highlights, one candelabra signed on underside "Tiffany Studios New York 22324" with Tiffany Glass & Decorating logo, other signed "Tiffany Studios New York D886" with Tiffany Glass & Decorating logo, very good to excellent condition, 12" high.* **$4,010**

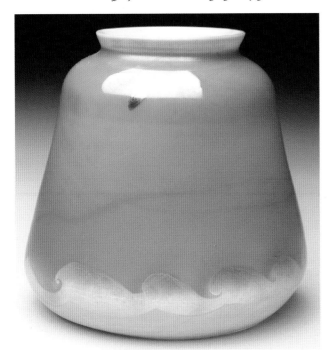

▲ *Rare art glass shade with varying gold iridescent finish with Cypriot texture, iridescence with red, green and blue highlights, signed on fitter rim L.C.T., very good to excellent condition, 4 1/4" high, 2 1/4" fitter.* **$2,489**

*Shade with green slightly iridescent body with gold iridescent wave design near lip that borders white area at lip, shade unsigned, very good to excellent condition with small bruise on interior of fitter rim, 4 1/4" high, 2 1/4" fitter.* **$1,067**

Courtesy of James D. Julia Auctioneers, Fairfield, Maine, www.jamesdjulia.com

*Rare vase with black iridescent background with light gold iridescent wavy and entwined band encircling shoulder, signed on underside "L.C. Tiffany O588 Favrile," very good to excellent condition, 3 1/2" high x 4 1/2" diameter.* **$3,022**

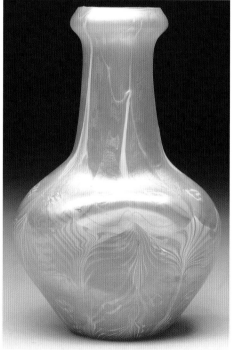

Courtesy of James D. Julia Auctioneers, Fairfield, Maine, www.jamesdjulia.com

*Monumental vase with gold iridescent body shading to blue at shoulder, blue and green iridescent swirling lines and green leaf and vine pattern descending from lip, blue iridescence at top with purple flashes, gold iridescence at bottom with pink highlights, interior with iridescent exterior atop amber glass body shading to red at top, signed in polished pontil "Louis C. Tiffany 0454" with remnants of original paper label with Tiffany Glass & Decorating Co. logo, very good to excellent condition, 19" high.* **$18,664**

Courtesy of James D. Julia Auctioneers, Fairfield, Maine, www.jamesdjulia.com

*Vase with bulbous body with dimpled front and back, random pulled feather design extending from foot to neck, gold iridescent zipper pattern, amber yellow glass background with light iridescence, signed on underside "L.C.T. A1513," very good to excellent condition, 9 1/8" high.* **$4,740**

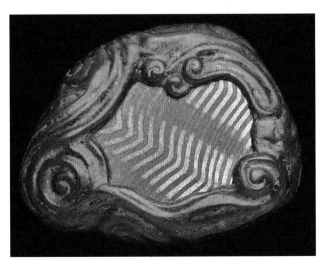

Courtesy of James D. Julia Auctioneers, Fairfield, Maine, www.jamesdjulia.com

▲ *Four wine glasses with opalescent inverted saucer foot, clear stem and pastel lavender bowls with vertical bands of white opalescence and white opalescent lip, each wine signed "LC Tiffany Favrile," very good to excellent condition, 7 3/4" high.* **$2,248**

Courtesy of James D. Julia Auctioneers, Fairfield, Maine, www.jamesdjulia.com

◄ *Rare inkwell with wide squat body with impressed waves with koi swimming among waves, brown patina with green highlights, signed on underside "Tiffany Studios New York 854," very good to excellent condition, missing original insert, small blue iridescent insert glued into opening as replacement, small professional repair on lip beneath lid, 7" diameter x 3 3/4" high.* **$3,555**

Courtesy of James D. Julia Auctioneers, Fairfield, Maine, www.jamesdjulia.com

◄ *Paperweight with bronze wave design frame encircling decorated green Favrile glass center with iridescent wavy lines in platinum to purple against green background, bronze with brown patina with green highlights, signed on underside "Tiffany Studios New York 932" with Tiffany Glass & Decorating Co. logo, very good to excellent condition, 3 5/8" long x 2 3/4" wide.* **$3,555**

Courtesy of James D. Julia Auctioneers, Fairfield, Maine, www.jamesdjulia.com

*Large flower form vase with translucent pulled feather design ascending from foot and terminating at flaring shoulder near top of vase, finished on top with slightly ribbed mouth and white lightly iridescent finish, mounted in cast bronze foot with stylized fleur-de-lis design, signed on underside "Louis C. Tiffany Furnaces, Inc. Favrile 500," very good to excellent condition, 14 1/2" high.* **$11,850**

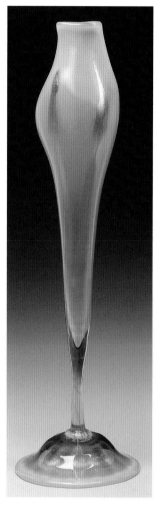

Courtesy of James D. Julia Auctioneers, Fairfield, Maine, www.jamesdjulia.com

*Large calyx vase with inverted saucer foot with opalescent rim and iridescent interior with blue, green, and purple highlights, foot supports translucent green stem leading to calyx form vase, gold iridescent pulled feather design against lightly iridescent background, translucent green lip, signed on underside "L.C.T. W2041," very good to excellent condition, 19 1/2" high.* **$11,850**

Courtesy of James D. Julia Auctioneers, Fairfield, Maine, www.jamesdjulia.com

*Rare candlestick with three bronze legs with cat's paw feet atop bronze disc, mounted with center gold Favrile body and candle cup, candlestick topped with gold Favrile shade with vertically ribbed body, iridescence on shade and candle cup with platinum highlights, shade signed on inside of fitter rim "L.C.T." and candlestick signed on underside "Tiffany Studios New York 1218," 15 3/4" to top of shade.* **$11,850**

◄ *Large bowl with swirled blue iridescent body with black iridescent swirling bands encircling body, interior in blue iridescence with purple highlights at bottom, signed on underside "Louis C. Tiffany R4424," very good to excellent condition with two open bubbles on shoulder from making, 7" high x 9 1/2" diameter.* **$4,444**

*Grapevine thermometer with acid-etched design with double row of beaded trim backed with brown, blue, green and purple glass, brown patina and strong green highlights, signed on backside with small applied tag "Tiffany Studios New York," very good to excellent condition, 3 3/4" x 8 1/4".* **$2,133**

*Decanter with gold iridescent finish and red and green highlights, original stopper, six shot glasses with gold iridescence with pink and green highlights, decanter signed "L.C. Tiffany Favrile," one shot glass signed "L.C.T. Favrile," others signed "L.C.T.," three numbered, very good to excellent condition, decanter 11 1/2" high, shot glasses 1 3/4" high.* **$2,430**

Courtesy of James D. Julia Auctioneers, Fairfield, Maine, www.jamesdjulia.com

▶ *Shade with gold iridescent pulled leaf design descending from fitter, background shading from orange to tan with light iridescence, shade signed on inside of fitter "L.C.T.," minor flake to fitter rim, 3 3/4" high x 5 1/2" diameter.* **$1,126**

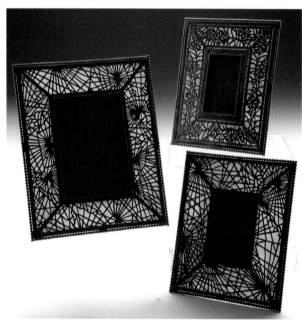

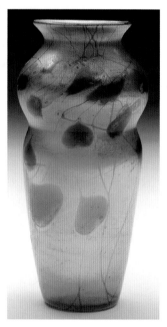

Courtesy of James D. Julia Auctioneers, Fairfield, Maine, www.jamesdjulia.com

*Three etched metal picture frames, two in pine needle pattern, one in flowering vine pattern, each frame with brown patina and green highlights, all patterns backed by green slag glass, largest frame signed "Tiffany Studios New York 947," smaller pine needle pattern frame signed "Tiffany Studios New York 948," flowering vine pattern frame signed "Tiffany Studios New York" with no number, very good to excellent condition, large pine needle 8" x 9 1/2" with 4" x 5 1/2" opening, small pine needle 6 1/2" x 7 1/2" with 2 1/4" x 3 1/4" opening, flowering vine 6 1/4" x 7 1/2" with 2 1/4" x 3 1/4" opening.* **$2,666**

Courtesy of James D. Julia Auctioneers, Fairfield, Maine, www.jamesdjulia.com

*Vase with green heart and vine decoration against gold iridescent background, sprays of white millefiori flowers encircling shoulder, signed on underside "L.C. Tiffany Favrile 6921A," very good condition with scuff mark encircling side of vase, 6" high.* **$3,555**

Courtesy of James D. Julia Auctioneers, Fairfield, Maine, www.jamesdjulia.com

*Three Byzantine desk pieces, stamp box, letter scale, and ashtray, letter scale and stamp box inset with gold Favrile glass, stamp box marked "Tiffany Studios New York," letter scale stamped "Tiffany Studios New York 870," ashtray not marked, overall very good condition, stamp box missing its four ball feet, ashtray 4 1/4" x 2 3/4".* **$3,645**

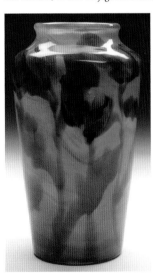

Courtesy of James D. Julia Auctioneers, Fairfield, Maine, www.jamesdjulia.com

▲ *Favrile vase with allover flower design with green stems and leaves and orange poppies against translucent, slightly iridescent paperweight background, signed on underside "LC Tiffany Favrile 3518L," drilled, tight hairline extends from drill hole up side of vase terminating below neck, 9 1/2" high.* **$2,370**

Courtesy James D. Julia Auctioneers, Fairfield, Maine, www.jamesdjulia.com

◀ *Vase with blue iridescent heart and vine decoration against bronze iridescent shading to green swirled background, purple and green highlights, silver collar of grape leaves and grape clusters, vase signed on underside with original paper label "Tiffany Favrile Glass Registered Trademark" with Tiffany Glass & Decorating Co. logo, silver collar signed "Tiffany & Co. Makers Sterling Silver C," very good to excellent condition, 14 1/2" high.* **$25,478**

Courtesy of James D. Julia Auctioneers, Fairfield, Maine, www.jamesdjulia.com

*Monumental Favrile vase with blue iridescence shading to gold at top, signed on underside "L.C. Tiffany Favrile 4454H," very good to excellent condition, 17" high. Provenance: Edward C. Moore family, Paris through Millon & Associe. The vase was a gift from Louis Comfort Tiffany to Moore, circa 1890, who became manager and artistic director of Tiffany & Co. in 1868.* **$9,480**

Courtesy of James D. Julia Auctioneers, Fairfield, Maine, www.jamesdjulia.com

*Cabinet vase with red slightly iridescent body with blue iridescent pulled leaf design zigzagging around body, signed on underside "L.C.T. 8043A," very good to excellent condition, 3 1/4" high.* **$5,333**

Courtesy of Rago Arts

▶ *Rare scarab inkwell, 1900s, patinated bronze, Favrile glass, clear glass, stamped "TIFFANY STUDIOS NEW YORK 1501," 2 1/4" x 3 1/2".* **$25,000**

Courtesy of James D. Julia Auctioneers, Fairfield, Maine, www.jamesdjulia.com

*Vase with white iridescent hooked feather design encircling shoulder, feathers outlined in gold iridescence with gold iridescent slender lines extending to lip against blue iridescent background, finished on bottom half in blue iridescence with darker blue iridescent pulled lines surrounding vase, signed on underside, "L.C. Tiffany Favrile, 1329H," very good to excellent condition, 6 1/2" high.* **$5,036**

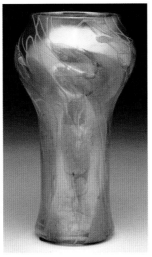

Courtesy of James D. Julia Auctioneers, Fairfield, Maine, www.jamesdjulia.com

*Rare paperweight vase with red and white nasturtiums against translucent iridescent background with purple highlights, signed on underside "LCT R2058," tight hairline at bottom edge of foot, 10 1/4" high.* **$4,148**

Courtesy of James D. Julia Auctioneers, Fairfield, Maine, www.jamesdjulia.com

*Flower form vase with decorated inverted saucer foot with green pulled feathers and gold iridescence with red, blue and green, foot supports applied to translucent green stem leading to orange iridescent bowl with green pulled feather design, signed on underside "L.C.T. O1965," very good to excellent condition with some dark inclusions near lip, 9 7/8" high.* **$4,740**

Courtesy of James D. Julia Auctioneers, Fairfield, Maine, www.jamesdjulia.com

◄ *Picture frame with acid-etched pine needle design against green slag glass background, beaded border and oval picture opening, reddish-brown patina with green highlights, signed "Tiffany Studios New York 917," very good to excellent condition, 12 1/4" x 14 1/4", oval opening 8 1/4" x 10 1/4".* **$3,851**

# Halloween Collectibles

By Mark B. Ledenbach

As a collector of vintage Halloween memorabilia for nearly 25 years, I find the evolution of the imagery for this fun hobby endlessly fascinating.

Halloween became quite the event in the first decade of the last century, mainly through the exchange of festive postcards. Those cards, with the art drawn by such luminaries as Winsch and Clapsaddle, typically accented the agricultural roots of Halloween, then branched out into the more whimsical realm of witches, black cats, blazing jack-o-lanterns, bats, cavorting devils, and the like.

As Halloween became an event to be celebrated with parties – primarily given by and for adults through the 1920s – the imagery began to change. From about 1909 through 1913, manufacturers of party supplies like Dennison of Framingham, Massachusetts, simply offered an array of seasonally decorated crepe papers from which the host would fashion decorations and party favors. The imagery from this period tends to be more subdued and somewhat pedestrian. However, as the manufacturers became more entranced by the business possibilities of offering finished goods for sale, the lines of available products exploded into a dazzling array of seals, silhouettes, tally cards, place cards, invitations, die-cuts, aprons, and costumes. To keep up with the seemingly endless kinds of products to be sold to adults, the imagery became more complex, scary, and perhaps sometimes chilling.

The most innovative purveyor of such complex Halloween imagery was the Beistle Co. of Shippensburg, Pennsylvania. They provided nut cups, die-cuts, lanterns, games, table decorations, and other small paper decorations that are especially coveted by collectors today. The firm's design sensibilities are easily recognized today for their ingenuity in extending Halloween imagery beyond what was offered previously by other manufacturers. Examples of this would be Beistle's 1930-1931 identical dual-sided lantern and 1923 fairy clock.

**MARK B. LEDENBACH,** longtime collector and expert on all things Halloween, is the author of *Vintage Halloween Collectibles,* 3rd edition, published in 2014. His website is HalloweenCollector.com.

*Candy holder,
skeleton pushing
jack-o-lantern
in wheelbarrow,
U.S.A., G.M.
Co., 1950s, heavy
cardboard, marked
RH-6A, 7 1/2"
high x 3" wide x
10 3/4" long.* **$195**

    Imagery through about 1940 tends to be more adult-focused. However, as trick-or-treating become more of an entrenched feature of Halloween celebrations, the target market segment for parties ceased to be adults and moved inexorably toward juveniles. The impact on Halloween imagery was profound. Out were the more complex and scary images of devils, witches and black cats, to be replaced by less threatening, less interesting, and less memorable imagery of apple-cheeked witches, grinning, plump devils, and friendly black cats. The air of implied menace, so evocative of early Halloween imagery, had been replaced by a sugar-high-inducing cuteness that any retailer could carry without censure.

    Through the present day, cuteness has been dethroned by goriness. One can shop at any mass retailer and find die-cuts of skulls with worms wriggling through eye sockets, costumes complete with wretch-inducing masks trumpeting various deformities or tortures, and other horrors meant to shock and perhaps dismay. The sense of subtlety and artistry so apparent in the majority of decorations made prior to 1940 is nowhere in evidence today.

    As with many hobbies, certain sub-categories have done better than others. Hotter categories are embossed German die-cuts;

**RECOMMENDED READING**

**Vintage Halloween Collectibles, 3rd edition,** contains nearly 550 new photographs showing over 600 new Halloween items, all in full color. Most of the new items shown have never appeared in other books on vintage Halloween. **http://HalloweenCollector.com.**

U.S. die-cuts, especially those made by Dennison and Gibson; Beistle paper products; boxed seals, silhouettes and cut-outs from Dennison; tin tambourines; and German candy containers and figurals as well as Halloween-themed games. Colder categories include tin noisemakers, U.S. pulp, and hard plastic.

Collecting vintage Halloween memorabilia became a red-hot hobby complete with skyrocketing prices and always scarce supply in the early 1990s. Even with all of the economic cycles since then and the rise of more efficient supply channels like eBay, prices continue to climb for nearly all genres of near-mint condition or better items. For example, embossed German die-cuts sold then for between $30-$75. Today many examples bring $100-$400, with the rarest items like a winged bat devil and a large fireplace screen topping $2,250. Even ephemera like a 1932 Beistle grandfather clock mechanical invitation bring astronomical prices. One recently sold for over $1,700.

As referenced above, not all categories have benefited. The garish hard plastic made in such huge quantities during the 1950s used to command head-scratching prices of $40-$1,000. Today prices have decreased to about half of the market's height given more collector awareness of the ubiquity of these items.

Unlike Christmas items, Halloween decorations were purchased with the intention of using them once, then tossing them out after the event with no sentiment. This is the primary supply driver behind the rapid escalation of prices today. The primary demand driver is the large number of new collectors entering this fun field as each Halloween season comes around.

As with all hobbies wherein the values have risen tremendously, reproductions and fantasy pieces are a problem. Consult other collectors and buy the right references before plunking down cash. Get in the habit of asking a lot of questions. Don't be shy!

*Tin clanger, U.S.A., T. Cohn, 1950s, 3 3/4" diameter.* **$85**

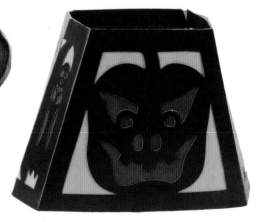

*Dual-sided jack-o-lantern shade with different expressions, U.S.A., Beistle, no mark, late 1930s, 6 1/4" high x 3 1/4" wide x 8 1/2" long.* **$165**

*Skull and crossbones, U.S.A., Hallmark, early 1950s, glossy-stock light cardboard, plain reverse side typically colored red, non-embossed, 8 1/4" high x 6 1/4" wide.* **$60**

▲ *Tin ratchet with mice, crows, cats, owls, and witches on brooms, Germany, late 1920s, 4 3/4" high.* **$140**

◄ *Here's Your Fate game, U.S.A., Whitney Co., Worcester, Massachusetts, 1920s, 10" high x 7 3/4" wide. Spin the center arrow to discover the name of your future spouse and his or her occupation and background. Your spin would also direct you to a listing of 24 fortunes on the reverse. A typical fortune reads, "You will soon receive news of great importance by telephone on a rainy evening." The instructions include this admonishment: "It is bad luck to try this more than one time in 24 hours."* **$200**

◄ *Placecard with witch at cauldron, bats, and cat atop chair, U.S.A., Dennison, sold with stock number H8, first appeared in 1920* Bogie Book, *3" high x 5" wide.* **$125**

*Tri-fold invitation with stooped witch, U.S.A., Dennison, sold with stock number H82, first appeared in 1922* Bogie Book, *3 1/4" square, closed.* **$135**

*Crawling baby boy, Germany, late 1920s, heavily embossed, back legs with perforated hinge giving 3-D effect, 8 1/4" high x 7 1/2" wide.* **$500**

*Surprised moon with attached witch on broom, U.S.A., Beistle, no mark, mid-1950s, non-embossed, witch separately attached to die-cut, unusual, 12" high x 12" wide.* **$200**

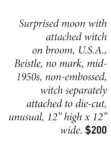

*Pumpkin house invitation, U.S.A., Dennison, sold with stock number H87, first appeared in 1924 Bogie Book, 4" high x 3 1/2" wide.* **$125**

Enveloped set of five pumpkin head cut-outs, U.S.A., Beistle, no mark, early 1920s, envelope 12 1/4" high x 9 1/2" wide, contents 5" to 8" diameter. **$350**

Composition candy container, jester creature playing lute, opens at neck, Germany, pre-1920s, jester's conical blue and white hat rests on ground between his legs, 6 1/4" high. **$725**

Boxed set of 20 cat with bowtie seals, U.S.A., Gibson Art Co., Cincinnati, Ohio, 1920s, 1 3/4" high x 1 1/4" wide. **$70**

*Spook Cat Game, U.S.A., Beistle, no mark, 1928, 11" high x 6 1/2" wide; pieces include main body, four legs and one tail, all made from black construction paper – variation of a standard "pin-the-tail" game; the envelope is the most compelling aspect because it does not rise to the design standard Beistle typically produced during the late 1920s.* **$275**

*Slot and tab candy container, owl on stump, U.S.A., Fibro toy manufactured by Dolly Toy Co. of Dayton, Ohio, mid-1930s, 5 1/2" high x 2" diameter.* **$20**

*Celluloid jack-o-lantern-headed boy with owl and squirrel on stump, U.S.A., Viscoloid Co. of Leominster, Massachusetts, early 1920s, 3 1/4" high x 2" wide. Provenance: From the collection of Barry Koester and Tammy Martin.* **$600**

*Suitcase candy container, 1910-1914, marked "Made in Saxony," lithographed paper, thicker cardboard slide box to hold hard candies, covered with stickers saying Black Cat Hotel, Oct 31st, Pumpkin Hotel, Great Witch Railway, and Halloween Express, 1 1/4" high x 1/2" wide x 1 3/4" long.* **$900-$1,000**

Candy container, jack-o-lantern-faced book, Germany, 1916-1921, made from lithographed paper over cardboard with simulated leather corners and spine, yellow string extends from back to small metal clasp at front, front lid opens, 3" high x 3/4" wide x 2 1/4" long. **$1,500**

Blow mold, orange slanted haunted house, U.S.A., Empire Plastic Corp. of New York, 1969, 13 1/4" high. **$65**

Candy container, jack-o-lantern-headed woman with cat, complex and well-made in Germany between 1910-1914, opens at neck, green circular wood base, 8" high. **$1,000-$1,200**

Bogie Book *envelope, U.S.A., Dennison, 1917, 5 1/2" high x 8 1/4" wide.* **$375**

*Soft cover* Bogie Book, *U.S.A., Dennison, 1917, 36 numbered pages, very best wraparound cover art of all editions with such covers, 7 1/2" high x 5" wide.* **$400**

# JEWELRY

# Jewelry
## Styles

Jewelry has been a part of every culture throughout time, reflecting the times as well as social and aesthetic movements. Jewelry is usually divided into periods and styles. Each period may have several styles, with some of the same styles and types of jewelry being made in both precious and non-precious materials. Elements of one period may also overlap into others.

**Georgian, 1760-1837.** Fine jewelry from this period is quite desirable, but few good-quality pieces have found their way to auction in recent years. Sadly, much jewelry from this period has been lost.

**Victorian, 1837-1901.** Queen Victoria of England ascended the throne in 1837 and remained queen until her death in 1901. The Victorian period is a long and prolific one, abundant with many styles of jewelry. It warrants being divided into three sub-periods: Early or Romantic period dating from 1837-1860; Mid or Grand period dating from 1860-1880; and Late or Aesthetic period dating from 1880-1901.

Sentiment and romance were significant factors in Victorian jewelry. Often, jewelry and clothing represented love and affection, with symbolic motifs such as hearts, crosses, hands, flowers, anchors, doves, crowns, knots, stars, thistles, wheat, garlands, horseshoes and moons. The materials of the time were also abundant and varied. They included silver, gold, diamonds, onyx, glass, cameo, paste, carnelian, agate, coral, amber, garnet, emeralds, opals, pearls, peridot, rubies, sapphires, marcasites, cut steel, enameling,

Courtesy of Heritage Auctions

*Diamond and silver-topped gold pendant-brooch, European-, mine- and rose-cut diamonds weighing approximately 7.35 carats, set in silver-topped 14k gold, pendant wire, removable pinstem and catch on reverse, 1 1/8" x 1 3/8".* **$4,780**

*Edwardian diamond, platinum and gold brooch, European-cut diamond measuring 6.92 x 6.85 x 4.71 mm and weighing approximately 1.35 carats, European-cut diamonds weighing approximately 1.30 carats, set in platinum, 14k gold pinstem and catch, total diamond weight 2.65 carats, gross weight 8.50 grams, 2 5/8" x 1/2".* **$4,062**

tortoise shell, topaz, turquoise, bog oak, ivory, jet, hair, gutta percha and vulcanite.

Sentiments of love were often expressed in miniatures. Sometimes they were representative of deceased loved ones, but often the miniatures were of the living. Occasionally, the miniatures depicted landscapes, cherubs or religious themes.

Hair jewelry was a popular expression of love and sentiment. The hair of a loved one was placed in a special compartment in a brooch or a locket, or used to form a picture under a glass compartment. Later in the mid-19th century, pieces of jewelry were made completely of woven hair. Individual strands of hair would be woven together to create necklaces, watch chains, brooches, earrings and rings.

In 1861, Queen Victoria's husband, Prince Albert, died. The queen went into mourning for the rest of her life, and Victoria required that the royal court wear black. This atmosphere spread to the populace and created a demand for mourning jewelry, which is typically black. When it first came into fashion, it was made from jet, fossilized wood. By 1850, there were dozens of English workshops making jet brooches, lockets, bracelets and necklaces. As the supply of jet dwindled, other materials were used such as vulcanite, gutta percha, bog oak and French jet.

By the 1880s, somber mourning jewelry was losing popularity. Fashions had changed and the clothing was simpler and had an air of delicacy. The Industrial Revolution, which had begun in the early part of the century, was now in full swing and machine-manufactured jewelry was affordable to the working class.

**Edwardian, 1890-1920.** The Edwardian period takes its name England's King Edward VII. Though he ascended the throne in 1901, he and his wife, Alexandria of Denmark, exerted influence over the period before and after his ascension.

*Early Victorian Vacheron & Constantin diamond, enamel and gold hunting case pocket watch with accompanying brooch, fob and key, circa 1850. Victorian gold mourning brooch with applied black and white enamel accents supports watch, key and fob. Case: 38 mm, hinged, circular 18k yellow gold with smooth edge and decorated case front and back, black champleve enamel, rose-cut diamonds; No. 83139 dial: white enamel with black Roman numerals, gilt "moon" hour and minute hands. Movement: 31 mm, gilt, 13 jewels, detached lever, keywind and set, No. 83139, signed Vacheron & Constantin on center bridge, lateral bridge escapement; signed and numbered Vacheron & Constantin in Geneve. E. E. Rodgers on cuvette, triple signed Vacheron & Constantin on dial, movement and dustcover.* **$3,107**

▲ ABOVE *Art Nouveau leaves brooch, demantoid garnet, diamond, plique à jour enamel, and silver-topped gold, round-shaped demantoid garnets weighing approximately 2.30 carats, European- and single-cut diamonds weighing approximately 0.90 carat, green plique à jour enamel, set in silver-topped gold, pinstem and catch, gross weight 13.55 grams, 3" x 2 1/8".* **$4,687**

TOP OF PAGE *Arts & Crafts moonstone, sapphire and diamond necklace, Louis Comfort Tiffany, circa 1915, designed as cabochon moonstone within twisted ropework frame with circular-cut sapphires and diamonds, three row fancy link chain and clasp similarly set, signed Tiffany & Co., approximately 18 1/2" long.* **$25,103**

The 1890s was known as La Belle Epoque. This was a time known for ostentation and extravagance. As the years passed, jewelry became simpler and smaller. Instead of wearing one large brooch, women were often found wearing several small lapel pins.

In the early 1900s, platinum, diamonds and pearls were prevalent in the jewelry of the wealthy, while paste was being used by the masses to imitate the real thing. The styles were reminiscent of the neo-classical and rococo motifs. The jewelry was lacy and ornate, feminine and delicate.

**Arts & Crafts, 1890-1920.** The Arts & Crafts movement was focused on artisans and craftsmanship. There was a simplification of form where the material was secondary to the design. Guilds of artisans banded together. Some jewelry was mass-produced, but the most highly prized examples of this period are handmade and signed by their makers. The pieces were simple and at times abstract. They could be hammered, patinated and acid etched. Common materials were brass, bronze, copper, silver, blister pearls, freshwater pearls, turquoise, agate, opals, moonstones, coral, horn, ivory, base metals, amber, cabochon-cut garnets and amethysts.

**Art Nouveau, 1895-1910.** In 1895, Samuel Bing opened a shop called "Maison de l'Art Nouveau" at 22 Rue de Provence in Paris. Art Nouveau designs in the jewelry were characterized by a sensuality that took on the forms of the female figure, butterflies, dragonflies, peacocks, snakes, wasps, swans, bats, orchids, irises and other exotic flowers. The lines used whiplash curves to create a feeling of lushness and opulence.

**1920s-1930s.** Costume jewelry began its steady ascent to popularity in the 1920s. Since it was relatively inexpensive to produce, it was mass-produced. The sizes and designs of the jewelry varied. Often, it was worn a few times, disposed of and then replaced with a new piece. It was thought of as expendable, a cheap throwaway to dress up an outfit. Costume jewelry became so popular that it was sold in both upscale and "five and dime" stores.

During the 1920s, fashions were often accompanied by jewelry that drew on the Art Deco movement, which got its beginning in Paris at the "Exposition Internationale des Arts Décoratifs et Industriels Modernes" held in 1925. The idea behind this movement was that form follows function. The style was characterized by simple, straight, clean lines, stylized motifs and geometric shapes. Favored materials included chrome, rhodium, pot metal, glass, rhinestones, Bakelite and celluloid.

One designer who played an important role was Coco Chanel. Though previously reserved for evening wear, the jewelry was worn by Chanel during the day, making it fashionable for millions of other women to do so, too.

With the 1930s came the Depression and the advent of World War II. Perhaps in response to the gloom, designers began using enameling and brightly colored rhinestones to create whimsical birds, flowers, circus animals, bows, dogs and just about every other figural form imaginable.

**Retro Modern, 1939-1950.** Other jewelry designs of the 1940s were big and bold. Retro Modern had a more substantial feel to it and designers began using larger stones to enhance the dramatic pieces. The jewelry was stylized and exaggerated. Common motifs included flowing scrolls, bows, ribbons, birds, animals, snakes, flowers and knots.

Sterling silver now became the metal of choice, often dipped in a gold wash known as vermeil.

Designers often incorporated patriotic themes of American flags, the V-sign, Uncle Sam's hat, airplanes, anchors and eagles.

**Post-War Modern, 1945-1965.** This was a movement that emphasized the artistic approach to jewelry making. It is

Jewelry courtesy of Robin Deutsch Collection

*Filigree faux amethyst, pearl, and enamel hinged Art Deco bangle bracelet, circa 1930, pierced filigree with faceted unfoiled glass amethyst stone surrounded by pearls and bordered with enamel, chromium-plated base metal, rectangular central element 1 1/2" x 1".* **$850-$950**

also referred to as Mid-Century Modern. This approach was occurring at a time when the Beat Generation was prevalent. These avant-garde designers created jewelry that was handcrafted to illustrate the artist's own concepts and ideas. The materials often used were sterling, gold, copper, brass, enamel, cabochons, wood, quartz and amber.

**1950s-1960s.** The 1950s saw the rise of jewelry that was made purely of rhinestones: necklaces, bracelets, earrings and pins. The focus of the early 1960s was on clean lines: Pillbox hats and A-line dresses with short jackets were a mainstay for the conservative woman. The large, bold rhinestone pieces were no longer the must-have accessory. They were now replaced with smaller, more delicate gold-tone metal and faux pearls with only a hint of rhinestones.

At the other end of the spectrum were psychedelic-colored clothing, Nehru jackets, thigh-high miniskirts and go-go boots. These clothes were accessorized with beads, large metal pendants and occasionally big, bold rhinestones. By the late 1960s, there was a movement back to Mother Nature and the "hippie" look was born. Ethnic clothing, tie-dye, long skirts, fringe and jeans were the prevalent style, and the rhinestone had, for the most part, been left behind.

Jewelry courtesy of ChicAntiques.com

*Miriam Haskell pastel necklace, circa 1950s, pastel beads and rhinestones with silver simulated baroque pearls, marked Miriam Haskell, necklace 15" long with 3 1/4" centerpiece.*
**$375-$425**

# Costume Jewelry

By Pamela Y. Wiggins
All images by photographer Jay B. Siegel, except where noted.

Jewelry, whether old or new, offers an unparalleled way to enhance self-expression. But collectible jewelry takes the notion one step further when design, artistry, and craftsmanship come together to create works of art we not only admire but enjoy wearing as well.

One of the most interesting aspects of jewelry collecting is the influence of popular culture, historical events, and fashion on adornment worn during various periods. Celebrities, royalty, and the fashionable set have all had an impact on jewelry and how it has been worn throughout the decades. Jewelry was mentioned in fictional works penned early on, illustrated in magazines as soon as mass printing was feasible, and then photographed on the rich and famous even before designers became celebrities in the era of Coco Chanel and Elsa Schiaparelli's rivalry. What was in vogue from a fashion perspective also heavily influenced the jewelry styles of the day, especially with Queen Victoria's sway in the 1800s, and later on runways in Paris, New York, and Milan.

One thing to remember when dating jewelry by period is that styles were fluid. That is, Victorian-style jewelry most often found by collectors didn't stop being produced the moment Queen Victoria died in 1901, nor did late-Victorian jewelry have the same styling as earlier Victorian pieces. Bold 1950s rhinestones didn't go out of style the moment the clock rang in 1960, and so on. You'll often find an overlapping of periods, which means transitional pieces with a number of influences were made and worn during those timeframes. For example, you might find a piece that includes elements of Edwardian design but offers a taste of Art Deco flair as well. You'll also notice that prolific companies like Napier produced fashion forward styles in the early 1970s using components similar to designs they made in the 1950s.

And don't forget about those all-important revival pieces that have been made throughout jewelry history. Egyptian revivals occurred not only in the 1920s when King Tut's tomb was opened, but also prior to that time in the Victorian era and also the 1970s when the Boy King's treasures were on tour once again. Victorian

**PAMELA Y. WIGGINS'** passion for jewelry includes studying pieces in her own collection and items she offers through her business, Chic Antiques by Pamela Wiggins, as well as exploring how popular culture and historical events shaped adornment worn decades ago. She is the co-founder of Costume Jewelry Collectors International, a global organization dedicated to costume jewelry education and events for collectors. She is the author of *Warman's Costume Jewelry Identification and Price Guide* and contributes to a number of national and regional publications.

Jewelry courtesy of Brigitte Gervais

▶ *Blue stomacher, circa late 1800s, heavy brass construction with tiny eyes to be sewn on garment, prong set in geometric pattern with white, royal blue, and dark blue pastes, 6" wide.* **$350-$450**

Jewelry courtesy of ChicAntiques.com

▲ *Porcelain pin, circa late 1890s, porcelain set in brass backing with transfer print of woman, hand-applied gold paint and simulated turquoise jewels, fastens with "C" catch, 1 1/4" diameter.* **$95-$125**

revivals have been around now longer than the Queen's lengthy reign, and there have been many interpretations through the decades. Recently, bold rhinestones and showy gold-tone pieces have become popular again with the advent of the "statement" necklace, and some of those pieces also revive styles of the past. Those are just a few examples of how designers have been inspired by the looks of yesterday when creating fashion jewelry.

Even though the Internet has brought an equalizing factor to the table, values for collectible costume jewelry vary widely across the country and around the globe. For instance, in larger cities and tourist areas, shops carrying these goods tend to command higher prices. Internet sites catering to a high-end clientele may command higher prices than online auctions, and so on.

Rarity, designer/manufacturer attribution, quality, craftsmanship, and past selling history are all taken into consideration when determining estimates of value. Keep in mind the prices denoted here are simply guidelines to follow based on the estimated values provided by the owners of the items depicted.

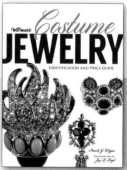

**RECOMMENDED READING**

**Warman's Costume Jewelry Identification and Price Guide** by Pamela Y. Wiggins provides a visual and educational feast for readers who enjoy buying, selling or collecting costume jewelry.
www.krausebooks.com

Jewelry courtesy ChicAntiques.com

*Pierced earrings in original box, circa 1890s, brass stampings with rhinestone dangles, in original crushed velvet box, pierced with screw posts, earrings just over 1 1/4" long.*
**$50-$75**

Jewelry courtesy Brigitte Gervais

▲ *Scarab pin, circa late 1800s, brass with molded art glass body set into scarab with tabs acting as prongs, 1 1/4" long.*
**$75-$95**

Jewelry courtesy of Brigitte Gervais

▶ *Moon man pin, circa late 1800s, heavy gold plate on brass with high domed faceted paste set into star, man in moon pale blue molded glass with mirror backing, fastens with "C" catch, 1 3/8" diameter.* **$300-$400**

Jewelry courtesy of Brigitte Gervais

*Pearl earrings, circa 1910-1920, pot metal with nickel plating, screw backs, glass button pearls and pastes set into pear-shaped drop, 3" long.* **$125-$150**

Jewelry courtesy of ChicAntiques.com

*Diamonbar sterling bracelet, circa 1917, transitional piece with Edwardian and Art Deco influences, sterling silver with clear and blue rhinestones, buckle-style clasp patented in 1917, bracelet 7" long.* **$125-$175**

Jewelry courtesy of ChicAntiques.com

*E.A. Bliss brooch, circa 1910, filigree silver-tone metal with old style flat-back rhinestones and small jewel and colored bead accents in blue, green, clear, purple, and amber, closes with "C" clasp, marked E.A. Co. for E.A. Bliss, forerunner to Napier, 2 7/8" x 2 1/2".* **$150-$200**

Jewelry courtesy of
Brigitte Gervais

▲ *Bird articulated sew-
on, circa 1910-1920, base
metal with white metal
plating, wings articulated
and attached to shoulders
by simple hook, set with
tiny pavé-set pastes,
meant to be sewn onto
garment via circular
attachments, 8 1/2" wide.*
**$200-$250**

Jewelry courtesy of
LinsyJsJewels.com

▶ *Jade glass necklace,
circa 1920s, jade green
melon-shaped beads
with stamped silver-tone
metal links and pendant
with layered stampings,
unmarked, 16" long.*
**$400-$550**

Jewelry courtesy of Pamela Y. Wiggins

*Napier bracelet, circa late 1920s,
gold-plated fine filigree metal
with topaz glass bezel-set stones,
fastens with hidden clasp, marked
Napier, 7 1/4" long x 1 1/4" wide.*
**$200-$250**

Jewelry courtesy of LinsyJsJewels.com

▶ *Eisenberg Original fur clips, circa 1935, red rhinestones and clear accents, marked Eisenberg Original, each clip 1 3/4" long.* **$450-$600**

Jewelry courtesy of Robin Deutsch Collection

▶ *Art Deco faux ruby diamond paste sterling earrings, circa 1935, rhodium-plated, each earring in three sections, fully articulated, screw back surmounts support geometric pendant comprised of bead set pastes with navette center with black enamel with large square-cut ruby glass stone, 2 1/4" long x 1 1/4" wide, marked STERLING GERMANY.* **$675-$875**

Jewelry courtesy of Robin Deutsch Collection

▼ *KTF "invisibly" set faux ruby bracelet, circa 1936, made of rhodium-plated base metal with 10 bead-set rhinestone pavé links and channel-set baguettes running down center, and invisibly set simulated rubies, fully articulated links slightly curved to mold to wrist, fold-over clasp integrates into design, marked KTF and 53 for stonesetter, 7" long x 3/4" wide.* **$1,650-$1,850**

Jewelry courtesy of Robin Deutsch Collection

◀ *Ciner sterling Art Deco swirl dress clip, circa 1937, with navette, baguette, and round rhinestones in three-dimensional scrolled millegrain setting, all stones set open back, dress clip fastening mechanism, marked CINER STERLING.* **$275-$375**

Jewelry courtesy of ChicAntiques.com

*Necklace, circa late 1930s, rare example of Monet Jewelers rhinestone and enamel jewelry, Victorian Revival festoon-style with pink and blue rhinestones and navy blue and white enameling, marked with "Monet Jewelers" hangtag, filigree centerpiece, 3 3/4" long, 16" long overall.* **$550-$650**

Jewelry courtesy of Robin Deutsch Collection

*Ciner bracelet, circa 1937, sterling silver articulated line bracelet set with unfoiled square-cut simulated sapphires set open backed with articulated central rhinestone-embellished element with bow motif, marked CINER PAT NO 2074046 STERLING, 7" long.* **$475-$675**

Jewelry courtesy of LinsyJsJewels.com

*Eisenberg Original bracelet, circa late 1930s, red rhinestones on clasp with hidden closure, marked Eisenberg Original, 7" long with 1 3/8" clasp.* **$850-$1,000**

Jewelry courtesy of LinsyJsJewels.com

▲ *Eisenberg Original fur clip, circa 1940, glass opalescent blue stones with simulated sapphire bullet cabochon accents and clear rhinestones with simulated pearls in heavy cast setting, marked Eisenberg Original, 4" long.* **$1,100-$1,300**

Jewelry courtesy of ChicAntiques.com

▲ *Eisenberg ring in box, circa early 1940s, large clear emerald-cut rhinestone with side accents set in silver-tone metal, adjustable sizing, marked Eisenberg.* **$225-$275**

Jewelry courtesy of Robin Deutsch Collection

▼ *KTF bracelet, circa 1937, rhodium-plated base metal, prong-set emerald-cut faux emeralds with bezel-set rhinestones, channel-set baguettes, and pavé-set round rhinestones, fold-over clasp integrated into design, marked KTF, 1 1/4" wide, central element 3/4" high.* **$5,000-$6,000**

*Joseff bracelet, circa 1940s, Russian gold-plated metal with purple and clear unfoiled stones, marked Joseff Hollywood, 7 1/2" long x approximately 1" wide.* **$375-$450**

◀ *Coro horse head Duette, circa late 1940s, red, green and clear rhinestones, can be worn as brooch or two pin clips, marked Corocraft on each horse and Coro Duette on frame, 2 1/2" wide.* **$275-$375**

▲ *Lightning bolt brooch, circa 1940s, unfoiled stones in blue, green, and red with clear accents, marked Sterling.* **$125-$150**

◀ *Sultan brooch, circa 1940s, sterling silver set with large teal rhinestone in turban and turquoise bead accents, marked Sterling.* **$225-$325**

Jewelry courtesy of ChicAntiques.com

*Mazer earrings, circa early 1940s, molded blue glass leaf-shaped stones and blue glass moonstone cabochons with clear rhinestone accents in rhodium-plated settings, marked Mazer, 1" long.* **$95-$125**

Jewelry courtesy of LinsyJsJewels.com

*Miriam Haskell sweater guard, circa late 1940s, unusual style with pink glass flowers with bead and rhinestone accents, marked Miriam Haskell horseshoe mark, 3 1/4" wide.* **$325-$450**

Jewelry courtesy of Pamela Y. Wiggins

*Hinged cuff bracelet, circa 1950s, double hinge cuff with large rock-shaped pink stones surrounded by pale purple and ice blue rhinestones set in silver-tone metal, unmarked, 2" wide.* **$525-$625**

*Original by Robért necklace, circa 1950s, simulated pearls with pink and purple rhinestones on gold-tone filigree backing with clear rose montee and gold vine accents, marked Original by Robért, 16" long, centerpiece 2 1/2" wide.* **$200-$250**

▼ *Regency bracelet, circa 1950s, green oval foiled cabochons with pastel yellow and green rhinestones in brass-tone metal, marked Regency, 7" long.* **$125-$150**

*Vendôme bracelet, circa late 1950s, iridescent cabochons surrounded by yellow and blue aurora borealis rhinestones in silver-tone setting, marked Vendôme, 7 1/4" long x 1 1/4" wide.* **$150-$200**

Jewelry courtesy of ChicAntiques.com

*Florenza Maltese cross set, circa 1950s, purple, blue, and aurora borealis rhinestones set in antiqued silver-tone metal, marked Florenza, pendant 2 1/2" wide, bracelet 7 1/4" long, earrings 1 1/8".* **$175-$225**

Jewelry courtesy of Pamela Y. Wiggins

*Schreiner adjustable ring, circa 1950s, large oval simulated turquoise art glass cabochon surrounded by emerald-cut brown rhinestones, marked "Schreiner New York" on back, 1 3/4" long.* **$175-$225**

*Schiaparelli angelfish brooch, circa late 1950s, simulated pearls and aurora borealis rhinestones in gunmetal setting, marked Schiaparelli, 2 3/4" long.* **$200-$250**

*Alice Caviness brooch set, circa late 1950s, gray, clear, and aurora borealis rhinestones in gold-tone metal, marked Alice Caviness, brooch 2 1/2" wide, earrings 1 1/2" long.* **$175-$225**

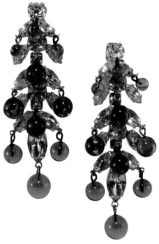

*Kramer earrings, circa 1958, clear rhinestones with emerald green glass bead dangles, 2 1/2" long.* **$175-$200**

*Hobé mesh necklace, circa late 1950s-early 1960s, silver-tone metal mesh wrapped with light and sapphire blue rhinestones, silver-tone beads with blue rhinestone embellishments dangle below, marked Hobé, 16" long.* **$100-$125**

Jewelry courtesy of Pamela Y. Wiggins

*Dior garland necklace, circa 1962, collar necklace with sapphire blue navette and pear-shaped rhinestones along with red accents, marked Chr. Dior © 1962, 16 3/4" long, front centerpiece 3 3/4".* **$850-$1,000**

Jewelry courtesy of LinsyJsJewels.com

▲ *Mimi Di N geometric brooch, circa 1960s, matte gold-tone metal with four large pear-shaped clear rhinestones, designed by Mimi di Nascemi, marked Mimi Di N, 3 1/4" wide.* **$200-$250**

Jewelry courtesy of ChicAntiques.com

◀ *Hattie Carnegie necklace, circa 1960s, bib-style with green and clear rhinestones, marked Hattie Carnegie, 16 1/2" long with 6" drop at front.* **$375-$475**

Jewelry courtesy of Pamela Y. Wiggins

▼ *Green rock bracelet set, circa 1960s, emerald green glass rock stones with spring green rhinestones in gold-tone setting with toggle clasp, bracelet 7 1/2" long x 1" wide, earrings 1" long.* **$125-$150**

Jewelry courtesy of ChicAntiques.com

*DeLizza & Elster "carved" glass parure, circa 1960s, blue molded glass ovals with fuchsia accent stones amid rhinestones of varying shades of blue, necklace 16" long, bracelet 7 1/4" long, earrings 1 1/4" long.* **$475-$575**

Jewelry courtesy of ChicAntiques.com

*Alice Caviness necklace set, circa 1960s, molded glass frosted amber stones with brown and purple aurora borealis rhinestone accents, all pieces marked Alice Caviness.* **$175-$250**

Jewelry courtesy of
LinsyJsJewels.com

◄ *Kenneth Jay Lane frog
brooch, circa late 1960s,
gold-tone body with clear
rhinestones, faux jade
back, red rhinestone eyes,
marked K.J.L, 1 5/8"
long.* **$100-$135**

Jewelry courtesy of LinsyJsJewels.com

*Boucher convertible flower brooch, circa early 1960s,
flower head opens and closes to reveal simulated
pearl inside, accented with clear rhinestones, marked
©Boucher, 4 1/4" long.* **$200-$275**

Jewelry courtesy of ChicAntiques.com

*Bib necklace set, circa 1960s, green, orange,
and yellow rhinestones with dangling beads in
complementary colors, necklace 15 1/2" long with
front drop of about 3", earrings 2".* **$125-$150**

Jewelry courtesy of ChicAntiques.com

*Rhinestone necklace set, circa 1960s, orange, olive
green, and pale yellow oval rhinestones with emerald
green accent stones, likely of European origin,
necklace adjusts to 16 1/2", earrings 1 1/8" long.*
**$170-$225**

Jewelry courtesy of ChicAntiques.com

*Napier dangle earrings, circa early 1970s, metal filigree hoops with heavy gold plating embellished with dangling crystal beads and metal filigree "leaf" shapes, marked Napier, over 3 1/2" long x 1 7/8" wide.* **$125-$150**

Jewelry courtesy of Pamela Y. Wiggins

*Monet "Princesa" necklace, circa early 1970s, gold-plated pierced metalwork with East Indian influence, marked Monet, adjusts to 17 1/2" long, centerpiece 4 1/4" long.* **$150-$175**

Jewelry courtesy of ChicAntiques.com

*Miriam Haskell Egyptian Revival necklace, circa 1970s, glass and ceramic scarabs and King Tut masks suspended from metal mesh necklace with antiqued gold-tone filigree findings, marked Miriam Haskell, adjusts to 17 1/2".* **$600-$750**

Jewelry courtesy of Pamela Y. Wiggins

*Simone Edouard star earrings, circa 1980s, gold-tone backings with clear rhinestones in round elongated navette and trillion shapes, marked Simone Edouarde, 3" long.* **$125-$150**

Jewelry courtesy of ChicAntiques.com

*Handcrafted Wendy Gell collage necklace, circa 1985, faux pearls and rhinestones with broken vintage jewelry parts, marked Wendy Gell 1985, 15" long, front embellished plate 2 1/2" wide.* **$325-$400**

Jewelry courtesy of ChicAntiques.com

◀ *Chanel cuff bracelet, circa 1980s, red and green Gripoix glass surrounded by faux pearl accents on gold-tone base, marked Chanel 2 CC 5 Made in France, 2 1/2" wide at front.* **$6,000-$6,500**

Jewelry courtesy of Pamela Y. Wiggins

*Dominique butterfly brooch, circa mid-1990s, large brooch by Dom DeToro with red, clear, and opaque black rhinestones in silver-tone setting, marked Dominique, 4 5/8" wide.* **$275-$375**

Jewelry courtesy of ChicAntiques.com

*Chanel 2.55 handbag charm brooch, circa 1994, named 2.55 for famous Chanel flap handbag style introduced in February 1955, gold-tone polished metal with CC coin medallion at top, marked Chanel 94 CC A made in France, 3 1/8" long.* **$375-$425**

Jewelry courtesy of ChicAntiques.com

◄ *Elizabeth Taylor Egyptian Revival earrings, circa 1993, created by Avon and based on fine jewelry from Taylor's collection, turquoise blue enamel with faux lapis and turquoise cabochons on matte gold-tone metal, excellent quality, marked Elizabeth Taylor Avon, 3" long.* **$150-$200**

# Lamps & Lighting

By Martin Willis

**MARTIN WILLIS** is the Director of the Decorative Arts at James D. Julia, Inc., one of the nation's premier auction galleries. Formerly of New Hampshire, Willis comes from a family of auctioneers: His father, Morgan Willis, developed and ran the Seaboard Auction Gallery in Eliot, Maine, which Martin eventually took over. He has 40 years of experience in the antique auction business with companies in Maine, New Hampshire, Massachusetts, Colorado and California. He spent six years with Clars Auction Gallery of Oakland, California, as senior appraiser, cataloger and auctioneer, handling the estate of TV mogul Merv Griffin as well as talk show host Tom Snyder. In 2009, Martin launched Antique Auction Forum, a biweekly podcast on the art and antiques trade with followers across North America and throughout the world.

A fine lamp provides illumination as well as a decorative focal point for a room. This dual-purpose trend had its origins in the mid-to-late 1800s with American lighting. As with most game-changing style movements, timing was key in this evolution.

Arguably, the vanguard name of decorative lighting was Louis Comfort Tiffany (1848-1933) of New York City. Urban homes became electrified on a wide scale near the end of the 19th century; it was then that Tiffany was becoming recognized as a designer as well as a commercial success.

Tiffany's first stained glass shade for an electric lamp was designed by Clara Driscoll around 1895. Since their introduction over a century ago, Tiffany's shades have always had a unique, glowing quality to them due to their masterful designs and chemically compounded stained glass colors. Today, Tiffany Studios lamps remain collectors' favorites. Rare and unusual designs – including the Hanging Head Dragonfly, Peony, Apple Blossom, and Wisteria patterns – generate the most interest and dollars; outstanding examples have commanded up to $2 million. More common items such as Acorn, Tulip, or Favrile art glass shade lamps have experienced falling prices relative to a decade ago.

Tiffany's commercial success catalyzed the creation of many new stained glass lamp companies. Contemporaries included Duffner & Kimberly, Suess, Chicago Mosaic, and Wilkinson. See *Mosaic Shades II* by Paul Crist for more information.

There were several other companies in the United States making fine glass lamps at the turn of last century. These included Handel, from Meriden, Connecticut, and Pairpoint, from New Bedford, Massachusetts. Handel was known primarily for its reverse painted shades. Fine examples of the company's landscape, aquarium, and other unusual motifs have garnered prices up to $85,000. Pairpoint opened in 1880 and soon merged with Mt. Washington Glass of Boston. They created reverse painted shades as well, the most popular being their "Puffy" shade. Prices for Pairpoint lamps start around $1,000 and peak about $25,000 for top examples.

Perhaps the most notable European glass lamp manufacturer from the late 19th century was Daum, founded by Jean Daum in France in 1878. The company is still in business today, manufacturing crystal art glass. Daum's lamps were made of cameo glass, produced through a proprietary technique of using acid to cut through layers of fused glass. This creates dramatic color reliefs. During the heyday, 1895-1914, Daum produced beautiful cameo glass lamp bases and shades. Today, early examples can be purchased starting at $1,000. Exceptional pieces may garner up to $80,000.

It is important to note that when it comes to vintage lamps, reproductions and fakes dominate the secondary market. If a

Courtesy of Heritage Auctions

*Pair of Walter von Nessen Space Age aluminum lamps, tiered, with inset bands of brass and Bakelite, designed for Pattyn Products, Detroit, circa 1935-1936, marked Model 310, 19 1/4" high.*
**$5,322**

price seems too good to be true, it probably is. It is imperative to buy from a reputable dealer or an auction house that will stand behind an item's authenticity. If a piece has the word "style" as part of its description, i.e., a "Tiffany style" lamp, this indicates that it is either a reproduction or that the seller is uncertain of its origins. Always ask plenty of questions before investing in a fine art lamp.

As always, anything is worth whatever someone will pay, and there are often good buys available – even from top manufacturers. With the exception of the very rarest examples, enthusiasts should be able to find and afford a nice authentic vintage lamp to admire and enjoy.

Courtesy of Heritage Auctions

*Pair of Empire-style patinated and gilt bronze six-light candelabra on marble pedestals, 20th century, marble pedestals with patinated bronze claw feet and decorative mounts, marble foot to candelabra atop pedestals, gilt bronze acanthus leaf socle supporting patinated bronze caryatid, issuing gilt trumpet-form arms and electrified candle-form lights, 96" x 12" x 12" including base.* **$7,813**

Courtesy of Burchard Galleries

*Empire vintage filigree table lamp, six-panel domed caramel slag glass shade with floral filigree metal, two-socket pull chain, bronzed metal base with caramel glass, shade 19" diameter x 23" high.* **$710**

Courtesy of Direct Auction Galleries

*Antique spelter figural lamp with woman holding two lanterns, 18" high.* **$460**

Courtesy of Cottone Auctions

▲ *Tiffany Studios Poppy lamp, overlay filigree shade signed Tiffany Studios NY 1461, bronze blown out base signed Tiffany Studios NY 2621, 24" high, shade 17" diameter.* **$69,000**

Courtesy Jeffrey S. Evans & Associates

◄ *Rare English cameo floral and leaf pattern art glass miniature lamp, white to citron yellow, with satin finish, white floral leaf and butterfly décor, and period burner.* **$11,500**

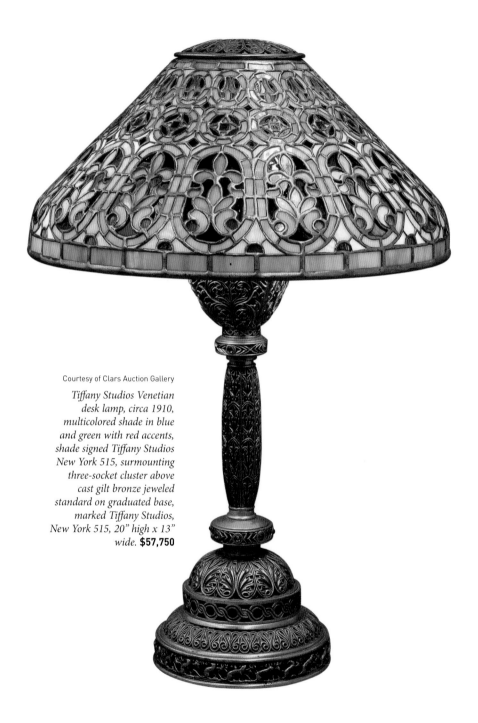

Courtesy of Clars Auction Gallery

*Tiffany Studios Venetian desk lamp, circa 1910, multicolored shade in blue and green with red accents, shade signed Tiffany Studios New York 515, surmounting three-socket cluster above cast gilt bronze jeweled standard on graduated base, marked Tiffany Studios, New York 515, 20" high x 13" wide.* **$57,750**

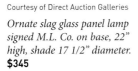

Courtesy of Direct Auction Galleries

*Ornate slag glass panel lamp signed M.L. Co. on base, 22" high, shade 17 1/2" diameter.* **$345**

Courtesy of Midwest Auction Galleries

*Leaded slag glass lamp, Mosaic Lamp Co. of Chicago, acanthus leaf base, cap and finial, granite back texture slag glass shade, 25 1/2" high.* **$325**

Courtesy of Direct Auction Galleries

*Slag glass lamp, green and pink glass, signed Bradley & Hubbard, 15" square shade x 21" high.* **$460**

Courtesy of World of Décor

*Pairpoint Puffy lamp, butterfly and rose shade, lamp base with matching signed Pairpoint reverse-painted Papillon shade in "Butterfly and Roses" pattern with large red and pink roses and green leaves and large yellow, red, and blue butterfly against white and green-streaked frosted ground, 22" high.* **$9,500**

Courtesy of Louis J. Dianni LLC

*Williamson leaded glass table lamp, early 20th century, geometric leaded glass shade of cream and amber over two-socket bronze base with overlapping petals, 23" high x 18" diameter.* **$1,122**

*Rare hanging cast iron miniature triple-arm chandelier lamp fitted with three colorless glass tapered fonts, each embossed "FIRE FLY" and with correct opaque glass chimney-shade, frame 10 1/4" high.* **$8,625**

*Prairie School stained glass table lamp, lighted base with matching six-panel shade, hand-cut glass wrapped in copper foil, in cream, honey and green, on hexagon base with metal brad trim with glass beads, 25" high.* **$472**

*Rare figural Santa miniature lamp, Consolidated Lamp & Glass Co., fourth quarter 19th/early 20th century, opaque white glass fired in yellow and brown, head and body of Santa serve as shade, matching base is pair of boots, period nickel burner with thumbwheel marked PAT FEB'Y 27.1877, shade ring and chimney, 9 1/4" high to top of shade, 4 1/8" high to top of collar, base 3" diameter.* **$6,900**

Courtesy Jeffrey S. Evans & Associates

◄ *Rare cameo "Fuchsia Glory and Leaf" pattern art glass miniature lamp.* **$8,625**

Courtesy of Louis J. Dianni, LLC

▲ *Metal overlay lamp, Handel Lamp Co., early 20th century, slag glass shade with metal overlay in landscape motif, three sockets with three acorn finial pull chains, bronze base marked "Handel Lamps" and decorated with flowers and foliates, both base and shade are property signed, 23" high.* **$2,430**

BACK-VIEW!

Courtesy of Roan's

*Artist-signed electric table lamp marked Pairpoint 3070 on bronze-tone cast metal base with reverse-painted dome shade in peacock, urn and floral motif, 17 1/2".* **$2,700**

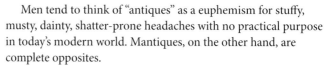

# Mantiques

By Eric Bradley

**ERIC BRADLEY** is one of the young guns of the antiques and collectibles field. Bradley, who works for Heritage Auctions, is a former editor of *Antique Trader* magazine and an award-winning investigative journalist with a degree in economics. His work has received press from *The New York Times* and *The Wall Street Journal.* He also served as a featured guest speaker on investing with antiques. He has written several books, including the critically acclaimed *Mantiques: A Manly Guide to Cool Stuff.*

Men tend to think of "antiques" as a euphemism for stuffy, musty, dainty, shatter-prone headaches with no practical purpose in today's modern world. Mantiques, on the other hand, are complete opposites.

If you think about the premise of most of the "found money" collecting television shows dominating every channel, it's easy to see why they all star men. Mantiques are fun and, as it turns out, pretty lucrative. The trend isn't limited to American television; dealers and collectors in Europe are also celebrating the renewed attention to items that appeal to men. U.S. auction houses are developing the trend as well, with Heritage Auctions, the world's largest collectibles auctioneer, now holding a Gentleman Collector auction every year.

Although the word "mantiques," used to describe items appealing to guys, has existed for about 30 years, the concept of the mantique is ancient. When they weren't chasing mammoths

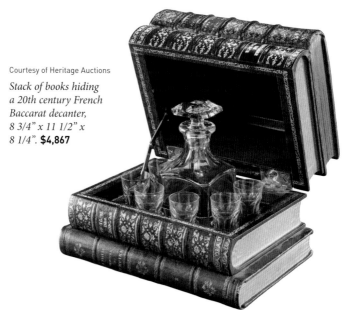

Courtesy of Heritage Auctions

*Stack of books hiding a 20th century French Baccarat decanter, 8 3/4" x 11 1/2" x 8 1/4".* **$4,867**

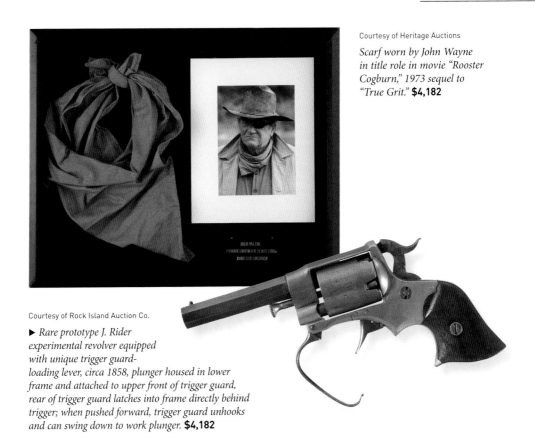

*Scarf worn by John Wayne in title role in movie "Rooster Cogburn," 1973 sequel to "True Grit."* **$4,182**

▶ *Rare prototype J. Rider experimental revolver equipped with unique trigger guard-loading lever, circa 1858, plunger housed in lower frame and attached to upper front of trigger guard, rear of trigger guard latches into frame directly behind trigger; when pushed forward, trigger guard unhooks and can swing down to work plunger.* **$4,182**

off cliffs, our ancestors were saving interesting stones, carving ivory tusks, or trading with other tribes. Why go through the trouble? The dude with the coolest stuff was seen as better able to care for offspring or lead the tribe to greatness. From Alibaba's lamp to Luke Skywalker's lightsaber (it is a hand-me-down, remember), mantiques are in our DNA.

Fast forward to the 21st century and we've got television shows devoted to them. The mantiques movement is big and chances are you're already a part of it.

For more information on mantiques, see *Mantiques: A Manly Guide to Cool Stuff* by Eric Bradley.

**RECOMMENDED READING**

**Mantiques: A Manly Guide to Cool Stuff.** From signs, tools, and technology to vintage cars, barware, and movie posters, the book surveys the stuff dudes like best, with more than 400 photographs. www.krausebooks.com

Courtesy of Heritage Auctions

*"Quick Change," Brown & Bigelow calendar illustration, Gil Elvgren (American, 1914-1980), 1967, oil on canvas, signed lower right, 30" x 24".* **$110,500**

Courtesy of Sotheby's

▼ *Pair of karat gold and enamel "bull's head" cufflinks by David Webb, each terminal designed as bull's head, blue enamel with red enamel eyes, mounted in 18k yellow gold, signed.* **$3,060**

Courtesy of Sewmanity (etsy.com)

*Late 1940s hand-painted naked island girl tie.* **$250**

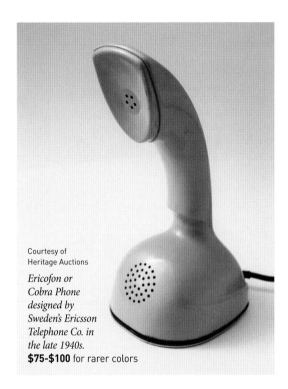

Courtesy of
Heritage Auctions

*Ericofon or
Cobra Phone
designed by
Sweden's Ericsson
Telephone Co. in
the late 1940s.*
**$75-$100** for rarer colors

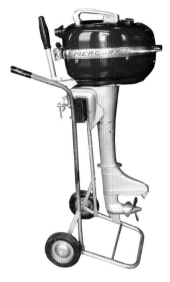

Courtesy of Lang's Auction

▲ *1950 Mercury Mark 5 boat
motor, professionally restored.*
**$350**

Courtesy of Hake's
Americana
& Collectibles

▶ *Money clip with
woven design, 14k
yellow gold and
gross weight 28
grams, 2 1/4" x 1".*
**$597**

Courtesy of Heritage Auctions

▲ *First edition of Hugh Hefner's*
Playboy *magazine with Marilyn
Monroe on cover and nude photo
spread of her inside.* **$55,000**

Courtesy of Heritage Auctions

◀ *Chromed metal and glass
airplane lamp from Sarsaparilla
Deco Designs by Ray A. Schober,
12" long.* **$468**

Courtesy of Heritage Auctions

◀ *Patek Philippe platinum wristwatch (Ref. 5004P), extremely rare, split-seconds chronograph, registers, perpetual calendar, moon phases, leap year adjustment and 24-hour indication.* **$242,500**

Courtesy of Auction Team Breker

*1867 Malling Hansen typewriter, most valuable vintage typewriter.* **$123,125**

Courtesy of Lang's Auction

◀ *William Mills & Son hard rubber Fairy Trout reel made for use with lightweight Catskill fly rods, with original leather case, 2 3/8" diameter, 5/8" wide spool reel. Provenance: From the Jerry Zebrowski Collection.* **$1,200**

◀ *Lithographed Stanley sign with bench plane and curling shaving, N. Y. Metal Ceiling Co., 9" x 18".* **$1,595**

◀ *1950s Royal Stetson Ivy League fedora.* **$85**

▶ *Rare duck call by James Tillman "J.T." Beckhart of Buckspoint, Arkansas, circa 1905, set record in 2013 as most valuable duck call ever sold at auction.* **$103,500**

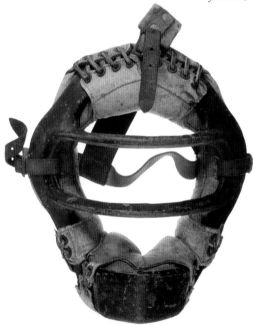

▲ *Catcher's mask worn by Hall of Famer Yogi Berra while playing for the New York Yankees, black cast iron shell with padded brown leather strapped with leather bands.* **$16,730**

▶ *Charles Miller No. 50 plane with 90 percent of original copper wash.* **$9,350**

Courtesy of Heritage Auctions

*Floor radio designed by John Vassos (American, 1898-1985) and manufactured by RCA, New York, 1936, 40" high.* **$5,000**

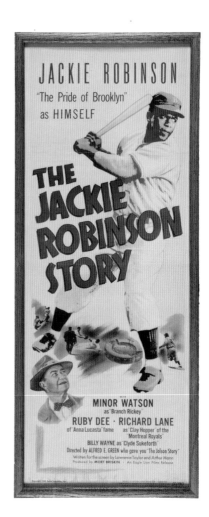

Courtesy of Heritage Auctions

*"The Jackie Robinson Story" insert format poster issued to cinemas screening film of Major Leagues' first African-American player to hit the silver screen, 1950, 14" x 36".* **$657**

Courtesy of Surfing Heritage Vintage Surf

*Rare 1949 Pete Peterson model surfboard, hollow balsa/plywood composite. Peterson is an innovative designer and the greatest California waterman of the first half of the 20th century, winning West Coast Championships four times (1932, 1936, 1938, and 1941). One of the most sought-after surfboards to exist.* **$32,400**

Courtesy of Heritage Auctions

*Zeppelin- or dirigible-shaped cocktail shaker with nickel-plated exterior and gold-plated interior, nose unscrews to expose cover over strainer/juicer opening to flask, base opens to four graduated measures and funnel, four spoons stored in gondola-form compartment, 12 1/4" high.* **$2,000**

Courtesy of Heritage Auctions

*French Art Deco and bronze floor lamp in form of cobra emerging from basket, circa 1920, by Edgar Brandt (French, 1880-1960), 58 5/8" high.* **$4,687**

# Maps & Globes

Throughout the ages, pictorial maps have been used to show the industries of a city, the attractions of a tourist town, the history of a region, or its holy shrines. Ancient artifacts suggest that pictorial mapping has been around since recorded history began. "Here be dragons" is a mapping phrase used to denote dangerous or unexplored territories, in imitation of the medieval practice of putting sea serpents and other mythological creatures in blank areas of maps.

Courtesy of Dreweatts & Bloomsbury

*English celestial star globe, Kelvin & Hughes, London, circa 1975, 12 gores printed with stars and principal constellations labeled, solstitial colure divided for annual calendar, equinoctial graduated in degrees, northern hemisphere with key for star magnitude above oval label STAR GLOBE, KELVIN & HUGHES LTD., EPOCH 1975, printed by George Philip & Son, Ltd., pivoted between poles within lacquered brass meridian circle divided for degrees and resting via divided horizon ring, annotated with principal compass cardinal points and inscribed PATT. 160133, No. 7120/BHS/10437, with four-arm restraint with each sector divided for degrees and fitted with friction sliding recording pointers, stained wood box with KELVIN HUGHES STAR GLOBE (1975) / (Twilight Setting Pattern) / INSTRUCTIONS FOR USE label pasted to inside of lid, exterior with leather carrying handle, 10 3/4" wide, globe 7".*
**$620**

**CLOSE-UP!**

Courtesy of Dreweatts & Bloomsbury

*Terrestrial table globe, George Philip and Son, London, early 20th century, 12 polychrome printed gores incorporating oval label PHILIP'S / 14 INCH / TERRESTRIAL GLOBE / LONDON / GEOGRAPHICAL INSTITUTE / GEORGE PHILIP & SON LTD. 32 FLEET STREET and annotated with principal towns, cities, rivers, mountain ranges, and transcontinental railway routes to land masses, oceans with principal steamship routes annotated in nautical miles, pivoted via poles within cast iron meridian circle divided for degrees and resting in wooden stand with printed paper horizon ring graduated in degrees, days of month and houses of zodiac with names and symbols, on three inverted baluster-turned supports with cross-stretcher, 19" maximum diameter, 22" high, globe 4".* **$1,630**

Courtesy of Pook and Pook, Inc.

*Five American maps, 18th/19th century: "Sketch of the Country Illustrating the Late Engagement in Long Island," 8" x 12 1/2"; German map of Virginia, Johan Smith, 6 1/4" x 9"; "A Chart of Delaware Bay and River From the Original by Mr. Fisher of Philadelphia 1776," 7 1/2" x 9 1/2"; Delaware, 7 1/2" x 6"; and hand-drawn pencil map of Virginia, 19th century, 9 3/4" x 12 1/2".* **$1,400**

Courtesy of Swann Auction Galleries

*Richard Cushee, "A New Globe of the Earth," hand-colored 12-gore pocket terrestrial globe, London, 1731, abraded and stained along equator, original black shagreen case lined with 12 bisected hand-colored celestial gores, original hardware, 2 3/4".* **$9,375**

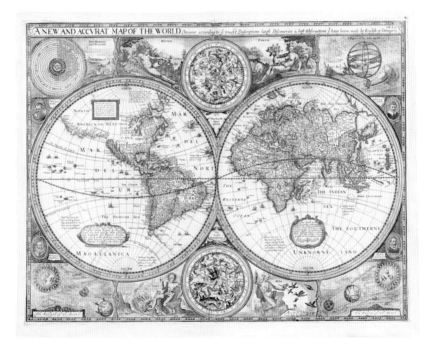

Courtesy of PBA Galleries

*Copper-engraved double-hemisphere map of world, hand-colored, in double-sided archival mat, based on William Grent's rare, separately issued map of 1625, surrounded by two celestial hemispheres, figural allegorical representations of water, earth, air, and fire, plus portraits of Ferdinand Magellan, Oliver vander Noort, Thomas Cavendish, and Sir Francis Drake; corners filled with astronomical table, armillary sphere, and eclipses of sun and moon; imprint of George Humble, map dated 1626 but was known to be published through 1632 with this imprint; this is one of the earliest published world maps to be printed in English, first atlas map to show cartographic curiosity of California as an island, one of first to show settlement of New Plymouth; "Southerne Unknowne Land" shows large conjectured continent covering much of southern hemisphere; engraver unknown but most likely Abraham Goos, 15 1/2" x 20 1/4".* **$15,990**

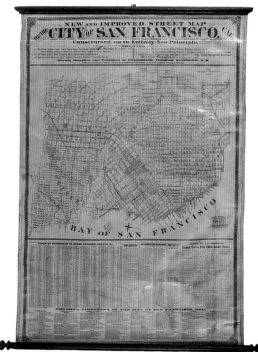

Courtesy of PBA Galleries

Manhattan / A Weekly for Wakeful New Yorkers, No.1 Vol. 1, Jan. 18, 1933 (New York, 1933), first and only printing, 16 pages, 12" x 16", unfolding to 16" x 24", centerfold by E. Simms Campbell, "A Night-Club Map of Harlem," dated 1932 in print, "The stars indicate the places that are open all night. The only important omission is the location of the various speakeasies but since there are about 500 of them, you won't have much trouble," numerous small cartoon vignettes illustrating Harlem street scenes, map considered a rarity of Harlem Jazz age in last days of Prohibition. **$12,300**

Courtesy of PBA Galleries

Wall map of San Francisco, lithographed, colored, backed with linen, on rollers with "General Directory of the City" and index to minor streets, locations of fire alarm boxes, U.S. Post Office letter boxes, Wells, Fargo & Cos. letter boxes, and "streets, avenues, courts, lanes... public squares, parks, cemeteries, military reservations, fortifications... railroads, street car lines... ferry connections...," overall 40" x 28". **$2,767**

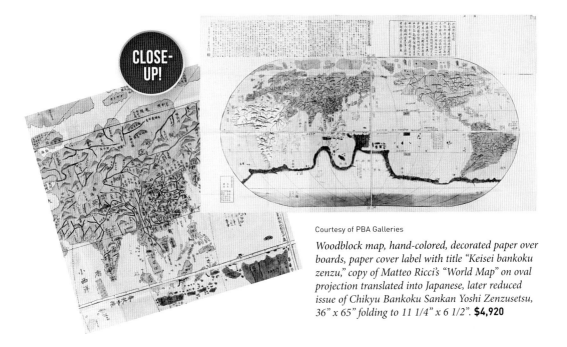

**CLOSE-UP!**

Courtesy of PBA Galleries

*Woodblock map, hand-colored, decorated paper over boards, paper cover label with title "Keisei bankoku zenzu," copy of Matteo Ricci's "World Map" on oval projection translated into Japanese, later reduced issue of Chikyu Bankoku Sankan Yoshi Zenzusetsu, 36" x 65" folding to 11 1/4" x 6 1/2".* **$4,920**

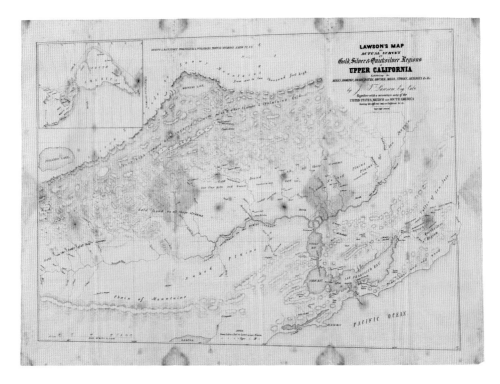

Courtesy of Heritage Auctions

*California Gold Rush map, "Lawson's Map from Actual Survey of the Gold, Silver & Quicksilver Regions of Upper California, Exhibiting the Mines, Diggings, Roads, Paths, Houses, Mills, Stores, Missions," New York by DeWitt & Davenport in 1849, lithographed by G. Snyder, normal folds, scattered stains, 16 1/2" x 22 3/4".* **$7,500**

Courtesy of PBA Galleries

*Lithographed map on blue laid paper, issued as pictorial lettersheet, first sheet of four-page lettersheet, important map of California Gold Region from Monterey and Tulare counties in south to Klamath and Siskiyou in north, with portion of Nevada (called Utah) in east; "Table of Distances from the Capital Sacramento City to the principal towns" in upper right corner, at center right is table of "Population of California 300,000," with San Francisco leading at 50,000, 1855 second issue, George Holbrook Baker, lithographed by Fishbourne, San Francisco, 10 3/4 x 8 3/4".* **$4,612**

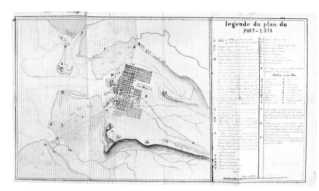

Courtesy of Swann Auction Galleries

*Mascarene Islands and Madagascar archive of maps, manuscripts, and early local imprints spanning more than 50 years of French colonial history in southern Indian Ocean, primarily Mascarene Islands, 1760s onward, consistent edge wear and oxidation throughout.* **$11,250**

Courtesy of PBA Galleries

*Copper-engraved, hand-colored map of Western Hemisphere as known at end of 16th century by grandson of Gerard Mercator; following death of Mercator in 1594, his son, Rumold, published last three parts that formed the famous atlas, Atlantis Par Altera; American map given to grandson Michael; coloring is early, if not original, French text on verso with folio no. 69 and signature mark S, a feature of editions published in 1633, 1635 and 1639, 14 1/2" x 18".* **$3,382**

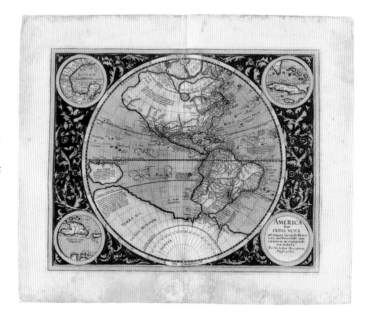

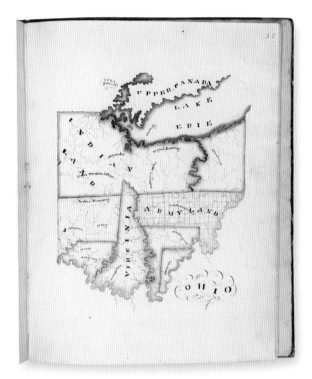

*Harriet E. Baker,* Book of Penmanship & Maps at Mr. Dunhams School Windsor Vermont, *Vermont, 31 March 1819, 14 manuscript maps of American subjects, along with text copied from near-contemporary sources, 4to, 250 x 200 mm, early 19th century, red straight grain Morocco gilt.* **$8,125**

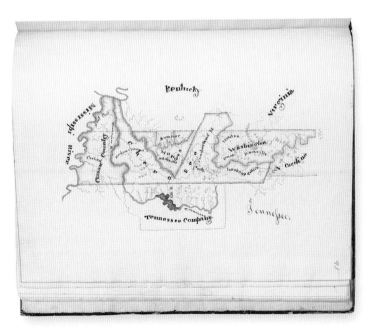

INSIDE LOOK!

Courtesy of Heritage Auctions

*J. De Cordova, map of State of Texas (1849), compiled from records of the General Land Office of the state by Robert Creuzbaur, signed by De Cordova, first edition of famous map and first official map of State of Texas, original condition, lithographed, colored by hand, showing counties, colonies, cities and towns, roads, rivers, and Indian villages, West Texas absent and only portion of Panhandle shown; next to title is printed, "Without my signature all copies of this map have been fraudulently obtained," followed by De Cordova's signature; relief designated by hachures, folded into original black blind- and gilt-stamped cloth covers with title in gilt on front cover, inset along left edge titled "Reference to Land Districts" lists corresponding counties of each district, official seals of State of Texas and General Land Office with printed comments regarding map from noted Texans Sam Houston, Thomas Rusk, John C. Hays, etc., with facsimile signatures; oval inset map at lower right depicts original boundaries of Republic of Texas surrounded by United States and northern Mexico; scattered light foxing, two stains, some separation at intersections with no loss of paper, 32" x 35 1/4".* **$149,000**

Courtesy of Heritage Auctions

*Pair of similar globes, mid-19th century, one with compass inlaid to base, loss of information to areas, otherwise surface wear commensurate with age, taller globe 24" high.* **$1,875**

Courtesy of Swann Auction Galleries

*William Harvey, Geographical Fun: Being Humourous Outlines of Various Countries, London: Hodder and Stouchton, possibly 1869, 11 (of 12) chromolithographed caricature maps of European countries (lacking France), 4to, 275 x 230 mm, publisher's pictorial boards, worn and chipped, backstrip perishing, subtle foxing, top margin shaved, partially obscuring country names.* **$2,750**

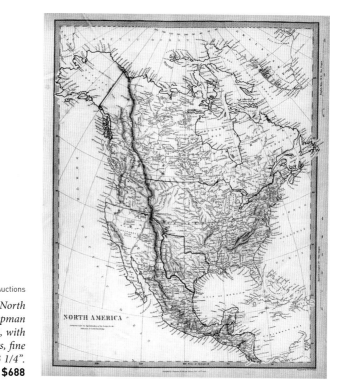

*Early map of North America, London: Chapman and Hall, 1843, with hand-colored borders, fine condition, 16" x 13 1/4".*
**$688**

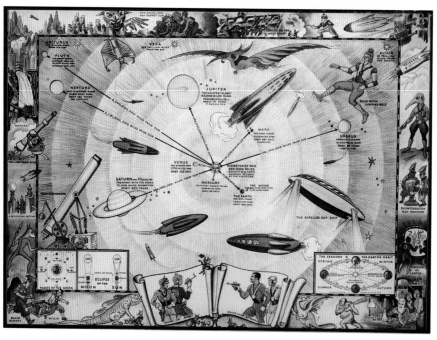

*Original Cocomalt premium Buck Rogers Solar System map, R. B. Davis Co., 1933, part of rare Solar Scouts campaign available only by mail order, poster originally sent rolled in tube, fine condition, 18" x 25", professionally matted and framed with glass to 30" x 23".* **$598**

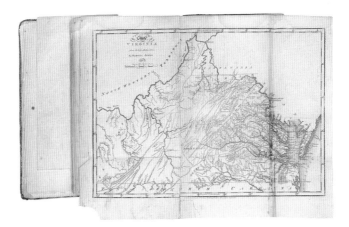

Courtesy of Doyle New York

Carey's American Atlas: Containing Twenty Maps and One Chart, *Philadelphia: Mathew Carey, 1795, first edition, contemporary calf backed marbled boards, with letterpress title and 20 engraved maps and chart by Samuel Lewis and Amos Doolittle, most folding or double page, some printed on blue paper; worn with covers detached, tear into title, various ownership signatures, chipped edges, damp staining to upper margin affecting most maps, tears to folds, spotting, small stains, very rare, first atlas engraved and printed in America, contains first printed map of Virginia as a state, map of "Tennassee Government" is in second state with that spelling (Tennessee would not become a state until following year), 14 3/4" x 8 1/2".* **$10,625**

Courtesy of PBA Galleries

*Copper-engraved map, hand-colored in outline, glued down on backing board, later issue of important map previously published by Robert Morden, William Knight, and Philip Lea; colonizing powers indicated, notes of shipping routes and practices, engraving at bottom left forms part of title cartouche with group of sailors presenting shoes to native in exchange for chest of gold coins, 23 1/2" x 40".* **$2,214**

# Maritime Art & Artifacts

By Martin Willis

**MARTIN WILLIS** is the Director of the Decorative Arts at James D. Julia, Inc., one of the nation's premier auction galleries. Formerly of New Hampshire, Willis comes from a family of auctioneers: His father, Morgan Willis, developed and ran the Seaboard Auction Gallery in Eliot, Maine, which Martin eventually took over. He has 40 years of experience in the antique auction business with companies in Maine, New Hampshire, Massachusetts, Colorado and California. He spent six years with Clars Auction Gallery of Oakland, California, as senior appraiser, cataloger and auctioneer, handling the estate of TV mogul Merv Griffin as well as talk show host Tom Snyder. In 2009, Martin launched Antique Auction Forum, a biweekly podcast on the art and antiques trade with followers across North America and throughout the world.

For extended periods, sometimes even years, a sailor was at sea on a whaling expedition. But little of that time was spent doing actual whaling work. Often months would pass between whale sightings. Sailors had hours of idle time, and some filled that time creating trinkets and art.

Sailors' artwork includes scrimshawed whale's teeth and bone; fancy rope knot work; wood and ivory carvings, such as whimsies, cane heads, pie crimpers, pipe tampers, fids (made for splicing rope); and more. There were valentines made with seashells, swifts (yarn winders), corset busks, and many more interesting and beautiful pieces.

The art of scrimshaw began in the early 1800s and is still practiced today. A scrimshaw artist is called a scrimshander. Starting with a raw tooth in its natural state with ridges, a scrimshander would spend hours polishing it to a smooth surface. He would then begin his design using a sharp needle and India ink. Most of the time black ink was used, but sometimes other colors were also used, mostly red.

I have been lucky enough to see some fabulous whale's tooth scrimshaw work. In the 1980s I spent several days with collector Barbara Johnson in Princeton, New Jersey. Her entire collection was a premier selection of some of the finest pieces known, considered the foremost in the world.

Scrimshaw can tell a story, often with a design of the captured whale on the verso side. The work may be valued as primitive or folk art. In general, most collectors want extensive detail and a great subject, including beautiful maidens, couples, portraits, whaling ships, American eagles and political designs, whaling scenes, and home ports or ports visited. Sometimes a tooth is completely covered with art telling intricate stories, some with named places and dates. Surprisingly, most scrimshaw work is

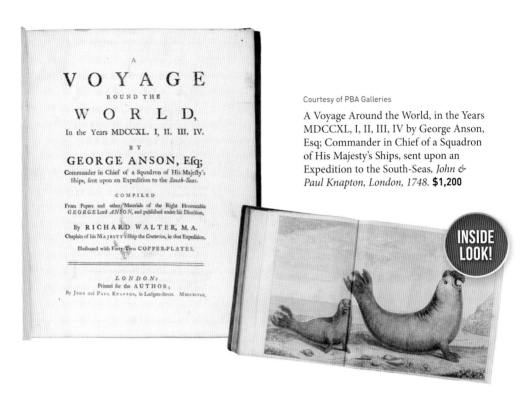

A Voyage Around the World, in the Years MDCCXL, I, II, III, IV by George Anson, Esq; Commander in Chief of a Squadron of His Majesty's Ships, sent upon an Expedition to the South-Seas, *John & Paul Knapton, London, 1748.* **$1,200**

INSIDE LOOK!

not signed by the scrimshander.

An original period scrimshaw tooth is very desirable and can sell from several hundred dollars to $50,000. In rare cases a few have sold for as much as $100,000, including one called Susan's Tooth from the whaling ship "Susan," by scrimshander Frederick Myrick.

However, the record goes to the scrimshander known only as "The Pagoda Artist." An unsigned and attributed tooth sold several years ago in Portsmouth, New Hampshire, for $303,000.

Before purchasing a vintage scrimshawed tooth, seek an expert's opinion. An old tooth should have a mellow patina, and the ink should be somewhat faded. Resin fakes can fool a novice, and antique whale's teeth can be recently scrimshawed. The ink is usually very dark on these pieces.

Whale's teeth are hollow on the underside, unless cut. Later teeth usually look very white. Sometimes people confuse walrus or elephant ivory with whale ivory. Walrus tusks are scrimshawed as well but are worth a fraction of the value of whale's teeth.

Collecting scrimshaw fell out of favor for many years until President John F. Kennedy was elected. He was an avid collector, and this spawned a renewed interest in the hobby. Today there are many collectors all around the world.

Fine examples of scrimshaw are exhibited at the New Bedford Whaling Museum (www.whalingmuseum.org) and the Peabody Essex Museum (www.pem.org) in Salem, Massachusetts.

Courtesy of Louis J. Dianni, LLC

*Scrimshaw on sperm whale tooth, 1810-1830, 7" long x 3 1/4" wide.*
**$3,750**

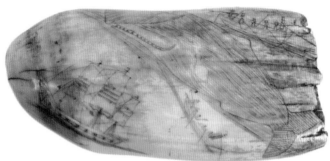

**CLOSE-UP!**

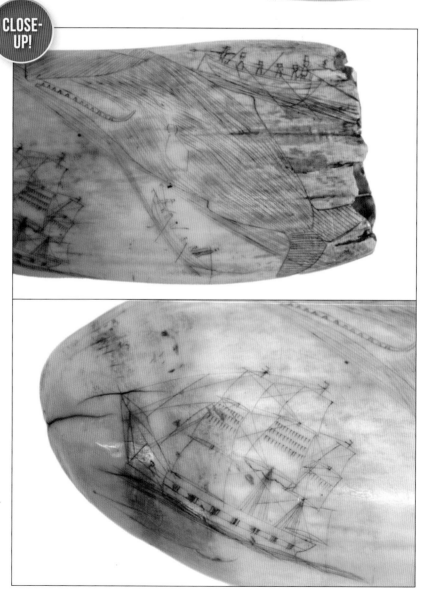

Courtesy of Sotheby's

*Two engraved documents (one shown) signed by James Madison: ship's passport and naval commission; commission on vellum, Washington, Dec. 10, 1814, signed by Madison as president of United States, countersigned by Secretary of Navy "BW Crowinshield" and registrar E. W. DuVal, engraved martial and maritime vignettes at top and bottom, embossed paper seal of Navy Department; ship's passport on vellum, Washington, March 15, 1817, signed by Madison as president of the United States, countersigned by Secretary of State "Jas Monroe" and collector of port of Charlestown, Massachusetts, being a pass for brig Hindu, commanded by Michael Whitney, mounted with two guns and carrying a crew of 15, engraved maritime vignettes at top, embossed paper seal of United States; vellum 18" x 13 1/8", ship's passport on vellum 15" x 10 7/8".* **$2,125**

Courtesy of Actionata

*Maritime painting by Jan Christianus Schotel (1787-1838), Dutch marine painter, oil on canvas, 19th century, signed lower right "J. C. Schotel," 44" x 56" framed.* **$17,734**

Courtesy of Swann Auction Galleries

*"Ship Constitution Capt. Peabody of Boston, off South Point, New Orleans" ink wash with white highlights on paper, circa 1841, on original stiff mount with ink caption, New Orleans, 14 1/4" x 21".* **$2,875**

Courtesy of Louis J. Dianni, LLC

*"American Steamboats on the Hudson" lithograph by Parsons & Atwater, published by Currier & Ives, 1874, once belonging to President Franklin D. Roosevelt and hanging in the Oval Office, with documentation including photograph of it hanging in his office, 25" x 38", 38 1/4" x 50 1/2" x 1 3/4" framed.* **$2,750**

Courtesy of John Moran Auctioneers, Inc.

*"Southern Cruiser" maritime nocturne with ship in rough water, oil on canvas laid to canvas, circa 1930, signed indistinctly lower left, titled partially indistinctly on stretcher, 28" high x 36" wide.* **$25,000**

Courtesy of Thomaston Place Auction Galleries

*Small scale, fully dimensional spread-wing maritime eagle, in original gold and polychrome paint, mounted on museum plinth, circa 1880, 28 1/2" wingtip to wingtip, 23 1/2" high overall, including plinth.* **$1,600**

Courtesy of Swann Auction Galleries

*"Wreck of the Steamship Central America – Appalling Disaster" hand-colored lithograph by John Childs, Philadelphia, circa 1858, 14" x 17 3/4".* **$3,000**

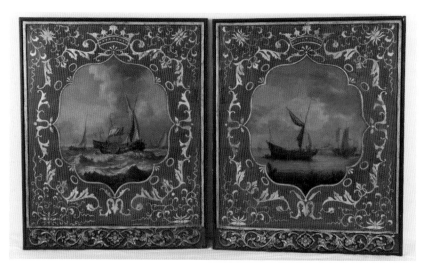

Courtesy of Grogan & Company

*Pair of Dutch School decorative maritime oil paintings, 18th century, probably Dutch East India Co., with lacquered gilt and carved border, 27" x 22" each.* **$2,250**

Courtesy of Heritage Auctions

*Three-masted schooner Andrew C. Pierce, 1905, oil on canvas, by Antonio Gasparo Jacobsen (American, 1850-1921), signed, dated, and inscribed lower right "Antonio Jacobsen 1905 / 31 Palisade N. West Hoboken, NJ," 30" x 50".* **$17,500**

*The William H. Conner built in Searsport, 1877, oil painting by Antonio Gasparo Jacobsen (American, 1850-1921), lower right "Jacobsen 1893 31 Palisade Ave West Hoboken, NJ," signature "Jacobsen" lower right, date of work 1893; 22" high x 36" wide, 26" high x 40" wide x 2 1/4 deep framed.* **$4,250**

*Ship model of Corsair IV in wood and glass case with table, 27 1/2" x 56 1/2" x 16 1/4".* **$3,750**

Courtesy of Ahlers &
Ogletree Auction Gallery

*Handmade model of ship constructed at Plymouth Dock Yard, England, for Royal Navy in 1832, approximately 60" long x 18" wide at main spar, 12" wide at hull.* **$4,000**

Courtesy of Sotheby's

◄ *Audemars Piguet rare enamel, yellow gold and diamond-set open-faced watch, ref 35715BA, mvt 264043, case C3669, 5020 manual winding nickel lever movement, 20 jewels, mono-metallic balance, gilt dial, Roman numerals, outer minute track, blued steel Breguet hands, 18k yellow gold case, back with painted polychrome enamel maritime scene of caravel on turbulent sea, signed Ni. Gi. Barna, encircled by diamonds, case band in rope form case, dial and movement signed.* **$72,500**

CLOSE-UP!

Courtesy of Louis J. Dianni, LLC

*Wine cooler, silver over base metal, three pieces, conjoined parts from SS Imperator (1913) Grand Ballroom, repoussé is Poseidon with dolphins on each side, floral patterns in high relief on surface of wine cooler, lid decorated in geometric pattern (high relief) with eagle wearing crown, script at bottom base: anchor with shield "H.A.P.A.G." and "Eigentum Von SS Imperator" HAPAG Line.* **$7,500**

Courtesy of Boston Harbor Auctions

*Nantucket sailor's box with inlaid ivory, pearl, and wood decorations, decorated with stars, geometric patterns, hearts, diamonds, etc., lid with ivory plaque with name "T. Nickerson" scrimshawed into it (there was a "T Nickerson" on board infamous Nantucket whale ship Essex of mid-1800s), interior fitted with five ivory spindles, four with ivory spools with thread that pass through pierced holes to exterior of box, interior holds approximately 40 pieces of baleen strips, possibly for garment making, 9 1/2" x 6" x 5 1/2".* **$25,000**

Courtesy of Boston Harbor Auctions

*Silk yacht ensign from J. Pierpont Morgan's private steam yacht "Corsair," hand-stitched relic of yachting history, with single appliquéd stars and anchor, panels of red and ivory silk, hoist marked "C.O. & K.R. Wilson Makers. 89 West St. New York. O.C. and K.R.," 153" x 9 1/2".* **$3,500**

Courtesy of Louis J. Dianni, LLC

*Moro lantaka cannon, 19th century, bronze, with detailed decoration including dolphins, on custom-made mahogany stand of recent fabrication, 18th/19th century, cannon 47" long x 5" wide x 6" high; stand 37" high x 22" wide x 20" deep. A lantaka is a type of bronze cannon mounted on merchant vessels traveling the waterways of the Malay Archipelago, and its use was greatest in pre-colonial Southeast Asia especially in Malaysia, the Philippines, and Indonesia; the guns were used to defend against pirates demanding tribute for the local chief, or potentate.* **$2,200**

# Movie Posters

By Noah Fleisher

**NOAH FLEISHER**
received his Bachelor of
Fine Arts degree from
New York University
and brings more than a
decade of newspaper,
magazine, book, antiques
and art experience to
his position as Public
Relations Director of
Heritage Auctions, one
of the country's foremost
auction houses. He is the
former editor of *Antique
Trader, New England
Antiques Journal* and
*Northeast Antiques Journal,*
is the author of *Warman's
Modern Furniture,* and
has been a longtime
contributor to *Warman's
Antiques & Collectibles.*

There is magic in old movie posters; the best directly channel the era from which they came. The totality of movie poster art, the oldest and rarest going back more than a century, taken as a whole, is no less than a complete graphic survey of the evolution of graphic design and taste in Western culture.

The broad appeal of movie posters stems from that nostalgia and from the fact that so many pieces can be had at very fair prices. This makes it an attractive place for younger collectors, many of whom don't even realize they are starting on the incredible journey that collecting can be. Most are simply looking to fill space on a wall or give a gift, and they fill it with art from a movie they loved when they were kids, or one that meant something to them at a specific point in their lives.

"There's a natural evolution with many of them," said Grey Smith, director of movie posters at Heritage Auctions. "As they progress in their lives, they tend to progress as collectors, trading up as they go. When it's all said and done, you see accomplished, broad-based collections."

Movie posters can rightly be called a gateway collectible for that very reason. Very few true collectors just collect one thing and, for more than a few, the first taste comes in the form of movie posters.

So where, exactly, is the top of the market and how has it fared in the last few years?

"As always, Universal horror is the top of the market," said Smith. "Top examples of any great film – the older the better – will always bring respectable prices. As a whole, though, the market is off from five and 10 years ago when top posters were bringing $250,000 and $350,000, but it's been steady at the bottom of the high end and in the middle."

What does this mean to today's collectors? It means that a cooled market constitutes incredible opportunity to the trained eye. The untrained eye can benefit by association with reputable dealers and auction houses, by keeping a steady eye on prices in various auctions and on eBay, and by learning what they like, where to get it and when to buy.

Any dealer or auction house worth its salt is going to spend some

*"Thunderball" subway poster, United Artists, 1965, starring Sean Connery and Claudine Auger, folded, minor staining in bottom right, fold wear with small tears and light wrinkling, very fine condition.*
**$1,076**

time with you – if you want – at whatever level you are collecting, to help you figure out what you can get within your budget. From $100 to $1,000 and up into five and six figures, there are relative bargains to be had right now and, to go back to the top of this discussion, the artwork just can't be beat.

"Ultimately, I would tell anyone looking to buy a movie poster to buy it because they like it," said Smith, echoing the first rule of the business across all categories. "It's all about individual taste. Never get into something for the money because you'll be disappointed."

Besides buying online or from auction houses – at least a few of which, like Heritage, have weekly offerings online to complement its larger thrice yearly events – good posters can be found, for the intrepid explorer, in country auctions, flea markets, and antiques shows across the country.

The movies are universal and every town had a movie house. The result is that posters were distributed everywhere and, while not meant for display purposes in the long-term, many found second lives as insulation in walls or as a single layer in a thick, glued board of movie posters, as theater owners would wallpaper the posters over each other from week to week. The erudite eye can pick out the corners of one of these constructs, or can recognize the quality of paper and the neat folds of a quietly stashed one-sheet. The result can often be a treasure, financially and artistically.

Two aspects of movie poster collecting that get much attention and much misinformation are restorations versus forgeries and fakes.

Every collector should be wary of fakes and forgeries: If it seems too good to be true, ask questions and consult reputable sources. There are always unscrupulous people looking to take advantage of the unsuspecting. A pro will know, based on a variety of factors, whether you have a once-in-a-lifetime find or if you're looking at a clever reprint.

This should never be confused, however, with respectable restoration. Older posters often come with the damage of age – they were not printed on the highest quality paper, as they were not meant to be lasting mementos. Movies played for a few weeks and were replaced, as were the posters. If a poster is linen-backed or framed, there has likely been restoration work on it, and a good dealer or auctioneer will be very up front about this.

"Oftentimes a poster would not have been saved had it not been for quality restoration," said Smith. "Good restoration work is respectful of the original and will enhance the value of a piece, not hurt it. A fake is a fake, no matter what, and should never be portrayed as an original. Educate yourself, check your sources and you should do just fine."

Courtesy of Heritage Auctions

*"Casablanca" insert, Warner Bros., 1942, starring Humphrey Bogart, Ingrid Bergman, and Paul Henreid, vertical rippling and toning along edges, touchup to extra horizontal creases, tear in right and bottom corner and pinholes in corners, archival tape on verso along three folds, fine-plus condition, 14" x 36".* **$83,650**

Courtesy of Heritage Auctions

*"Casablanca" Style B half-sheet poster, Warner Bros., 1942, starring Humphrey Bogart, Ingrid Bergman, and Paul Henreid, small chips in bottom corners, stain in right border, surface paper loss in side borders and top corners, light horizontal creasing, edge wear and pinholes, rolled, in fine-plus condition, 22" x 28".* **$71,700**

*"Swing Time" 24-sheet poster, RKO, 1936, starring Fred Astaire and Ginger Rogers, minor edge tears, crossfold tears just under Astaire's sleeve, paper tape on verso, small pinholes, fine/very fine condition, 104" x 232".* **$15,535**

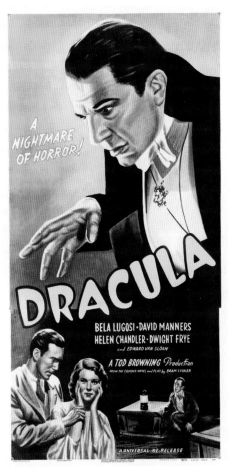

*"Dracula" three-sheet poster, Universal, R-1947, only known copy for 1947 re-release of 1931 classic film starring Bela Lugosi, David Manners, Helen Chandler, and Dwight Frye, fine-plus condition, on linen, 41 1/4" x 79 1/2".* **$71,700**

*"The Wolf Man" insert, Universal, 1941, starring Claude Rains, Ralph Bellamy, Lon Chaney, and Bela Lugosi, pinholes in corners and tear from right border into artwork up to "s" in "Rains," bend in upper left corner and small tear from center of upper border into Wolf Man's head, folded, fine/very fine condition, 14" x 36".* **$47,800**

Courtesy of MoviePosterExchange.com

*"Forbidden Planet" insert, MGM, 1956, starring Leslie Nielsen, Anne Francis, Walter Houston, and Robby the Robot, fine-plus condition, pinholes in corners and around border, small border tears, scratch to upper center title area and one along left image area, 14" x 36".* **$1,800**

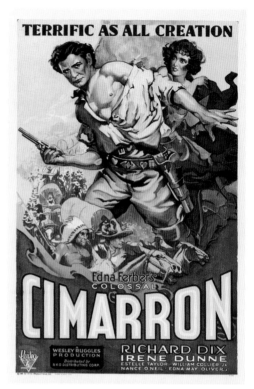

Courtesy of Heritage Auctions

*"Cimarron" one-sheet poster, RKO, 1931, starring Richard Dix and Irene Dunne, art by illustrator Frederic C. Madan, restored, top and right border replaced, chips and tears in bottom corner and small chips in title area, very good/fine condition, on linen, 27" x 41 1/2".* **$50,788**

Courtesy of Heritage Auctions

*"King Kong," Style A French double grande poster, RKO, 1933, starring Fay Wray, Robert Armstrong, and Bruce Cabot, touchup to correct signs of wear, small chip in center and lower-left corner, fine-minus condition, on linen, 61 1/2" x 92".* **$56,763**

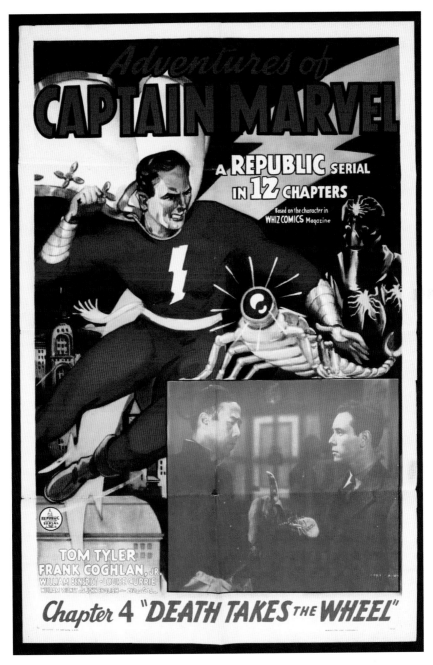

Courtesy of MoviePosterExchange.com

*"Adventures of Captain Marvel, 'Chapter 4: Death Takes the Wheel'"* one-sheet poster, Republic, 1941, starring Tom Tyler and Frank Coghlan, fine-plus condition, folded with light wear to two lower cross folds, one pinhole per corner, 1" tear along bottom border and light border-edge wear, 27" x 41". **$1,500**

Courtesy of
Heritage Auctions

*"Stage Door" photo gelatin poster, RKO, 1937, starring Katharine Hepburn, Ginger Rogers, and Lucille Ball, restored, light edge wear and slight creases in background, fine-plus condition, on linen, 40" x 60".* **$5,378**

Courtesy of Heritage Auctions

*"Platoon" original Mike Bryan poster artwork, Orion, 1986, airbrush, inks, and colored pencil over blueprint, ghosted image on ammonia-based paper, with "The History of the 'Platoon' Poster" document, signed by Bryan, detailing production of piece; small blemishes, including white paint splatters in lower left of image, very fine condition, 30" x 44".* **$21,510**

Courtesy of Heritage Auctions

*"It Came From Outer Space" 3-D Style Y poster, Universal International, 1953, starring Richard Carlson and Barbara Rush, restored, fine-plus condition, 30" x 40".* **$2,868**

Courtesy of Heritage Auctions

*"Follow the Fleet" six-sheet poster, RKO, 1936, starring Fred Astaire and Ginger Rogers, stains, small chips and slight paper lifts along folds and at crossfolds, very good condition, on linen, 79" x 80".* **$16,730**

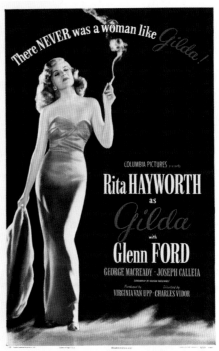

Courtesy of Heritage Auctions

*"The Phantom of the Opera" one-sheet poster, Universal, 1925, starring Lon Chaney, Norman Kerry, and Mary Philbin, minor color touchups to fold line, wrinkles in background, edge chips and light horizontal crease in top and bottom borders, professional restoration, fine/very fine condition, 27" x 41". Provenance: From the collection of Nicolas Cage.* **$203,150**

Courtesy of Heritage Auctions

*"Gilda" Style B one-sheet poster, Columbia, 1946, starring Rita Hayworth, George Macready, and Glenn Ford, professional restoration with touchup to small chips in borders and along folds, creasing and tears in top border, restoration including touchup to folds and borders, fine/very fine condition, on linen, 27 1/2" x 41".* **$77,675**

*"Bullitt" 24-sheet poster, Warner Bros., 1968, starring Steve McQueen, edge ware, staining in borders, minor creasing and two small chips in background, very fine condition, 104" x 232".* **$7,768**

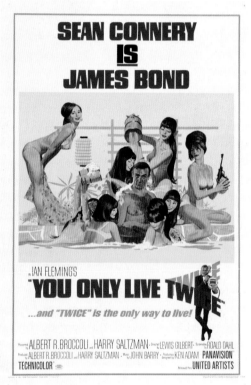

*"You Only Live Twice" Style C one-sheet poster, United Artists, 1967, starring Sean Connery, art by Robert McGinnis, surface paper loss on verso, with bottom right corner bend, very fine condition, on linen, 27 1/2" x 41".* **$1,315**

◄ *"A Day at the Races" insert, MGM, 1937, starring the Marx Brothers, Allan Jones, and Maureen O'Sullivan, with art by Al Hirschfeld, small tears in top border, pinholes in corners, smudging in credits and fold wear, fine-plus condition, 14" x 36".* **$11,353**

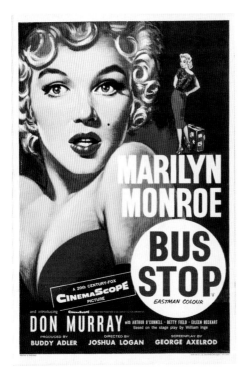

◀ *"Bus Stop" British Double Crown poster, 20th Century Fox, 1956, starring Marilyn Monroe and Don Murray, artwork by Tom Chantrell, light edge wear and wrinkled bottom left corner, rolled, very fine condition, 20" x 30".* **$3,884**

▲ *"La Dolce Vita" Style B Italian Foglio poster, Cineriz, 1959, starring Anita Ekberg and Marcello Mastroianni, on linen, with chip in top vertical cross fold, small tear in upper left, touchup to small tar, smudging in top border, very fine-minus condition, 55" x 77".* **$8,963**

◀ *"The Endless Summer" Day-Glo silk screen poster, Cinema 5, 1966, documentary film about surfing filmed by Bruce Brown in Africa, Australia, New Zealand, Tahiti, Hawaii, and California, minor signs of handling including edge wear, horizontal creases and tears in top and bottom borders, folded, fine/very fine condition, 40" x 60".* **$1,554**

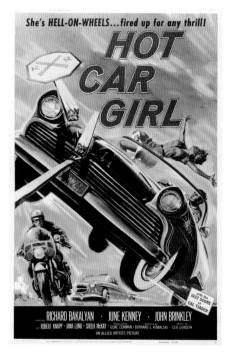

Courtesy of Heritage Auctions

*"Hot Car Girl" poster, Allied Artists, 1958, starring June Kenney and Richard Bakalyan, light smudging to left border and minor handling wear, rolled, very fine-plus condition, 40" x 60".* **$5,676**

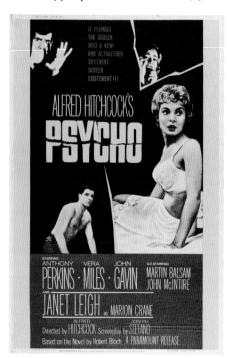

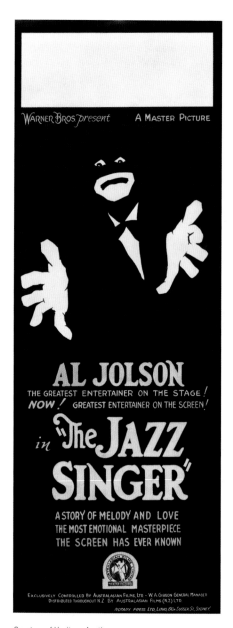

Courtesy of Heritage Auctions

*"The Jazz Singer" pre-war release Australian daybill, Warner Bros., 1927, restored, fine-plus condition, on linen, 15" x 40".* **$28,680**

Courtesy of Heritage Auctions

◄ *"Psycho" Style Y poster, Paramount, 1960, starring Janet Leigh and Anthony Perkins, rolled, light stains in top border, creasing, corner bends, light edge wear and pinholes, very fine-minus condition, 40" x 60".* **$4,183**

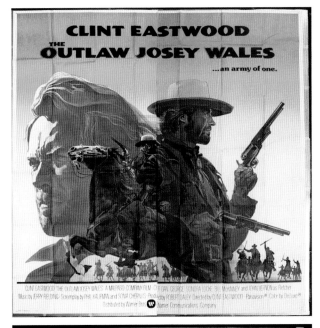

◀ *"The Outlaw Josey Wales" six-sheet poster, Warner Bros., 1976, starring Clint Eastwood, Dan George, and Sondra Locke, very fine-plus condition, unused with light fold/cross-fold wear only.* **$1,310**

▲ *"Invasion of the Body Snatchers" insert, Allied Artists, 1956, starring Kevin McCarthy and Dana Wynter, very fine condition, 14" x 36.* **$1,400**

◀ *"You Said a Mouthful" one-sheet poster, First National, 1932, starring Joe E. Brown, Ginger Rogers, Preston Foster, Allen "Farina" Hoskins, and Harry Gribbon, gel-backed, fine condition, minor border wear, some tearing and minor damage at upper border area, 27" x 41".* **$1,377**

# Music Memorabilia

By Susan Sliwicki

The state of the hobby for those who collect music and related memorabilia is healthy, according to Jacques van Gool of Backstage Auctions. Based in Houston, the boutique online auction house specializes in authentic rock memorabilia consigned directly by legendary musicians and entertainment professionals.

"I have not seen a massive exodus or departure from collecting music memorabilia as a hobby," van Gool said. "I think the number of collectors and buyers is just as high as it was three or five years ago. But there is definitely a bigger interest for lower- to mid-range items."

Before the economy went south in 2008, multiple buyers might be in the market for a pricey item, such as a fully signed photo of The Beatles. The resulting bidding battle could drive that lot's price up to $10,000. These days, fewer people are looking for that type of lot to begin with, and those who are interested likely would pay less for it, too. Instead, buyers are gravitating toward low- to mid-price lots that previously might not have been considered for auction, van Gool said. And, the acts that buyers are interested in aren't necessarily your parents' favorites.

"There is definitely a new generation of collectors, which is people that currently age-wise are between 35 and 55, who didn't grow up listening to '60s music," van Gool said.

Artists from the late 1970s and 1980s, especially hard rock, heavy metal and pop acts, are poised to be the next generation of headlining acts for collectors, van Gool said. He listed Guns N' Roses, Motley Crüe, Bon Jovi, U2, Prince and Madonna as prime examples.

And just as the desired artists are changing, so, too, are some of the items that are being collected.

"Obviously, concert posters are becoming more and more extinct because there hardly is a need to do concert posters anymore," van Gool said. "Back in the '60s, it was almost the only way to communicate that there's a concert coming, and you would

**SUSAN SLIWICKI'S** favorite childhood memories are of hours spent hanging out with her oldest brother, who let her listen to his collection of albums, including Pink Floyd's "Dark Side of the Moon" and Deep Purple's "Machine Head," in exchange for her silence as long as the record was still spinning on the turntable. A journalist by trade, Sliwicki brought her two greatest passions – words and music – together when she joined *Goldmine* magazine in 2007 and became its editor in 2011.

see these posters staple-gunned to phone poles. These days, you announce concerts via e-mail and websites and text messages and Facebook and Twitter and all of that."

Also on the endangered species list: ticket stubs, printed magazines, handbills, and promotional materials. The sharp decline of many record companies and the rise of CD and digital formats have combined to reduce the production of promotional items, van Gool said.

T-shirts, on the other hand, have come into their own.

"T-shirts really didn't start taking off as either a promotion or concert merchandise item until the mid-'70s or beyond," van Gool said. "The whole T-shirt collection is more of a next-generation kind of thing. Of course, there are exceptions; there are old concert shirts for Led Zeppelin and the Stones. But in terms of sheer volume and numbers, that's not anything like the next decade."

And those reports you've heard about the pending demise of vinyl records in the wake of digital formats? Don't believe 'em.

"Vinyl is far from dead. Vinyl is alive and kicking," van Gool said. "Of '60s artists, vinyl is a prime collectible. But the same holds true for collectors of '80s bands or artists. They are just as intrigued and as interested in vinyl as the previous generation."

Whatever your interest in music and memorabilia, van Gool offers one key piece of advice.

"I have never looked at collecting music memorabilia as an investment," he said. Instead, he recommends building a collection around your passion, be it punk music, concert posters, or all things Neil Diamond.

"If you just collect for the sheer and simple fact of pleasure and passion, then the money part, the investment part, becomes, at best, secondary," van Gool said. "In a way, collecting represents pieces of history. Whether it's an old handbill or a ticket stub or a T-shirt, every picture tells a story. When you buy that 1978 Blue Öyster Cult Wichita, Kansas, T-shirt, you've bought a piece of history."

## Collecting Tips

There are a few things you should consider as you invest in your hobby, according to van Gool.

▶ **Condition, condition, condition.** Strive to acquire items that are in the best condition possible, and keep them that way.

"One universal truth will always be condition," van Gool said. "Obviously, the more mint an item, the more it'll hold its value. That was true back then, it's true today, and it'll be true 40 years from now."

From poster frames to ticket albums to record storage sleeves, bags and boxes, there are ways to preserve basically every collectible you might seek. "It's money well spent to make sure you preserve your items well," van Gool said.

Courtesy of Heritage Auctions

*Gibson Custom Shop 2004 Les Paul Jimmy Page signature black solid-body electric guitar, serial no. Jimmy Page No. 6, of limited run of 25, signed and played by guitarist Page of Led Zeppelin fame, with certificate of authentication, original hard case and accompanying case candy, very good condition.*
**$26,250**

Courtesy of Gotta Have
Rock and Roll

*Original Marquee Club
poster for The Who,
which hung inside the
front door of the club
when the band appeared
there on Tuesday nights;
with letter of provenance
from Geoff Harris, who
acquired it from the
club sometime between
December 1964 and
February 1965; very good
condition, light staining
and 1" tear on left edge
and along middle crease,
20" x 30".* **$8,500**

▶ **Put a priority on provenance.** Some collectors feel that personal items, like an artist's jewelry, stage-worn clothing or even a car, have more value than other pieces. But the personal nature of a piece doesn't matter if you can't prove its pedigree.

"Personal items are considered valuable, but you'd better have the provenance to back it up, and provenance is harder to come by than the actual item," van Gool said.

Working with reputable auctioneers and dealers is a great way to boost the likelihood that an item is everything you want. But even if you acquire a personal item with an impeccable provenance, keep in mind that doesn't necessarily make it more valuable than something of a less personal nature.

"What I've seen is that a fully signed Beatles item may be worth $10,000. But there's an enormous amount of non-personal items that are worth more. We've seen certain concert posters sell for $20,000, $50,000, even $100,000," van Gool said.

▶ **Weigh quantity and rarity.** "You always want to collect those types of items that there are the fewest of – promotional items or items that are local, for instance," van Gool said. "Anything that is made in smaller quantities or made for promotional purposes or a local purpose, like a concert, eventually will be more collectible."

▶ **Take advantage of opportunities geared toward collectors.** "Record Store Day is once a year, and I really think that it pays to go to your local record store and buy the releases that will be unique for Record Store Day only," van Gool said. "The vinyl that is going to be offered is typically limited to 1,000 or 3,000 or 5,000 copies, and those limited editions will always become more valuable as time goes by."

Today, some bands release limited-edition vinyl LPs or singles in addition to CDs and MP3s. Van Gool recommends music lovers buy one format to enjoy (be it CD, vinyl, or MP3) and buy a copy of the vinyl record to keep – still sealed, of course – in your collection.

"Because there are fewer records pressed, if you keep yours sealed, 20-30 years from now, there's a good chance that you'll be happy you did that," he said.

▶ **Refine the focus of your collection.** The hottest acts tend to

have the most collectors and, by extension, the most items you can collect, van Gool said. If you try to collect everything that is available, you'll need a lot of time to chase pieces down and a lot of money to acquire them.

"Figure out what really excites you as a collector," van Gool said. "If you do that, you make the hobby a lot more fun for yourself. You set some parameters so you protect yourself from spending an enormous amount of money."

▶ **Think before you toss.** Good condition, once-common items that date back before World War II – like advertising posters, Coca-Cola bottles, 78 RPM records, and hand tools – are cherished by collectors today.

"Nothing saddens me more than people going through their basements, garages, storage facilities, attics, etc., with big plastic bags and just putting them out for the trash," van Gool said. "Eventually, true historic treasures are just being thrown away. Why keep that concert poster? Well, you can pitch it, but that might be the only piece of evidence for that particular venue, and now it's gone."

*Courtesy of Heritage Auctions*

*Jimi Hendrix owned and worn long velvet vest with multicolored paisley and flower design with orange frog-style closures, with letters of authenticity from Hendrix's father, Al, and from Concerts West, Inc., excellent condition, 33 1/2" from top of neck to back hem.* **$43,750**

*Feb. 26, 1966, poster designed by Chet Helms for concert featuring Great Society (with Grace Slick), The Grass Roots, Quicksilver Messenger Service, and Big Brother & The Holding Co. (prior to Janis Joplin) at Fillmore Auditorium; second Family Dog event and first poster with Wes Wilson's classic Family Dog logo; restoration to all four corners and some outer borders, very good-minus condition, 14 x 20".* **$37,500**

▲ *Custom yellow cloud-shape solid-body electric guitar owned and played onstage and in studio by Prince from late 1980s to mid-1990s, gold-colored Schaller tuners, Floyd Rose Original tremolo with bar, and fretboard markers in shape of Prince's symbol, label indicating guitar is property of Prince's Minneapolis-based PRN Music Corp.* **$30,000**

*Bruce Springsteen poster signed by Springsteen and The E Street Band, very good condition.* **$1,504**

*The Beatles "Please Please Me" mono U.K. first pressing album, 1963, signed by all four Beatles, Parlophone PMC 1202, cover in very good/ excellent condition, record in excellent condition.* **$62,500**

*RIAA Platinum sales award for "Tattoo You" album, very good condition.* **$1,391**

*Elvis Presley red wool jacket worn on cover of "Kissin' Cousins" albums and in several publicity photos for film, jacket signed by Presley and inscribed "To the March of Dimes, the best of luck to you and may God bless you, Elvis Presley"; only known piece of clothing that Presley wore on album cover and also signed.* **$12,081**

Courtesy of Heritage Auctions

*Harley-Davidson 1976 FLH motorcycle owned, customized, and used by Mötley Crüe members Mick Mars and Nikki Sixx, S&S Super E turbojet carburetor, kick and electric start, performance machine braking system, dual front disc brakes, single disc back brake, chain drive, four-speed transmission, dual gas tanks and custom flame paint job and leather seats (including extra P-pad passenger seat signed by Sixx), Mötley Crüe "Dr. Feelgood" gold emblem on tank and Sunset Strip Tattoo sticker on rear fender, with certificate of authenticity signed by Sixx.* **$32,500**

CLOSE-UP!

Courtesy of Heritage Auctions

*Elvis Presley owned and worn brick red leather overcoat, circa 1960s, by Lansky Brothers, label reads "Custom Tailored for Elvis Presley" on inside breast, coyote fur on collar and cuffs, with letter of authenticity and original Lansky Brothers hanger.* **$35,000**

Courtesy of Julien's Auctions

*Michael Jackson stage-worn black leather loafers, each signed in silver marker, wear to soles and heels.* **$32,000**

◀ *Bob Dylan concert poster for Dec. 3-12, 1965 dates at California venues in Berkeley, San Francisco, and San Jose, very good-minus condition with tack holes, corner damage and minor creases, 13 1/2" x 21 3/4".* **$25,000**

*Frank Sinatra oil on canvas painting, signed "Sinatra '89" in lower right-hand corner, gifted by singer to Elvina Joubert, his maid of more than 30 years, unframed 42" x 48 1/2".* **$27,500**

▲ *Ray Charles owned and played Yamaha KX88 keyboard, serial no. 1788, with photo of Charles playing keyboard onstage, 57" x 13 1/2".* **$3,840**

◀ *Gibson Custom Shop 2007 Jimmy Page EDS-1275 cherry solid body double-neck electric guitar (12-string and six-string), serial no. Jimmy Page No. 2, of limited run of 25 (Page kept No. 1 for himself), hand-signed, hand-numbered and played by Page of Led Zeppelin fame, meant as replica of Page's original guitar used with Led Zeppelin, with original hard case, lacking certificate of authenticity binder originally issued with guitar, good condition.* **$17,500**

Courtesy of Julien's Auctions

*Elvis Presley owned and worn size 10 ring with 1853 U.S. Gold Liberty $250 coin surrounded by 35 full-cut round diamonds (0.70 total carat weight) in 14-karat yellow gold setting, with letter of authenticity from Elvis Presley Museum, 19 grams.* **$14,080**

Courtesy of Julien's Auctions

◄ *Gibson R-B-250 five-string banjo owned and used by The Byrds' one-time drummer Gene Parsons, flat-head tone ring given by Earl Scruggs, pair of original Scruggs Pegs and first experimental strap-actuated StringBender ever installed on a banjo, serial no. 100698, with hardshell case and letter of authenticity from Parsons, 40" x 16" x 16".* **$15,360**

Courtesy of Julien's Auctions

▲ *Joni Mitchell owned and stage-used Ibanez arch-top blonde electric guitar and flight case, engraved "Joni Mitchell" in mother of pearl at 21st fret, serial no. I786634, with maple neck, arched spruce top and arched maple back and sides, with signed letter of authenticity from Mitchell that guitar was one of six used on her 1979 "Shadows and Light" and 1983 "Refuge of the Roads" tours.* **$31,250**

Courtesy of Julien's Auctions

*Guns N' Roses MTV Moonman Video Music Award for 1987-88 Best New Artist for its song "Welcome to the Jungle," band's second single from debut LP "Appetite for Destruction," 12" high.* **$17,920**

Courtesy of Heritage Auctions

**LEFT AND ABOVE:** *Fender Custom Shop 2004 Stevie Ray Vaughan No. 1 Stratocaster, serial No. JC181, Sunburst solid-body electric guitar master built by John Cruz, with original hard case with "case candy" and Cruz-signed certificate of authenticity, excellent condition.* **$30,000**

Courtesy of Julien's Auctions

◄ *Custom-made scarlet satin jacket worn by Michael Jackson during press conference during HIStory tour in Sheffield, England, 1997, gold-tone buttons, eagle badges, gold cord work, gold lamé armband, Dennis Tompkins Michael Bush label, with rhinestone and gold tone brooch.* **$51,200**

Courtesy of Julien's Auctions

*Miles Davis 22-karat yellow gold ring with square-cut H-I color, VS clarity diamond 5.5 mm x 3.65 mm and 0.85 carats, inside of size 5 ring inscribed "Dewey."* **$12,800**

Courtesy of Julien's Auctions

▶ *Levi's jeans worn by Bruce Springsteen on "Born in the U.S.A." tour, size 30" waist, 32" inseam.* **$1,280**

# Native American Indian Artifacts

By Russell E. Lewis

**RUSSELL E. LEWIS** is a university professor, anthropologistyt, collector and author of several books, including *Warman's North American Indian Artifacts Identification and Price Guide.*

Our interest in Native American material cultural artifacts has been long-lived, as was the Indians' interest in many of our material cultural items from an early period.

During recent years, it has become commonplace to have major sales of these artifacts by at least four major auction houses, in addition to the private trading, local auctions, and Internet sales of these items.

Anthropologists have written millions of words on American Indian cultures and societies and have standardized various regions of the country when discussing these cultures.

We have been fascinated with the material culture of Native Americans from the beginning of our contact with their societies. The majority of these valuable items are in repositories of museums, universities, and colleges, but many items that were traded to private citizens are now being sold to collectors of Native American material culture.

Native American artifacts are now acquired by collectors in the same fashion as any material cultural item. Individuals interested in antiques and collectibles find items at farm auction sales (an especially good place for farm family collections to be dispersed), yard sales, estate sales, specialized auctions, and from private collectors trading or selling items.

Native American artifacts are much more difficult to locate

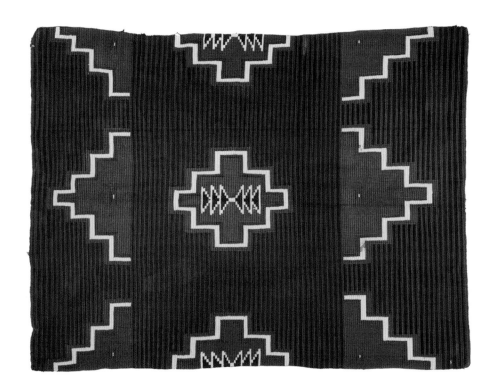

*Navajo Germantown Moki weaving, circa 1890, aniline-dyed Germantown yarns in ivory, red, purple, and black, with nine large-scale stepped elements, each centering geometric motif against banded Moki ground, overall very good condition, no holes, warp and weft intact, stains on both sides, breaks in selvedge, minor loss on sides and at corners, no apparent restoration, 76 x 57".*
**$13,750**

for a variety of reasons including the following: scarcity of items; legal protection of items being traded; more vigorous collecting of artifacts by numerous international, national, state, regional, and local museums and historical societies; frailties of the items themselves, as most were made of organic materials; and a more limited distribution network through legitimate secondary sales.

However, it is still possible to find some types of Native American items through the traditional sources of online auctions, auction houses in local communities, antique stores and malls, flea markets, trading meetings, estate sales, and similar venues. The most likely items to find in the above ways would be items made of stone, chert, flint, obsidian, and copper. Most organic materials will not have survived the rigors of a marketplace unless they were recently released from some estate or collection and their value was unknown to the previous owner.

For more information on Native American collectibles, see *Warman's North American Indian Artifacts Identification and Price Guide* by Russell E. Lewis.

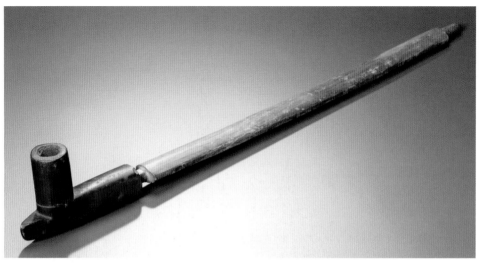

Courtesy of Heritage Auctions

*Chippewa wood and stone pipe with old tag attached, inscribed Sioux, Chippewa, or Gros Ventre, circa 1875, 19" long.* **$594**

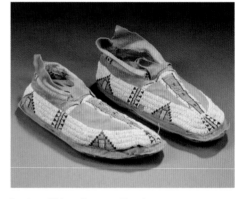

Courtesy of Skinner, Inc.; www.skinnerinc.com

*Pair of Cheyenne beaded hide moccasin tops, circa last quarter 19th century, rawhide soles detached and sewn to cloth inset, some bead loss, 10" long.* **$400**

Courtesy of Skinner, Inc.; www.skinnerinc.com

*Apache pictorial basketry olla, circa early 20th century, with human and animal forms and zigzag designs from neck, 14" high.* **$3,690**

Courtesy of Allard Auctions, Inc.

*Anasazi pottery jar, Soccoro black-on-white water olla with checkered medallions, hatched elements, arrows around neck, and rare built-in finger holes on bottom, circa prehistoric, very good condition, some professional restoration, 12 1/2" x 15".* **$3,250**

Courtesy of Allard Auctions, Inc.

◄ *Rare Hopi low-profile polychrome pottery jar by Fannie Nampeyo in her famous "migration" pattern, circa mid-1900s, very good condition, minor scuffs, 6 1/2" x 10 3/4".* **$4,250**

Courtesy of Allard Auctions, Inc.

*Acoma wide-mouthed polychrome pottery jar with traditional motif, circa 1930-1940s, very good condition, excellent patina, 8 1/4" x 8 1/4".* **$1,000**

Courtesy of Heritage Auctions

*Nine strands of Anasazi shell and stone beads, circa 1000 AD, each approximately 12" long.* **$1,125**

Courtesy of Skinner, Inc.; www.skinnerinc.com

*Cree beaded hide and cloth pouch, circa late 19th century, multicolored floral designs on white background, 9" x 7 1/2".* **$277**

*Courtesy of
Heritage Auctions*

*Bear claw necklace
presented to Buffalo
Bill by Sitting Bull,
10 grizzly bear claws
varying in length
from 3" at ends to
4 1/2" in middle,
beads, and sinew,
with unbroken
documentation of
ownership up to
and including letter
of transmittal to
consigner, 19 3/4"
long overall.* **$40,625**

Courtesy of Allard Auctions, Inc.

*Karuk "catch basket" (flour tray) of bear
grass, maidenhair fern, and woodwardia
fern, Florence Jacobs Harrie, circa 1925,
excellent condition, 6" x 18". Harrie
considered this her life's masterpiece.*
**$5,000**

Courtesy of Skinner, Inc.; www.skinnerinc.com

*Navajo pictorial weaving, circa first quarter 19th century, with
central cornstalk, eight-point stars, and feather and arrow devices
on variegated background, stains, 76" x 49 1/2".* **$2,091**

Courtesy of Skinner, Inc.; www.skinnerinc.com

*Lakota beaded hide and cloth cradle, circa 1880s, buffalo hide form with muslin lining and flannel back, rawhide tab at top and sides beaded with classic Lakota designs on white background, bead loss, one side of back unsewn, 24" long.* **$3,998**

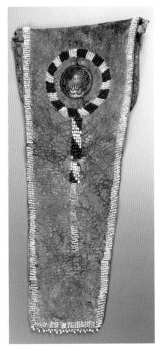

Courtesy of Heritage Auctions

*Navajo beaded leather belt pouch, circa 1890, 11" long.* **$813**

Courtesy of Skinner, Inc.; www.skinnerinc.com

*Great Lakes loom-beaded cloth bandolier bag, circa last quarter 19th century, multicolored geometric and abstract floral designs on pink and crystal background, green wool tassels from bottom, bead loss, 38" long x 10 1/2" wide.* **$923**

Courtesy of Heritage Auctions

*Laguna polychrome storage jar, Arroh-ah-och, circa 1895, painted in red and black over white slip with four large-scale stepped elements, each enclosing diamond, hatched background, surmounted by three bands of geometric designs, dark brown underbody, one restored area beneath rim, 13 1/2" diameter.* **$10,000**

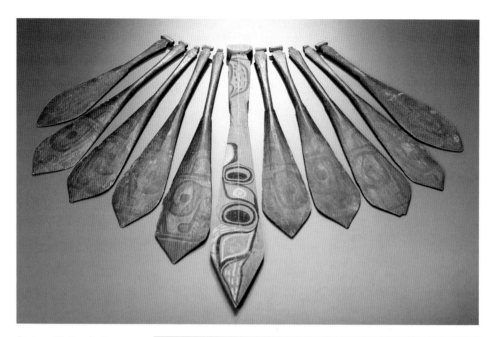

Courtesy of Heritage Auctions

*Eleven Northwest Coast painted model paddles, circa 1890, overall good condition, wear commensurate with age, no apparent restoration, longest 18 1/4".* **$563**

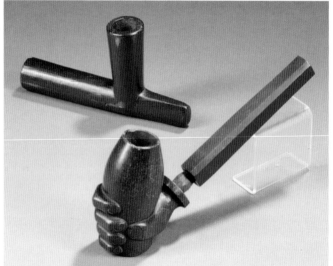

Courtesy of Skinner, Inc.; www.skinnerinc.com

▶ *Two Plains catlinite pipe bowls, circa last quarter 19th century, classic T-bowl labeled "Dawson Co. Mont." and two-piece pipe, bowl being grasped by human hand, T-bowl 5 1/4" long, second pipe 7 1/4" long.* **$2,214**

Courtesy of Heritage Auctions

*Pima coiled bowl, circa 1890, 10 1/2" diameter.* **$275**

**676** *Warman's* Antiques & Collectibles

**N**

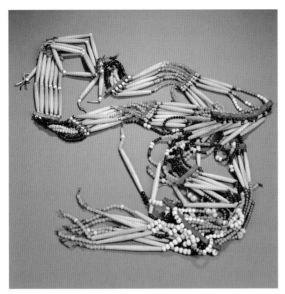

Courtesy of Skinner, Inc.; www.skinnerinc.com

*Plains woman's hairpipe necklace, circa late 19th century, bone hairpipes alternating with variety of large glass trade beads with commercial leather spacers, broken in spots.* **$461**

Courtesy of Heritage Auctions

*Sioux beaded hide baby carrier, circa 1890, sinew sewn and lane-stitched in classic Sioux bead colors, body with geometric elements of alternating design, surmounted by rawhide tab decorated with banded beadwork and hide fringe, overall very good condition, minimal bead loss, moderate soiling at top, brittleness to hide fringe at top, no apparent restoration, 24" high.* **$8,125**

Courtesy of Heritage Auctions

◄ *Plains quilled hide war shirt once belonging to Sioux Chief Runs the Enemy, circa 1880, overlaid over shoulders and across sleeves with hide strips, decorated with elongated triangles and cross motifs, stitched in natural, yellow, purple, and red-dyed porcupine quills, rectangular bibs with four lanes of banded beadwork stitched in blue and white beads, trimmed overall with hair locks, 54" long across sleeves.* **$35,000**

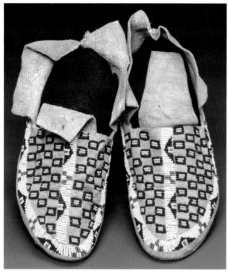

Courtesy of Heritage Auctions

*Sioux beaded hide moccasins, circa 1900, stitched with sinew in various shades of glass seed beads, each with band of small geometric motifs overlaying checkered pattern on vamp, similar band of geometric motif encircling foot, rawhide soles, each 9 1/2" long.* **$656**

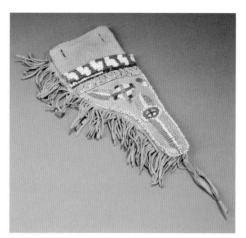

Courtesy of Skinner, Inc.; www.skinnerinc.com

*Plains beaded hide holster for small frame revolver, circa 1900, 9 1/4" long without fringe.* **$308**

Courtesy of Heritage Auctions

*Ute beaded hide dress yoke, circa 1890, decorated overall with yellow ochre pigment, sinew sewn and lane-stitched in various shades of glass seed beads, geometric motifs on neck and shoulders, alternating blue and white bands to edges, fine hide fringe, 36" long excluding fringe.* **$3,750**

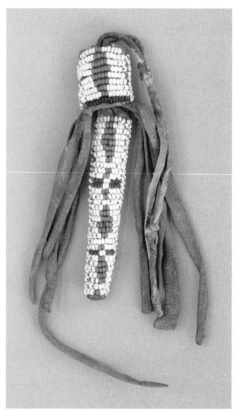

Courtesy of Heritage Auctions

*Ute beaded hide needle case, circa 1880, 3 1/2" long.* **$163**

Courtesy of Allard Auctions, Inc.

◀ *Pomo twined conical-shaped traditional burden basket with geometric designs in red fern, circa 1890, good condition, 21 1/4" x 25 1/2".* **$20,000**

Courtesy of Allard Auctions, Inc.

▶ *Zuni polychrome pottery olla with traditional rosettes and other typical figures and symbols, circa 1900, very good condition, 9 1/2" x 11".* **$2,250**

Courtesy of Skinner, Inc.; www.skinnerinc.com

*Two Woodlands items, circa last quarter 19th century, pair of Seneca beaded cloth and hide moccasins and cloth wall pocket, both with multicolor floral designs, pocket 9 1/2" high, moccasins 10" long.* **$246**

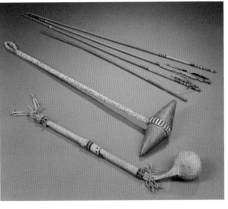

Courtesy of Skinner, Inc.; www.skinnerinc.com

*Six weapons, Plains skull cracker club with bead-wrapped handle, Apache slingshot club with partially beaded handle, and four arrow shafts, three with painted decoration, skull cracker 24" long.* **$1,046**

# Perfume Bottles

By Kyle Husfloen

**KYLE HUSFLOEN,**
Southern California
representative for
Kaminski Auctions, is a
well-respected expert on
antiques and collectibles.
He was with Antique
Trader publications for
more than 30 years.

Although the human sense of smell isn't nearly as acute as that of many other mammals, we have long been affected by the odors in the world around us. Science has shown that scents or smells can directly affect our mood or behavior.

No one knows for certain when humans first rubbed themselves with some plant or herb to improve their appeal to other humans, usually of the opposite sex. However, it is clear that the use of unguents and scented materials was widely practiced as far back as Ancient Egypt.

Some of the first objects made of glass, in fact, were small cast vials used for storing such mixtures. By the age of the Roman Empire, scented waters and other mixtures were even more important and were widely available in small glass flasks or bottles. Since that time glass has been the material of choice for storing scented concoctions, and during the past 200 years some of the most exquisite glass objects produced were designed for that purpose.

It wasn't until around the middle of the 19th century that specialized bottles and vials were produced to hold commercially manufactured scents. Some aromatic mixtures were worn on special occasions, while many others were splashed on to help mask body odor. For centuries it had been common practice for "sophisticated" people to carry on their person a scented pouch or similar accoutrement, since daily bathing was unheard of and laundering methods were primitive.

Commercially produced and brand name perfumes and colognes have really only been common since the late 19th and early 20th centuries. The French started the ball rolling during the first half of the 19th century when D'Orsay and Guerlain began producing special scents. The first American entrepreneur to step into this field was Richard Hudnut, whose firm was established in 1880. During the second half of the 19th century

*Baccarat Monne Toute l'Egypte perfume bottle, cover, inner stopper, 1917, clear/frost crystal, molded label, black patina, Baccarat mark, box, 4 1/8".* **$30,000**

most scents carried simple labels and were sold in simple, fairly generic glass bottles. Only in the early 20th century did parfumeurs introduce specially designed labels and bottles to hold their most popular perfumes. Coty, founded in 1904, was one of the first to do this, and they turned to Rene Lalique for a special bottle design around 1908. Other French firms, such as Bourjois (1903), Caron (1903), and D'Orsay (1904) were soon following this trend.

People collect two kinds of perfume bottles – decorative and commercial. Decorative bottles include any bottles sold empty and meant to be filled with your choice of scent. Commercial bottles are any that were sold filled with scent and usually have the label of the perfume company.

The rules of value for perfume bottles are the same as for any other kind of glass – rarity, condition, age, and quality of glass.

The record price for perfume bottle at auction is something over $200,000, and those little sample bottles of scent that we used to get for free at perfume counters in the 1960s can now bring as much as $300 or $400.

For more information on perfume bottles, see *Antique Trader Perfume Bottles Price Guide* by Kyle Husfloen.

Courtesy of Perfume Bottles Auction

*Austro-Hungarian scent bottle, circa 1880, ruby crystal, engraved hand-cut silver mount, faux jewels, hinged cover, stopper, 4".* **$950**

Courtesy of Perfume Bottles Auction

*French perfume bottle, circa 1840, clear crystal, ball stopper, raised gold enamel with faux emerald jewels, bronze mounted tip, shoulder, and stopper cover, gilt bronze and marble figural tripod holder, 9".* **$2,700**

Courtesy of Perfume Bottles Auction

*European vinaigrette, 18k three-tone gold, 19th century, various textures, applied floral motif set with turquoise, rubies and pearls, cover set with 42-carat faceted amethyst, engraved hinged grill, ram's head gold marks, 1 3/4" diameter.* **$4,000**

Courtesy of Perfume Bottles Auction

◄ *French scent bottle, circa 1850, painted porcelain, gilt border with porcelain beaded edge, original porcelain inner stopper formed as bead, gilt metal screw top, 2 1/2".* **$500**

Courtesy of Perfume Bottles Auction

► *Palais Royal scent caddy, circa 1850, hand-painted porcelain, gilt bronze mounts, two Baccarat crystal bottles, stoppers, gilt hardware framing hand-painted miniatures, bottles 2 3/8".* **$2,000**

Courtesy of Perfume Bottles Auction

◄ *Palais Royal Sèvres porcelain scent tantalus, circa 1850, painted porcelain of four floral bouquets, gold detail, engraved gilt bronze cap, holds four Baccarat crystal bottles with gilt detail, reserves in feet for removed stoppers, bottle 6 1/4".* **$4,250**

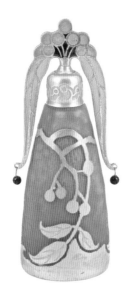

Courtesy of Perfume Bottles Auction

*Austrian chatelaine scent bottle, circa 1900, gilt silver, enameled detail, set with garnets and sapphires, glass liner, dauber-stopper, depicting Eve as half woman/half serpent in Garden of Eden, 2 3/8".* **$1,400**

Courtesy of Perfume Bottles Auction

*DeVilbiss perfume bottle, 1927, acid cut glass in Cherry Drop motif, enameled orange interior, gilt relief finish, gilt bronze fitting and tiara stopper head, champleve enamel, dauber, 5 1/8".* **$8,000**

Courtesy of Perfume Bottles Auction

*DeVilbiss Imperial Series atomizer, 1926, interior painted glass shaded green to white, gilt metal hardware and elaborate mounting, hanging pink faceted jewels (one tip chip), DeVilbiss mark, 8 1/2".* **$3,000**

Courtesy of Perfume Bottles Auction

Courtesy of Perfume Bottles Auction

Courtesy of Perfume Bottles Auction

*Austrian perfume bottle, black crystal, circa 1930, green crystal stopper, enameled gilt bronze collar, jeweled gilt metal base, Austrian label, base marked France, 9 1/4".* **$3,000**

*Limoges enamel scent bottle, circa 1870, gold mounts, glass stopper, shaped as hinged etui box, gold mark D&V, 3".* **$1,000**

*J. Viard, Monna Vanna Bouquet Cavalieri, perfume bottle and stopper, 1900, frosted glass with clear panels, cattail motif, multicolor patina and enamel decoration, 5 1/4".* **$2,000**

Courtesy of Perfume Bottles Auction

*Delyna Nuit Romantique perfume bottle and stopper, 1925, clear/frost glass, molded high relief surface star motif and labeling, cord sealed, 6 1/4".* **$1,000**

Courtesy of Perfume Bottles Auction

*L'Berty & Co. Ame de Fleur floriform perfume bottle and stopper, 1920s, frost glass formed as leaves and flower head with lady bugs, gray-black enamel detail and label, 4 3/4".* **$1,300**

Courtesy of Perfume Bottles Auction

*Baccarat Jovoy Gardez Moi perfume bottle and stopper, 1926, black crystal, on stand (recreated), Baccarat mark, 4 7/8".* **$3,750**

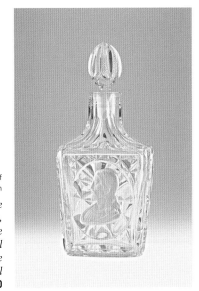

*Baccarat perfume bottle and stopper, circa 1860, clear crystal, sulphide portrait of Jesus, wheel cut pattern on opposite side, chips to one vertical corner, 5 3/4".* **$850**

▲ *Hoffmann, Czechoslovakian perfume bottle, opaque white crystal, circa 1930, matching red crystal stopper, dauber stub, unmarked, 7 1/2".* **$1,900**

◄ *Czechoslovakian perfume bottle and stopper, circa 1930, clear/frost blue crystal, reclining nude basking in rays of stylized sun stopper, 7 7/8".* **$2,200**

▶ *Ricksecker perfume bottle,
circa 1900, hand-painted
porcelain, hanging flask-form,
painted label, metal sprinkler
cap, 3 3/8".* **$250**

◀ *Depinoix figural perfume
bottle and stopper, 1920s,
clear glass, molded rose arbor
and gate, gilt and enamel
details, 4 1/2".* **$2,400**

▶ *Emilia (Caron) Royal
Emilia perfume bottle and
stopper, circa 1899, clear
glass, label, box, rarely seen
example by ancestor of Caron
Co., 4 1/2".* **$1,200**

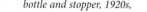

Courtesy of Perfume Bottles Auction

*R. Lalique Violet Gri-Gri perfume bottle and stopper, 1924, clear glass, relief coral pattern overall, Lalique mark, 3 3/4".* **$2,400**

Courtesy of
Perfume Bottles Auction

▲ *Ingrid Czechoslovakian perfume bottle, circa 1930, black crystal, figural malachite crystal stopper, dauber, MIC in oval, 5 7/8".* **$4,250**

Courtesy of
Perfume Bottles Auction

◄ *Palais Royal perfume casket, circa 1860, turquoise opaline glass, gilt metalwork and holder, faceted crystal bottle, metal cover, tiny frozen stopper, 6 3/4".* **$350**

# Petroliana

Petroliana covers a broad range of gas station collectibles from containers and globes to signs and pumps and everything in between. As with all advertising items, factors such as brand name, intricacy of design, color, age, condition, and rarity drastically affect value.

Beware of reproduction and fantasy pieces. For collectors of vintage gas and oil items, the only way to avoid reproductions is experience: making mistakes and learning from them; talking with other collectors and dealers; finding reputable resources (including books and websites), and learning to invest wisely, buying the best examples one can afford.

Marks can be deceiving, paper labels and tags are often missing, and those that remain may be spurious. Adding to the confusion are "fantasy" pieces, globes that have no vintage counterpart, and that are often made more for visual impact than deception.

How does one know whether a given piece is authentic? Does it look old, and to what degree can age be simulated? What is the difference between high-quality vintage advertising and modern mass-produced examples? Even experts are fooled when trying to assess qualities that have subtle distinctions.

There is another important factor to consider. A contemporary maker may create a "reproduction" sign or gas globe in tribute of the original, and sell it for what it is: a legitimate copy. Many of these are dated and signed by the artist or manufacturer, and these legitimate copies are highly collectible today. Such items are not intended to be frauds.

But a contemporary piece may pass through many hands between the time it leaves the maker and wind up in a collection. When profit is the only motive of a reseller, details about origin, ownership, and age can become a slippery slope of guesses, attribution, and — unfortunately — fabrication.

As the collector's eye sharpens, and the approach to

Courtesy of Ron Garrett

*Hood Tire Dealer Man die-cut sign, single-sided porcelain, 36" x 12". Multiple variations of this sign exist.* **$100-$500**

Courtesy of Heritage Auctions

*Penn Auto Refinishing calendar, 1931, offset and color lithograph of work by Spanish painter Luis Ricardo Falero (Spanish, 1851-1896), 29 1/2" x 17-12". Provenance: From the estate of Charles Martignette.* **$275**

Courtesy of Matthews/Morphy Auctions

*Five-pound metal can for Packard cup grease by Wolverine Lubricants.* **$375**

Courtesy of Matthews/Morphy Auctions

▲ *Packard universal joint graphite grease 25-pound round bucket.* **$200**

inspecting and assessing petroliana improves, it will become easier to buy with confidence. And a knowledgeable collecting public should be the goal of all sellers, if for no other reason than the willingness to invest in quality.

For more information about petroliana, consult *Warman's Gas Station Collectibles Identification and Price Guide* by Mark Moran.

◄ *Tiolene Oil double-sided porcelain curb sign, "Property of the Pure Oil Company," embossed cast iron base, "Guaranteed 100% Pure Pennsylvania Oil – Permit. No. 37," The Pure Oil Co., excellent condition, 27" x 66" high.* **$2,875**

*Texaco Sky Chief porcelain sign/pump plate, white T and "Gasoline Super-Charged with Petrox" slogan, 22 1/4" x 12".* **$1,500**

*"Value-Checked For Your Protection" sign, 34 3/4".* **$500**

Courtesy of Matthews/Morphy Auctions

▲ *Mobil Diesel single-sided porcelain shield-shaped sign with iconic Pegasus graphic.* **$3,300**

Courtesy of
Matthews/Morphy Auctions

▲ *Shell shark-tooth shape sign, 48" x 48".* **$1,750**

Courtesy of Morphy Auctions

◀ *Pontiac Service sign, circa 1930s to 1940s, good to excellent condition, 42 1/2" diameter.* **$3,300**

*Ferrari with horse logo self-framed sign, 34" x 18".* **$8,500**

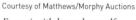

CLOSE-UP!

*Fogg's Drug Store sign, circa 1920s, hand-painted tin, pieces of sheet metal fastened to original wood stretcher frame, "You Au-to Trade at Fogg's Drug Store," marked "Ithaca Sign Works, Ithaca, N.Y.," excellent condition, 73" wide x 48" high.* **$14,220**

◄ *Mohawk Gasoline sign with rare orange background, 15" single lens.* **$3,200**

*Greyhound with graphics sign, 24" x 40".* **$450**

Courtesy of
Matthews/Morphy Auctions

*Reliable Premium
Regular 13 1/2" lenses
in original Capco
globe body.* **$7,700**

Courtesy of
Matthews/Morphy Auctions

*Original, hard-to-find
Porsche Stuttgart sign
with classic crest, 1960s.*
**$4,500**

Courtesy of Matthews/Morphy Auctions

*Shell milk glass globe.* **$600**

Courtesy of
Matthews/Morphy Auctions

*Gilmer Super-Service
Moulded Rubber Fan
Belt countertop metal
cabinet display, 22" x
16" x 26".* **$175**

Courtesy of
Matthews/Morphy Auctions

*Incredibly rare
Authorized Mack
Truck Service
"Performance
Counts" shovel nose
style sign.* **$9,500**

Courtesy of Oliver's Auction Gallery

◀ *Standard Oil gasoline, 1940, tin sign, image of Mickey Mouse licensed as part of the most elaborate marketing campaign of Walt Disney's lifetime, lasting 1938-1940, involving an animated short, newspaper supplements, and a line of service station signs, marked Walt Disney Productions, 23 1/2" diameter.* **$4,000-$5,000**

Courtesy of Matthews/Morphy Auctions

*Small Amoco flame sign, lighted plastic.* **$100**

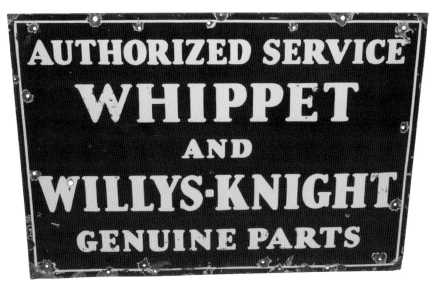

Courtesy of Brian Maloney

*Whippet and Willys-Knight double-sided porcelain enamel sign, 36".* **$800**

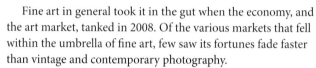

# Photography

By Noah Fleisher

**NOAH FLEISHER**
received his Bachelor of
Fine Arts degree from
New York University
and brings more than a
decade of newspaper,
magazine, book, antiques
and art experience to
his position as Public
Relations Director of
Heritage Auctions, one
of the country's foremost
auction houses. He is the
former editor of *Antique
Trader, New England
Antiques Journal* and
*Northeast Antiques Journal*,
is the author of *Warman's
Modern Furniture*, and
has been a longtime
contributor to *Warman's
Antiques & Collectibles*.

Fine art in general took it in the gut when the economy, and the art market, tanked in 2008. Of the various markets that fell within the umbrella of fine art, few saw its fortunes fade faster than vintage and contemporary photography.

Unless the name on your pictures was Mapplethorpe, Avedon, Weston, Sherman – or among the handful of photographers who transcended – then the value of your pieces fell, precipitously in some cases.

It's been a bit of a slog coming back, but six years later there is a sign of stirring in the photography market.

Burt Finger is the owner of Photographs Do Not Bend (PDNB) Gallery on Dragon Street in Dallas (PDNB.com), the center of the city's Design District, and is a longtime recognized expert from his nearly 20 years in his gallery championing both individual artists and collectors.

"Photography, like the other disciplines, has been a struggle since the recession," he said, "but it seems things are moving forward. Good pieces between $1,000 and $50,000 are selling again. People have some new-gained confidence from what's been going on and there's a new-found equilibrium between buyer and seller."

That's good news for collectors and dealers alike, though the market still favors buyers at auction a little more, with a large concentration of offerings all at once giving collectors a chance to get good buys on a great many pieces in the middle range. Unless you really know your stuff, though, buying photographs at auction can be a daunting world to just jump into.

That is where dealers like Finger come in. While he's in the business of selling photography, like the best of his ilk, he does not approach it from the financial standpoint. His is an artist's eye, and he curates from inspiration; he educates from a love of the imagery and its meaning. He's the sort of dealer who embodies the ethics you want when you are looking for guidance starting or propping up a collection.

*Brett Weston
(American, 1911-
1933), "Holland
Canal," 1971, gelatin
silver print, signed
and dated in pencil,
19 1/4" x 15 1/4".*
**$12,500**

In fact, a few weeks after talking with Finger and visiting him at his Dallas gallery, I found myself in conversation with a longtime client (and now friend) of Finger's – a lawyer from Dallas – who related the following assessment of Finger:

"When I first started thinking about collecting, back in the mid-1990s, I wandered into Burt's gallery. I didn't have much discretionary income back then, but he took the time and talked with me and soon was sending me home with books and catalogs, pointing me to shows and specific artists and galleries. He was more like a teacher than a dealer. Soon I was ready to start buying."

He noted that he recently purchased his first William Eggleston. That would be music to any good dealer's ears, and business.

Where does Finger see the market right now, besides on the rebound? He casts a philosophic glance on where it stands.

"Collectors and collections have to move forward," he said, "and there's definitely a shift forward right now as a new generation ages in and the previous generation moves up. While

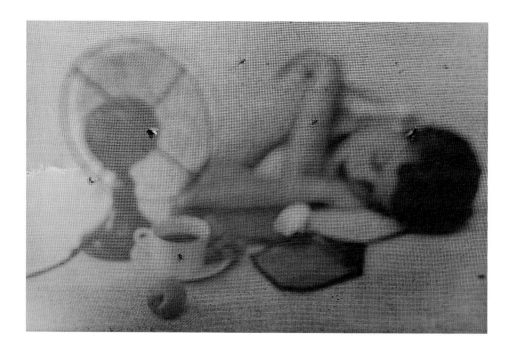

Courtesy of Phillips

*Irving Penn, "Summer Sleep, New York," 1949, dye transfer print, printed 1959-1960, signed, titled, dated in ink, Condé Nast and "Photograph by PENN" copyright credit reproduction limit, 14 3/8" x 21 1/8".* **$112,000**

the 1940s and 1950s were very popular a decade ago, right now vintage pieces from 1960s and 1970s are very attractive to collectors – the '70s in particular."

Another element that the world of photography has had to contend with is the lightning quick progress of technology.

How does photography keep up and stay relevant in a world where iPhones and applications can imbue any photograph with any range of effect that photographers used to have to study years to master?

"A good camera does not make someone an artist," Finger points out. "I'm not concerned with it being 'digital photography,' I'm concerned with the finished product. I think the bar has been changed, it's risen. We have photographers now that are thinkers, that buy into a whole concept."

Finger cautions against getting too stuck on a particular era or artist, however, as you'll miss opportunities to learn, and to collect, in a variety of venues. A good relationship with a dealer prepares you for gallery buying, but it will also get you set to enter the auction market and to look for hidden gems in the corners of markets, shops and shows all over the country, if not the world.

"It's a thrill to be expansive rather than reductive," he said. "Find out what your interests are individually, not what someone tells you. When it comes to photography it has to be something you really love, not an investment. You are going to live with this image."

Courtesy of Phillips

*Irving Penn, "Vogue Fashion Photograph (Café in Lima), Peru (Jean Patchett)," selenium toned gelatin silver print made in 1984 from 1948 photograph, signed, titled, dated, initialed twice in ink, annotated "Passage Print" in unidentified hand in pencil, Condé Nast copyright credit reproduction limitation, credit and edition stamps on reverse of mount, one from edition of 25, 19 1/4" x 18 1/2".* **$137,000**

Courtesy of Phillips

*Ahmet Ertug, "The Library of Trinity College, 'The Long Room,' Dublin," 2008, chromogenic print, flush mounted, signed in ink, printed title, date and number 3/3 on artist's label accompanying work, 88 1/2" x 71 1/4".* **$137,000**

*Elliott Erwitt, "New York City," 1974, gelatin silver print, printed later, signed in ink in margin, 11 5/8" x 17 1/2".* **$8,000**

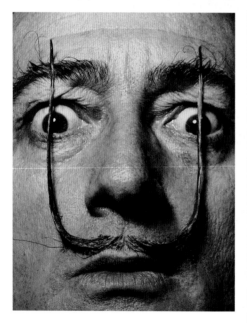

*Philippe Halsman, "Dali's Mustache," 1953, gelatin silver print, signed, dated 1954 in pencil, copyright credit, "33 West 67th Street" credit and reproduction limitation stamps on verso, 13 5/8" x 10 5/8".* **$6,875**

*Ernst Haas, "Leaping Horse on set of 'The Misfits,' Nevada," 1960, gelatin silver print, printed later, signed, titled, dated and numbered 4/15 by Alexander Haas, photographer's song, in ink on studio label affixed to reverse of frame, 33 7/8" x 23 1/4".* **$5,000**

Courtesy of Phillips

*Alex Prager, "Sophie From Week-End," 2009, chromogenic print, flush mounted, signed, titled, dated and numbered 3/5 in ink on label accompanying work, 34 1/2" x 46".* **$22,500**

Courtesy of Phillips

*Albert Watson, "Monkey With Gun, New York City," 1992, gelatin silver print, signed, titled and dated in pencil on verso, 14" x 19 1/4".* **$6,875**

Courtesy of Phillips

*Bill Brandt, "Grand Union Canal, Paddington," 1938, gelatin silver print, printed later, signed in ink on mount, 13 1/8" x 11 1/2".* **$8,125**

Courtesy of Phillips

*Henry Wessel, Jr., "Walapai, Arizona," 1971, gelatin silver print, signed, titled and dated in pencil on verso, 10 3/8" x 15 5/8".* **$8,750**

Courtesy of Phillips

*Horst P. Horst, "Coco Chanel, Paris," 1937, gelatin silver print, printed later, signed in pencil on verso, 14 3/8" x 13 7/8".* **$16,250**

Courtesy of Phillips

*Sebastião Salgado, "The Eastern Part of Brooks Range, Arctic National Wildlife Refuge, Alaska, USA," 2009, gelatin silver print, flush mounted, signed, titled "Alaska" and dated in pencil on verso, accompanied by signed copy of* Genesis: Sebastião Salgado, Collector's Edition, *Volumes 1 and 2, 64 7/8" x 48.* **$68,750**

Courtesy of Phillips

*Annie Leibovitz, "Queen Elizabeth II, Buckingham Palace, London," 2007, archival pigment print, signed in ink, printed title, numbered 4/25 and copyright credit reproduction limitation stamp on label accompanying work, 15" x 22 5/8".* **$40,000**

Courtesy of Phillips

*Carrie Mae Weems, "Untitled (woman and daughter with children)," 1990, gelatin silver print, signed, dated and numbered 4/5 in pencil on verso, 27" x 27".* **$32,500**

Courtesy of Bonhams

*Ansel Adams, "The Grand Tetons and the Snake River, Grand Teton National Park, Wyoming," 1942, gelatin silver print, probably printed in late 1950s, signed in pencil on mount, 15 1/4" x 19 5/8".* **$25,000**

Courtesy of Phillips

*Man Ray, "Jean Cocteau, Paris," 1922, gelatin silver print, 11 1/8" x 8 5/8".* **$28,750**

Courtesy of Phillips

*August Sander, "Jungbauern (Young Farmers), Westerwald," 1914, gelatin silver print, printed in 1998, Köln-Lindenthal blindstamp on recto, signed and dated by artists' estate in pencil on verso, copyright credit and edition tamps on verso, numbered 1/12 in unidentified hand in ink, copyright credit stamp and "Menschen des Zwanzigsten Jahrhunderts" label on reverse of mount, 10 1/8" x 7".* **$7,500**

Courtesy of Phillips

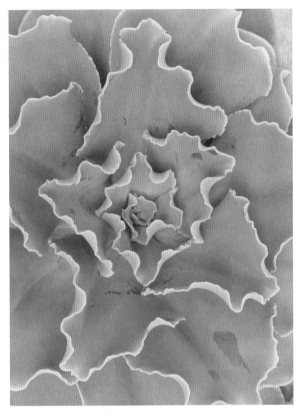

◀ Horst P. Horst, "Echeveria Gibbiflora Crispa," 1945, platinum print, printed later, signature blindstamp in margin, signed in pencil by artist, titled, dated and numbered 6/25 in unidentified hand in pencil on verso, 19" x 14 3/8". **$10,625**

Courtesy of Phillips

▼ Nick Brandt, "Lion Before Storm, Close Up, Maasai Mara," 2006, archival pigment print, signed, dated and numbered 23/25 in pencil in margin, 18 1/8" x 25 7/8". **$27,500**

Courtesy of Bonhams

*Margaret Bourke-White (1904-1971), "At the Time of the Louisville Flood, Kentucky," 1937, gelatin silver print with black borders, mounted, titled in unidentified, with "Photo by Margaret Bourke-White" credit stamp on mount verso, 10 1/4" x 13 5/8"; photo of flood refugees lining up for supplies at emergency relief station in black quarter of Louisville, was taken in February 1937 for* Life Magazine. **$161,000**

Courtesy of Bonhams

▲ *Edward S. Curtis (1868-1952), "Oasis in the Badlands," 1905, orotone, signed by photographer in image, in original studio frame with Seattle, Washington, studio label on frame verso, 8" x 10".* **$6,875**

Courtesy of Phillips

▲ *Henri Cartier-Bresson, "Behind the Gare Saint Lazare, Paris," 1932, gelatin silver print, printed later, signed in ink and copyright credit blindstamp in margin, 17 1/2" x 11 3/4.* **$26,250**

Courtesy of Bonhams

◀ *Sandy Skoglund (born 1946), "Germs Are Everywhere," 1984, cibachrome print, signed, titled, dated and numbered 6/20 in ink on image, 26" x 31/1/2".* **$3,750**

Courtesy of Doyle New York

*Group of seven images from "Camera Work XLII/XLIII," 1913, includes Edward Steichen's "Late Afternoon-Venice" (pictured), photogravure in tissue paper, 6 1/4" x 7 1/2"; Yvette Guilbert's "Together With Vitality," photogravure on tissue paper, 9 1/2" x 6 1/2"; and five other "Camera Work" gravures by Steichen and Arthur Stieglitz (one duplicate).* **$2,375**

Courtesy of Phillips

*Richard Avedon, "Bob Dylan, singer, 132nd Street and FDR Drive, November 4," 1963, gelatin silver print, signed in ink in margin, signed, numbered 2/25 in pencil, copyright credit reproduction limitation, title and date stamps on verso, 9 3/4" x 7 7/8".* **$62,500**

Courtesy of Swann Galleries

*Mourning ribbon with attached tintype miniature portrait of Abraham Lincoln in brass frame, affixed to flag ribbon of similar size, mounted and framed with 1909 relief postcard of Lincoln, 1" x 3/4".* **$875**

Courtesy of Phillips

*William Wegman,*
*"Fay Ray," 1988,*
*gelatin silver print,*
*signed and dated*
*in pencil on verso,*
*6 3/8" x 6 3/8".*
**$8,125**

Courtesy of Swann Galleries

*Hand-tinted, quarter-plate daguerreotype*
*of saddle maker, in original seal and leather*
*case, circa 1850s.* **$6,000**

Courtesy of Swann Galleries

*Group of 23 images (one shown) of scenes*
*and portraits, 14 ambrotypes (including two*
*hand-tinted quarter-plate size images) and*
*nine tintypes, circa 1850s-1860s, subjects*
*include siblings, card players, boys with*
*dogs, nursing mother, laborers, soldier and*
*pugilists, most in full cases.* **$3,000**

Courtesy of Phillips

*Anton Bruehl, "Untitled," 1927, gelatin silver print, printed later, signed in pencil in margin, signed and annotated "No. 89" in pencil on verso, 16 7/8" x 13 3/8".* **$4,000**

Courtesy of Bonhams

*Margaret Bourke-White (1904-1971), "Fort Peck Dam, Montana," 1936, gelatin silver print with black borders, mounted, titled in unidentified hand in pencil "A Margaret Bourke-White Photograph," credit stamp on mount verso, 13" x 10 3/4"; image appeared on Nov. 23, 1936, cover of* Life Magazine. **$149,000**

Courtesy of Swann Galleries

*R.A. Beck, group of 13 cyanotypes of Chicago preparing for 1893 World's Fair Columbian Exposition, 1892, locations and dates appear in negative, 7 3/8" x 9 3/8" each.* **$1,625**

# Quilts

Each generation made quilts, comforters and coverlets, all intended to be used. Many were used into oblivion and rest in quilt heaven, but for myriad reasons, some have survived. Many of them remain because they were not used but stored, often forgotten, in trunks and linen cabinets.

A quilt is made up of three layers: the top, which can be a solid piece of fabric, appliquéd, pieced, or a combination; the back, which can be another solid piece of fabric or be pieced; and the batting, which is the center layer, which can be cotton, wool, polyester, a blend of polyester and cotton, or even silk. Many vintage quilts are batted with an old blanket or even another old, worn quilt.

The fabrics are usually cotton or wool, or fine fancy fabrics like silk, velvet, satin, and taffeta. The layers of a true quilt are held together by the stitching, or quilting, that goes through all three layers and is usually worked in a design or pattern that enhances the piece overall. The term "quilt" has become synonymous with "bedcover" to many people, so tied quilts, comforters, and quilt tops – none of which are true quilts in the technical description – fall into this category.

Quilts made from a seemingly single solid piece of fabric are known as wholecloth quilts, or if they are white, as whitework quilts. Usually such quilts are constructed from two or more pieces of the same fabric joined to make up the necessary width. They are often quilted quite elaborately, and the seams virtually disappear within the decorative stitching. Most wholecloth quilts are solid-colored, but prints were also used.

Courtesy of
Pook & Pook, Inc.

*Pennsylvania appliqué quilt, 19th century, 77" x 100".* **$456**

*Victorian crazy quilt, late 19th century, 80" x 82".*
**$369**

Whitework quilts were often made as bridal quilts and many were kept for "best," which means that they have survived in reasonable numbers.

Wholecloth quilts were among the earliest type of quilted bedcovers made in Britain, and the colonists brought examples with them according to inventory lists that exist from colonial times. American quiltmakers used the patterns early in the nation's history, and some were carried with settlers moving west across the Appalachians.

Appliqué quilts are made from shapes cut from fabric and applied, or appliquéd, to a background, usually solid-colored on vintage quilts, to make a design. Early appliqué quilts dating back to the 18th century were often worked in a technique called broderie perse, or Persian embroidery, in which printed motifs were cut from a piece of fabric, such as costly chintz, and applied to a plain, less expensive background cloth.

Appliqué was popular in the 1800s, and there are thousands of examples, from exquisite, brightly colored Baltimore Album quilts made in and around Baltimore between circa 1840 and 1860, to elegant four-block quilts made later in the century. Many appliqué quilts are pictorial, with floral designs the predominant motif. In the 20th century, appliqué again enjoyed an upswing, especially during the Colonial Revival period, and thousands were made from patterns or appliqué kits that were marketed and sold from 1900 through the 1950s.

Pieced or patchwork quilts are made by cutting fabric into shapes and sewing them together to make a larger piece of cloth. The patterns are usually geometric, and their effectiveness depends heavily on the contrast of not just the colors themselves, but of color value as well. Patchwork became popular in the United States in the early 1800s.

Colonial clothing was almost always made using cloth cut into squares or rectangles, but after the Revolutionary War, when fabric became more widely available, shaped garments were made, and these garments left scraps. Frugal housewives, especially among the westward-bound pioneers, began to use these remnants to put together blocks that could then be made into quilts. Patchwork quilts are by far the most numerous of all vintage-quilt categories, and the diversity of style, construction, and effect that can be found is a study all its own.

Dating a quilt is a tricky business unless the maker included the date on the finished item, and unfortunately for historians and collectors, few did. The value of a particular example is affected by its age, of course, and educating yourself about dating methods is invaluable. There are several aspects that can offer guidelines for establishing a date. These include fabrics, patterns, technique, borders, binding, batting, backing, quilting method, and colors and dyes. For more information on quilts, see *Warman's Vintage Quilts Identification and Price Guide* by Maggi McCormick Gordon.

Courtesy of Thomaston Place Auction Galleries

*Summer cotton quilt in red and yellow stripes, circa 1920s, minor wear, one edge cut, 72" x 88".*
**$115**

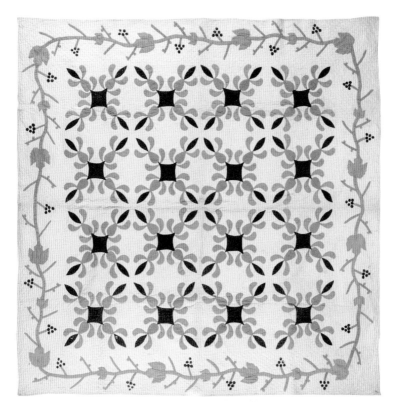

Courtesy of
Pook & Pook, Inc.

*Pennsylvania floral
appliqué quilt, circa
1900, 92" x 90".* **$215**

Courtesy of
Pook & Pook, Inc.

*Trip Around the
World quilt, early 20th
century, 80" x 80".*
**$540**

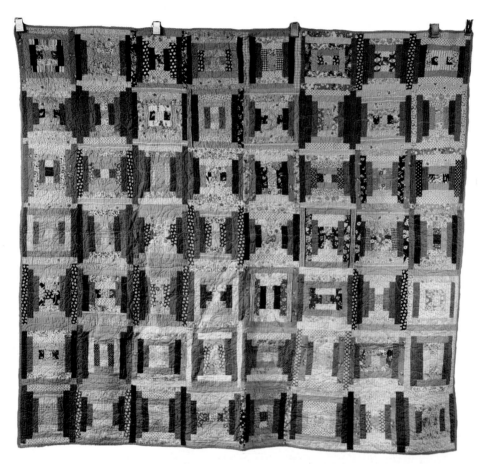

Courtesy of Thomaston Place
Auction Galleries

▲ *Summer cotton parti-colored quilt in Log Cabin pattern, circa 1900, some wear, 70" x 76".* **$316**

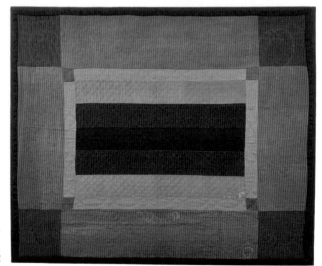

Courtesy of Pook & Pook, Inc.

*Amish bar crib quilt, 49 1/2" x 39".* **$652**

▲ *Pieced crib
quilt, 19th century,
purportedly made by
Sarah Marshall Allen,
34 1/2" x 46".* **$385**

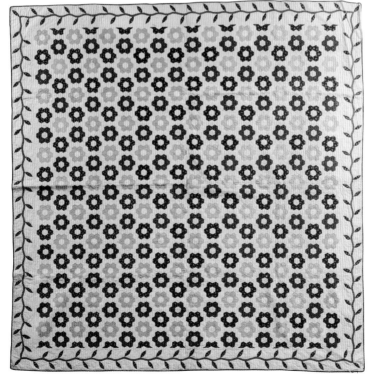

◄ *Pieced quilt with
honeycomb pattern
and vine border, 87"
x 85".* **$474**

Courtesy of
Pook & Pook, Inc.

▲ *Amish pieced
diamond and square
quilt, 82" x 82".* **$593**

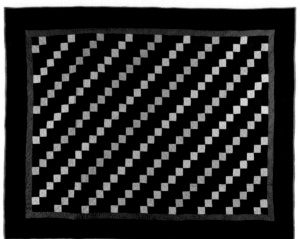

Courtesy of
Pook & Pook, Inc.

▶ *Amish Stepping
Stone quilt, 20th
century, 87" x 67".*
**$415**

Courtesy of Pook & Pook, Inc.

▲ *Amish pieced quilt, 20th century, 81" x 71".* **$415**

Courtesy of Pook & Pook, Inc.

◄ *Ohio Amish reversible pieced cotton quilt, circa 1930, in bar pattern, 72" x 84".* **$246**

Courtesy of
Pook & Pook, Inc.

*Pennsylvania nine-patch quilt, late 19th century, 82" x 84".* **$180**

Courtesy of
Pook & Pook, Inc.

*Lone Star quilt, 86" x 84", with Dresden Plate quilt, 82" x 72".* **$420**

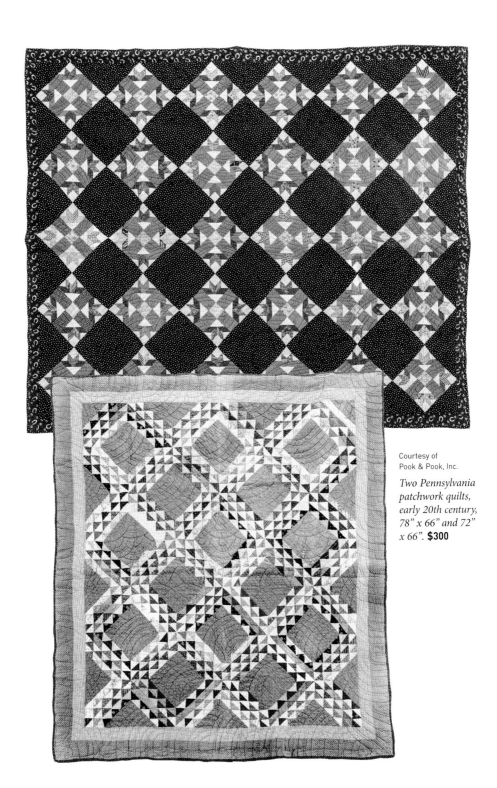

Courtesy of
Pook & Pook, Inc.

*Two Pennsylvania
patchwork quilts,
early 20th century,
78" x 66" and 72"
x 66".* **$300**

# Records

By Susan Sliwicki

**SUSAN SLIWICKI'S**
favorite childhood
memories are of hours
spent hanging out with
her oldest brother, who let
her listen to his collection
of albums, including Pink
Floyd's "Dark Side of the
Moon" and Deep Purple's
"Machine Head," in
exchange for her silence
as long as the record
was still spinning on the
turntable. A journalist by
trade, Sliwicki brought
her two greatest passions
– words and music –
together when she joined
*Goldmine* magazine in
2007 and became its
editor in 2011.

Values for records – much like those for other collectibles – are dependent on a mix of factors, including condition, rarity, overall demand, market trends, and past sales results. Here are some key points to remember as you buy, sell, and value your records.

*Discern the record's quality,* which is not the same thing as condition. Quality relates to the materials that were used in the first place. When 78 RPM blues records were pressed in the 1920s to 1930s, manufacturers used either stock shellac or laminated discs. Stock shellac discs had a lower-quality playing surface, which made them prone to more noise at playback, while laminated discs (which were used by labels including Columbia and OKeh) featured a higher quality playing surface.

Likewise, quality can vary for vinyl records. For 12" records, the low end of the scale is 120 gram vinyl (4.23 ounces), with 150 grams (5.29 ounces) considered a "heavy" weight, and anything pressed on 180 grams (6.35 grams) or more deemed audiophile grade. The higher the weight, the higher the quality and durability.

*Be ruthless when you assess condition. Goldmine* magazine established (and continues to follow) the Goldmine Grading Standard, which determines how well a record, cover, or sleeve has survived since its creation. These are high standards, and they are not on a sliding scale. A record or sleeve from the 1950s must meet the same standards as one pressed today.

*Rarity does not guarantee value.* You thought you bought a copy of Lynyrd Skynyrd's "Street Survivors" album; the cover and labels were correct, after all. But when you put it on the turntable, you discovered the A-side was actually Steely Dan's "Aja." Or maybe the labels were wrong, but the music was what you thought you bought. Or perhaps you bought a still-sealed record that advertised one group on the cover and contained a completely different artist's album inside. These types of scenarios happened more often than you might think at a record pressing plant. While these records are snowflakes, they don't possess the types of errors that draw big bucks from collectors; if anything, they negatively impact value. Depending

*The Beatles, "Magical Mystery Tour," Capitol 2835, still sealed mono LP, 1967.* **$1,625**

on the music fan, these errors may only be a source of frustration, because the listener was anticipating "What's Your Name" and got "Black Cow" instead.

*A record can be old without being valuable, and vice versa.* Head to a garage sale, a thrift store or a relative's attic, and chances are good you'll find some old records. We're not saying you'll never find a beauty or two in the mix, but you're far more likely to find copies of Frankie Yankovic's "40 Hits I Almost Missed," Tom Jones' "Live In Las Vegas," and Glenn Miller's "The Carnegie Hall Concert" (worth $5 or less apiece) than a rare 78 RPM of Charley Patton's "High Water Everywhere" Parts 1 and 2 on the Paramount label, which sold for $5,000 in March 2012. Condition, quality, demand, and rarity are far more important than age when determining value.

*The laws of supply and demand rule.* Meat Loaf's claim that "Two Out of Three Ain't Bad" doesn't count if the missing No. 3 is demand. No demand means no value; it doesn't matter how fine or rare the

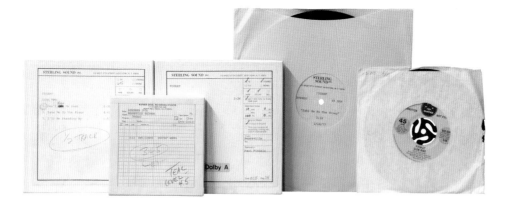

*Foghat, 1975-1977, original recording reels, 10" acetate.*
**$656**

record is unless others want to buy it and own it. Supply figures in, too. A quality record in great condition that also is in great supply means buyers deem what the market is worth.

Trying to sell a record but not getting the price you seek? *Get a second, third, or more opinion* on the record in question. Has your record gotten a better grade than it deserves? Is it a first pressing? Or is it a reissue or a counterfeit? Are similar-condition copies selling for wildly different amounts on the Internet or with other dealers? This will give you a better picture of what you have, what it's worth, and how in-demand it really is.

If you feel a dealer is offering an unfair price, make a counter offer. If the dealer shows no interest in negotiating, ask why he or she arrived at the price offered. Keep in mind that reputable dealers offer what they feel are fair prices, based on the costs and risks they assume for the items they acquire.

*Collect what you love and what you can afford.* Don't raid your 401(k) account to buy a too-good-to-be-true rarity under the guise that it is an investment. Enjoy the thrill of the chase within your budget, buy the best that you can afford, and always take time to appreciate what you have, from super-cool sleeves and covers to great-sounding music.

## Goldmine's Record Grading Guide

Record grading uses both objective and subjective factors. Our advice: Look at everything about a record – its playing surface, the label, the record's edges, the cover and/or sleeve – under a strong light. If you're in doubt, assign the record a lower grade. Many dealers grade records, sleeves, or covers and sometimes even labels separately. The grades listed below are common to vinyl records, including EPs, 45s, LPs, and 12" singles.

**MINT (M):** Perfect in every way. Often rumored, but rarely

*Original 1966 First State stereo copy of The Beatles' "Yesterday and Today" (Capitol ST 2553) with butcher photo cover design later withdrawn; this copy, which was supposed to be destroyed, was produced at Modern Album Co. in Burbank, California, and salvaged by an employee who took it home with him.* **$5,670**

seen. Never played, and often still factory sealed. Never use Mint as a grade unless more than one person agrees that a record or sleeve truly is in this condition. Mint price is best negotiated between buyer and seller.

**NEAR MINT (NM OR M-):** Nearly perfect. Looks and sounds like it just came from a retail store and was opened for the first time. Jackets and sleeves are free of creases, folds, markings, or seam splits. Records are glossy and free of imperfections. Many dealers won't use a grade higher than NM, implying that no record or sleeve is ever truly perfect.

**VERY GOOD PLUS (VG+) or EXCELLENT (E):** Except for a few minor things – slight warps, scuffs, or scratches that don't affect playback, ring wear on the labels, a turned up corner, cut-out hole, or seam split on the sleeve or cover – this record would be NM. Most collectors, especially those who want to play their records, are happy with a VG+ record, especially if it's toward the high end of the grade (VG++ or E+). Worth 50 percent of NM value.

**VERY GOOD (VG):** Many of the imperfections found on a VG+ record are more obvious on a VG record. Surface noise, groove

*The Beatles, 1962 Decca audition, two-sided EX acetate with 15 tracks, recorded before Ringo Starr joined band.* **$2,000**

wear, and light scratches can be found on VG records. You may find stickers, tape, or writing on labels, sleeves, and covers, but no more than two of those three problems. VG records are among the biggest bargains in record collecting. Worth 25 percent of a NM record.

**GOOD (G), GOOD PLUS (G+), or VERY GOOD MINUS (VG-):** Expect a lot of surface noise, visible groove wear and scratches on the vinyl, as well as more defects and repairs to labels, sleeves, and covers. Unless the record is unusually rare, G/G+ or VG- records are worth 10 to 15 percent of the NM value.

**POOR (P) and FAIR (F):** Records are cracked, impossibly warped, or skip and/or repeat when an attempt is made to play them. Covers and sleeves are heavily damaged, if they even exist. Unless they are incredibly rare, P and F records sell for 0 to 5 percent of the NM value (if they sell at all).

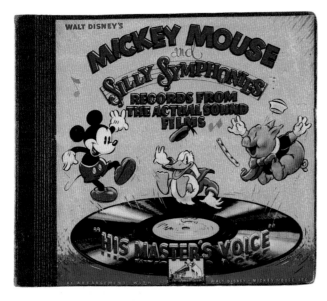

◄ *Mickey Mouse and Silly Symphonies, 1936, 78 RPM set of six records in 10" x 11 1/2" cardboard cover, released by The Gramophone Co., Ltd. of England, an RCA affiliate; cover and all records have "His Masters Voice" text and Nipper logo, choice paper label on front cover depicts Mickey, Donald Duck, and Fifer Pig on spinning record, inside front cover with attached plate with image of Mickey carrying records, inside back cover with attached plate of Mickey holding picture of Nipper logo design. Album has six bound-in paper sleeves to hold records; each record with same label illustration of Mickey, Donald, and Fifer Pig dancing. Recordings are from actual sound films, including "Who Killed Cock Robin," "The Orphans Benefit," "Mickey's Grand Opera," "Three Little Wolves," "Three Little Pigs," "Mickey's Moving Day," "The Grasshopper and the Ants," "Lullaby Land," and "The Pied Piper." Records appear to be unplayed, minor aging to illustrated labels.* **$575**

◄ *Lowest-possible numbered copy (A0000001) of The Beatles' 1968 "White Album," U.S. pressing, Apple 101, sleeve in mint condition, with two LPs in excellent condition. This album was among approximately two dozen copies given out as promotional items to Beatles' and Capitol Records' executives; no copies with this number were sealed or sold to the public.* **$35,000**

Courtesy of Heritage Auctions

*The Beatles, "Sgt. Pepper's Lonely Hearts Club Band," Mobile Fidelity Sound Labs (MFSL UHQR 1-100), half-speed, mastered, limited-number vinyl box set with inserts, 1982, NM/still sealed box.* **$750**

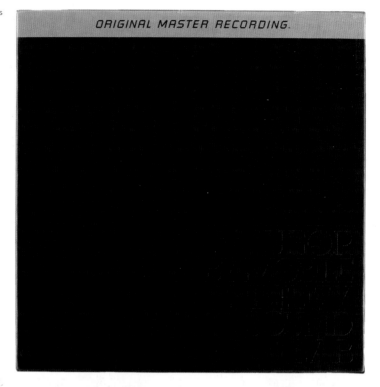

Courtesy of Heritage Auctions

*Various artists, "The Amazing Beatles & Other Great English Group Sounds," Clarion 601, still-sealed LP, 1966; four early pre-Ringo Starr Beatles recordings (three with Tony Sheridan) and five Beatles covers by The Swallows.* **$750**

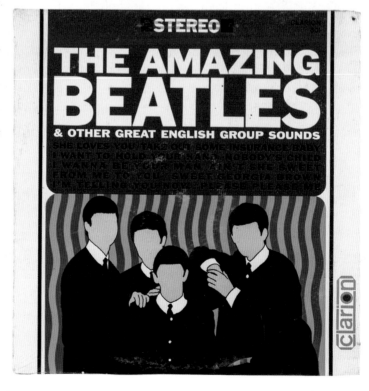

▲ *Five Buddy Holly-related 45s: The Crickets, "That'll Be the Day" b/w "I'm Lookin' For Someone to Love," Brunswick 9-55009, EX, 1957; The Crickets, "It's So Easy" b/w "Lonesome Tears," Brunswick 9-55094, EX, 1958; Buddy Holly, "Early in the Morning" b/w "Now We're One," Coral 9-62006, EX, 1958; Buddy Holly, "True Love Ways" b/w "That Makes It Tough," Coral 9-62210, EX blue-label promo copy, 1960; Buddy Holly, "Rock Around With Ollie Vee" b/w "I'm Gonna Love You Too," Coral 62390, EX, 1964.* **$325**

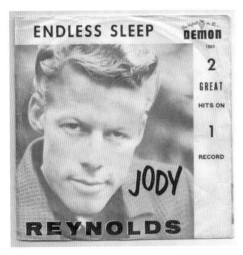

◄ *Jody Reynolds, "Endless Sleep" b/w The Olympics, "Western Movies," Demon 1801, EX/VG+ 45 with EX/VG+ picture sleeve.* **$140**

*Various artists, "Merry Christmas Baby," Hollywood Records 501, NM mono LP, 1956; various artists, "Whoppers!," Jubilee 1119, reissue of "Best of Rhythm and Blues," still-sealed mono LP, 1960.* **$65**

Courtesy of Heritage Auctions

Courtesy of Heritage Auctions

◄ *The Beatles, "Can't Buy Me Love" b/w "You Can't Do That," NM picture sleeve only, 1964, rarest of Capitol's commercial picture sleeves for The Beatles.* **$875**

▲ *Rolling Stones, "England's Newest Hit Makers," 1964 white-label promo LP (London LL3375 (DJ), signed on back cover by all five original members: Mick Jagger, Brian Jones, Bill Wyman, Charlie Watts, and Keith Richards; "Promotion Copy Not for Sale" sticker on front cover, record and sleeve both very good/ excellent condition, record has minor warp that does not affect play.* **$18,750**

Courtesy of Heritage Auctions

*Buddy & Bob, "Take These Shackles From My Heart" b/w "I'll Just Pretend," Acetate Recordisc, G 78 RPM, 1952, featuring Buddy Holly. Provenance: From Maria Elena Holly's personal collection.* **$3,000**

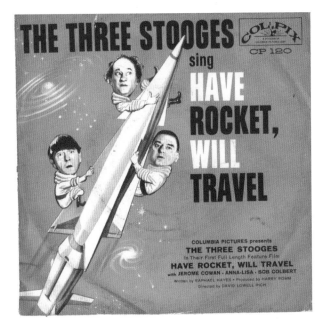

Courtesy of Heritage Auctions

▲ *Tony Sheridan and The Beat Brothers, 1962, "My Bonnie"/"The Saints" 45 single (Decca 31382). Sheridan was backed by the band later known as The Beatles, which featured Stu Sutcliffe on bass and Pete Best on drums. Promotional copies of this record outnumber commercially released copies because few of the latter survived in listenable condition. Experts estimate that only 20-25 copies of the commercially released single still exist, and of those, even fewer survive in this copy's near mint condition.* **$18,750**

Courtesy of eBay seller lsdinlv

◄ *The Three Stooges, "Have Rocket, Will Travel," Colpix (CP 120), VG+ picture sleeve, 1959, no record.* **$822**

Courtesy of Gotta Have Rock and Roll

▶ *Nirvana "Nevermind" cassette liner signed by band members Kurt Cobain, Krist Novoselic, and David Grohl; Cobain signed and inscribed "Kurdt" next to his image with heart and arrow and word "HELP" circled (next to baby) in black felt-tip pen; Grohl signed in green felt-tip pen "David" (above baby) and "David Grohl" next to his image; Krist Novoselic signed "Krist" in blue ballpoint pen under baby; very good condition, 9 1/2" x 4", unfolded.* **$533**

▲ *Bruce Springsteen, "Blinded By the Light" b/w "The Angel," Columbia 4-45805, VG 45 (scratches on both sides), 1973; "Spirit in the Night" b/w "For You," Columbia 4-45864, VG 45 (short scratches) 1973; both records with one sticker each that reads "Promotional Record for Broadcast and Review Not For Sale," and each with original record company sleeve.* **$5,977**

▶ *Charlie Parker Septet/Quintet, "Charlie Parker Septet/Quintet," Dial 201, VG+ 10" LP, F cover, mono recording.* **$400**

◀ *Test pressing for "Beat Bop, Version One, Volume One," 1983, Tartown Record Co., New York, white vinyl edition, screen-printed jacket and label, 12 1/4" x 12 1/4", minor soiling and handling creases, wear to spine and corners of jacket, record has not been played to confirm its condition, record's cover and labels with artwork of New York graffiti artist Jean-Michel Basquiat (1960-1988), credited as producer for project; record was collaboration between rap artists K-Rob and Rammellzee.* **$1,185**

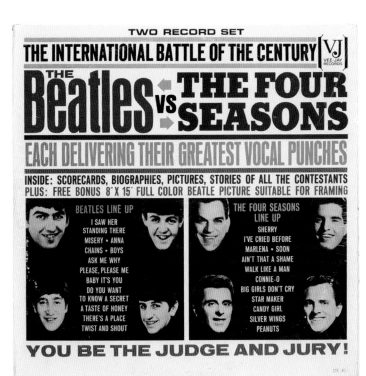

*The Beatles and The Four Seasons, "The Beatles Vs. The Four Seasons," Vee-Jay DX-30, two LPs, 1964, reissues of "Introducing The Beatles" and "Golden Hits of The Four Seasons," both NM/M- condition.* **$813**

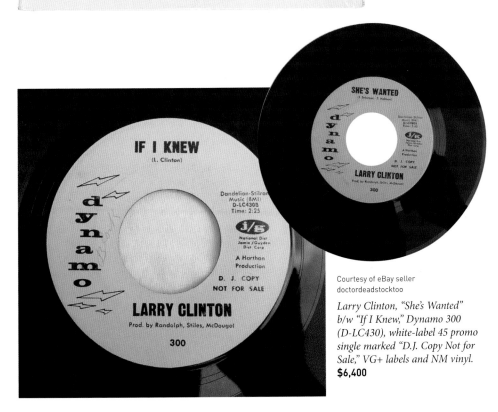

*Larry Clinton, "She's Wanted" b/w "If I Knew," Dynamo 300 (D-LC430), white-label 45 promo single marked "D.J. Copy Not for Sale," VG+ labels and NM vinyl.* **$6,400**

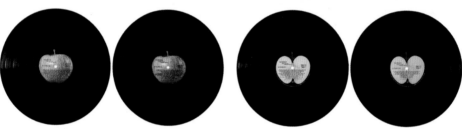

*The Beatles, "The Beatles," (aka "The White Album"), Apple 101, two LPs, numbered A0000004, 1968, VG photos and poster, EX records and cover. Capitol Records President Stan Gortikov forwarded the albums numbered A 0000001 to A 0000025 to George Harrison at Apple's Saville Row headquarters, except for 0000005, which Gortikov told Harrison he kept.* **$18,750**

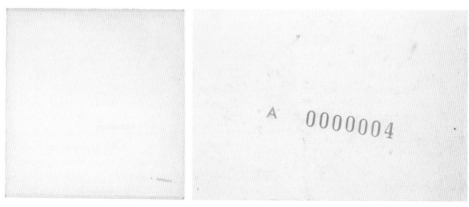

*Beatles "Please Please Me" b/w "From Me to You," Vee-Jay (VJ-581), VG/EX 45 RPM white-label promo with rare promo sleeve, 1964; sleeve is rarer and more valuable than promo disc.* **$6,250**

Courtesy of Heritage Auctions

*The Beatles, "Sgt. Pepper's Lonely Hearts Club Band," Capitol (SMAS 2653), EX LP, 1967. Rare cover with 40 Capitol Records executives' faces, rather than original collage of celebrities. It is believed only 40 to 50 copies were ever produced; this copy belonged to Capitol National Sales Director Marvin Beisel, who is among those pictured on the cover. The records were distributed at a Capitol party in late 1967, after the initial pressings of the album earlier in the year, as indicated by the correct printing of "With a Little Help From My Friends" on the record.*
**$32,500**

# Science and Technology

By Eric Bradley

**ERIC BRADLEY** is one of the young guns of the antiques and collectibles field. Bradley, who works for Heritage Auctions, is a former editor of *Antique Trader* magazine and an award-winning investigative journalist with a degree in economics. His work has received press from *The New York Times* and *The Wall Street Journal.* He also served as a featured guest speaker on investing with antiques. He has written several books, including the critically acclaimed *Mantiques: A Manly Guide to Cool Stuff.*

Scientific models, diagrams, and lab equipment are now hot collectibles, thanks to a boost in the Steampunk design movement and the rise of "geek chic."

It's cool to be smart and it's a cool collector who has at least a few fascinating objects devoted to mankind's pursuit to knowing more about the world we live in. From books to microscopes to calculators and even quack medical devices, this collecting category spans several object classes.

Increasingly, auction houses are pursuing this trend with specialty-themed sales. Bonhams, Heritage, Skinner, and even Sotheby's have all offered major technological auctions, many

Courtesy of Heritage Auctions

*Nikkormat FT2 single lens reflex camera, serial #5172071, with lenses, flashes, and case. Provenance: From the personal collection of longtime NASA photojournalist Andrew "Pat" Patnesky.* **$188**

Courtesy of Heritage Auctions

*Holt 75 1.3 scale operational four-cylinder gas engine for 1916 tractor with radiator, mounted on oak stand with power source for ignition, 22 1/2" x 20 1/2" x 13 1/2". Provenance: From the Glen Reid Collection of Mechanical Models.*
**$6,875**

with strong results. However, the undisputed leader in this category is based in Germany. Auction Team Breker, located in Cologne, offers several sales each year on office antiques, photographica, and film. The sales are just one more example of how auction houses are seeking to cater not only to what collectors collect, but how collectors collect.

Trends in this area are likely to be centered on the dawn of personal computing. The first personal computer sold to the public was Simon, a hulk of wire and cabinetry holding a simple mechanical brain. It debuted in 1950 for $600 ($5,723 in today's dollars) and was able to perform addition, negation, greater than, and selection. It's rare for these early computers to come to market, however, when they do collectors and investors take notice.

A rare 1976 Apple I computer brought $374,500 at a June 2012 auction. Similar models don't sell for nearly as much money, with provenance, condition, and exposure key to an object's auction value.

Rare examples aside, collecting scientific and technology collectibles is a very affordable hobby and one that stands an excellent chance to grow as today's tech-savvy youth become the nostalgic collectors of the future.

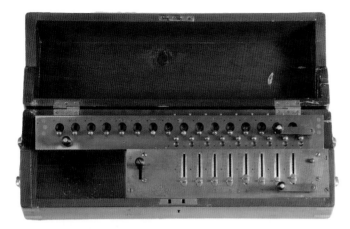

Courtesy of Dreweatts & Bloomsbury Auctions

▲ *Mahogany cased lacquered brass Tates Arithmometer from C. and E. Layton of London, circa 1900, stepped-drum crank-wound mechanism with two-section top plate, lower plate for setting with eight numbered slides with divisions labeled 0-9 flanked by crank handle and selection lever labeled ADD, SUB, MULT, DIV, above inscription TATES ARITHMOMETER, C. & E. LAYTON, LONDON to lower margin, 24" wide; fuller pattern cylindrical slide rule/calculator of Stanley, London, circa 1900, in telescopic form with logarithmic spiral scale printed on outer sleeve, inscribed Fullers Spiral Slide Rule, 17 3/4" wide.* **$1,450**

Courtesy of Heritage Auctions

*Robot sculpture by Midwestern scrap metal folk artist Sonny Dalton, 70 1/2" high. Provenance: From the Glen Reid Collection of Mechanical Models.* **$938**

Courtesy of Heritage Auctions

▶ *Assembly of Maxwell Hemmens steam engines designed as shop floor with central vertical boiler, street lamps at corners, 27" x 28" x 28". Provenance: From the Glen Reid Collection of Mechanical Models.* **$10,625**

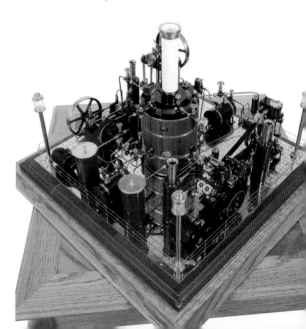

Photo Courtesy of Material Culture

▲ *Vintage optics: six brass Leitz lens canisters, opera glasses, and ophthalmologic measuring device, 3" x 5".* **$90**

Courtesy of Dreweatts & Bloomsbury Auctions

◄ *Ebonized barograph by Yeates and Son, Dublin, Ireland, early 20th century, eight-segment aneroid chamber within lacquered brass armature operating via system of pivoted levers, with inked pointer for recording change in barometric pressure on clockwork-driven rotating paper-scale lined drum, inscribed YEATES & SON, DUBLIN, 14 1/4" wide.* **$613**

Courtesy of Heritage Auctions

▼ *Two Victorian models, brass live steam vertical engine and iron model of treadle-operated spinning wheel, both in glass and brass display cases, taller model 6 1/4" high.* **$594**

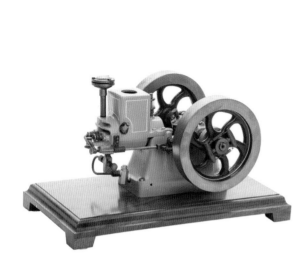

Courtesy of Heritage Auctions

*Scale demonstration model "Hit and Miss" engine, restored, finished by Kirk White, on wood stand, 8" x 12 1/2" x 7 1/2". Provenance: From the Glen Reid Collection of Mechanical Models.* **$1,375**

Courtesy of Heritage Auctions

*Victorian demonstration hydraulic pump, presumably unique, hand-built cast iron and brass scale model of hand-operated pump mechanism, on wood stand, 15 1/2" x 11" x 7 1/4". Provenance: From the Glen Reid Collection of Mechanical Models.* **$188**

Courtesy of Heritage Auctions

*▼ Two German demonstration instructional scale driving models, steering assembly model by Emil Hohm and Werner Degener model gear box, circa 1950 and 1978, each with original base and legend, fitted for electrical power drive, 11" x 13" x 10".* **$688**

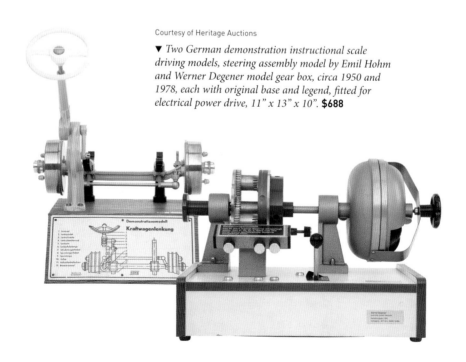

Courtesy of Heritage Auctions

*Model Saito FA-325 five-cylinder radial aircraft engine, 1.4 scale model of four-stroke World War I engine designed for large radio-control models, 18" x 11 1/2" x 11 1/2".* **$750**

Courtesy of Heritage Auctions

*Live steam triple-expansion engine, Stuart standard small scale vintage model of mid-Victorian British marine pumping engine, on wood stand, 8" x 8" x 5 1/2". Provenance: From the Glen Reid Collection of Mechanical Models.* **$3,250**

Courtesy of Heritage Auctions

*Vintage Carl Zeiss microscope in original oak case, 13" high.* **$594**

*French mariner's lacquered brass hand-held sighting compass, signed Doninelli a Nice, with silvered compass engraved with eight cardinal points within outer scale calibrated in degrees set behind beveled glass, 3"; English black japanned brass sextant from H. Hughes and Son, Ltd., London, early 20th century, with diamond lattice-pierced 6" radius frame with pivoted arm, fitted with sighting tube opposing mirror with wooden grip handle, 10 3/4" overall; and patina brass aneroid surveyor's barometer, early 20th century, with circular silvered scale calibrated in barometric inches, 3".* **$613**

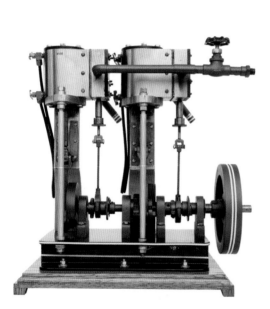

*Scale model double-cylinder vertical gas engine, restored vintage operational demonstration model with single drive wheel, on wood stand, 19 1/2" x 17" x 12 1/2".* **$469**

*British dumpy level by E.R. Watts & Sons of London, circa 1920, on original folding tripod stand, 17" long.* **$531**

Courtesy of Heritage Auctions

▲ *Brass zeppelin cigarette dispenser with tray on bottom, accurate representation of ship with spinning propeller, central body opens to load cigarettes, some wear along tray edge, 7" wide x 4 1/2" high.* **$203**

Courtesy of Heritage Auctions

◄ *Demonstration model vertical hot air engine, water-cooled, fashioned after early 19th century design by Robert Stirling in Scotland, with circa 1900 steam indicator kit by Star Brass of Boston, in oak case, 25" x 11 1/2" x 10".* **$500**

Courtesy of Heritage Auctions

▼ *German vintage machine shop model with belt-driven lathe, sander and drill operated by electric motor marked EKT, circa 1930, 8 1/4" x 14" x 10 1/4".* **$469**

Courtesy of Heritage Auctions

*Live steam model Henry Greenly marine engine and boiler, scarce vintage British model of 1/2 horsepower marine engine of steam barge type, with vertical wood-staved boiler with gauge and whistle, 63" x 36" x 18". Provenance: From the Glen Reid Collection of Mechanical Models.* **$1,125**

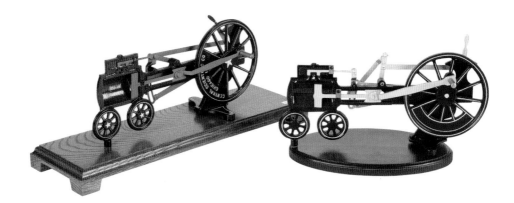

Courtesy of Heritage Auctions

*Two restored vintage cutaway demonstration models of railroad locomotive engines by Central Scientific Chicago, circa 1925, 9 1/2" x 21" x 7 1/8".* **$250**

Courtesy of Heritage Auctions

*▲ Original aluminum LP albums of 1937 National Air Races; four-disc audio recording of 17th annual races at Great Lakes Exposition in Cleveland, Ohio in 1937, of flyers Rudy Kling and Earl Ortman duking it out to last second; it was so close, Kling didn't know he'd won until he was back on the ground; in original sleeves and handle-bag wrapper with special needle required to play albums.* **$191**

Photo courtesy of Dirk Soulis Auctions

*Telegraph receiver printer by Max Kohl A.G., late 19th century, with nearly full roll of paper tape, Max Kohl maker plate to top, circuit in good condition, 4 1/2" x 10" x 5".* **$300**

▲ *Scratch-built vintage brass scale demonstration model of 1866 George W. Warren patent horizontal chamber piston engine, with original feeder shovel, on original wood stand with title plaques of Warren as inventor and Martin, Allen of Danville, New York, as makers, 11" x 31" x 10 1/2". Provenance: From the Glen Reid Collection of Mechanical Models.* **$875**

▶ *Two vintage surveyor's dumpy levels, Ulmer military level and brass level by David White of Milwaukee, Wisconsin, larger level 15" long.* **$406**

Courtesy of Heritage Auctions

▼ *Cased portable steam boiler gauge kit (below, right) and Richard's Indicator calibration device in original oak case (below), circa 1920s. Provenance: From the Glen Reid Collection of Mechanical Models.* **$438**

Photo courtesy of Thomaston Place Auction Galleries

▲ *Rare steam engine diagnostic device, Richard's Patent Steam Engine Indicator manufactured by Elliott Brothers, Opticians, London, circa 1872, solid brass, recording cylinder mounted like whistle with pressure cylinder alongside, with various springs changed out to alter resistance, with lever relief valve; in original mahogany case with springs, instruction card, and 9 3/4" x 9 3/4" x 3 1/2" box; gauge in good condition, box worn.* **$360**

# Silver

Silver has been realized since ancient times and has long been valued as a precious metal, used to make ornaments, jewelry, tableware and utensils, and coins.

Pure silver is too soft to be fashioned into strong, durable, and serviceable utensils, but adding alloys of copper and nickel to it gave it the required degree of hardness. Silversmithing in America goes back to the early 17th century in Boston and New York and the early 18th century in Philadelphia. Boston artisans were influenced by the English styles; New Yorkers by the Dutch.

Silver-plated items are made from a base metal coated with a thin layer of silver.

For more information on sterling silverware, see *Warman's Sterling Silver Flatware,* 2nd edition, by Phil Dreis.

Courtesy of Dreweatts & Bloomsbury Auctions

*Oval twin-handled tray by Hung Chong, Shanghai, late 19th century, marks: SHANG.HAI, character artisan mark and retail silversmith's mark HUNG CHONG, engraved with bamboo, prunus and peony, border similarly decorated and with characters at incurved angles, with foliate and ribbed handles, on four scroll panel feet, 23 3/4" long, 55.6 troy oz.* **$7,135**

Courtesy of Rago Arts

*Reed & Barton "chambord" sterling flatware service for 12: 12 dinner forks, 8"; 12 teaspoons, 5 1/4"; 12 knives, 9 1/2"; five serving spoons, 8 1/2"; five soup spoons, 7"; monogram "E," 46 pieces total, 46.6 troy oz. (excludes hollow handle utensils), in quartersawn oak box.* **$938**

Courtesy of Heritage Auctions

*Silver and silver gilt figural sardine fork, George W. Shiebler & Co., New York, circa 1880, leaf-form ribbed handle, center leaf folded over at terminal end, three gilt tines modeled as fish, marks: (winged S), STERLING, 2851, 6 1/2" long, 2.0 oz.* **$1,125**

Courtesy of Heritage Auctions

*Polish silver and silver gilt etrog box, Jan Polgorzelski, Warsaw, Poland, circa 1862, chased decoration of fruit, scrolls and Hebrew text to hinged lid, three sides centered with stylized foliate and scrolls, opening to gilt interior, raised on four spherical feet, marks: POGORZELSKI (partially effaced), IB, 1863, 84, (city mark), (stag head), 3 1/2" x 6 1/4" x 5 1/8", 21.9 oz.* **$1,250**

▲ *Dressing table set by
Barrowclift Silvercraft,
Birmingham 1989, circular
swing mirror in stem that fits
onto circular stand with pair of
fixed vases and brush rests, pair
of circular pots and covers and
six make-up tools, in fitted case,
22.25 oz.* **$527**

*English cigar case with camel
finial and match safe, Grey
& Co., London, 1899, 8 1/2";
three antique Continental
snuff boxes; Georgian
arched snuff box with later
inscription; and American
Elks Fraternal match safe,
18th-19th century.* **$1,000**

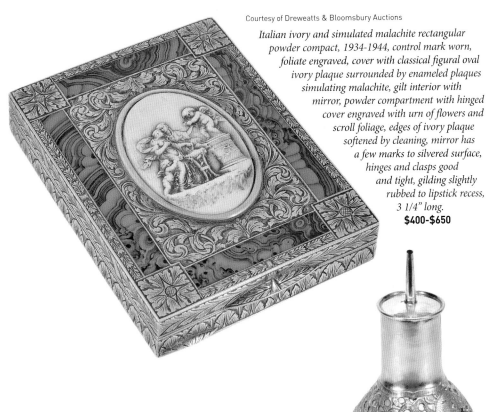

*Italian ivory and simulated malachite rectangular powder compact, 1934-1944, control mark worn, foliate engraved, cover with classical figural oval ivory plaque surrounded by enameled plaques simulating malachite, gilt interior with mirror, powder compartment with hinged cover engraved with urn of flowers and scroll foliage, edges of ivory plaque softened by cleaning, mirror has a few marks to silvered surface, hinges and clasps good and tight, gilding slightly rubbed to lipstick recess, 3 1/4" long.*
**$400-$650**

▼ *Set of eight Italian beakers by Fabbrica Argenteria Fiorentina, Florence 1944-1968, .800 standard, retailed by Saviotti, Rome, with scroll engraved borders, girdle for nesting and on circular bases, interiors gilt, 28.1 oz.* **$346**

▶ *Chinese export cagework and glass Angostura bitters bottle, marked "Sterling," "Hong Kong" and "K," of triangular dimple form, pierced and engraved with dragons amidst clouds, 4 3/8" high.*
**$130-$200**

Courtesy of Heritage Auctions

*Victorian silver-plated wagon-form wine cradle, circa 1900, chased foliate to rim, on four wagon wheels with curved handle, 19" long.* **$287**

Courtesy of Heritage Auctions

Courtesy of Dreweatts & Bloomsbury Auctions

*Vincent Astor commemorative Galapagos penguin modeled by James L. Clark for Gorham, dated 1930, base with some light surface wear, penguin in very good condition, marks: (lion-anchor-G), STERLING, JAS.L.CLARK. SC30, 11 1/2" high.* **$6,250**

*George III oval baluster cream jug by Peter & William Bateman, London 1809, with reed and stitch high clip handle, reeded border, engraved with band and on oval foot, 12 cm long; Edwardian helmet-shaped cream jug by George Nathan & Ridley Hayes, Chester 1902, with reeded high clip handle, engraved with band, foliate decoration and wreath, on circular foot and square base, 14.5 cm high; Edwardian oval sauce boat by William Aitken, Birmingham 1904, with leaf-capped flying scroll handle, gadrooned border and three shell and pad feet, 14.5 cm long, 12.7 oz. gross; George III cream jug, hallmarks visible, engraving rubbed in places; Edwardian cream jug, hallmarks visible, engraving rubbed in places; Edwardian sauce boat, hallmarks rubbed.* **$230**

Courtesy of Dreweatts & Bloomsbury Auctions

◄ *George III barrel-shaped straight-tapered silver tankard by John Carter II, London 1774, flat cover engraved with flower spray, bright-cut border and open work thumb piece, square section loop handle, two threaded "coopered" girdles and engraved with swags, interior gilt, marks clear to base, applied oval plate with later initials, engraving crisp, interior possibly regilded, base has partially erased inscription (illegible), 7 1/2" high, 25.95 oz.* **$800-$1,200**

Courtesy of Heritage Auctions

▲ *Figural letter opener, 20th century, good condition with surface wear and scratching commensurate with age and indicative of use, marks: P.L. KRIDER & CO., STERLING, 10 3/8" long, 2.8 oz.* **$87**

Courtesy of Dreweatts & Bloomsbury Auctions

▶ *Victorian novelty horn vinaigrette by Thomas Johnson I, London 1870, stamped for Thornhill, 144 Bond St., as retailers, cover applied with monogram, gilt interior with Patent Office design registration mark for 22nd August 1869 and star-pierced and engraved grille, with suspension chain, marks slightly rubbed, monogram edges softened, 4 1/4" long.* **$270-$350**

Courtesy of Heritage Auctions

*Pair of Mexican silver and silver gilt duck-form boxes, Tane Orfebres, Mexico City, Mexico, circa 1950, naturalistic chased repoussé feathers and turquoise eyes, body bisected to form lid and base, marks: TANE, HECHO EN MEXICO, 0925, (eagle-71), LUNT STERLING, 5" x 5 3/4" x 4", 37.9 oz.* **$1,250**

Courtesy of Dreweatts & Bloomsbury Auctions

*Indian or Ceylonese twin-handled rectangular tray, unmarked, 20th century, handles molded as twin elephant heads, hunting scene to border and engraved foliate cartouche to well, 21 1/2" long, 46 oz.* **$1000-$1,200**

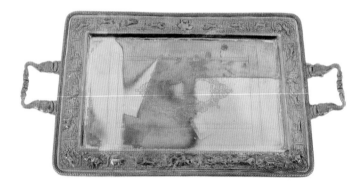

Courtesy of Dreweatts & Bloomsbury Auctions

*Edwardian twin-handled tray by Cooper Brothers & Sons Ltd., Sheffield, 1905, gadrooned instep border and threaded rim, well engraved with swags and floral sprays and geometric wrigglework borders, on domed feet, ring-turned hardwood handles with pierced scroll supports, 25" long.* **$2,100**

▲ *Continental rectangular stamp
box, import marked for London
1907, sponsor's mark of Arthur
Graf, hinged cover embossed with
banqueting scene, interior with
five compartments, scene is after
painting by Bartholomeus van der
Helst "Banquet at Crossbowmen's
Guild in celebration of Treaty of
Munster of 1648," in museum in
Rijksmuseum, Amsterdam, 4 3/4",
5.75 oz.* **$400-$550**

◄ *Pair of English silver-plated
four-light candelabra, 20th century,
overall surface wear commensurate
with age, 22" high.* **$1,062**

*Victorian mug by Joseph & Albert
Savory, London 1855, with loop
handle, embossed with flowers and
scrolls, engraved "D.R.D" and on
circular foot, 9 cm high; pair of
Edwardian shaped rectangular trays
by Henry Matthews, Birmingham
1901, embossed with flower sprays
and shaped vacant reserves to
centers, 15 cm long; trophy cup,
maker's mark obscured, Birmingham
1931, engraved with presentation
inscription, on circular foot and
mounted on socle, 19 cm high; and
Victorian Fiddle, Thread and Shell
pattern dessert fork by George Adams,
London 1840, engraved with two
crests, 16.5 cm long, 11.75 oz.* **$247**

# Sports

Sports and sports memorabilia are eternally intertwined. Since sports began, there have been mementoes to draw in audiences, attract attention to the games or invite future fans to the stadiums. And because the games tend to evoke fond memories, many times those mementoes are kept for a long time. Sports memorabilia is our connection to sporting events we remember and the players we loved to watch.

Today, sports memorabilia is used for more than simply waking up the memory bank or providing a connection to the past. These items are also increasingly used for home or office décor, as well as investments. Sports collectibles are more accessible than ever before through online auctions, with several auction houses dedicating themselves solely to that segment of the hobby. Provenance and third-party authentication is extremely important when investing in high-ticket sports collectibles. In today's market, high-quality and rare items are in most demand, with a heavy nod toward stars and Hall of Famers. Condition is everything – keep an eye toward temperature, humidity and exposure to sunlight with pieces in your collection.

Courtesy of Heritage Auctions

*Unopened 1973 Topps Baseball Series 4 wax pack box with 24 uncirculated packs contained inside, with Gaylord Perry, Willie McCovey, Juan Marichal, and Phil Niekro, various teams/ coaches, and "All-Time Leader" cards.* **$2,987**

For Energy..Eat **Grape=Nuts**

"BOYS! GIRLS! GET MY VALUABLE PRIZES FREE!" — *Dizzy Dean*

DETAILS ON Grape=Nuts PACKAGE

Courtesy of Heritage Auctions

▲ *Grape Nuts die-cut sign with Dizzy Dean, circa 1930s, cardboard with easel back, scattered staining and general wear at edges, 40" high x 26" wide.* **$2,629**

*1887 N28 Allen & Ginter "The Worlds Champions" advertising banner with cards of baseball greats Cap Anson, John Clarkson, Charles Comiskey, Tim Keefe, Mike "King" Kelly, and John Ward; pugilist John L. Sullivan; gun enthusiasts "Buffalo Bill" Cody and Annie Oakley; and rowers, wrestlers, and billiards players, 50 names total.* **$478**

*Jersey Lou Gehrig wore when the Yankees dominated baseball in 1927.* **$717,000**

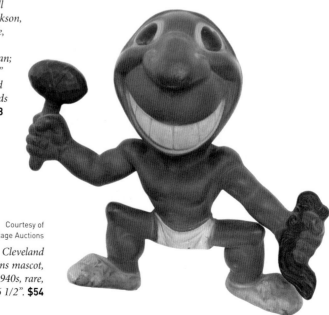

*Cleveland Indians mascot, circa 1940s, rare, 6 1/2".* **$54**

◄ *Baseball game with players of 1937 World Series including DiMaggio, Gehrig, Dickey, Chapman, etc., at bat and Medwick, Dykes, Dean, Averill, etc., in outfield, 40" wide x 54" high x 29 1/2" deep. After a coin is deposited, a ball appears from the umpire's chest (standing behind pitcher) and is handed to the pitcher, who then throws it in one of a variety of pitches, and you swing your bat. The accurate system of balls and strikes is kept by means of steel balls in marked troughs.* **$33,350**

▶ *Circa 1932 Babe Ruth game-worn New York Yankees cap.* **$200,000**

*1969-1970 Topps basketball complete set, 99-card series, with 25 basketball hall of famers including Jerry West, Oscar Robertson, and Wilt Chamberlain, with rookie cards of Lew Alcindor (Kareem Abdul-Jabbar), John Havlicek, Bill Bradley, Wes Unseld, and others.* **$209,125**

Courtesy of Saco River Auction

*White satin Everlast trunks worn by Muhammad Ali in a Heavyweight Championship bout against Joe Frazier, known as "Thrilla in Manilla," written in black marker on front: "Ali - Frazier Fight, Trilla (sic) in Manila, Pres. F. Marcos, Manila, Philippines, Oct. 1, 1975."* **$155,350**

Courtesy of Heritage Auctions

*1952 Topps Mickey Mantle card, an American icon.* **$77,675**

Courtesy of Saco River Auction

*1971 Panini Olympia unopened pack of cards with Cassius Clay on back of pack, GAI Gem Mint 9.5; Cassius Clay's "B" issue seen through yellow wrapper.* **$101**

Courtesy of Heritage Auctions

*Circa 1965-1967 Fuzzy Thurston game-worn Green Bay Packers helmet, during Vince Lombardi era.* **$6,572**

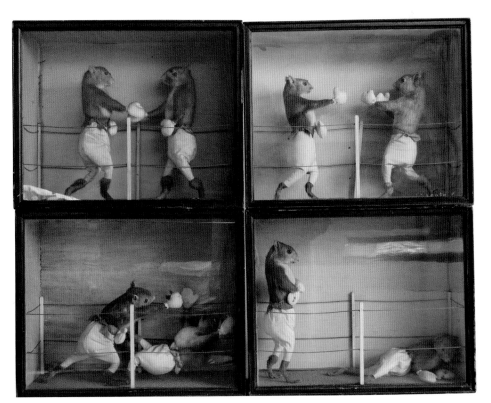

Courtesy of Heritage Auctions

*Four 19th century shadow boxes of boxing squirrels, circa 1850s, by William Hart & Sons, displayed at Great Exhibition of the Works of Industry of all Nations in 1851, each 14 3/4" x 19" x 7".* **69,000**

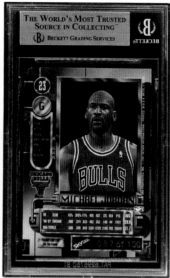

*1997-1998 Metal
Universe Precious Metal
Gems Michael Jordan
Red #23 basketball card,
BGS 9.5 rating, rare.*
**$41,825**

*1894 N302 Mayo's Cut
Plug complete set of
football cards.* **$35,850**

▲ *Turn-of-the-century football
nose mask, heavy rubber shield
covered nose and was held in
place by cloth strap, molded "bite
plate" fit between teeth, tooth
marks visible.* **$15,535**

Courtesy of Brunk Auctions

*Home Run Cigarettes cardboard sign, copyright 1909, stone lithographed advertisement with baseball illustration, by American Tobacco Co., very good condition, 11 1/2" wide x 17 1/2" high.* **$5,750**

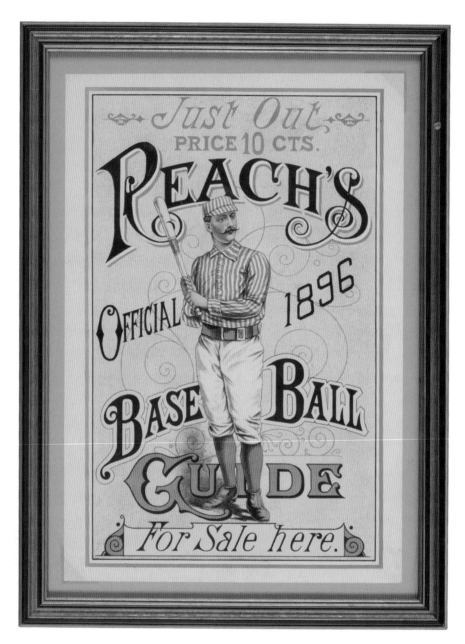

Courtesy of Heritage Auctions

Reach's Official Base Ball Guide
*sign, 1896, age toning and*
*horizontal center fold, print 12" x*
*18", 15" x 21" framed.* **$4,481**

*Replica metal
advertising piece
with authenticated
signature by Ted
Williams, 10" x 15".*
**$131**

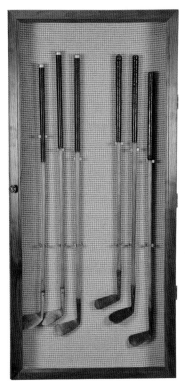

*Old bicycle used as sign for repair shop in Thompsonville,
Connecticut.* **Value unknown.**

*Six golf clubs in shadowbox.* **$325**

# Toys

Toy collecting has gone through dramatic changes over the years, but the premise of collecting remains the same – holding onto something from childhood that brings a smile to your face every time you see it.

Toys are fun. There are no hidden messages when it comes to toys. They are produced for entertainment, and while they can also be quite valuable, that is not the driving force behind collecting toys.

If you collect now, during a challenging economy and high gas prices, you're doing it as a passion. And that's what toys are all about, a piece of nostalgia that can grow into a fascination that fills rooms in houses and provides endless stories for relatives and friends.

Over the past few years, one aspect of the hobby is becoming apparent: More people are becoming acquainted with toys and their values than at any other point in American history, thanks to the exposure the hobby has garnered from the collectible-based reality programs broadcast on television.

The best weapon in the battle for equitable prices for toys is acquiring knowledge: Education is power. Learn about the toy and its backstory, know its manufacturer and date of production, as well as its importance in the realm of popular culture.

When estimating the value of a toy, you must first evaluate its condition. Mint toys in mint packaging command higher prices than well-played-with toys whose boxes disappeared with the wrapping paper on Christmas day. Mint is a rare condition indeed as toys were meant to be played with by children. Realistic evaluation of condition is essential, as grading standards vary from class to class. Ultimately, the market is driven by buyers, and the bottom line final value of a toy is often the last price at which it is sold.

For more information on toys, see *Toys & Prices,* 19th edition, by Mark Bellomo.

Courtesy of Morphy Auctions

*Smith-Miller Bank of America truck with decals and original lock on back doors, very good all original condition, some chipping and edge wear throughout, 14" long.*
**$300-$400**

Courtesy of Bertoia Auctions

▲ *Marklin "Chicago" paddle wheeler, Germany, circa 1900-1902, No. 1080/2, hand-painted lower deck curtains, blue and brown band stacks and matching paddle wheel covers, side guns, all hanging lifeboats, with six original figures of captain and crew, 31" long.* **$277,150**

Courtesy of Morphy Auctions

◄ *Diamond Planet robot, made in Japan by Yonezawa, tin-litho and painted, blue variation, key is vintage replacement and works, 10 1/2" high.* **$13,200**

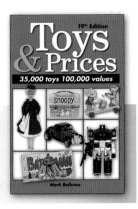

**RECOMMENDED READING**

**Toys & Prices, 19th edition.** The most trusted guide devoted to postwar toys, with more than 35,000 toys and 100,000 values, as well as more than 2,000 black-and-white images.
**www.krausebooks.com**

Courtesy of Bertoia Auctions

*Mother Goose tin wind-up toy, Louis Marx, Mother Goose with cat riding large goose, box, 8 3/4" long.* **$680**

Courtesy of Heritage Auctions

*Freighter Venus vintage live steam model toy, German-built, original finishes intact with live steam engine, 58 1/2" x 68 1/2" x 19".* **$6,785**

▲ *Arcade "White" moving van, painted black, marked "Lammerts" on both sides, considered finest example known, with seated driver, opening rear doors, silver trimmed grille and painted disc wheels, 13" long.* **$31,330**

◄ *Gunthermann open phaeton with passengers, German, lithographed luxury toy touring auto with four hand-painted seated figures, rubber spare wheel attached to curved bonnet, blue and white color scheme, front headlamps with glass fronts, clockwork driven, 9 1/2" long.* **$54,000**

*Tipp and Co. wind-up motorcycle, tin, made in Germany.* **$2,700**

▲ *Atom Jet racer with original box, Yonezawa, Japan, teal color, extensive graphic images, enclosed cockpit with nickel-plated cage frame, friction driven, rubber tires with nickeled hubs, 26 1/2" long.* **$19,000**

▶ *Tootsietoy 4630 U.S. Mail delivery van, die-cast, gold.* **$4,600**

*Lehmann Zig-Zag tin toy with original box, Germany, early 20th century, lithographed in red, white, and blue with spring motor and black and white riders, 5" long.* **$3,250**

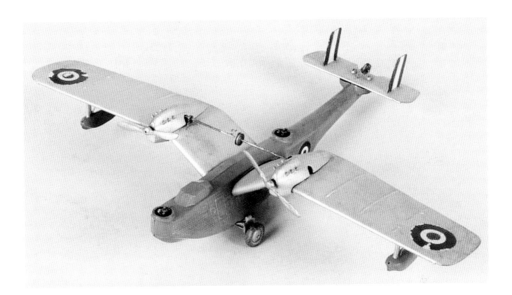

▲ *Britains Flying Boat monoplane, die-cast, made in 1936 only, with scarce original box marked "Short Monoplane Flying Boat No. 1520 W. Britain," 14 1/4" wingspan; one of rarest and most valuable airplane toys ever made.* **$13,800**

*Polychromed clown nine-piece skittle holder/pull-toy supported by two wooden wheels in front and hidden cast iron wheel mounted beneath upturned legs, 23" long.* **$25,000**

*Mego World's Greatest Super-Heroes Robin with original box, Burbank Toys, copyright 1977 DC Comics, item No. 81302, never removed from box, 9" high Robin the Boy Wonder scaled for 12" figure line.* **$5,693**

Courtesy of Bertoia Auctions

*Vindex John Deere combine, circa 1929, cast iron, silver overall with green trim throughout, yellow spoke wheels, operating front cutter wheel in green, large harvest hopper, front-mounted engine, standing figure on railed platform, 18 1/2" long.* **$4,750**

Courtesy of Bertoia Auctions

*Shutter-Bug battery-operated toy with original box, TN, Japan, lithographed tin boy holds camera in standing pose with rubber hands, 8 3/4" high.* **$988**

Courtesy of Bertoia Auctions

*Ferris wheel tin wind-up toy, General Metal Toys, Canada, lithographed tin carnival ride with four gondolas, 12 1/2" high.* **$463**

Courtesy of Noel Barrett

*Althof-Bergmann Santa sleigh, late 19th century, three-wire scroll support structure with no skirting, 20" long.* **$101,640**

Courtesy of RSL Auction Co.

▼ *Tin Central Station, Marklin, Germany, circa 1910, with detachable canopy over train tracks, platform 17" wide x 13" deep.* **$3,388**

Courtesy of RSL Auction Co.

▶ *Scarce wood, papier maché, cloth, and tin clockwork toy, Ives, Blakeslee Co., Bridgeport, Connecticut, circa 1875, young black musician strums fiddle, excellent condition.* **$7,530**

Courtesy of RSL Auction Co.

*Rare hand-painted tin lighthouse, Doll & Cie, Germany, circa 1905, steam attachment can be hand-cranked, boats go up and down as lighthouse beacon turns around, overall pristine condition, one boat missing sail, 15" high.* **$6,000-$9,000**

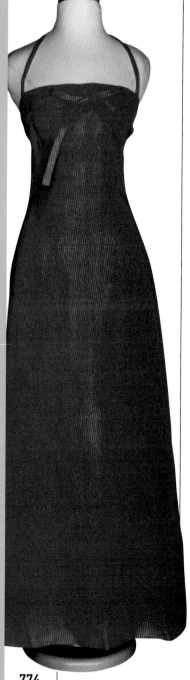

# Vintage Fashion
## Accessories

The history of fashion is a mirror to the future. Nearly every style has already been done in some form and is reproduced with variations today. The popularity and demand for vintage pieces are growing because clothing and accessories are great collectibles that are also a good investment.

Many factors come into play when assessing value. When shopping vintage fashion, keep the following in mind:

**Popularity:** How well known the designer is affects the price.

**Condition:** Collectors tend to want the original design condition with no modifications or repairs.

**Relevance:** The piece should be a meaningful representation of a designer's work.

**When you're hot, you're hot:** As a trend develops, it is shown in fashion magazines, and the original vintage pieces go up in

CLOSE-UP!

Courtesy of Augusta Auctions

*Pink silk and linen floor-length empire-style gown with self-fabric halter strap and bow detail on bust, built-in corset, label reads "Christian Dior Printemps-Ete Paris 02225," from Christian Dior spring-summer 1973 collection, bust 29", waist 23", hips 40", total garment length 50", bottom hem edge dirty.* **$2,040**

*Hermès matte Himalayan Nilo crocodile Birkin Bag, considered one of the rarest Hermès bags ever made, with 9.84 carats of diamonds: cadena lock of 68.4g 18k white gold with 40 white round brilliant diamonds (1.64 carats), seven on touret, 16 on pontets, and 182 on plaques de sanglons; pristine condition with original plastic protection on both sides of plaques de sanglons, lock and all four clou, 12" wide x 8" high x 6" deep.* **$185,000**

*Two sterling silver cigarette cases: Battin & Co. sterling silver and 14k gold case with striped two-tone exterior, and small unmarked repoussé cigarette case with engraved inscription "Edward K, Rast from J.N.H.C., 1894," larger case 4 5/8" long, approximately 6.7 troy oz.* **$185**

value (and plummet when it goes out of favor).

**Location:** Prices fluctuate from one geographic region to another.

**Value:** The appeal of vintage fashion items has greatly increased over the last few years. Our rule of thumb is to buy quality.

For more information on vintage fashion, see *Warman's Handbags Field Guide* by Abigail Rutherford, *Vintage Fashion Accessories* by Stacy LoAlbo, and *Warman's Shoes Field Guide* by Caroline Ashleigh.

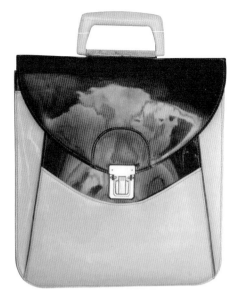

Courtesy of Augusta Auctions

▲ *Marie Leavell mod colorblock handbag in red and white patent leather, one exterior and two large interior pockets with one zipper pocket, stamped "Made in France Ref. 1007" and "Brevete No. 882369," circa 1960s, very good condition, 13" square, handle 2 1/2".* **$270**

Courtesy of Augusta Auctions

◀ *Unlabeled Christian Dior tulip dress, circa 1950s, built-in silk bodice foundation and narrow inner silk skirt, outer skirt of strapless black silk faille with diagonally overlapping front panels, excellent condition, bust 33" to 34", waist 24," length 30 1/2".* **$6,600**

INSIDE LOOK!

Courtesy of Heritage Auctions

*Bulgari 18-karat yellow gold Melone minaudiere evening bag with 1.21 carat round diamond push-lock clasp and four interchangeable tassels in black, green, purple, and gold, circa 1960s, believed to be one of only a handful made, interior with two sections and center mirror divider, excellent condition, includes dust bag, 6 1/2" wide x 4" high x 2" deep.* **$22,000**

Courtesy of O'Gallerie

*Vintage Louis Vuitton wardrobe trunk, French, early 20th century, opens to original fitted interior, one side with hangers and hanger bar, other with rank of six drawers, exterior covered with standard Louis Vuitton monogram toile canvas with wood staves, leather corner trim and brass hardware, good overall condition with light to moderate wear commensurate with age and use, some cracking and losses to leather, 44 1/2" long x 22" high x 22" wide.* **$10,000**

Courtesy of John Moran Auctioneers

*Art Deco enamel and jadeite compact, circa 1925, black, white, ivory, and green enamel work with carved jadeite plaque with rose-cut diamond surround, case trimmed with 14k gold with emerald push clasp that opens to reveal two lidded compartments and mirror, overall good condition commensurate with age, 3" x 1 3/4" x 3/8".* **$5,206**

Courtesy of Heritage Auctions

*Prada tote bag with python front and back exterior, brown canvas sides and base and plastic tortoiseshell chain strap, fabric interior with one zip pocket, no closure, excellent condition with light bending of python scales, 11" wide x 11" high x 2" deep, shoulder strap with 12" drop.* **$1,150**

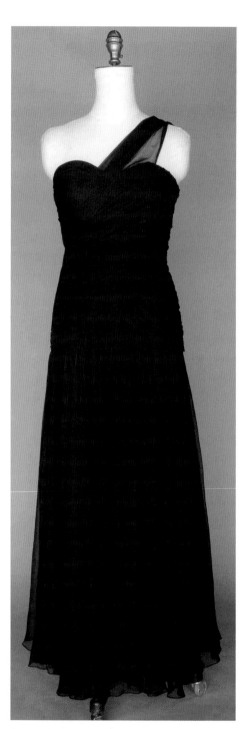

Courtesy of Augusta Auctions

*Adele Simpson black silk chiffon evening gown, circa 1977, single shoulder strap, draped and pleated fitted bodice extends to low hip with full two-layer skirt, excellent condition, bust 34", waist 26", length 60".* **$390**

Courtesy of Skinner, Inc.; www.skinnerinc.com

*Ben Kahn full-length white mink coat with front-clasp closures, wide collar, embroidered silk lining and interior and exterior pockets.* **$400**

Courtesy of Skinner, Inc.; www.skinnerinc.com

*Christian Dior red lamb's wool women's overcoat with braided black front closures and exterior pockets, size 14.* **$154**

Courtesy of Skinner, Inc.; www.skinnerinc.com

*Russian sable coat with round collar and silk lining.* **$2,520**

**BACK VIEW!**

Courtesy of John Moran Auctioneers

*Large crocodile and burgundy leather attaché case, top handle and shoulder strap marked Ghepard, central flap ends with lock-and-key closure, interior with two large compartments and central zippered pocket with small side-zippered pocket, gold-tone metal hardware, 16" high x 23" wide x 10" deep.* **$420**

Courtesy of Skinner, Inc.; www.skinnerinc.com

▲ *Two Emilio Pucci velvet- and silk-lined women's jackets, one with purple and blue floral pattern on cream-colored ground, other color-blocked pattern with teal, turquoise, royal blue, grass green, purple, and cream design elements, Florence, Italy, both size 14.* **$185**

Courtesy of Heritage Auctions

▼ *Prada red Saffiano leather hard-sided hatbox with round body, hinged opening and three silver-buckle closures, red leather top handle and luggage tag, flat bottom, interior lined with red fabric printed with Prada logo, elastic pouch, mirror and ties, good to very good condition, light scratching throughout exterior, includes Prada dust bag, 19 1/2" wide x 18 1/2" high x 8" deep.* **$813**

Courtesy of Skinner, Inc.; www.skinnerinc.com

▲ *Chanel black velour smoking pantsuit with black silk shawl collar and gold-tone and imitation pearl buttons, ladies' European size 38/U.S. size 8.* **$277**

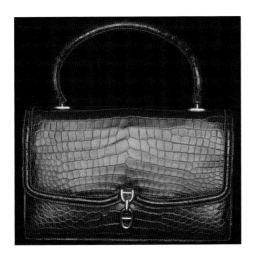

Courtesy of Augusta Auctions

*Hermès crocodile Escale handbag, circa 1968, short leather handle, brass fittings and three-section interior with chestnut brown leather lining, two interior square pockets and one snap-close envelope pocket, "Hermès Paris" stamped on front inside section, very good condition with minor wear to raised, corded edge on outside of bag and handles near brass fixtures, pen mark on lining, 6" x 10" x 3".* **$1,440**

Courtesy of A.B. Levy's

*Crocodile skin briefcase stamped Italy with croc handle, gold brass locking hardware and leather lining, interior with various slots and storage compartments, 12 1/2" high x 17 1/4" wide x 3 3/4" deep.* **$550**

Courtesy of John Moran Auctioneers

*Two 14k gold money clips, overall good condition with normal signs of wear, 46.9 grams combined weight.* **$1,020**

BACK VIEW!

Courtesy of Heritage Auctions

◄ *Hermès special-order horseshoe orange, vert anis and jaune togo leather Birkin bag with palladium hardware, interior jaune chevre leather with one zip pocket and one slip pocket, pristine condition with plastic still on hardware, includes lock, keys, clochette, dust bag and box, 14" wide x 10" high x 7" deep.* **$35,000**

Courtesy of
Heritage Auctions

▶ *Hermès matte bois de rose Nilo crocodile clutch bag with palladium hardware, interior bois de rose chevre with one slip pocket, pristine condition, plastic still on hardware, includes dust bag and box, 12" wide x 5" high x 1" deep.* **$50,000**

Courtesy of Heritage Auctions

◀ *Prada shoulder bag with leopard-print pony-hair exterior, one adjustable shoulder strap, gold hardware, Prada luggage tag and magnetic snap closure, brown fabric interior with one slip pocket and one zip pocket, excellent condition, color loss to metal feet, includes Prada dust bag, 16" wide x 11" high x 4 1/2" deep, 9" shoulder drop.* **$900**

Courtesy of Heritage Auctions

▶ *Gucci bifold wallet, waxed monogram canvas exterior with brown patent leather bow detail on front, brown leather interior with two large slip pockets and 12 smaller card slip pockets, rear snap coin compartment, very good to excellent condition, smudging to patent leather and scratches to interior, 5" wide x 4 1/2" high.* **$80**

Courtesy of Heritage Auctions

▲ *Christian Dior white leather saddlebag with silver hardware, leather-covered hook-and-loop closure, center straps hang from flap, shoulder strap with silver CD on both sides, interior brown logo fabric with one zip pocket, very good to excellent condition with faint markings on exterior flap, 9" wide x 7 1/2" high x 2" deep with 7" shoulder drop.* **$263**

Courtesy of Heritage Auctions

▼ *Chanel orange patent leather East-West flap bag with silver and orange leather chain and silver hardware, orange calf box leather interior, very good condition, 10 1/2" wide x 5 1/2" long x 1 1/2" deep.* **$775**

Courtesy of Skinner, Inc.; www.skinnerinc.com

*Jean Paul Gaultier floor-length gown, black pleated virgin wool, Paris, late 1990s.* **$369**

# World War II
## Collectibles

During the nearly seven decades since the end of World War II, veterans, collectors, and nostalgia-seekers have eagerly bought, sold, and traded the "spoils of war." Actually, souvenir collecting began as soon as troops set foot on foreign soil. Whether Tommies from Great Britain, Doughboys from the United States, or Fritzies from Germany, soldiers eagerly looked for trinkets and remembrances that would guarantee their place in the historic events that unfolded before them. Helmets, medals, Lugers, field gear, daggers, and other pieces of war material filled parcels and duffel bags on the way back home.

As soon as hostilities ended in 1945, the populations of defeated Germany and Japan quickly realized they could make money selling souvenirs to the occupation forces. The flow of war material increased. Values became well established...a Luger was worth several packs of cigarettes, a helmet just one pack. A Japanese sword was worth two boxes of K-rations, an Arisaka bayonet was worth a Hershey's chocolate bar.

Over the years, these values have remained proportionally consistent. Today, that "two-pack" Luger might be worth $5,000 and that one-pack helmet, $1,500. The Japanese sword might fetch $1,200 and the Arisaka bayonet $95. Though values have increased dramatically, demand has not dropped off a bit. In fact, World War II collecting is the largest segment of the miltaria hobby.

For more information on World War II collectibles, see *Warman's World War II Collectibles Identification & Price Guide,* 3rd edition, by John Adams-Graf.

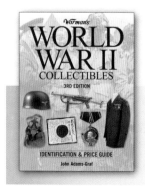

**Warman's World War II Collectibles Identification & Price Guide, 3rd ed.** by John Adams-Graf. Comprehensive full-color guide with 1,250 images, listings, and values for uniforms, footwear, weapons, medals, headgear and more. **ww.krausebooks.com**

RECOMMENDED
READING

# Uniforms

◄ *British RAF warrant officer navigator's battle dress uniform.* **$565-$625**

▲ *German SS Judicial Service Sturmführer black tunic.* **$10,000-$12,000**

◄ *German reversible lace-up camouflage smock.* **$11,000-$13,000**

Courtesy of AdvanceGuardMilitaria.com

*USMC 1st Marine Division staff sergeant's dress blue uniform.*
**$145-$175**

Courtesy of AdvanceGuardMilitaria.com

*U.S. 82nd Airborne soldier's jump jacket and trousers, including paratrooper M2 knife.*
**$3,200-$3,865**

Courtesy of AdvanceGuardMilitaria.com

*U.S. Red Cross Woman's Military Welfare Service uniform.*
**$385-$425**

Courtesy of AdvanceGuardMilitaria.com

*U.S. AAF 13th Air Force 5th Bomb Group aerial gunner's painted A2 flight jacket.* **$2,650**

# Headgear

*French kepi for general officer of the Medical Service, 1930-1940.*
**$1,000-1,400**

*British MK II paratrooper helmet.*
**$1,250-$1,700**

*German M35 SS double-decal helmet.* **$8,000-$11,000**

*Luftwaffe Fallschirmjäger helmet, 2nd Model.* **$5,500-$7,000**

Courtesy of Hermann-Historica.de

*Luftwaffe tropical visor cap.*
**$4,000-$6,500**

Courtesy of Hermann-Historica.de

*Kriegsmarine rear admiral's service cap.* **$8,000-$9,000**

Courtesy of AdvanceGuardMilitaria.com

*Polish Infantry enlisted field cap.*
**$1,000-$1,200**

Courtesy of AdvanceGuardMilitaria.com

*U.S. D-Day Utah Beach 1st Engineer Special Brigade NCO's painted helmet.* **$4,000-$5,000**

Courtesy of Heritage Auctions

*U.S. Army officer's summer cap owned and used by General Joseph W. "Vinegar Joe" Stilwell.* **$3,585**

Courtesy of HistoryHunter.com

*Japanese Army combat helmet with field cover.* **$1,000-$1,600**

# Accoutrements

Courtesy of AdvanceGuardMilitaria.com
*SS officer's belt plate.* **$1,500-$2,000**

Courtesy of Rick Fleury
*SS enlisted buckle, aluminum.* **$400-$500**

Courtesy of Heritage Auctions
▲ *British "Rupert" D-Day dummy paratrooper.* **$3,346**

Courtesy of Chris William
▶ *G-43 double magazine pouch.* **$600-$800**

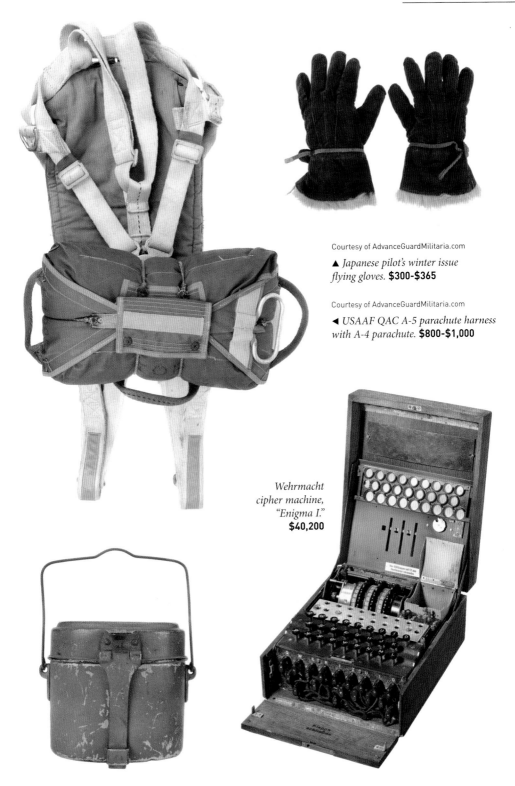

Courtesy of AdvanceGuardMilitaria.com

▲ *Japanese pilot's winter issue flying gloves.* **$300-$365**

Courtesy of AdvanceGuardMilitaria.com

◄ *USAAF QAC A-5 parachute harness with A-4 parachute.* **$800-$1,000**

*Wehrmacht cipher machine, "Enigma I."* **$40,200**

Courtesy of AdvanceGuardMilitaria.com

*Camouflage painted M31 mess kit.* **$325**

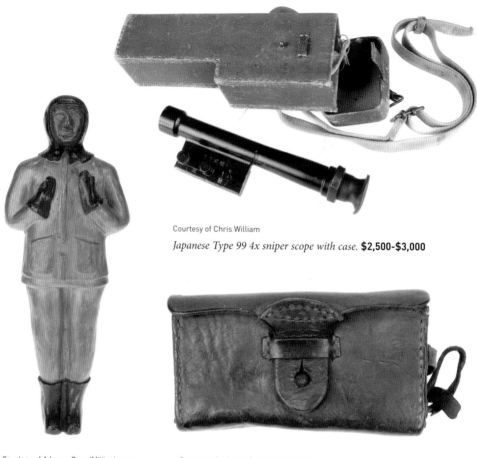

Courtesy of Chris William

*Japanese Type 99 4x sniper scope with case.* **$2,500-$3,000**

Courtesy of AdvanceGuardMilitaria.com

*U.S. paradummy decoy "Oscar."*
**$800-$1,000**

Courtesy of AdvanceGuardMilitaria.com

*Japanese Type 30 rear ammunition pouch.* **$400-$465**

Courtesy of AdvanceGuardMilitaria.com

*USN individual aviator's first aid kit.* **$295-$365**

Courtesy of AdvanceGuardMilitaria.com

*U.S. shotgun ammunition pouch.*
**$265-$325**

# Firearms

Courtesy of Chris William

▲ *Japanese Type 26 revolver.* **$300-$950**

Courtesy of Rock Island Auction Co.

▶ *Winchester T3 carbine with original pattern M-2 infrared sniper scope and accessories.* **$15,000-$30,000**

Courtesy of James D. Julia Auctioneers, Fairfield, Maine, www.jamesdjulia.com

▲ *British Bren Mk2 machine gun.* **$38,000-$42,000**

Courtesy of Rock Island Auction Co.

◀ *German factory-cased, gold-plated and relief-engraved Walther Model PP pistol as presented to SA officer, Viktor Lutze.* **$241,500**

# Index

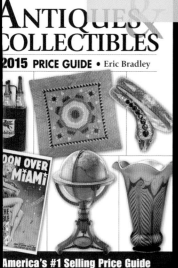
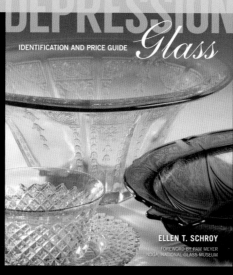
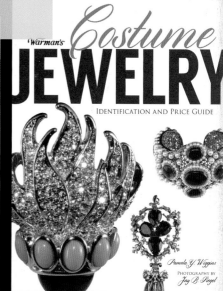

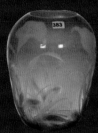

GURNEE ANTIQUE CENTER, L.L.C

The Gurnee Antique Center offers antiques and fine collectibles through the mid 20th century in a comfortable and spacious 24,000 sq. ft. building - a paradise for collectors, decorators, and casual shoppers.

Unlike many "antique" stores, we strive to sell true antiques and no reproductions. We have a 50+ years old rule, with very limited exceptions.

A large barn-like red structure visible from I-94, we're located in Gurnee near Six Flags Great America, & a short hop to the Naval Training Center, Great Lakes or the Gurnee Mills Outlets.

We're close to the Wisconsin Border, about an hour North of Chicago and ½ hour from O'Hare.

Now in our 14th successful year, we welcome antiquers & seekers of the rare, beautiful, and unusual.

Store-wide Sales occur 3 times a year: Labor Day and Memorial Day week-ends & mid-December. Call for dates.

## 5742 Northridge Dr., Gurnee, IL 60031

From I-94 Take Route 132 East. Turn right at Dilleys Road (1st stop light) follow Dilleys Road into Northridge Dr.

Closed only on Easter, Thanksgiving, and Christmas Day.

**Gift Certificates Available.**

# (847) 782-9094

## www.GurneeAntiqueCenter.com